D1320947

THE MAGIC OF A NAME
THE ROLLS-ROYCE STORY
PART THREE

We must keep our nerve. The BA decision was a big disappointment but not a killer. You can't read the whole market on two or three early 777 decisions.

Sir Ralph Robins in 1991, immediately after British Airways had selected the GE90 instead of the Trent 800 to power its Boeing 777s.

Independent audit of engineering activities was implemented, so that before a design could pass through to the next stage of development, it had to be scrutinised and passed off by an independent team. Emphasis was placed on getting the basic design right, first time; on using unified data throughout the project and on integration of design and manufacture into a seamless activity.

Philip Ruffles, former Director of Engineering and Technology at Rolls-Royce, on Project Derwent, which he introduced into Rolls-Royce engine development in the early 1990s

There is enormous respect in Munich for Rolls-Royce and especially for its Chairman, Sir Ralph Robins. Here in Germany, there are many engineers at the head of our companies. Engineering is a highly respected profession. In England, the structure of society is such that engineers do not have the same position. But Sir Ralph has made it. He is there at the top of one of your greatest companies. When I go round a factory with him he can pick up pieces of the engine and talk in detail to those working on the engine. He is highly respected here in Munich.

Eberhard von Kuenheim, responsible for building the modern BMW company

Our strategic approach builds on the common characteristics of power systems and our ability to adapt to customer requirements in the different market sectors. In doing so we maximise the transfer of capability and knowledge between business sectors. We aim to 'invest once and use many times'.

John Rose, Chief Executive of Rolls-Royce plc, in March 2002

He's been the principal architect in restoring Rolls-Royce's credibility and success. It's during his stewardship that Rolls has really come back.

Lord Marshall of British Airways on Sir Ralph Robins

THE MAGIC OF A NAME

THE ROLLS-ROYCE STORY

PART THREE

A FAMILY OF ENGINES

1987–2002

Peter Pugh

ICON BOOKS UK
TOTEM BOOKS USA

Published in the UK in 2002 by Icon Books Ltd.,
Grange Road, Duxford, Cambridge CB2 4QF
e-mail: info@iconbooks.co.uk
www.iconbooks.co.uk

Distributed in the UK, Europe, South Africa and Asia
by Airlife Publishing Ltd., 101 Longden Road,
Shrewsbury SY3 9EB

Published in Australia in 2002 by
Allen & Unwin Pty. Ltd., PO Box 8500,
83 Alexander Street, Crows Nest, NSW 2065

Published in the USA in 2002 by Totem Books
Inquiries to: Icon Books Ltd., Grange Road,
Duxford, Cambridge CB2 4QF, UK

Distributed to the trade in the USA by
National Book Network Inc.,
4720 Boston Way, Lanham,
Maryland 20706

Distributed in Canada by Penguin Books Canada,
10 Alcorn Avenue, Suite 300,
Toronto, Ontario M4V 3B2

ISBN 1 84046 405 4

Typesetting by Hands Fotoset, Woodthorpe, Nottingham

Design and layout by Christos Kondeatis

Cover design by Nicholas Halliday

Printed and bound in the UK by
Biddles Ltd., Guildford and King's Lynn

CONTENTS

INTRODUCTION

As I said in the Introduction to the first two parts of this history, many books have been written about Rolls-Royce. Most of them are either biographies of the leading personalities, or works that tackle specific aspects of the cars or aero-engines.

The last publication to attempt a truly comprehensive history of Rolls-Royce was Harold Nockolds's *The Magic of a Name*, published by Foulis in 1938 and reprinted several times until a third edition was finally printed in 1972. These three books are the first attempt since then to cover comprehensively the story of Rolls-Royce from its earliest days until the present. The Rolls-Royce name *is* magic, made so by the calibre of its people and its products, and the title *The Magic of a Name* is singularly appropriate. Foulis, now owned by Haynes Publishing, has kindly allowed us to use the title again.

The first part of this trilogy took the story from 1904 to 1945 with all the excitement of the meeting of the great engineer, Henry Royce, and the aristocratic motor-car enthusiast and salesman, the Hon. C.S. Rolls, through the early pioneering days with the best car in the world, the Silver Ghost, on to the design by Royce and production by Rolls-Royce of the leading aero-engine of the First World War, the Eagle. We moved on to Royce's design of an aero-engine which enabled Britain to retain the Schneider Trophy. This association with the aircraft designer R.J. Mitchell led on to the Spitfire and Rolls-Royce's Merlin engines. As we saw, without the Spitfire and the

Hurricane, and the Merlins that powered them, the Battle of Britain would have been lost. Finally, we saw how Ernest (later Lord) Hives realised the significance of the jet engine and how he backed Sir Frank Whittle to the hilt.

Part Two was the story of Rolls-Royce's realisation that it must tackle the US civil-airliner market if it was to remain a world player in the aero-engine business. The British civil-aircraft industry faded away in the 1960s after the success of the Vickers Viscount and the initial triumphs of the de Havilland Comet before its tragic accidents.

The USA was where Rolls-Royce had to be and, to their credit, Sir Denning Pearson and Sir David Huddie knew it and went for it. Unfortunately, Rolls-Royce did not have the resources to withstand the inevitable development setbacks entailed in bringing the revolutionary three-shaft RB 211 to market, and the company was forced into receivership in February 1971.

Nevertheless, the vision was right, and the RB 211 won further orders as the company recovered in its Government-ownership days in the 1970s and 1980s.

Meanwhile, the Motor Car Division was floated as a separate company and continued to develop the Rolls-Royce and Bentley brands, first on its own and then in conjunction with Vickers. In this period also, Rolls-Royce broadened its activity to provide gas-turbine power to the Royal Navy and other navies, and also to the oil and gas industries.

By the mid-1980s, Rolls-Royce was sufficiently robust to be returned to the private sector, and that's where Part Two ended.

This book starts with Rolls-Royce coping with the competitive world without Government protection. As always, the competition from its two arch-rivals, General Electric and Pratt & Whitney, was as fierce as ever, and Rolls-Royce had to decide whether it wanted to compete with them across a range of engines or only in certain sizes. We saw in Part Two how it flirted with the idea of leaving the big-engine field to General Electric. This was the plan of Chairman Bill Duncan, but when he died his successor, Lord Tombs, and the Managing Director, Sir Ralph Robins, would have none of it. Rolls-Royce would compete across the range.

This book is the story of how Rolls-Royce moved from a company with a small number of engines supplying an equally small number of airlines to a company with a complete 'family' of engines supplying nearly all the world's major airlines and most of the smaller ones too. Thanks to strategic partnerships and acquisitions, it has also become a truly global operation in both civil and military aerospace, in the commercial and naval marine industry and in the energy markets of the world. This volume covers a period that matches the achievements of Rolls-Royce at any other point in its history.

Peter Pugh
June 2002

AUTHOR'S ACKNOWLEDGEMENTS

In researching this third volume of the history of Rolls-Royce, I have read all the books mentioned in the bibliography and quoted from several of them. I am grateful to the authors and to the publishers. I have interviewed many people, some of them several times, and I am grateful to them too. Most of the interviews took place in Britain, but I visited the Rolls-Royce Allison plant in Indianapolis again, Rolls-Royce North America's new headquarters in Chantilly, near Washington DC, and Rolls-Royce's plant in Montreal. I also had the privilege of interviewing Dr Eberhard von Kuenheim in Munich, Dr Bernd Pischetsrieder in Wolfsburg, Jean Pierson in Nice and Rod Eddington at Heathrow, as well as visiting the new Rolls-Royce Deutschland plant in Dahlewitz near Berlin and the ITP offices in Madrid. I also had the great pleasure of visiting Singapore and interviewing a number of present and former executives of Singapore Airlines, including Dr Cheong Choong Kong, Chew Choon Seng and Joe Pillay.

I would like to mention especially: Jonathan Asherson, Brian Allen, Peter Baines, Sam Beale, Tom Bowling, Ian Brackenbury, Sir Colin Chandler, John Cheffins, Charles Coltman, John Coplin, Bob Crabtree, Charles Cuddington, Nick Cumpsty, Nick Devall, Martin Duckworth, Norm Egbert, John Ferrie, Keith Garwood, Jack Gordon, Duncan Gorham, Tony Gott, Colin Green, Jim Guyette, Sir Terence Harrison, Dr Bob Hawley, Paul Heiden, Lord Heseltine, Dr Mike Hicks, Jock Hill, Darrel Hinder, Chris Hornblower,

Mike Howse, Charles Hughes, David Hygate, Gerry James, Neil Jennings, Tim Jones, Jim Keir, Ian Kinnear, Geoff Kirk, Saul Lanyado, Martin Lee, Ian Lloyd, Peter Lockton, George Lowe, Sue Lyons, Lord Marshall, Richard Maudslay, Martin Menrath, J. George Mikelsons, Riley Mixson, The Rt. Hon. Lord Moore, Barry Morgan, Mike Mundy, Frank Mungo, Mike Neale, Sir Robin Nicholson, Al Novick, Gordon Page, Peter Pavey, Jorge Montes del Pino, Fernando Pombo, Chris Pratt, Roy Quipp, Andrew Rice, John Rivers, Jim Roberts, John Rose, Tony Roulstone, Phil Ruffles, Michael Ryan, John Sandford, Rob Sellick, Jorge Sendagorta, David Sidaway, Sir Donald Spiers, Mike Steele, Andy Stephens, Bob Sunerton, Mike Terrett, Bill Thomas, Robin Thuillier, Stan Todd, Frank Turner, Mike Turner, Richard Turner, Gordon Waddington, David Watkins, David Whetton, Ray Whitfield, Derek Wilding, Phil Wilkins, Steve Williams, John Wragg, Sir William Wratten.

As with Parts One and Two of this history, I received constant help and advice from Mike Evans, whom I now reinstate as Chairman of the Rolls-Royce Heritage Trust, a post from which I inadvertently retired him in my acknowledgements in Part Two. Philip Hall, curator of the Sir Henry Royce Memorial Foundation at The Hunt House, Paulerspury, kindly read the motor-car chapter and also provided photographs of Rolls-Royce and Bentley motor cars.

In the USA, Dave Newill organised interviews for me when I visited Indianapolis, and provided photographs and helped with the captions for the Allison chapter. Mike Hudson kindly read the Allison chapter and made some very helpful suggestions.

The Rolls-Royce Corporate Communications Department at Buckingham Gate, Derby and Bristol were at all times extremely helpful in providing media cuttings and photographs, and in giving constant support to the project. I would like to mention Martin Brodie, David Howie, Andrew Siddons, Martin Johnson, Martin Nield, Roger Scriven and Zara Turner. I found the *Rolls-Royce Magazine* a great fount of information. It must be the best in-house magazine in British industry. I must not forget the Chairman's magnificent secretary Sally Cameron, who has replied instantly to my e-mail requests and who has fitted me into the Chairman's busy schedule whenever I have requested it.

Finally, I must thank most of all the Chairman himself, Sir Ralph Robins, whose idea it was to have this history written. His enthusiasm for it has never wavered, and he has been constantly available for help and advice for the whole of the five-and-a-half years it has taken to complete this project.

As you can see, the jacket on this book is green – perhaps British Racing Green – and I have to tell you why. When we were selecting a colour, everyone agreed it should be burgundy. Burgundy goes beautifully with the blue and silver of the first two volumes. We mocked up a burgundy cover, put it on a book, put it in a slip case with the other two volumes and took it to show the Chairman. Not wanting to dictate the colour to him, we also mocked up a black cover and a green one, but did not put them on a book. The Chairman said the burgundy, silver and blue looked fine, in fact perfect. Then he spotted the green cover, and I could see going through his head, 'That looks just like my Bentley.' 'That green looks rather good. Can I see it on a book? ... Oh yes, green, that's the colour.' I hope the Chairman in 2010 doesn't have a yellow Rolls-Royce!

Finally, I must thank all the people of Rolls-Royce with whom I have come in contact. Whether it's because I was writing for the Chairman or whether because I was writing about their company I don't know, but, without exception, every single person was extremely helpful and courteous, often going beyond the call of duty to make sure I received the necessary information. I said to the Chairman a few months ago how much I enjoyed interviewing people who work for Rolls-Royce, and I said I thought it was because they were all so knowledgeable. I remarked at the time that it was a bit strange, because very often clever and knowledgeable people can be a bit too 'clever' and overbearing – or, to put it more bluntly, a bit of a pain. A week later, I interviewed two of the engineers responsible for Rolls-Royce's achievements in securing the company's participation on Joint Strike Fighter, and it came to me why Rolls-Royce's clever people are not 'a bit of a pain'. It's because they are so modest. No one ever said to me, 'I did this.' It was always 'We did this' or 'Rolls-Royce did this.'

How will I ever write about another company?

Peter Pugh
June 2002

Photo Credits

The majority of the photographs have been provided either by the Rolls-Royce Heritage Trust or by Andrew Siddons in Rolls-Royce's media department.

The photographs relating to Rolls-Royce BMW between pages 82 and 83 were provided by Rolls-Royce Deutschland, and almost all between pages 114 and 115 by Rolls-Royce Allison in Indianapolis.

The photographs of Bentley and Rolls-Royce motor cars between pages 146 and 147 were provided by the Sir Henry Royce Memorial Foundation, and those of Henri Ziegler, Roger Beteille, Jean Pierson and Noël Forgeard by Airbus Industrie. The XG-40 Demonstrator Engine photograph was provided by Mike Neale.

The photographs of the Tornado aircraft and the Sea King helicopter between pages 210 and 211, and those of the *Iwate*, HMS *Invincible*, the submarine, Vickers machine gun and Vickers light tank between pages 274 and 275, are reproduced by kind permission of the Imperial War Museum.

THE VALUE OF MONEY

In a book about a business, we cannot ignore the changing value of money, and – with the exception of the inter-war years – the twentieth century has been inflationary. There is no magic formula for translating 1900 prices into those of 2000. Some items have exploded in price, others have declined. We have to choose some criterion of measurement, and I have chosen the average working wage.

The Victorian age was one of stable prices, but prices started to rise just before the First World War, and rose sharply at the end of it. (Wars are always inflationary, because they distort supply and demand.) Immediately after the war, prices were more than twice as high as in 1914, and although they declined somewhat in the depressed economic conditions of the 1920s and 30s, they remained about twice as high as those before the war.

Price controls and rationing were imposed in the Second World War, but as these were withdrawn, prices again doubled. Inflation continued at about 3 per cent a year through the 1950s and 60s, but then rose sharply, almost catastrophically, in the 1970s. Although it was brought under control by the end of that decade, there were two more nasty upward blips in the early and late 1980s before the more stable 1990s.

I have used the following formula:

Late nineteenth century – multiply by 110 to equate with today's prices
Early twentieth century – multiply by 100 to equate with today's prices
1918–45 – multiply by 50 to equate with today's prices
1945–50 – multiply by 30 to equate with today's prices
1950–60 – multiply by 25 to equate with today's prices
1960–70 – multiply by 18 to equate with today's prices
1970–74 – multiply by 15 to equate with today's prices
1975–77 – multiply by 10 to equate with today's prices
1978–80 – multiply by 6 to equate with today's prices
1980–87 – multiply by 3 to equate with today's prices
1987–91 – multiply by 2 to equate with today's prices
1991–97 – multiply by 1.5 to equate with today's prices

Since 1997, the rate of inflation, by the standards of most of the twentieth century, has been very low, averaging less than the present Government's stated aim of maintaining it at 2.5 per cent. You don't need me to tell you that some items, such as telephone charges, are going down in price, while others, such as houses, are going up very sharply.

CHAPTER ONE

A VERY HIGH-THRUST ENGINE

THE BIG FAN BATTLE
ALL SET FAIR
A CRITICAL BREAKTHROUGH
'WE DECIDED TO MAKE A NEW AIRPLANE'
'A BILLION-DOLLAR BILL IS NOW SMALL CHANGE'
'AN ENGINE A DAY FOR SEVEN YEARS'
PROJECT DERWENT

THE BIG FAN BATTLE

TORY PRIME MINISTER Harold Macmillan once remarked that privatisation was akin to 'selling off the family silver'. Yet as Rolls-Royce was floated on the Stock Exchange in 1987 – having been in Government ownership since 1971 – the *Observer* was able to write:

Rolls-Royce is arguably the flashiest piece of family silver that the Thatcher Government has put up for public auction via its privatisation programme. Rolls has the glamour of a global mega brand and the go-go promise of high-tech.

Rolls-Royce Managing Director Ralph Robins said that going public was to 'return back to where we should be, on our own two feet'. And Chairman Sir Francis Tombs added:

Rolls-Royce virtually went to sleep for sixteen years. It wasn't their fault, they just couldn't get decisions quickly enough.

Rolls-Royce had regained its freedom on 28 April 1987, and the Chairman, then Sir Francis Tombs, said in the prospectus inviting potential investors to buy shares in the famous company, as he announced a record pre-tax profit of £120 million for 1986:

With outstanding orders worth £3.1 billion, the prospects for 1987 are encouraging. We have a strong order book, there is a large civil and military engine market to be satisfied, and we have a broad product range with which to compete. Add to this the steady growth in productivity over the past five years, improved financial controls, an experienced management team and skilled workforce, and I am confident that we have the ingredients for a successful future.

On privatisation – 'Impact Day' – Rolls-Royce aero-engines were in service with more than 270 airlines, 700 executive and corporate operators and 110 armed services worldwide. The company also had over 175 industrial customers operating gas turbines for power generation, gas- and oil-pipeline pumping and other industrial uses. Its gas turbines powered the naval vessels of 25 countries.

Nevertheless, Rolls-Royce, if it were to survive and prosper as an independent company, would need to invest heavily and expand rapidly. Tombs, along with the rest of the Board and senior management, could hardly wait to move from the state to the private sector.

Rolls-Royce still only had 8 per cent of the world airline-engine market. As Stewart Miller, Director of Engineering in the late 1980s, said:

Where we'd been available we'd done well but we weren't available on enough aircraft.

For example, its sole Airbus application was the A320, powered by its joint-venture engine within the International Aero Engines consortium, the V-2500. Would Rolls-Royce now seize the opportunities that freedom from Government restraint would bring?

It would not be easy. The product range was limited, the number of customers small, the dependence on military spending heavy. On large civil engines, Rolls-Royce's market share was only 8 per cent. It was little more than a niche player compared with General Electric (GE) and Pratt & Whitney, supplying scarcely more than half a dozen of the world's major airlines.

This was not going to satisfy the freshly liberated Rolls-Royce. Sir Francis Tombs and Managing Director Sir Ralph Robins had already extricated the company from the onerous arrangement with GE that would have prevented Rolls-Royce manufacturing large engines in its own right. This was followed by the production of a strategy paper that outlined the plan to produce a family of engines based on a common core. The aim was no less than to place Rolls-Royce in a position from which it could produce an engine for every gas-turbine civil aircraft manufactured anywhere in the world.

The need for a higher-thrust engine became clear during 1987. The

42,000 lb thrust of the original RB 211 had been increased to 60,600 lb on the RB 211-524G/H, which powered the Boeing 747-400 and the 767. However, this was not going to be sufficient for the new wide-bodied airliners being developed by Boeing and Airbus, which would require a new payload/range capability as well as the need for a high initial cruise altitude.

The new aircraft – the Boeing 777, McDonnell Douglas MD-11 and the Airbus A330 and 340 – would all want to fly much further than the 747, DC-10 and TriStar that they would replace. Airlines could also benefit if their aircraft could start their cruise at high altitude, because in busy periods they were more likely to obtain operating slots at a favourable time of the day. The higher cruise altitude also reduced fuel consumption. The result of these requirements was the need for engines capable of thrust much higher than 60,000 lb for all but the A340, which was going to use four engines.

In devising its big-engine strategy, Rolls-Royce immediately had to make two fundamental decisions. Would the engine be a brand new one or a derivative, and would it be three-shaft or two-? In coming to conclusions, Rolls-Royce appreciated the key factor of reliability. The new twin-engined wide-body aircraft would demand absolute reliability from the very first days of service.

This certainly pushed Rolls-Royce towards the derivative and three-shaft approach. Giles Harvey, General Manager of the Trent, which, as we shall see shortly, would be Rolls-Royce's new big engine, said:

Our basic strategy was to build on what we were good at, which was a three-shaft engine, with its inherent advantages of stiffness, performance retention and fuel economy.

However, in pursuing the concept of an RB 211 derivative, they had to be aware of its supposed unfavourable weight comparison with its competitors. Harvey felt this would not be a problem, saying:

Although we knew the early RB211s were of conservative design and hence heavier than their competitors, we knew that, as we pushed the fan size up, the engine became relatively lighter. We'd obviously done design studies before, but we'd never appreciated the significance of the weight saving that would occur with this size of engine.

It was the higher thrusts that made the difference. The three-shaft engine had better stage matching which meant that each spool could be better optimised aerodynamically thereby working more efficiently and saving weight.

Stan Todd, Trent project director at the time, said:

The benefits were always there, but at smaller sizes, two-shaft designs could make up the difference with active clearance control and careful design.

Harvey maintained that, at high thrusts, the two-shaft design had limited options, adding:

To get adequate core flow they either have to put more booster stages on the fan, or increase the length of the high-pressure (HP) compressor. The larger fans of the new engines were limited in rotational speed because of noise and blade-off considerations, which meant that grafting extra stages on to the back of the booster was progressively less effective. So you had to think about more stages on the high pressure system. The problem there was that the HP compressor became longer while its diameter was constrained to control rotational speed. Then you were into shaft whirl problems and the bearing arrangement to control that was less than optimum.

Mike Howse, current Director of Engineering at Rolls-Royce, summed it up:

The three-shaft engine concept comprises a low-pressure system and a gas generator made up of an intermediate (IP) and high-pressure (HP) system. These three systems can then be individually designed to run at their optimum aerodynamic loading which gives high efficiency and a low number of compressor and turbine stages. This was one of the design intents when the concept was formulated in the mid 1960s.

The lower speed of the IP turbine (relative to the HP) means low mechanical loading so that the IP blade could be uncooled and has remained so on all Trents ever since. This provides further fuel savings.

The fan runs at its own slow correct speed allowing the core compressors, each of modest pressure ratio, to run close to their ideal higher speeds. Each stage can generate high pressure and so relatively few stages are needed with a minimum of variable geometry stators. Because the IP compressor creates high pressure rise, the short HP system, which runs even faster, can avoid the use of variables, allowing easier overhaul and lower cost maintenance.

The three-shaft design is therefore shorter, more rigid and lighter than the equivalent two-shaft engine. It performs its duties with fewer stages, fewer aerofoils, fewer total components, giving low unit cost. The short rigid engine can be designed with high structural strength incorporating double-skin casings and four bearing chambers, each located by a rigid radial support structure. This gives excellent support to each of the short rotating systems ensuring tight tip clearance control for the fan, compressors and turbine blades, giving excellent performance retention.

An inherent advantage of the three-shaft configuration is the flexibility of the arrangement, easily providing a family of engines with a range of bypass ratios or thrusts. This arises because the HP and IP systems can be designed without being compromised by the slow LP system. Individual scaling of components leads to a great number of options and this, combined with present day computer modelling, has made it possible to realise these options industrially in a practical cost effective way ...

With the more efficient structure, the reduced numbers of components and its ability to get more thrust out of a smaller fan diameter, the three-shaft concept has produced lighter engines relative to the two-shaft designs as engine thrust requirements have increased. The inherent thrust-to-weight benefits of the Trent engine can result in a payload advantage of over 8000 lb on the Boeing 777 aircraft.

The 'derivative approach' meant that, apart from material changes and improved aerodynamics, the Trent HP system would be similar to that of the RB 211-524G/H that was under development; whereas Rolls-Royce had introduced the -535E4 as the world's first high-bypass-ratio engine with a wide-chord, snubberless (clapperless) fan and followed suit with later -524s and then with the Trent. Titanium remained the chosen material because, as we saw in Part Two, the attempt to introduce composite blades on the original RB 211s failed in bird-strike tests. The wide-chord blades had proved their worth in thousands of hours of service, most notably when a 757 hit a flock of Canada geese on a take-off from Chicago. One engine ingested at least four 3-kilogram birds but continued to run for the go-around and landing. And this go-around would not be just a simple fly round and land. Regulations would demand that fuel would have to be dumped mid-air so that the aircraft would be much lighter than for take-off.

As we have already seen, Rolls-Royce had made the conscious decision to compete in the large-engine market. How was it going to fare and what was the competition?

The three combatants – Rolls-Royce, GE and Pratt & Whitney – were playing for even higher stakes than in the past. They were aiming specifically at the new breed of big twin-engined aircraft that would operate extensively in the extended-range twin-engine operations environment better known as ETOPS, which some dubbed 'Engines Turn Or Passengers Swim'.

The relevant Federal Aviation Regulation stipulated:

Unless authorized by the Administrator, based on the character of the terrain, the kind of operation, or the performance of the airplane to be used, no certificate holder may operate two-engine or three-engine airplanes (except three-engine turbine powered airplanes) over a route that contains a point farther than one hour flying time (in still air at normal cruising speed with one engine inoperative) from an adequate airport.

This meant the demand would be for the kind of reliability from the beginning of service that, in the past, had been expected only from engines with years of development history. There was also a continuing demand for better performance, reduced fuel burn, lower emissions and noise, and lower operating costs.

GE was the only one of the three developing an all-new core. Pratt & Whitney planned to extend its PW4000 core, and Rolls-Royce was going to develop the Trent from its RB 211 family. The key design feature of the GE90 engine was its huge 3.12-metre-diameter fan, which would boost the bypass ratio to between 9:1 and 10:1. It was expected to enter service at a thrust level of 342 kN, and at this level its wide-chord fan blades would pump through 1,520 kg/s of air at the top of the climb, compared with 830 kg/s for its existing 277 kN CF6-80C2. The bypass ratio of the CF6 was only 5:1. GE, like Pratt & Whitney, was adopting the wide-chord fan for the first time, and, for reasons of weight, GE was also hoping for the fan to be made of composite materials, but was aware of the dangers of delamination under stress or bird impact.

Pratt & Whitney was working on a 2.84-metre-diameter, hollow, shroud-less, titanium wide-chord fan-blade set, yet acknowledged that:

Composites may come into play later as we grow into the Advanced Ducted Prop.

It confidently announced that when the PW4073 went into service with United Airlines (Pratt & Whitney had won the first 777 order), the PW4000 core would have 14 million hours of flight experience behind it.

For its part, Rolls-Royce was promoting its lower turbine entry temperature (TET). According to statistics given to Boeing by all three engine makers, the Trent 665/668 TET would be up to 100°C cooler than the PW4000 on the MD-11 aircraft, and, for the Trent 770/772/775 on the A330 aircraft, 60°C cooler than the CF6-80E1 or the PW4164. The Trent 800 series was claimed to have a TET some 100°C lower for the Boeing 777 aircraft than the GE90. One of the advantages of running cooler would be greater reliability, while maintaining competitive fuel efficiency due to the three-shaft configuration.

Furthermore, the Trent was the lightest of the engines offered for the 777. Rolls-Royce had struggled against the GE CF6 and the Pratt & Whitney JT9 and PW4000 with the extra weight of the RB 211. Now Boeing agreed that the Trent would be lighter than both the Pratt & Whitney and GE engines. However, GE claimed when it announced its brand new GE90 that it would be quieter than the Trent. In a typical example of his humour, Robins retorted:

At the moment it's infinitely quieter than the Trent because it's only a wooden mock-up.

When the Trent engine was unveiled at the Farnborough Air Show in 1988, the father of the jet engine, Sir Frank Whittle, was invited by Rolls-Royce to come and look at it. His first engine had produced 480 lb thrust. Whittle said of the Trent:

The most powerful engine I designed had a thrust of 2,500 lb ... I would have said something like 10,000 lb was as far as we were likely to go. If we wanted more power for a particular aeroplane, we'd just have had more engines than, say, two of these enormous powerful jobs.

ALL SET FAIR

As Rolls-Royce faced its new life as an independent company in the spring of 1987, all seemed set fair on the economic and political fronts.

In June, the Prime Minister, Margaret Thatcher, won a third term in office. The result was decisive, with the Conservatives securing a 101-seat majority. This had not seemed likely earlier in the year when the Government was still suffering the effects of the Westland Helicopters affair.

Indeed, as late as January 1987 the Conservative and Labour parties were given equal backing in the opinion polls, and, in a by-election in the London constituency of Greenwich on 26 February, the Conservative share of the vote fell from 35 per cent, reached in the 1983 election, to just 11 per cent – the biggest decline in any by-election since Thatcher had come to power in 1979.

Nevertheless, with her popularity boosted by a successful and widely publicised visit to the Soviet Union for lengthy talks with Mikhail Gorbachev – someone she had earlier declared she 'could do business with' – Thatcher decided to call the election for 11 June, and won comfortably. In doing so, she became the first Prime Minister since Lord Liverpool 160 years earlier to win three consecutive general-election victories. Furthermore, she did so with a more radical agenda than in 1979 and 1983, spurning the advice of many senior Conservatives to pursue a policy of consolidation. The great psephologist David Butler summed up Thatcher's success in winning her third election:

Mrs Thatcher had gone through one or two bad patches but in Cabinet and parliament she remained overwhelmingly dominant ... and she was presiding over an economy that despite three million unemployed, was continuously growing. An expanding economy is the most generally accepted formula for electoral success.

By the autumn of 1987, the overall economic picture was not looking quite as rosy. In the middle of October, after a long bull-run stretching back to 1982, the world's stock markets crashed; but, in truth, the seeds of Thatcher's eventual downfall had already been sown when the Local Government Finance Act received the royal assent in July 1987. This law established the timetable for the abolition of rates and for its replacement by a flat-rate 'community charge', or 'poll tax' as it became popularly, or perhaps unpopularly, known. In principle, the poll tax was supposed to be simpler, which it probably was, and fairer, which it was not – at least in the sense that many of the poorer members of society would be paying more, while the richer would be paying less, than under the old system of rates. It was introduced at a time of relatively high inflation, and although the Government had estimated that the average charge would be £278 per person, the same as the average rates bill, the outcome was an average of £363. Gallup polls showed it to be the most unpopular reform the UK Government had introduced since the Second World War, and on 31 March 1990 a demonstration in London's West End turned into the worst riot in the city in the twentieth century.

Combined with economic difficulties, mainly caused by overheating, and the Conservative Party's obvious disarray over Europe, the poll tax was the final straw, and Conservatives, fearing that their once brilliant leader was now a liability, voted her out of office when a challenge was mounted by Michael Heseltine in the autumn of 1990. Thatcher gained 204 votes to Heseltine's 152, with 16 abstentions. This was only four votes short of the 56 majority she needed for victory. Her reaction was to fight on, but her cabinet colleagues advised her to quit. This left the way open for others to come forward to fight Heseltine. Two did so: John Major, Chancellor of the Exchequer, and Douglas Hurd, Foreign Secretary. One hundred and eighty-seven votes were required for victory: Major won 185, Heseltine 131 and Hurd 56. Heseltine and Hurd immediately conceded, and John Major, to the surprise of many, became Prime Minister – the youngest, at that point, of the twentieth century.

Nicholas Ridley, Thatcher's close friend, who had been forced to resign his position as Minister for Trade and Industry in 1990 for describing the European Union as a 'German racket', wrote later of the Conservative Party:

It is a very cruel animal … It is ruthless and cruel. Few that evening spared a moment to regret both the fact and the manner of her going, let alone permit themselves a tear. There was much unconcealed pleasure at the clever way they got her out.

David Childs wrote in his *Britain Since 1945*:

When the victory of John Major was announced, Margaret Thatcher said she was 'thrilled'. Labour's John Cunningham called him a Thatcherite and Liberal Democrat Paddy Ashdown said he was 'a Thatcherite with a different face'. The Liberal MP Alan Beith commented, 'I like him and he is a very competent man, but I do not understand what he believes.' His Cabinet colleague, Tony Newton, said he cared deeply about the plight of the under-privileged.

Margaret Thatcher did not remain 'thrilled' for long and irritated Major enormously throughout his six-and-a-half-year period as Prime Minister with her critical comments. Alan Beith had summed up Major accurately – he did not seem to believe in much except competence; but then, that's really what most of the electorate want from their government – competence.

A CRITICAL BREAKTHROUGH

Apart from political ups and downs, Rolls-Royce after privatisation was launched into a booming civil-airline market. Indeed, the major issue in the air transport industry in 1987 was the problem of insufficient airport capacity. The problem was at its worst in the USA, where demand was growing annually at 14 per cent. To cope with this growth in demand, forecasts were put forward for the need for new aircraft. Airbus Industrie calculated that 7,300 airliners would be needed in the next twenty years. Commercial aircraft designers continued to produce new or 'derivative' designs. For example, in February 1987 Airbus Industrie flew its 150-seat A320 for the first time and could boast orders and options for 400 aircraft.

Airbus Industrie also took a bold step when it announced in June 1987 that it would have a new wide-bodied, twin-engined airliner, the A330, which would meet the emerging demand for greater payloads in Europe and elsewhere over short-to-medium distances. Furthermore, it would have a wide-bodied, four-engined, long-range stablemate, the A340. The two aircraft would have a common wing design and many other common components, but different engines.

This was effectively a challenge to the three engine manufacturers to design and develop suitable engines. The A340 could possibly use enhanced versions of existing engines, but clearly the A330 would need something new. Rolls-Royce may have recently been liberated, but, as we have seen, the future looked pretty daunting. There were about 1,500 Rolls-Royce RB 211s flying worldwide – half the number of GE CF6s and Pratt & Whitney JT9Ds. Furthermore, two-thirds of those RB 211s were on Lockheed L.1011 TriStars, an aircraft no longer in production. As airlines looked for replacement aircraft, Rolls-Royce had to force its way on to those new aircraft if it was going to retain its customers.

Under Government control in the 1970s and early 1980s, Rolls-Royce had been acutely aware that its engines were not on enough aircraft types. However, big and radical investment decisions were not possible; only small investment decisions could be made. One of those was to try to get the RB

211 on to the 747. As we saw in Part Two, that was achieved in the late 1970s, and by the late 1980s the RB 211-524, introduced in 1977, had captured 25 per cent of the 747-200/300 market. Rolls-Royce had developed this engine to meet the 747's increasing thrust demands, and had held on to their BA, Qantas and Cathay customers for the extensively updated and higher-rated 747-400.

Perhaps the most important engine competition that Rolls-Royce ever won in the civil market was the one in 1988/9 to supply American Airlines with the RB 211-535E4 for its Boeing 757s. The 757 had originally been launched in 1978 (as we saw in Part Two, Eastern Airlines and British Airways launched it with Rolls-Royce RB 211-535C engines) but initially sold only in small numbers. Boeing's marketing manager for the 737 and 757, Brian Boyd, said:

In retrospect the 757 was developed too early. We didn't anticipate deregulation nor the steady fuel price. The market has grown to the 757.

After the rising fuel costs of the early 1970s, Boeing thought there would be a high demand for a fuel-efficient 727 replacement. However, high labour costs had been largely curbed by the airlines, and the fuel price stabilised, reducing the economic need to replace the three-cockpit-crew 727s with the two-crew 757s. By the mid-1980s, the market was changing. Congestion at airports and in the air combined with noise restrictions to increase the attractions of the 757. The airlines wanted more seats without more flights.

In May 1988, American Airlines ordered 50 757s with an option on another 50, and Chairman Bob Crandall cited the low noise of the RB 211-535 as an important influence on his specifying the Rolls-Royce engines to power the aircraft. For example, American could take the 757s into and out of John Wayne Airport, Orange County, California – which had some of the strictest noise regulations in the world – without any restrictions on the number of movements. Washington National (now Washington Reagan) quickly followed Orange County in imposing night-curfew noise limits. The 757, with Rolls-Royce's RB 211-535, was within these limits but not with Pratt & Whitney's PW2037. This enabled Rolls-Royce to place advertisements referring to 'The Quiet American'.

Richard Turner, currently Marketing Director of Rolls-Royce, said in 2001:

This was an absolutely critical breakthrough. It was a kind of coming-of-age. We had really been a marginal supplier in the States with engines on the TriStar, Fokker F28 and F100 and with a small share on 747s.

Sir Ralph Robins agreed. In his view, the 757 was one of the most important episodes in the growth of Rolls-Royce's position as a civil-engine manu-facturer. It was the first time a Boeing aircraft was launched with a Rolls-Royce engine, and the -535E4's subsequent domination of the market against the Pratt & Whitney 2037 was a major factor in building the airline customer base that Rolls-Royce would exploit to sell the Trent family.

Now Rolls-Royce needed to be on the planned Airbus Industrie twin-jet A330, the McDonnell Douglas tri-jet MD-11 and Boeing's planned 767X. The company certainly took up the challenge, and, a few months before he died in 1999, Stewart Miller told the author that the one thing he wanted to be remembered for was his persuading the Rolls-Royce Board, only a few months after privatisation, that the company should invest in developing the new 'very high thrust' engine, which in the Rolls-Royce manner of naming civil aero-engines after rivers, they called the Trent. Robins said:

We thought about Derwent and Clyde but I decided that Trent was the most appropriate.

There had been two previous Rolls-Royce Trent engines. The first was the 1945 prop-jet demonstrator based on the Derwent, which flew in the Meteor, and the second was the late-1960s fan-jet destined for a Fairchild airliner. Some 1960s Trents were built and ran well, but the aircraft project was abandoned.

The brief was given to the Rolls-Royce engineers to design the best engine to meet the needs of the new wide-bodies of the 1990s. It should be based on the RB 211 three-shaft concept, proven by 45 million hours of experience, and incorporate state-of-the-art technology to give the lowest weight and fuel consumption, highest reliability and a capability of meeting all foreseeable thrust needs as well as noise and emission regulations.

When the Rolls-Royce Board gave its approval for the Trent development programme, the forecast for the potential market in the 1992–2001 period was 2,650 engines, and the presumed Rolls-Royce share was 22 per cent. Rolls-Royce spread its risk by bringing in its old friends in Japan – Kawasaki Heavy Industries (KHI) and Ishikawajima Harima Heavy Industries (IHI) – who between them took up an 11 per cent risk-sharing stake in the Trent programme. This consolidated a relationship that Rolls-Royce had been building in Japan for fifteen years. Manufacturing agreements had been set up on the Orpheus and Adour engines and on early models of the RB 211-524. There had also been a partnership with Kawasaki on industrial and marine engines. And, of course, the three Japanese companies – Kawasaki, Ishikawajima Harima and Mitsubishi Heavy Industries – were members of the Japanese Aero Engines Corporation, which had joined the consortium that developed the V-2500. Apart from spreading the risks, Rolls-Royce hoped that the Japanese links would help penetration of the Trent in the Far East, where demand for wide-bodied aircraft was expected to be particularly strong.

Discussions were continuing with Boeing on the possibility of the Trent being the launch engine on the 767X. A product strategy had been developed that would make the Trent suitable for all three new wide-bodied aircraft being developed. There would be three basic engine ratings but with a high degree of component commonality to minimise the effect on the total launch costs. Based on the Trent being the launch engine in the 767X with one initial competitor, Rolls-Royce's view by late 1989 was that it would achieve a market share of 30 per cent rather than the 22 per cent forecast a year earlier.

At the time of the launch of the Trent, Boeing was studying a rewinged development of the existing 767. However, during 1989 the strategy changed, and Boeing proposed to develop a new aircraft with a competitive advantage over the rather larger Airbus A330 in terms of payload, range and cruise speed, but with a weight 12 per cent greater than the A330. This would need a higher-thrust engine, and by late 1989 a high-thrust version of the Trent had become a prime candidate for the possible launch customers, which included BA, United, American and Delta. BA was naturally seen as a key target customer, and a separate strategy was worked out to secure the British airline as the 767X launch customer.

The design of the 767X was aimed at the 4,000 nautical miles of intra-European and US domestic routes as a replacement for DC-10s and TriStars by 1995. The initial weight of the aircraft would be 495,000 lb, with growth to 550,000 lb to satisfy the 5,500 nautical miles of North Atlantic routes by 1997. A final growth step for an even higher-weight aircraft to tackle trans-pacific or high-density routes was planned for the year 2000.

'WE DECIDED TO MAKE A NEW AIRPLANE'

When Boeing had assembled a team to design a brand new aircraft for the 1990s, Alan Mulally, second-in-command to engineer Phil Condit on the design team, said to them:

The airlines of the world told us they wanted an airplane that was bigger than the 767 and smaller than the 747. And we said, 'Why don't you buy 767s?' And they said, 'We want an airplane that's bigger than the 767 and smaller than the 747 because on some of the city pairs that we fly we cannot get enough people to fill up a 747 and we have too many for a 767.' It took us two years to figure out that they really wanted an airplane that was bigger than the 767 and smaller than the 747. So we decided to make a new airplane.

Jeff Pearce, chief project engineer on the 777 in the early 1990s, said:

Our forecasters were telling us that the total requirement for the industry through 2005 would be about 8,400 aircraft, worth some $516 billion and that approximately $210 billion worth of those aircraft would be in the medium-sized range.

We initially considered simply building an enlarged derivative of the 767, designated 767X. We came up with some pretty wild configurations, including the 'humpback of Mukilteo', named after the shape of the fuselage and a small town near Everett, where Boeing builds its widebodies. This was a 767 with an upper deck, much like the 747, but the deck was situated aft and so the aircraft was much stranger looking. Most of us thought it was ugly, and when an aircraft does not look right, it probably is not the best solution ... That was when we decided to build a new aircraft family, the 777.

To help them, Boeing pulled together a team of representatives from eight of the world's largest airlines – United, American, Delta, British Airways, Japan Airlines, All Nippon Airways, Qantas and Cathay Pacific. These became known as the 'Gang of Eight'. In the end, the 777 was closer to the 747-100 in size, and 747-400 in systems, than it was to the 767. It was bigger than the other two large airliners – the twin-engined Airbus A330 and the triple-engined McDonnell Douglas MD-11.

The competition to supply the engines for this new aircraft would be close and fierce, as was illustrated in this remark by Gordon McKinzie of United Airlines, after he had selected Pratt & Whitney engines:

I'd say all three of the engines were technically very, very comparable. The GE engine was an excellent engine, but a brand-new-technology engine. There were three parts of that engine that were virtually new technology. It had a new wide-chord composite blade, a new combustor design, and a very high-pressure compressor which they had never tried before. But that engine also had a lot more growth potential than some of the others, and it had excellent fuel burn, so it was a real contender. The Rolls engine [was] also a great engine [with] a big core ... we spent a lot of time in Derby looking at that engine. But we knew the Pratt engine very well, we were flying the core engine on the 747s and the 767s and we looked at the new engine they were looking at for this airplane, which was a kind of an extension of that design and we felt comfortable. But, in all honesty, all three engines would have worked for us.

Rolls-Royce put in place a strategy for the Trent family of engines that could cope with the demands they anticipated from the airlines and therefore the airframe makers. The Trent 650 was for the McDonnell Douglas MD-11 and had the capability of 4 per cent growth to the Trent 660, which would be competitive if McDonnell Douglas developed the aircraft to higher weights.

In the event, Rolls-Royce concentrated on providing an engine for McDonnell Douglas's long-range, 375-seat MD-12 airliner. The Trent 680 was planned for the entry of the A330 into service in 1995, but a higher-thrust engine, the Trent 720, was planned for use by Cathay Pacific and Trans World Airlines (TWA). The Trent 720 would meet the requirements of Airbus's plans to increase the weight of the A330 from 208 to 223 tonnes. The Trent 760 would meet the requirements of Boeing's planned 550,000lb 767X. However, Boeing's plans for the ultimate development of the 767X to a maximum weight of 600,000lb would require a take-off thrust around 85,000 to 90,000lb. This would mean Rolls-Royce producing an engine with an increased fan diameter of up to 120 inches, with further core improvements and a new nacelle.

In looking at the competition, Rolls-Royce came to a number of conclusions. In terms of thrust, the Trent family was well matched to the competition and possessed adequate growth potential. For example, it would enhance the MD-11 capabilities from 'hot and high' airfields. Pratt & Whitney offered similar thrust capability, but the GE CF6-80C2 had limited growth potential and could not meet the thrust requirements of the heavier-weight versions of the A330 and 767X. As a result, it was thought GE was considering the development of a brand new, large-diameter engine.

The RB 211 had always been heavier, thrust for thrust, than its competitors, and the Trent gave Rolls-Royce a chance to eradicate this disadvantage. The Trent was similar in weight to its Pratt & Whitney competitors and, although it was heavier than the GE CF6-80E1 proposed for the A330, the GE engine did not possess adequate thrust for the higher-weight versions of the A330.

On fuel consumption, it was difficult to tie down an exact position. McDonnell Douglas said that the Trent was about 1 per cent worse than Pratt & Whitney and 1 per cent better than GE. Boeing had audited both the Trent and the Pratt & Whitney engine for the 767X and found them about equal. The GE90, a new high-bypass-ratio engine, was better but lost advantage from installation costs and high weight. Airbus showed the Trent to be worse than its competitors. One per cent of the deficit was due to the Trent long nacelle – a disadvantage Rolls-Royce expected to overcome after wind-tunnel testing. Rolls-Royce put the remaining deficit down to Airbus conservatism or unreal bids from Pratt & Whitney and GE. Rolls-Royce therefore entered discussions with Airbus to ensure a competitive representation of the Trent.

On reliability, Rolls-Royce showed the airlines and airframe manufacturers that the Trent was the fourth generation of the RB 211 and that intense attention was being given to ensure that the service experience of the earlier RB 211s would be fed into the Trent design. Rolls-Royce could show that such attention to detail had been applied with great success to the -535.

Crucial to the success of the Trent family of engines was Rolls-Royce's successful development of the wide-chord fan. To appreciate the significance of this development, we need to understand in basic terms how a gas-turbine aero-engine works.

The engine sucks in air, compresses it, adds fuel and burns it, and ejects the resultant gas as a hot stream that drives the turbines, and thereby the compressors and the aircraft forwards. The function of the large fan at the front of the engine is to act as the first stage in the sequence of compressing the air that is ingested. The fan is like a multi-bladed propeller, some 8 feet or more in diameter in modern gas-turbine engines, and is driven by the rearmost turbine in the engine. The fan sucks in more than half a tonne of air every second, and more than 80 per cent of that air bypasses the gas-generator section of the engine, while the other 20 per cent is greatly compressed and then mixed with vaporised fuel and burned to provide the hot gas exhaust stream. At the rear of the engine, the bypass air is mixed with the hot gas exhaust to provide a massive rearward force that drives the engine and aircraft forward at high speed.

The front fan is one of the most vital parts of the engine. It is driven by 50,000 to 100,000 horsepower or more, which is extracted from the hot gas flow by means of the low-pressure turbine in the engine. This huge power is essential because the rotating fan is required to pump enormous volumes of air through the engine. The fan blades provide thrust in the same way as the wings of an aircraft produce lift, but the speed at which a fan blade meets the intake air increases along its span. Near its root, the twisted aerofoil sections of a fan blade act like the wing of a subsonic aircraft, progressively changing to that of a fighter flying at supersonic speed near the tip. Effectively, the fan provides propulsion efficiency.

Because the fan produces so much of an engine's thrust, any improvement in its overall design that improves its efficiency has a beneficial effect on fuel consumption. Producing blades with a wider chord (i.e. the width in relation to the length) means the blades can be made stiffer and aerodynamically more stable, which in turn means fewer blades to achieve the same task. Thus, there is a saving in weight and, as it happens, greater foreign-object damage resistance.

After almost 25 years of development, Rolls-Royce produced the wide-chord fan with hollow blades filled with a metal honeycomb core. Viability was only achieved after many extremely exacting requirements had been satisfied in relation to adequate fatigue life, the minimising of vibration stresses and the provision of resistance to impact by birds and other foreign objects.

The wide-chord fan also brought significant benefits in noise reduction, thanks to the smaller number of blades and the blockage effect produced by the wider fan blades, making it more difficult for noise to escape forwards through the fan on a landing approach. At high thrust – on take-off or climb – the more rigid wide-chord fan blades produce less of the 'buzz-saw' sound that results from the supersonic flow over the tips of more flexible, narrower-chord blades.

Rolls-Royce's first wide-chord fan went into service in late 1984 on the RB 211-535E4 powering the Boeing 757. It immediately showed its strengths in better fuel consumption, lower noise and increased reliability, and was soon used at different sizes on four other engines: the Tay turbofan, the V-2500, the higher-thrust developments of the RB 211-524 and the Trent.

By October 1989, the decision by the Board in June 1988 to proceed with the Trent programme seemed to be fully justified. Launch orders had been secured on the McDonnell Douglas MD-11 with Air Europe and on the Airbus A330 with Cathay Pacific. An order had also been placed by Trans World Airlines for Trent-powered A330s. Firm and option orders had reached 228, including those from the International Lease Finance Corporation (ILFC).

A progress report for the Board said:

Discussions have continued with Boeing, who are now finalising the specification of the 767X. This is a totally new and highly competitive aircraft for which we have an opportunity to be launch engine and therefore secure a market share equivalent to that achieved by the 535. A further development of the Trent for this new aircraft has been studied and Boeing now require formal proposals from the engine manu-facturers, prior to a submission to their Board at the end of October.

A product strategy has been developed for the application of the Trent to all three new wide bodied aircraft and their future developments. Three basic engine ratings are identified to meet the different requirements of these aircraft, but a high degree of component commonality between the ratings has minimised the effect on the total launch costs.

On current sales, orders and options, the Trent was achieving a 60 per cent share on the A330 but only a 6 per cent share on the MD-11. However, the report saw opportunities about to rise on the MD-11 – especially in the Pacific Basin with Japanese Airlines, All Nippon Airways and Singapore Airlines, as well as with Continental in the USA.

Success with Airbus Industrie was particularly sweet because, apart from the International Aero Engines (IAE) V-2500 on the A320 and its A319 and A321 derivatives, Rolls-Royce had never powered an Airbus aircraft. Jean Pierson, the charismatic Managing Director of Airbus Industrie, when asked in May 1991 if he was not stretching the company by launching the A330 and A340 at the same time, said characteristically:

No. The most risky time for us was between 1978 and 1984, when we were introducing the A310 and developing the A300-600 and A320. For the next ten years we are looking at less investment than the last ten ... There was a debate within Airbus. Some people said we should launch a twin, others a quad. Finally, the engineers promised they could do both aircraft with a common airframe for half a billion less. Let's go! ... The A330 and A340 do not represent a technology goal. The goal is to increase market share and, using the technology of the A320, to make money with that share. It's a business goal. When you launch an aircraft you have to decide your priorities. These aircraft have already helped us to increase our market share from 20 per cent to 30 per cent in the last four years. We've sold more than 200 aircraft of both types and the A340 is not due to fly for five months.

'A BILLION-DOLLAR BILL IS NOW SMALL CHANGE'

The strong market conditions that Rolls-Royce had enjoyed at privatisation in 1987 continued into 1988, with Boeing, McDonnell Douglas and Airbus Industrie all stretched to capacity. Boeing was the top producer, with 747s coming out of its Seattle plant at the rate of one per week. The 757 suddenly received a large spate of orders, and by the end of September 1988 Boeing had sold 368, compared with 307 of the 767s. Selling more than any of these three was Boeing's smaller aircraft, the 737. Europe's competing Airbus A320 entered service in February 1988, and, by the end of the year, orders and options had reached 700, comfortably above the 600 break-even level.

Rolls-Royce, full of confidence and renewed energy after its successful privatisation, began to increase its market share. As we saw earlier, on 26 May 1988 it was announced that American Airlines had ordered 50 Boeing 757-200 airliners to be powered by twin Rolls-Royce RB 211-535E4 engines. The contract was worth more than £500 million to Rolls-Royce over the life of the aircraft and could be worth over £1 billion if American took up its option of another 50 aircraft. Francis Tombs said that Rolls-Royce's share of the world civil aero-engine market had reached 20 per cent and was still rising. Bob Crandall, Chairman and President of American Airlines, said that they had chosen the Rolls-Royce engine in preference to the Pratt & Whitney 2037 because:

It is a very quiet, fuel-efficient and extremely reliable engine that is also exceptionally cost effective to operate. The first 757s came in even quieter than we thought they would. Initial operating experience is very good, very good indeed.

By the late 1980s, American Airlines was the largest airline in the Western world, both in terms of fleet size and passengers carried. Based in Dallas, Texas, it had been founded in 1929 out of a combination of no fewer than 85 small airlines. Since then, led for many years by the legendary C.R. Smith, who eventually became Lyndon Johnson's Secretary of Commerce in 1968 (the appointment caused American to change its mind about buying the British-made RB 211 for its Douglas DC-10s, as we saw in Part Two), American pioneered many new features of the US airline industry scene. For example, it offered the first sleeper service on its Curtiss Condors in the early 1930s, and it also offered the first non-stop coast-to-coast service in both directions in 1953 with the Douglas DC-7.

Bob Baker, American's Vice-President of Operations, said that American's experience with Rolls-Royce's RB 211-535E4 had been 'outstanding', adding:

We haven't had any problems. They are doing just what Rolls told us they would do.

Looking to the future, he said:

Clearly big twins are coming into their own. The next big competition, or challenge if you will, for the manufacturers and the airlines to deal with will be the replacement of the widebodies. My own view is that it will probably be a big twin so the implication to a manufacturer like Rolls-Royce is larger engines [with] more thrust, which is represented by Rolls's Trent.

And on into 1989 the boom went. Boeing's flagship, the new 747-400, entered service in February. The industry was being swamped by record-breaking orders. The Californian-based International Lease Finance Corporation had ordered 130 Boeing and Airbus transporters in May 1988, but this order was eclipsed in April 1989 by Guinness Peat Aviation's order, worth $16.8 billion, for 308 airliners spread over all three manufacturers. The leasing industry had become very significant because airline profits could not finance the 8,500 aircraft Boeing estimated would be needed over the next decade (a huge increase on Airbus Industrie's calculation of 7,300 aircraft over twenty years, made two years earlier). On a single day in February, McDonnell Douglas announced orders worth $11 billion from five airlines, including an order for 50 MD-11 tri-jets from American Airlines. And in April, United ordered 370 aircraft worth $15.7 billion, prompting *Flight International* to write:

A billion-dollar bill is now the small change of aircraft buying.

As Michael Donne wrote in the *Financial Times* on 7 June 1989:

The world's aerospace industries go to the Paris International Air Show with order books fuller than ever before, and an optimistic view of business through to the end of the century … In military aviation, despite cuts in some defence budgets, there is still

TOP: The Rolls-Royce Tay, already successful on the Gulfstream GIV, was also selected for the Fokker regional jet, the F100: the twin-engined, short-range airliner. It was selected not only by huge airlines such as American but also by smaller ones such as China Eastern.

BOTTOM: Fokker developed a regional jet, the Fokker 70, which was also powered by the Rolls-Royce Tay.

TOP: Rolls-Royce sold the RB 211-524H to British Airways to power its Boeing 767s.

BOTTOM: The new-generation Boeing, the 747-400, entered service in February 1989. Here, a Qantas 747-400 takes off from Heathrow, powered by Rolls-Royce RB 211-524s, on a record-breaking non-stop flight to Sydney, Australia.

Sir Ralph Robins, as Managing Director of Rolls-Royce,
and Bob Crandall, as President of American Airlines, shake hands
on the deal specifying the Rolls-Royce RB 211-535 to power the
100 Boeing 757s ordered by American Airlines in 1988.
Crandall cited the low noise levels of the RB 211-535 as a critical
factor, giving credence to Rolls-Royce's advertisements referring
to 'The Quiet American'.

Phil Ruffles, Rolls-Royce's Director of Engineering and Technology in the 1990s, was largely responsible for implementing Project Derwent, which did so much to improve the development of new engines within the company.

Sir Frank Whittle, pioneer of the jet age, could scarcely believe the power of the engines of the 1990s. Here, he celebrates the progress with Sir Ralph Robins, standing in front of a Rolls-Royce Trent prototype.

Mike Terrett, President of International Aero Engines from 1998 to 2000 – a period of strong growth for the consortium.

OPPOSITE TOP: After some severe teething problems in development, the V-2500 engine – a collaborative venture between Rolls-Royce, Pratt and Whitney, MTU, Fiat and the Japanese Aero Engines Corporation – enjoyed great success throughout the 1990s and into the new millennium, powering the Airbus A320 and its derivatives: the A319 and A321.

OPPOSITE BOTTOM: Lufthansa expressed concerns about the early V-2500s that it originally ordered for its A320s, but eventually ordered the engine for its A321s.

Powered by International Aero Engines V-2500s, the Airbus A320
and A319 were bought in large numbers by United Airlines, British
Airways and the Latin American Alliance of Grupo Taca,
TAM Brazil and LanChile.

substantial spending on aircraft and associated weapons systems of all kinds ... Several important projects are under development, including the French Dassault Rafale and the Anglo-German-Italian-Spanish European Aircraft. Other countries are making massive purchases of aircraft and associated weapons systems. One example is the recent Saudi Arabian weapons deal with the UK, Al Yamamah II, believed initially to be worth some £35 billion but ultimately perhaps as much as £150 billion. It provides for eventual maintenance of the equipment in service over many years, including Tornado and Hawk fighters, Westland helicopters, new air bases and new systems.

Donne went on to point out that the same boom conditions existed on the civil side. More than 1,000 new jet airlines had been added to order books in the previous twelve months. At the end of 1989, there were about 2,000 new jet airliners on order, worth some £40 billion. The next ten years were expected to bring £367 billion of business for aircraft, £130 billion of which would be accounted for by aero-engines. Over a billion passengers travelled by air in 1989, and forecasters expected this number to double by the end of the century.

Flight International did sound a note of caution in its issue of 10 June 1989. In an article with the heading 'Countdown to 1,000 Whitetails?', it wrote:

The new airlines have ordered 3,000 new jets, and at Paris they will buy more. Fifty million new passengers a year will be needed to fill them. If the present traffic boom falters, one third of the new orderbook could be surplus by 1995.

In the meantime, Rolls-Royce's success continued. On 8 February 1989, it announced that it had won its first order for a civil airliner manufactured by McDonnell Douglas since 1965, when the Rolls-Royce Conway was chosen for the DC-8. (It had supplied engines for the British-designed Hawk trainer and Harrier fighter made by McDonnell Douglas in the 1980s.) This was the first order for the RB 211-524L (soon to be called the Trent), on which Rolls-Royce was spending up to £500 million in development, and came from International Leisure Group – the parent company of UK-based Air Europe, run by the ebullient, if mercurial, Harry Goodman. The firm order for eighteen engines was worth £100 million.

This order was somewhat eclipsed a month later when American Airlines placed a massive order worth $4 billion (£2.3 billion). Included in the deal were 75 Fokker F100 twin-engined, short-range airliners, with an option on another 75, and 25 Boeing 757 twin-engined, short-to-medium range airliners with fifteen options and the possibility of buying up to another 70 Boeing airliners, of which 40 would probably be 757s. In the firm order category came ten Boeing 767-300ER (extended range) twin-engined

19

aircraft. Rolls-Royce was a huge beneficiary as the Fokker F100 was powered by Tay engines and the 757 by RB 211-535E4Bs. If all the options were confirmed, over 500 Rolls-Royce engines would be bought. Sir Ralph Robins said:

We worked hard for ten years to convince American Airlines that our engines were the best for its business. That hard work has paid off.

More good news followed in April when Cathay Pacific Airways ordered ten Airbus Industrie A330 twin-engined airliners and specified the Rolls-Royce RB 211-524L engine. If Cathay also took up the ten options, the order would be worth $600 million to Rolls-Royce. David Gledhill, Chairman of Cathay, said the A330, seating 315 passengers, with deliveries starting in January 1995, would replace Lockheed TriStars and was ideal for medium-range operations in the Asia-Pacific market, enabling Cathay to increase flight frequency and open new routes. Rolls-Royce was also involved in an update of Cathay's orders for long-range Boeing 747-400s, whereby it increased its firm contract from five to six aircraft, with another eighteen on option.

We saw in the second volume of this history how Cathay's chief engineer, Stewart John, had evaluated very carefully the engines being offered by Rolls-Royce, GE and Pratt & Whitney before choosing the Rolls-Royce RB 211 for its first 747 in 1978, and how Ralph Robins, then Rolls-Royce's Commercial Director, had gambled by giving Cathay the sort of concessions normally reserved for orders of tens of engines. The gamble paid off, for Cathay's services – and therefore purchases of aircraft – grew like topsy in the 1980s, and all of its fleet of Lockheed TriStars and Boeing 747s were powered by RB 211s.

By 1990, Cathay was operating eighteen TriStars and seventeen 747-200s and -300s. It had taken delivery of its first 747-400 in June 1989, and by the end of 1990 was operating six. All these 747-400s were powered by RB 211-524 engines. The earliest were powered by the -524G, rated at 58,000 lb thrust, but from May 1990 the more powerful -524H, rated at 60,600 lb, had been fitted. Indeed, Cathay was the launch customer for the -524H, and though it did not need the 60,600 lb thrust for most of the time, it did for the hot days at Gatwick (there is a hill at the end of the runway) and for the 33°C days, common for five months of the year, at Hong Kong's Kai Tak airport.

Such experience gave Cathay great confidence in Rolls-Royce and in the potential of the Trent. Stewart John had now ordered it for the A330, and if Cathay were to buy the Boeing 777, which he saw as a complementary rather than a competing aircraft, then he could buy the Trent 800 for the 777 to go with the Trent 700 for the A330.

On 19 June 1989, Rolls-Royce announced that it had won orders and options so far in 1989 for more than 700 civil engines, worth over £1.5 billion. It calculated that, with the subsequent sales of spares over the lives of these engines, the ultimate value of the orders could reach £3 billion. There were orders for 188 Tay engines for use in the Fokker F100 airliner, with options on another 180 engines. In the RB 211 family, there were 148 orders and 24 options for the -535E4 in the Boeing 757, 61 orders and 27 options for the -524G and -H engines in the 767 and 747, and 38 orders and 56 options for the -524L in the twin-engined Airbus A330 and the tri-jet McDonnell Douglas MD-11.

Rolls-Royce worked closely with Airbus Industrie to offer its RB 211-524L, renamed the Trent, on the A330 – the first high-capacity twin in the marketplace. This would make the A330 the first Airbus aircraft to be powered by Rolls-Royce engines, although the A320 was already flying with V-2500 engines from the International Aero Engines consortium in which Rolls-Royce had a 30 per cent stake.

The A330 aimed to fill two roles. First, it aimed to replace the 300-to-350-seat Lockheed TriStar and McDonnell Douglas DC-10 and provide the economy of having only two engines as well as the advantages of a completely new design. Second, Airbus felt it was the logical next step-up for the many operators of Airbus A300 and Boeing 767 airliners as they sought to increase their carrying capacity above 250 passengers.

Cathay Pacific, the first to choose Rolls-Royce engines for its A330s, and Trans World Airlines both chose the aircraft to replace their ageing three-engined wide-body aircraft. In June 1989, it was announced that TWA had ordered twenty A330s with an option on a further twenty. The aircraft would be powered by Rolls-Royce's new 'big thrust' engine, the Trent. Rolls-Royce said that when the Trent entered service in 1993/4, it would be the most powerful jet engine available, capable of thrusts up to 72,000 lb in the variant engineered for TWA, but with development capacity to take it up eventually to 80,000 lb. TWA had specified the Trent because it would enable its A330s to fly non-stop from New York to Rome, or from St Louis to Frankfurt, or from Los Angeles to London. Sir Ralph Robins, by now Deputy Chairman and Managing Director, said that the TWA deal brought total orders and options for the Trent engine up to 174, and added:

It firmly establishes the Trent as the best-selling engine for the A330 airbus, with the largest market share of firm orders and options, over 60 per cent. Since we unveiled the engine at Farnborough last year [in 1988], the Trent has been launched on two of the airframes for which it is targeted – the A330 and the McDonnell Douglas MD11.

And even though the world economic clouds darkened in 1990, the orders for commercial aircraft still flowed in; unfortunately, not all of them to be powered by Rolls-Royce engines. British Airways signed for 33 747-400s at a cost of $130 million each, China reserved 72 Boeing aircraft worth $4 billion, International Lease Finance Corporation put in orders and options for 87 Boeing airliners worth $4.5 billion, Singapore Airlines ordered 50 Boeing 747s and McDonnell Douglas MD-11s worth $8.6 billion, Delta Airlines ordered 50 McDonnell Douglas MD-90s and 50 Boeing 737-300s worth $10 billion, and All Nippon Airways ordered 35 aircraft from Boeing and Airbus Industrie in orders worth $5.8 billion. BA's Boeing 747-400s would be powered by Rolls-Royce RB 211s. The order, for 160 engines and spare parts, would be worth £600 million.

And in October, United Airlines ordered 34 Boeing 777s at a cost of $11 billion. Boeing expected the 777 to enter service in 1995. As we saw earlier, United did not break from their long tradition of specifying Pratt & Whitney engines.

'AN ENGINE A DAY FOR SEVEN YEARS'

We read in Part Two how Rolls-Royce teamed up with Pratt & Whitney, MTU of Germany, Fiat of Italy and the Japanese Aero Engines Corporation of Japan to form this consortium to develop the V-2500 ('V' for five countries, and '2500' for the 25,000 lb initial thrust of the engine). The targets for the engine were the Airbus A320 and the MD-90. It might also be used in new derivatives of the smaller Boeing 737, such as the 737-300, and in some versions of the McDonnell Douglas DC-9. The first order was won in January 1985 when Pan Am ordered it for sixteen Airbus A320s due to go into service in the late 1980s.

We also read of the horrendous problems Rolls-Royce encountered in getting the compressor on the engine to work. Jock Hill, head of aerothermal technology under Phil Ruffles at the time, recalled that:

Once Tom Harper [from Pratt & Whitney] and Mike Williams [from Rolls-Royce] had put some sense and direction into the enterprise, the V2500 produced the most intense and concentrated recovery effort that Derby has ever seen. We were told that if the project was cancelled, and if we survived the financial fallout, we would never be entrusted again with a major project.

To concentrate minds further, a letter jointly signed by Stewart Miller, Director of Corporate Engineering, and Phil Ruffles, Director of Design Engineering, was sent on 18 November 1987 to everyone on the project, including those as senior as Jock Hill, which said *inter alia*:

The Company is totally dedicated to the achievement of certification and entry-into-service on time of the -524G, V2500 and Tay 650 programmes, recognising the total workload that this implies. The coming weeks are of particular significance.

We have become increasingly aware of the need to maintain adequate standards of professionalism in the conduct of our Derby engineering programmes. It is your responsibility as Managers to ensure that this applies to your subordinates as well as to yourself. It is also your responsibility to highlight any situation which could hazard the attainment of the Company's objectives.

The pressures in the current certification programmes are very great and the response has in general been excellent, although we are conscious that a relatively small number of individuals are carrying the heaviest load. Visibility within the industry of errors of judgement in engineering practice is very high and the consequences for the Company could be serious and far-reaching.

Any failures to achieve the necessary standards may result in disciplinary action including, in the most serious of cases, the possibility of dismissal.

We regret having to write to you in this way but it is vital that all those involved clearly understand the situation.

This came as a great shock to many but clearly served its purpose, and, as we saw, the V-2500 programme was rescued and the engine certificated on time. At that point, Sir Ralph Robins wrote to Stewart Miller, saying:

I should like to congratulate you and your whole team on the amazing recovery of the V2500 programme to certificate on time. Now all that remains is to bring the 95B [HP compressor] in as fast as possible and we have got a respectable engine.

Please pass on my congratulations to all those concerned.

After this dramatic start, the engine originally envisaged emerged, and the IAE consortium and the V-2500 competed very successfully with the well-established GE/SNECMA CFM56.

The V-2500 was designed to be the most reliable, cost-efficient and environmentally conscious civil engine ever produced. The advanced technology included wide-chord fan blades, single-crystal turbine blades, powder-metallurgy discs and Full-Authority Digital Engine Control (FADEC). The engine also had one of the most comprehensive heat-management systems ever developed, designed to use the minimum of air-bleed for cooling. It used fuel instead and, for the majority of any flight, diverted fuel back through the aircraft's wing tanks, using them as giant coolers. This brought a 2 per cent benefit in specific fuel consumption compared with the traditional air-bleed method. As for the question of its competing with the CFM56, 'very well' is the answer, though as with all consortia there have been moments of tension. There was an immediate setback in February 1988 when Lufthansa, which had ordered fifteen Airbus 320s with an option on 25 more, changed the engine specification from the V-2500 to the GE/SNECMA CFM56 on the grounds that the V-2500 did not show indications of being sufficiently reliable. This decision immediately prompted Pan Am to review its engine position on the sixteen A320s, with 34 on option, that it had ordered. This caused the IAE consortium to worry about other orders – from Cyprus Airways, Adria of Yugoslavia, Indian Airlines, Australian Airlines and Royal Jordanian.

Lufthansa did not pull any punches, saying:

The risk of delayed deliveries of the A320 with V2500 engines, and of a technical engine reliability not matching Lufthansa's quality standard, seemed too high for the airline. Lufthansa wants to avoid repeated modifications necessary to obtain the final configuration of these engines. Overall, the CFM engine is said to have a secure growth potential, whereas there is some doubt concerning the V2500. It has also proved its reliability on different types of aircraft and meanwhile matches the V2500 in terms of operating cost.

Nick Tomassetti, President of the IAE consortium, responded by saying that although there had been problems, these were 'now behind us'. He claimed that, as a result of improvements, the V-2500 was now 'a modern, efficient and quieter power-plant than its competitor'. The engine was on target to enter passenger service in April 1989, a date set when the engine was launched in January 1984.

In spite of these reassurances, life was going to be tough for the consortium. Michael Donne put it this way in the *Financial Times*:

Mr Tomassetti and his team will be required by his remaining customers fully to document and support these claims. He may well also be asked why, if they are true, and if Lufthansa was aware of them, that airline still remained sufficiently sceptical to change its mind at such a late stage in the A320's own development stage, and opt for the rival engine. Upon satisfactory answers to that question rest not only the retention of remaining customers, but also the chances of winning new ones in what is already a fiercely competitive fight.

The consortium managed to hold on to the orders from Cyprus Airways, Indian Airways and Adria, and in 1990 was part of a deal whereby America West Airlines bought 118 A320s. We shall see how thin on the ground airline orders were once the recession of 1990–92 set in and how great a relief it was when United Airlines announced in July 1992 that it was buying 100 A320s to be powered by the V-2500. The first aircraft was due for delivery in November 1993. It was understood that Airbus had put together a very attractive deal to win the order in competition with Boeing's 737-400. Boeing said:

We made a very attractive offer and went as far as prudence would dictate. Obviously Airbus could do more.

And Airbus put the squeeze on IAE to come up with a very good price for the engines. It was reported to the main Board at Rolls-Royce that:

The United Airlines fifty firm plus fifty options order for A320s had been a significant boost both for Airbus and for IAE, but the terms, certainly for the latter, had been very tough. IAE management had committed concession levels far higher than those approved by the Company. Mr [Frank] Turner [a director of IAE] was now in the United States looking to see what procedures and protection were practicable and to see how far it would be possible to claw back the concessions given in drawing up the formal contract. It might be more sensible to hand over management formally to Pratt & Whitney so that they would carry responsibility for unauthorised commitments. This prospect was being investigated.

The success of the bid had knocked Boeing, who now felt that it would have to rejuvenate the 737 to be competitive and offer the V-2500 as an alternative to the CFM56.

Whatever the short-term financial pain for IAE, the breakthrough into United – the second biggest airline in the USA – at least brought further orders. By 2001, United had bought 113 A319s and A320s. Whether it had an effect or not, Lufthansa also came back and selected the V-2500 for its A321s.

It was rumoured, if not said openly, that Lufthansa was concerned about the noise and vibration of the CFM56, which it felt could affect the life of the A321 and reduce its resale value.

In what Mike Terrett – now President of Civil Aerospace at Rolls-Royce, but also President of IAE from 1998 to 2000 – described as Phase Three in the life of IAE from 1992 to 1995, 'not much happened' – except, presumably, the routine production and delivery of engines.

By the middle of 1994, of the 450 Airbus A320s and A321s in service, just over 300 were powered by CFM International engines and 150 by V-2500s. However, IAE seemed to be gaining market share. Since 1989, more than 50 per cent of orders had gone to them, and since 1992 IAE's share had reached 80 per cent. One of the V-2500's advantages over the CFM56 was its consistent specific fuel consumption (about a 6 per cent advantage).

Phase Four, from 1995 to 2000, was a period of great activity on the sales front, spearheaded initially by Barry Eccleston, who came from a spell in charge of Rolls-Royce Canada with a strong marketing-skills reputation.

By June in 1997, IAE had won seven of the eight engine competitions on the A320 that year, the latest being British Midland's selection of the V-2500 for its twenty new A320s and A321s. Up to that point, British Midland had been operating CFM56-powered 737s. However, Eccleston expressed 'frustration at not being on a Boeing aircraft'. By this time, CFM had 55 per cent of the units on the Airbus A320 family, while IAE had 55 per cent of the customers. As the GE CFM56 had enjoyed a considerable head-start on the V-2500, this represented a strong catch-up by IAE. IAE was predicting that over the next fifteen years it would triple its current customer base of 70 and would expect to increase its 700 engines in service to 4,000.

By this time, the V-2500 engine had been expanded in both directions from its original 25,000 lb thrust. There were eight variants, from 22,000 lb for the latest and smallest Airbus – the 124-seat A319 – to 33,000 lb for the largest Airbus – a single-aisle 200-seat A321-200. This versatility meant the engine was ideal not only for charter airlines using their aircraft for 1,300 hours a month in the peak holiday season, but also for a US non-stop coast-to-coast operation run by United Airlines and Trans-Asia's short commercial routes in Taiwan.

The year 1998 brought a slightly odd move by Pratt & Whitney when it launched a new engine, the PW8000, announcing that it would 'offer up to 10 per cent lower operating costs than competing engines for the Airbus A320 and Boeing 737 families, the V-2500 and CFM International CFM56'. Rolls-Royce was unimpressed by the announcement of a competitor to the consortium in which Pratt & Whitney was a 30 per cent shareholder. At the Asian Aerospace Show in Singapore in April 1998, Sir Ralph Robins describing the PW8000 as a 'two-and-a-half shaft engine', said it was 'thirty years too late' and 'an extremely retrograde step'.

Pratt & Whitney President, Karl Krapek, responded by saying that Rolls-Royce had taken the compressor of the V-2500 and scaled it down for use in the BMW Rolls-Royce BR715 engine (we shall read about Rolls-Royce's collaboration with BMW in Chapter Three), adding:

They didn't ask us, they just went ahead and did it. [In fact, the compressor was a Rolls-Royce product and did not belong to IAE.]

In wondering why Pratt & Whitney launched this competitive engine, Mike Terrett felt it was because they were failing to get the V-2500 on to Boeing's CFM56-powered variants of the 737 and had recently lost US Air to the CFM56.

Undeterred, Barry Eccleston pulled two big deals in the summer of 1998. British Airways bought 187 A319s and A320s, all with V-2500 engines, and Grupo Taca, TAM Brazil and LanChile – the 'tres amigos' of the Latin American Alliance – also bought 175 A319s and A320s, again all powered by the V-2500.

While Eccleston should have credit for persuading the 'tres amigos' to take the V-2500 engine, the credit for persuading them to take the Airbus aircraft should probably go to Tracy Taylor. At a dinner to celebrate the order, Airbus Industrie Chief Executive Jean Pierson said:

You see what we have now – young ladies selling our aircraft and I note, smoking cigars as well. [She had forgotten her cigarettes and had been given a cigar.] What is the industry coming to?

The order from British Airways was significant because it was the first time BA had placed an order with Airbus Industrie. The order for A320s powered by the V-2500 was secured after a fierce battle with both Boeing and CFM International. BA also opted for IAE's fleet-hour-management support deal, which provided a guaranteed dollar-per-engine cost for off-wing maintenance.

Shortly after these coups, Eccleston moved on and was succeeded by Mike Terrett, who admitted to being concerned about the competition of the PW8000. Nevertheless, when asked about Pratt & Whitney at the Paris Air Show in June 1999 and, in particular, about the company's new president, Louis Chenevert, he said:

I fully expect continuity now that he is in position. Louis has come from the operations side at Pratt & Whitney; he will have seen all the benefits that the V2500 has brought to Pratt & Whitney and I have no doubt in my mind that he will continue to support both the V2500 and IAE. On a personal level, my observation is that the relationship between all of the IAE shareholders is extremely warm and cordial.

He remained sceptical about the PW8000, saying:

Pratt & Whitney does not have any applications for that so far and, as far as we can see, the A320 family will be selling for many years yet. Any developments planned for that airframe we believe we can match for at least the next 10 to 12 years.

It is perhaps relevant to say that Pratt & Whitney dominated the short- and medium-range airline market from the late 1960s through to the 1980s, with the JT8D on the 727, 737, DC-9 and MD-80 series – all big sellers. These types were not succeeded by exact equivalents. The 727 was succeeded by the 757, and Rolls-Royce stole the launch order. The 737 was lost to GE/SNECMA's CFM engines. The DC-9 and MD-80 series were succeeded by the MD-90, in which Pratt & Whitney did keep a share through the V-2500. Airbus came in with the A319, 320 and 321 and here GE got in first, but Pratt & Whitney again captured a share later with the V-2500. Under the circumstances, it was only natural that Pratt & Whitney would want to recapture some of the market that had been all its own in the past.

Chenevert went on to say that while 1999 was not so far as big a year for orders as the bumper year of 1998, with its record 440 V-2500 engines ordered and 265 produced, nevertheless it was shaping up well:

We have taken two out of three available orders … We have been able to announce orders from Spanish carrier, Spainair, and New York start up, New Air. Those are both green field customers to us and we particularly liked that. It fits well with our message that the V2500 is the perfect match for the A320. If you look over the past two years, it's interesting to note that we have taken a lot more new customers than CFM International. It seems that we have been particularly successful in those competitions where the airlines have choices. We have taken a lot of those deals.

By the end of 1999, IAE had delivered more than 1,200 engines and was looking at an order book of about 3,000. As Terrett put it, it was 'an engine a day, including Christmas Day, for seven years'. Nevertheless, the consortium knew it could not rest on its laurels, and in the middle of 2000 announced that it was developing a new generation of engines to meet the thrust needs of future Airbus and Boeing narrow-bodies from the year 2008. This appeared to lay to rest rumours that the IAE consortium had no long-term future, rumours fuelled by Pratt & Whitney's development of its PW8000. Now it looked as though that engine might be quietly laid to rest as Pratt & Whitney reaffirmed its commitment to the V-2500 and its successors.

PROJECT DERWENT

By 1989, the RB 211-535 had gained a substantial market share over the PW2037 on account of its superior reliability and lower operating costs, despite its worse fuel consumption. Concerned that Pratt & Whitney would improve the reliability of the PW2037, Rolls-Royce embarked on a programme to improve the RB 211-535's performance. At about the same time, operators such as Qantas required improved payload range capability on the B747-400, and so an RB 211-524G/H performance-improvement and weight-reduction programme was launched. This was to be achieved by using a more advanced HP system that was to be common with the Trent 700 and then applying the same technology to the RB 211-535. The RB 211-524 and -535 programmes were due to complete at the end of 1991 to make way for the Trent, but unfortunately the task turned out to be more difficult than expected, and it therefore became necessary to abandon both programmes. In the event, Pratt & Whitney failed to improve the reliability of the PW2037, and so the RB 211-535 remained the dominant engine on the Boeing B757. The Trent HP system was eventually fitted to the RB 211-524G/H in 1997 after the Trent 800 had entered service.

Phil Ruffles, who became Director of Engineering of the Aerospace Group at this time, had already lived through the near disaster of bringing the V-2500 into service. He recognised the risk to the Trent programme and set about changing the way engineering operated so that Rolls-Royce engines were designed and developed to a consistently high standard, thus avoiding the setbacks that were only too common through the 1980s. Whereas in 1971 the engineering failures were due largely to under-investment in technology, particularly high-temperature technology, these had been addressed by the launch of technology-demonstrator programmes.

The first programme was the High Temperature Demonstration Unit (HTDU), which was conceived by Geoff Wilde in 1968 and was eventually launched in 1972 to address the high-temperature problems that Rolls-Royce experienced in developing the revolutionary three-shaft engine, the RB 211, in the late 1960s. The aero-engine manufacturers in the USA had already put in place formal demonstrator programmes, and Geoff Wilde insisted that if they expected to compete Rolls-Royce must do the same. At the time, the Board were completely focused on solving the problems of the RB 211 and said that the company could not afford the expense or diversion of setting up such a unit. However, when Sir Stanley Hooker was brought out of retirement in order to take control of the RB 211's progress towards satisfactory production standards, Wilde was able to pursue this approach, Hooker asking him to take charge of High Temperature Research.

Wilde went at it with a will, involving the universities as well as the National Gas Turbine Establishment at Pyestock. His High Temperature Demonstration Unit first ran in 1972 and became the vehicle around which all high-temperature testing was developed. For Rolls-Royce, it was the start of a properly structured Research and Technology programme.

The problems in the 1980s were more related to how people were organised to carry out what had become a very complex task. Ruffles recognised that only a radically new approach would deliver the complex aero-engines demanded by the market within the required timescales and with the vital lower costs. He looked back into Rolls-Royce's history and found that the Derwent V had been developed quickly and at low cost. As we saw in Part Two, two Derwent V engines, installed on a Gloster Meteor, established a world speed record of 615.81 miles per hour on 7 September 1946. From launch of design on 1 January 1945 to its first flight, the Derwent V took just eight months, and all endurance and type tests were passed first time without any development modifications. The engine went into operational service in late 1947. Between 1947 and 1990, aero-engines had become more complex, and the accepted development time for a civil engine had grown to four to five years – and for a military engine to at least seven, and often over ten, years. In Ruffles' view, this was too long.

He wondered what lessons could be learnt from the Derwent V. It was a 0.855 linear scale of the Nene, chosen so that it would fit in the nacelle of the Meteor. Consequently, it was an 'off the shelf' design using proven technology and simple engineering and manufacturing processes. Furthermore, the development was carried out by an integrated team unrestrained by the organisational complexities that grew up in the subsequent 40 years.

Ruffles sought to replicate the approach taken with the Derwent, though of course he appreciated that the aero-engine of the 1990s was more complex than that of the 1940s. The application of generic designs to existing and new products using well defined and simplified processes would therefore have to be supported by electronic product definition to accommodate this increased complexity.

Project Derwent was launched in 1992 with the clear vision of enabling Rolls-Royce to become the world's best at developing aero-engines within the aircraft launch timetable, at lower cost, faster than its competitors and with a fully compliant specification. Its specific objectives were to reduce the timescale from project launch to certification to 30 months, to achieve a 30 per cent reduction in R&D costs from engine launch to engine certification (as Ruffles pointed out, this was an absolute necessity), to reduce the 'long lead-time items' procurement period to a maximum of nine months and to reduce the experimental build/test/strip timescales.

Reliability was another key factor. The new wide-body aircraft had two engines requiring ETOPS clearance either early in their service life, as on the A330, or at entry in service, as on the B777. The RB 211-535 was a world-class reliable engine, due in large part to the diligent approach adopted by Stewart Miller in ensuring that problems experienced on earlier variants of the RB 211 were systematically addressed during the design and development of the RB 211-535 engine. Rolls-Royce was determined that the Trent, the fourth generation of the RB 211, would be even more reliable and would benefit from all this knowledge being fed into the Trent design to ensure the utmost dependability. Testing was made more vigorous than previously, and every problem experienced during development, no matter how small, was properly investigated and solved to the satisfaction of Rolls-Royce, Boeing and the airworthiness authorities.

Phil Ruffles said later:

In practice, this meant that engineering activities carried out in isolation, such as stress, aerodynamics and mechanical design, were replaced with project teams, all operating to staged gateways during design, development and in-service support. Independent audit of engineering activities was implemented, so that before a design could pass through to the next stage of development, it had to be scrutinised and passed off by an independent team. Emphasis was placed on getting the basic design right, first time; on using unified data throughout the project and on integration of design and manufacture into a seamless activity.

It was a whole new world for Rolls-Royce. The Derwent Process initially caused a stir, and some resistance, as many employees had to physically move, co-locating into new premises, with new colleagues, working to new goals. So there was an enormous change-management task to undertake. But it paid off. We have since increased our retention of engineering staff by about 50 per cent, largely by creating broader roles, with more responsibility and supported by effective training.

Was the ambitious plan successful? Yes. The Trent 800, which entered service on the Boeing 777 in April 1996, showed what a difference Project Derwent made. Originally specified as an 84,000 lb-thrust engine, the Trent 800 was successfully certified three months ahead of schedule at 90,000 lb thrust. The product development was completed in 39 months and at 20 per cent lower cost than comparable product developments in the past. It became a world-beating engine in terms of noise levels, emissions, unit weight and cost of ownership. The Trent 500 programme followed the Trent 800 and was completed in 34 months and at a comparably low development cost.

Later, Phil Ruffles commented:

At the same time, the push to develop a cost-effective technology acquisition programme had reached a progressive stage. Teams of engineers were already focussed on refining those core technologies so that Rolls-Royce could feed the enhancements into new programmes or retrofit into existing ones. In order to get ahead Rolls-Royce had already embarked on a programme of employing colleagues in academia through the development of university technology centres (UTCs) and partnerships (UTPs). UTCs vary in scope but they generally deliver research based projects in highly specialised areas, for example, turbo machinery aerodynamics, advanced combustion concepts or new manufacturing technologies. Rolls-Royce have 18 UTCs today after taking the first steps with Imperial College and Oxford in 1990. They continue to make an enormous contribution to Rolls-Royce's R&D capacity. The combination has proved to be very successful; the boost to the in-house research capability and the increased knowledge gained from sharing data has given Rolls-Royce an advantage across many areas of engineering activity.

As we have already seen, one of the most significant technological advances made by Rolls-Royce in the 1980s was the introduction of the hollow wide-chord fan blade on the RB 211-535E4 in 1984. In the following few years, it was also built into the -524, the V-2500 in solid form in the Tay and, in a superplastically formed, diffusion-bonded (rather than honeycomb) form, into the Trents.

By early 1989, these engines had been specified for a range of new commercial aircraft. The Tay was powering the Gulfstream IV business jet and the Fokker F100 airliner, and plans were in hand for it to re-engine the British Aircraft Corporation BAC 111, the Boeing 727 and the McDonnell Douglas DC-9. The V-2500 was in production for the Airbus A320, while the RB 211-524G/H was on order for the long-range Boeing 747-400 and the twin-jet Boeing 767. The RB 211-524L, renamed the Trent at the Paris Air Show in June 1989, was being developed for the McDonnell Douglas MD-11, the Airbus A330 and advanced developments of the Boeing 747 and 767.

As we saw in the second volume, previous fan blades of solid-titanium construction were restricted in chord by a limit in blade weight, necessary to ensure successful containment in the event of failure. These relatively narrow blades required a snubber or damper to prevent flutter to make them aero-elastically stable, thereby increasing efficiency and capacity.

We also saw that the wide-chord fan blade had originally been developed for the RB 211 in the late 1960s using lightweight carbon-fibre material, encouraged by the performance of composite materials in the new RB 162 lightweight lift-jet engine for STOVL aircraft. Unfortunately, although the carbon-fibre Hyfil wide-chord fan blade was aerodynamically sound, it failed to withstand the impact of foreign objects – most notably, birds – and its development programme was stopped in 1970.

Nevertheless, Rolls-Royce retained its confidence in the concept and began a ten-year research programme into honeycomb-reinforced, hollow titanium wide-chord fan blades, which were first introduced in the RB 211-535E4.

As Phil Ruffles pointed out, there were three advantages to the wide-chord fan. The hollow titanium-alloy skin with honeycomb core eliminated the weight penalty of the wide-chord aerofoil. It also eliminated the need for narrow aerofoil snubbers. At the same time, it improved blade integrity, performance and noise. However, there were some limitations with the initial design of the wide-chord fan that Rolls-Royce was putting into these engines in the 1980s. The honeycomb design was increasing the load on the wall of the engine and also made the engine heavier. Where the honeycomb joined the titanium, there was a high stress concentration, and, finally, bonding the honeycomb to titanium was an intricate process bringing a high, and costly, scrap rate.

Further development led to the superplastically formed, diffusion-bonded configuration (SPF/DB) with a self-supporting internal structure without stress concentrations, allowing the reduction of panel thicknesses. The resulting blade weight was less, with additional benefits in the weight of the disc and containment system. Manufacturability was improved, reducing costs, and cost of operation for the airlines was reduced by the lower weight of the engine.

With regard to weight, the RB 211 had always been heavier than its competitors in the same thrust class, and Rolls-Royce saw an opportunity to correct this with the Trent. The Trent 700 was similar in weight to the comparable Pratt & Whitney engine, and, although it was heavier than the GE CF6-80E1 proposed for the A330, the GE engine did not possess the required thrust for the higher-weight versions of this aircraft. The Trent was still heavier on the MD-11, where it was competing against smaller engines.

Before Rolls-Royce was working on Project Derwent, the Chairman, Sir Francis Tombs, thought he had found a way to help with the onerous development costs of the Trent family. Why not buy a company in another industry that was in a mature stage of its life and was throwing off some cash?

CHAPTER TWO

Diversification

HOW WEINSTOCK MUGGED NEI

When northern engineering industries (NEI) was formed in 1977, the two components – Reyrolle Parsons and Clarke Chapman – employed 40,000 people. By the time Rolls-Royce took over the group in 1989, half of those employed had gone, during what Terry Harrison described as 'a decade of famine'. A first rationalisation programme in 1984, when Sir Duncan McDonald was Chairman and Harrison Chief Executive, did not go far enough, and a second in 1986 and 1987 – by which time Harrison was Chairman – was much more radical. Fourteen of NEI's 38 factories were shut, and 5,800 employees made redundant. Harrison cut the group back to its core activities, getting rid of peripheral businesses such as John Thompson's excavator and heavy truck production. Two companies in the electronics industry in the USA, Extel and IPM, acquired in an attempt at diversification, were sold. Extel had cost $35 million in 1980 and was sold for $4 million in 1986. What remained at NEI was organised into three groups: power engineering, general engineering and international and projects engineering.

Harrison did not only cut out factories but the number of machines in those remaining. He said in 1988:

In 1981 we had 3,300 machine tools. Now we have 1,300 but 250 are numerically controlled. We have quadrupled output per man compared with 10 years ago. But we are not making the same products faster. We are making different products much, much faster … We don't sell a pump anymore we sell pump systems.

The magazine *Business*, which was published jointly by Condé Nast and the *Financial Times* in the mid-1980s, printed an article under the heading 'Power Struggle: How Weinstock Mugged NEI' in May 1988. Its concluding paragraph read:

The power struggle now whirls on a global scale. Only last month, Westinghouse of the US joined with Europe's newlyweds, Asea and Brown Boveri, in an electrical team of frightening force. And GEC [General Electric Company], having been denied Babcock, lingers. It knows that a foreigner might try to get into Europe by snapping up NEI. The Tyneside group will probably get its turbine or boiler order [from the CEGB]. But it is doubtful whether it can retain what it values even more: its independence.

Sure enough, in November 1988 it was announced that neither GEC nor a foreign buyer but rather Rolls-Royce itself had secretly purchased a 4.7 per cent stake in NEI. Everyone, both at Rolls-Royce and NEI, was tight-lipped about the motive. Jim Rigg, Rolls-Royce's Finance Director, said:

It's a trade investment. I haven't any other comment to make.

Terry Harrison commented:

Until such time as Rolls-Royce makes its intentions clear the company has no further comment to make.

In the City, the analysts speculated, some wondering whether Rolls-Royce's interest was sparked by reports that none of the three large coal-fired power stations planned for the UK would be built and that instead there would be growing dependence on smaller, gas-turbine-powered and combined-cycle stations. If so, this would suit Rolls-Royce's manufacture of gas turbines for power-generation applications. Rolls-Royce had also signed a marketing and co-operation deal in 1987 with Asea Brown Boveri.

Talks on a merger between Rolls-Royce and NEI took place for the next few months, but on 21 December 1988 it was announced that these had been terminated. Rolls-Royce said the two had not been able to agree on price. *Lex* in the *Financial Times* commented:

The month of friendly talks between NEI and Rolls-Royce may have come to nothing, but that does not mean that the whole thing can be forgotten. Yesterday's statement was pointedly silent about Rolls' intentions, and it is quite possible that the next step will be a hostile offer … But even if Rolls does not wish to proceed, it should have little difficulty in selling its stake at a profit. While NEI only makes sense to Rolls as a way of diversifying away from aero engines and the US dollar, to any of the European heavies the fit would be much more direct: NEI would help them win British orders for private power stations.

However, Rolls did wish to proceed, and after further talks it was resolved at the Rolls-Royce Board meeting of 6 April 1989 'that negotiations should take place with its [NEI's] Board with a view to an offer being made for the whole of its issued ordinary share capital'. This time, the NEI Board was convinced of the logic of a deal, and four days later, on 10 April 1989, it was announced that Rolls-Royce would acquire NEI – or, to use the customary euphemism, the two companies would merge. The price, valuing NEI at £306 million, was no higher than Rolls-Royce had offered in 1988.

'WE WOULD SEEK TO EMULATE THESE'

As the Rolls-Royce Chairman, Sir Francis Tombs, announced the merger at a press conference, he spoke of two great international companies with big exports, excellent products, superb product names and huge skill and research bases.

Tombs also explained that he had long been keen to break free of what he described as Rolls-Royce's product cul-de-sac, its near dependence on the supply of aero-engines to the civil and military markets. He referred to the diversified character of its US competitors, GE and Pratt & Whitney:

We would seek to emulate these.

How was the merger received? In NEI's heartland, the North-East, it was given a cautious welcome. Jeremy Beecham, leader of Newcastle City Council, said it was good for Newcastle and the North-East. Combining with Rolls-Royce would keep NEI safe from predators with intentions of closing down factories. Nick Garnett, writing in the *Financial Times*, was not so sure:

Uncertainty surrounds the possibility of long-term rationalisation of NEI's business. Sir Francis Tombs says Rolls will help to continue development of NEI's core businesses. There are no plans for rationalisation as a result of the merger and NEI will keep its own culture. Whether, in the long run, Rolls will want to keep all NEI's operations must be a moot point.

Certainly, NEI needed to merge with someone. As we have seen, it had struggled in the 1970s and 1980s to cope in a more competitive environment against larger companies such as GEC, whose Managing Director, Arnold (now Lord) Weinstock, was adept at stalking the corridors of Westminster and Whitehall. Furthermore, NEI was perhaps too restrained in its approach. Having finally been awarded the contracts for all the turbine-generator work and switchgear for the Drax power station (Babcock International got the boilers), NEI then stood aside to give GEC a clear run for Hong Kong's Castle Peak power station. The £500-million contract that GEC won was Britain's biggest export order ever at the time. NEI had hoped for a good deal of subcontract work, but GEC looked after its own factories. When a similar situation arose over the contract for the Rihand power station in India, this time with NEI in the driving seat, GEC lobbied the Government to make sure GEC was given plenty of subcontract work. Dr Bob Hawley, who ran Reyrolle Parsons at the time, still remembers with great chagrin that Parsons did not even make the turbine generators. And finally, in 1984 when an Anglo-French bid was agreed for China's Guandong nuclear power station, GEC was the nominated supplier. Terry Harrison said:

The Chinese asked us to bid for the turbine generators but we were warned off by the Government.

STEAMING AT ASTONISHING SPEED

Undoubtedly, the most famous engineering name that Rolls-Royce acquired when it bought NEI was Parsons. The company, founded by Charles (later Sir Charles) Parsons in 1884 (the same year Royce set up his first business, F.H. Royce & Co.), became renowned throughout the world thanks to the development and exploitation of Parsons's steam turbine.

Born in London in 1854, Charles Parsons, the sixth son of the Third Earl of Rosse, spent most of his childhood in the family house in Old Castle in Parsonstown, Ireland. His father, a distinguished astronomer and scientist himself, arranged for him to be tutored at home, and young Charles spent much of his youth in the laboratory, workshops, forge and foundry built at the castle by his father for his own experiments. He continued his training and experimentation, first for a year at Trinity College, Dublin, and then at St John's College, Cambridge.

Leaving Cambridge in 1877, he became a premium apprentice at the Elswick Works of W.G. Armstrong in Newcastle upon Tyne and continued his experiments, first on an epicyclic engine and then on rocket propulsion for torpedoes. In 1884, he joined Clarke, Chapman & Company as a junior partner, taking charge of their recently formed electrical department. Becoming involved in the supply of electric-lighting equipment for ships, he decided to look into the steam turbine and the driving of the high-speed generator attached to it.

There was nothing new about the principle of the steam turbine. The first record of a turbine went all the way back to 60 BC, when Hero produced a device in which a hollow ball set in trunnions was rotated under the influence of steam issuing from tangentially directed nozzles. As it was the reaction to the steam emerging from the nozzles that produced the rotation, this machine is considered to be the first *reaction turbine*.

Nearly 1,700 years later, but still 250 years before Parsons began his experiments, an Italian architect, Giovanni Branca, built a different type of turbine with a steam jet directed into cup-shaped blades set in the periphery of a wheel. The impact of the steam on the blades produced the rotation and demonstrated the principle of the *impulse turbine*.

Parsons used both Hero's reaction and Branca's impulse principles in the development of his turbine blades. However, the great difficulty in 1884 when he began his experiments was the excessive velocity of the steam. Steam escaping into the atmosphere even at comparatively low pressures can travel at 1,000 feet per second (750 m/s, or over 2,700 km/h). Parsons himself said:

The steam flows through a turbine with a force about ten times as great as that of the strongest hurricane.

He realised that the steam speed would have to be reduced if a proper relationship between steam speed and turbine-blade speed was to be achieved. He began experiments that concentrated on using several bladed wheels on one shaft, the steam travelling parallel to the shaft so that the total steam-pressure drop was distributed through all the wheels in a series of individual stages. Behind each wheel was a set of fixed blades that redirected the steam to the next wheel. The drop of pressure at each stage was sufficient only to generate a velocity that could be efficiently utilised by blades running at moderate speeds. This division into stages, now known as pressure compounding, made possible only moderate peripheral speeds; but nevertheless, the useful external work obtained per pound of steam still exceeded that of any other engine.

Parsons possessed the engineering ability to put this theory into practice, and in 1884 he built the first really practical steam turbine, producing 7.5 kW at 18,000 rpm and giving a steam consumption of about 150 lb per kilowatt-hour. This plant worked regularly for some years, supplying current for lighting experimental shops, including the start-up of the Sunbeam Incandescent Lamp works at Gateshead. During his time as a partner at Clarke Chapman, which lasted until December 1888, about 360 turbo-generators with outputs from 1 kW up to 75 kW were constructed with an aggregate capacity of about 4200 kW. These were used mainly on ships for electric lighting, the first a 2 kW machine installed on the Tyne Tees Shipping Company's ship, the SS *Earl Percy*, in 1885. The 75 kW sets were constructed in 1888 for the Newcastle and District Electric Lighting Company and were installed in the Forth Banks power station. These were the first high-speed turbo-generators in a public power station.

By the end of 1888, Parsons felt it necessary to found his own company to develop the turbine to the full, and in 1889, with financial help from friends, he established Heaton Works. In June of that year – with 48 staff, a small machine-and-erection shop, a blacksmith's shop and a small time office and administration office – C.A. Parsons & Co. Limited began life. The area covered by the whole works measured less than two acres.

Unfortunately for Parsons, the deed of his partnership in Clarke Chapman meant that all patents taken out by a partner became the property of the firm. Parsons, of course, needed his patents and was prepared to buy them. However, valuing them was problematic, and after discussion both sides agreed to arbitration. There followed a long-drawn-out legal battle, but meanwhile the patents were retained by Clarke Chapman. Parsons was therefore prevented from building axial-flow turbines, the basis of his first patents. He was restricted to building radial-flow turbines, and by 1891 a unit of 100 kW had been constructed. This was the first condensing turbine, and when tested was found to have a steam economy equal to the best reciprocating engine of the day. The largest radial-flow turbine built for land purposes was a 150 kW turbo-generator supplied to the Portsmouth Municipal Electric Light station in 1893.

In her book about electricity in the Enlightenment, *An Entertainment for Angels*, Patricia Fara commented on the experiments of the poet Percy Bysshe Shelley, who was showing off his skills as early as 1810. One of his friends described how he would pull out an electrical machine from the clutter on his desk and charge himself up 'so that the fierce, crackling sparks flew forth; and his long, wild locks bristled and stood on end'.

Nevertheless, it was not until the 1890s that electrical power became generally available, as Michael Evans pointed out in his *In the Beginning: The Manchester Origins of Rolls-Royce*:

The years 1889 to 1892 saw the real beginnings of electric power generating stations. Prior to that only London had seen much in the way of development and then only because there were wealthy sections of the community willing to pay over the odds for the novelty of electric light. The cost of electricity in the early 1880s was about 9d or 10d [about £4 to £4.50 in today's terms] per kWh. By 1990 it had fallen to about 2d [still about 90p in today's terms]. Even so, it was not until 1911, with the advent of the drawn tungsten filament, that electric light became indisputedly [*sic*] cheaper than gas in this country, for the advent of the incandescent gas mantle had maintained its competitive position. From 1892 onwards power generator stations began to spread into the provinces. Manchester and Derby were among the first towns to establish facilities in 1893. By 1895 the industry was well established and, around 1900, there was a major boom in investment as the size of the stations began to grow. So it was in the 1890s that electricity became widely available and Royce's product grew apace.

Finally, in 1894, Parsons made an offer for the patents which Clarke Chapman accepted, and he was able to return to the axial-flow principle that he had always felt was the best method for the development of turbine machinery.

After this, progress was rapid. One of the first machines built was a 350 kW turbo-generator for the Manchester Square power station in London. By the turn of the century, machines of 1,000 kW were being constructed, and by 1912 the size had risen to 25,000 kW. In 1923, the first 50,000 kW machine was built. Coinciding with this progress came the increase in generator voltages. In the early days, it was customary to generate at 2,000 volts and to step up the pressure when required by means of transformers. In 1905, Parsons built a turbo-generator to generate at 11,000 volts, and this pressure became the norm for many years. Parsons turned his attention to generating pressure again in the 1920s, constructing a 25,000 kW machine to generate direct at 36,000 volts in 1928.

On ships, Parsons began the task of adapting the turbine to marine propulsion in 1893 – the same year, as we saw above, that he supplied a radial-flow turbine to the Portsmouth Municipal Electric Light station. In January 1894, he formed the Marine Steam Turbine Company Limited and began construction of a small vessel, the *Turbinia*. Although later in 1894, as we saw, he recovered the axial-flow patents, Parsons decided to stick to the radial-flow principle for the *Turbinia* as he had built machines of this type up to 150 kW, whereas he had built up to only 75 kW of the axial-flow type.

The first trials of the *Turbinia* took place at the end of 1894 but, due to the phenomenon of cavitation, little understood at the time, proved disappointing. Running the turbine at slower speeds was tried, as well as experiments with different diameters and various arrangements of propellers, but the best performance achieved was only 19.75 knots with a turbine speed of 1,780 rpm. Obviously, either the turbine was not developing its rated output or the efficiency of the propellers was extremely low. To settle this question, Parsons devised a special apparatus to measure the torque exerted by the turbine on the propeller shaft. This instrument was the prototype of the modern torsion meter, and by using it he convinced himself the fault lay with the propellers not the turbine. The trouble was the inability of the water to follow the rapidly moving propeller blades, with a consequent loss of propulsive power. To study the problem, he constructed a tank with glass sides in which a model propeller was strongly lit by intermittent light, the speed of the flashes being regulated in accordance with the revolutions of the propeller so that the blades could be made to appear stationary or as if revolving very slowly. The nature of cavitation was exhaustively studied in this way, with the result that Parsons modified the design of the propellers.

Meanwhile, the company had built axial-flow turbines up to 350 kW for use on land, and it was decided to replace the single radial-flow turbine on the *Turbinia* with an axial-flow turbine arranged with three separate annuli. Each annulus was coupled to a propeller shaft on which were fitted three propellers, making nine propellers in all. After further experiments with various forms of propellers, trials were resumed in April 1897, and the *Turbinia* eventually attained the remarkable speed of 34.5 knots.

Charles Parsons, as well as being a great inventor and courageous entrepreneur, was also an aggressive salesman. He organised a publicity stunt to show off the merits of his new engine which could have landed him in serious trouble. His plan was to steam the *Turbinia* southwards from the Tyne to Queen Victoria's Diamond Jubilee Review of the Fleet in Spithead, where a large array of ships from both the Royal Navy and overseas navies would be assembled. Present would be Lords of the Admiralty, high-ranking naval officers and ambassadors from other countries, and members of both Houses of Parliament. In short, the 'right' people, including the Prince of Wales, would be there.

The Fleet Review took place on 26 June 1897. The British Fleet was drawn up in four main lines with 140 ships stretching for 25 miles. The royal procession moving between the Fleet lines was led by the Trinity House yacht *Irene*, which piloted the way. Behind was the Royal Yacht *Victoria and Albert*, the P&O liner *Carthage*, and another royal yacht, the *Alberta*. Next came the *Enchantress* with the Lords of the Admiralty and the *Danube* carrying members of the House of Lords, the *Wildfire* with visiting colonial heads of state, the Cunard liner *Campania* with members of the House of Commons and finally the *Eldorado*, carrying foreign ambassadors.

Parsons, at the engine-room controls of *Turbinia*, waited. Then, soon after the royal procession passed, the *Turbinia* burst between a line of battleships and cruisers and a line of visiting foreign vessels. She reached the astonishing speed of 34.5 knots right in front of all the people Parsons wanted to impress. An Admiralty patrol boat began to chase her, but this only served to emphasise the *Turbinia*'s speed.

The Times wrote:

Among these [unauthorised vessels] was the now famous *Turbinia*, the fastest vessel in the world. At the cost of a deliberate disregard of authority, she contrived to give herself an effective advertisement by steaming at astonishing speed between the lines [of naval ships] shortly after the Royal procession had passed.

On the strength of the favourable publicity generated, Parsons formed the Parsons Marine Steam Turbine Company Limited with a registered capital of £500,000 [£55 million in today's terms]. He built the Turbinia works at Wallsend for the manufacture of marine steam turbines.

The Admiralty had been impressed by the speed of the *Turbinia* and with the possibilities of using steam turbines for naval vessels, and in 1898, after much deliberation [*plus ça change!*], placed an order with Parsons for a 30-knot turbine-driven destroyer, HMS *Viper*. Parsons was required to place a deposit of £100,000 [£11 million today] in case the performance was not up to expectation. At the same time, another destroyer under construction was also fitted with turbine machinery, and this vessel was also bought by the Admiralty and named HMS *Cobra*. Both performed up to scratch, but both vessels, in no way connected with the performance of the turbines, were lost at sea; the *Viper* when she ran ashore in fog on 3 August 1901, and the *Cobra* when she broke her back in a storm in the North Sea on 18 September 1901.

Next came a passenger vessel, the *King Edward*, which was ordered with turbine propulsion for service on the River Clyde. This was quickly followed by another for the same service, and then by turbine-driven cross-channel boats, and later by vessels for the Liverpool–Canada passenger trade. In 1907, the Atlantic liners *Mauretania* and *Lusitania* were launched. The *Mauretania*, displacing 38,000 tons, obtained a speed of 26.04 knots with her turbines developing 70,000 hp; she stayed in service until 1935. The *Lusitania* was sunk by a German U-boat in 1917 with the loss of 1,198 lives, many of them American – an action that was a considerable factor in bringing the USA into the First World War.

Meanwhile, the Royal Navy had acquired further destroyers, HMS *Velox* and HMS *Eden*, and a cruiser, HMS *Amethyst*. The Navy was delighted with their performance, and in 1905 a committee on naval design, appointed by the Admiralty, advised that in future only turbine machinery should be used in all classes of warship. The first battleship fitted with Parsons turbines, HMS *Dreadnought*, was commissioned in 1906.

And it was not only the Royal Navy that acted on the obvious technical breakthrough of Parsons's *Turbinia*. Prince Henry of Prussia had been at Spithead as a guest, and, as a result, the German Navy was soon introducing steam turbines into its ships.

Parsons continued to experiment to improve the performance of his turbine engines and in 1912 invented what became known as 'creep-cutting'. By this mechanism, the work table of the machine was caused to rotate slightly faster than the master wheel, with the result that any errors in the latter were distributed spirally round the wheel being cut, instead of being concentrated at one part of the circumference. The result was that the unavoidable defects of the master wheel were, for all practical purposes, eliminated. This created an entirely new standard of accuracy for mechanical gearing and made it possible to produce gear wheels that could transmit any desired power with quietness and durability.

In 1925, Parsons indulged his interest in optical equipment by buying the ailing optical glass firm Grubb & Sons, renaming it Sir Howard Grubb Parsons & Co., and transferred it from St Albans in Hertfordshire to Heaton. The firm continues to produce mirrors for telescopes and other specialised glassware.

GREAT NAMES COME TOGETHER

Sir Charles Parsons died in 1931, and by the purchase of his shares in C.A. Parsons & Co. Limited, Reyrolle of Hebburn – the third leg of what became Northern Engineering Industries (NEI) – began the financial involvement with its Heaton neighbour that would eventually culminate in their merger as Reyrolle Parsons in 1968.

Alphonse Reyrolle came to England from France as a young man of nineteen in 1883. After a period with Lege & Company, scientific instrument makers, he set up independently in a workshop off the Euston Road in London. He made components for larger electrical manufacturers such as Ferranti and British Thomson Houston. In 1901, Reyrolle formed his firm into a limited liability company and took it to the North-East, settling into premises in Hebburn-on-Tyne formerly used for the manufacture of chemicals and dyestuffs.

His speciality was switchgear, and Reyrolle Limited was the first company to make metal-clad, drawn-out switchgear. It also pioneered the manufacture of flameproof switchgear for use in mines, and of protective systems for electricity supply networks. It became involved with C.A. Parsons in the development of the public electricity supply in the North-East. As voltages in the public supply increased, a great deal of development work on substation switchgear was needed. Reyrolle's short-circuit testing station, built in 1929, was the first of its kind in the world. The company also developed small-oil-volume switchgear, designed to reduce the risk of fire, and air-break switchgear, as well as a comprehensive range of industrial plugs and sockets.

Alphonse Reyrolle died in 1919, but his work continued under the technical direction of H.W. Clothier. Reyrolle and Parsons moved closer together in 1934 with the foundation of the Parolle Electric Plant Company, a joint contracting and general engineering operation.

Clarke, Chapman & Company was founded in 1864 when an engineer, William Clarke, who had worked at the Bedlington Iron Works, opened a small factory at South Shore, Felling, on the south bank of the River Tyne. The background to its formation was the expansion of the shipyards on the Tyne and the conversion from sail to steam. Clarke began by manufacturing small hand-winches, and in 1868 he designed and built the first steam-driven cargo winch to be placed on the market. Donkey boilers were built to provide the required steam power. In 1874, he added a new product, the steam windlass. This necessitated both larger premises (the company moved from South Shore to the site it would occupy for over 100 years, Victoria (named after the Queen) Works in the grounds of Park House, Gateshead, alongside the Newcastle-to-South-Shields railway line) and more capital. Captain Abel Henry Chapman joined as a partner. Another partner was Joseph John Gurney, and until 1884, when Gurney resigned, the firm was called Clarke, Chapman & Gurney. On 1 January 1884, Charles Parsons bought himself a junior partnership for £20,000 [about £2.2 million in today's terms]. As we have already seen, Parsons took out two patents in 1884 covering steam turbo-dynamos, and in the five years he was with Clarke Chapman over 360 turbo-generators were constructed.

The company exhibited a turbine at the London Inventions Exhibition of 1885 and was rewarded by this entry in the journal *Engineering*:

If the motor invented by the Hon. Charles Algernon Parsons and constructed by Clarke, Chapman and Company accomplishes one half that is ascribed by rumour, viz, that it will run steadily at many revolutions per minute, then it will constitute by far the most noticeable feature in the Electric Lighting Department of the Exhibition and will even rank among the foremost novelties of the entire collection.

Clarke Chapman's catalogue of 1886 shows the company manufacturing a wide range of equipment, including various types of steam winches, wind-lasses, deck-, quayside- and works-cranes, winding engines for collieries, haulages, torpedo-boat hoisting engines and other hoists, ship's steering gear, capstans and pumps for use on and at sea. The catalogue also shows two types of vertical boiler and a 'Victoria' patent multi-tubular boiler. In the same year, Clarke Chapman made its first searchlight projector for use on ships.

By the following year, the company was supplying portable generating plants to ships that passed through the Suez Canal, recently opened in 1869. These generating plants consisted of a vertical boiler with engine and generator on a wheeled carriage. A searchlight was slung from a davit over the bows of the ship, with both the searchlight and its operator in a cage. Early generating plants for lighting were by this time being fitted aboard Admiralty vessels, and by the end of the 1880s Clarke Chapman was pioneering the use of electricity as a motive power for ship's deck and engine-room auxiliaries.

All three companies, Parsons, Clarke Chapman and Reyrolle, suffered heavily in the Depression of the 1930s, as did most of industry throughout the world, but all recovered sharply when war broke out in 1939 and their products were in great demand. There was no fear of unemployment while the War lasted, but what would happen when peace returned? All three of our companies benefited for the fifteen years after the War from the huge expansion programme put in place by the newly nationalised electrical supply industry. (We have already read in Part Two of this history about the nationalising zeal of the Labour administration elected in 1945.)

The 1948 Electricity Act established a Central Electricity Authority to control the general policy of the industry and to be responsible for power generation and its bulk transmission to fourteen Area boards. In 1957, a further Electricity Act replaced the Authority with the Central Electricity Generating Board, controlling power stations and transmission lines, and the Electricity council, whose role was to advise the Government on all matters relating to the industry and to take responsibility for finance, research and industrial relations. Separate arrangements were made for Scotland, and the North of Scotland Hydro-Electric Board and the South of Scotland Electricity Board split the country between them.

For more than a decade, the controlling body maintained a high level of ordering as the demand for electricity continued to rise sharply. Parsons and Reyrolle developed and extended their involvement with the power industry, and Clarke Chapman manufactured large utility boilers, which were in great demand. Sir Claud Gibb, who had worked at the Ministry of Supply during the War, became Chairman of both Parsons and Reyrolle and initiated large expansion programmes at both companies. He was also aware of the possibilities in the nuclear-power market, and by 1956 Parsons, Reyrolle and Clarke Chapman were all involved in the Nuclear Power Plant company, a consortium of eight firms that was awarded the contract for the Bradwell nuclear station (one of the first two nuclear stations in the UK) and was also employed in the construction of the Latina nuclear power station for the Societa Italiana Meridionale per l'Energia Atomica in Italy.

Unfortunately, Gibb, who had criss-crossed the world seeking orders, died suddenly in 1959 of a heart attack while changing aeroplanes at Newark, New Jersey. His energy and skills would be sorely missed. In the early 1950s, Canadian newspapers had carried photographs of him stripped to his vest, using a huge spanner to tighten the last nut on a 100-megawatt turbine – the largest Parsons had ever built – for a Toronto power station. After his death, the first suggestions of a Reyrolle–Parsons merger were mooted. Parsons certainly appeared vulnerable, and Associated Electrical Industries (AEI) were considered a potential predator. However, AEI itself fell prey to the expansionist General Electric Company.

In spite of the possibility of takeover, Parsons was still very busy in the 1960s. By 1961, the capacity of the biggest turbines had increased by a factor of five to 500 megawatts. Parsons supplied the first of the big machines to the Ferrybridge C station and then captured 28 of the 49 orders placed among the four UK manufacturers. In 1966, it clinched the first 600-megawatt contract, Dungeness B in Kent, Britain's first advanced gas-cooled nuclear reactor station.

Clarke Chapman, a supplier mainly to the shipbuilding, mining and construction industries, benefited from the shipping boom in the immediate post-war years, though British shipyards became less and less competitive from the 1950s onwards. Clarke Chapman developed its boiler-making activities to cash in on the constantly growing electrical power-generation industry. It coped better than Reyrolle and Parsons as the post-war boom slowed down in the 1960s.

The more competitive era brought some necessary rationalisation in many industries (we saw it in the aircraft and aero-engine industries in Part Two of this history), and electrical engineering was no exception. GEC, under Arnold (later Lord) Weinstock, a director of Rolls-Royce in the 1970s, sold its turbine-generator interests. One of the factories was at Erith, where Francis (later Lord) Tombs, Chairman of Rolls-Royce from 1985 to 1992, worked, and another was at Wilton in Birmingham. Both were sold to Parsons in 1965. However, when GEC bought AEI and English Electric, it found itself back in the turbine-generator business and, with greater resources than Parsons, was likely to squeeze Parsons out of the business.

Technologically, Parsons was superior and was still pioneering. For example, through its subsidiary, International Research and Development (IRD), it developed the first superconducting AC generator. However, on its own it lacked the resources to compete with GEC, and in 1968 it merged with Reyrolle. This merger was followed by the acquisition of the transformer manufacturer Bruce Peebles in 1969. If there was over-capacity in turbine generators, there was even more in the transformer business. In 1968, there were six manufacturers of 132 kVA and above, and four making transformers of 275 kVA and above. The Industrial Re-organisation Corporation (IRC), set up by Harold Wilson's Labour Government in the mid-1960s, was pressing for rationalisation in many industries, transformers included, and was using the ordering by the CEGB to enforce it. One of the advantages of buying Bruce Peebles was the acquisition of its more modern factory in Edinburgh, and in 1969 the manufacture of transformers at Heaton was transferred to Scotland.

However, it was in the turbine generator industry that Reyrolle Parsons had to succeed if it was to have a future as an independent electrical engineering group.

Government policy was to keep two UK turbine-generator manufacturers in business, and the CEGB promised in 1965 and again in 1970 to place future power-station orders first with one and then the other. Unfortunately, these promises were broken, and in 1969 the CEGB cancelled the Sizewell order it had given to Reyrolle Parsons. More export business seemed to be the solution, but lack of home business hindered the company here as well. For example, Ontario Hydro of Canada, a large customer for many years, criticised the lack of opportunity to test prototype features in the UK market. In 1970, the company set up a joint venture in the USA with Rockwell called Rockwell-Parsons. It was hoped that together they would capture a share of the power-generating industry in the USA, which was dominated by Westinghouse and General Electric. However, results were disappointing. Potential customers doubted the stability of the British economy [with good cause – throughout the 1970s, the country suffered from high inflation, incompetent government, chaotic labour relations and weak management]. The partnership with Rockwell was dissolved. Negotiations with Westinghouse that would have led to the US company acquiring a controlling interest in Reyrolle Parsons fell through, and by 1973 the company was in some trouble.

By this time, the Conservative Government of Edward Heath had decided it favoured the idea of a single turbine-generator company, and along with CEGB they urged Parsons and GEC to combine their turbine-generator operations. GEC made it clear they would be happy to take over the turbine-generator activities of Reyrolle Parsons, but not those of the rest of the group. Talks continued without conclusion for the rest of the decade. Talks also continued with the Government. (An election in early 1974 returned the Labour Party to power, and its new vehicle for involvement with industry was the National Enterprise Board.) By 1977, Reyrolle Parsons's future lay in the hands of the NEB and the Department of Industry. Would the company receive the order for the Drax B power station? The Government held out for the recommendations made by the Central Policy Review Staff (CPRS) that there should be only one turbine-generator manufacturer and that the Drax B order would not be placed until Reyrolle Parsons made a statement in favour of this recommendation and agreed to reduce their workforce. Although the company refused to do this, they were eventually given the Drax B order on 18 July 1977. However, by this time negotiations to merge with Clarke Chapman and form Northern Engineering Industries (NEI) had been concluded.

During the 1960s, Clarke Chapman, well managed by William Hanlon and his team, led the rationalisation that took place in crane manufacture. By

1970, the company was operating factories in Yorkshire, the Midlands, the North-West and Scotland, as well as on Tyneside. It also became involved in the rationalisation in the boiler-making industry, acquiring, again with encouragement from the IRC, the Wolverhampton-based and long-established company John Thompson. Much of the 1970s was taken up with making this acquisition work, and with trying to persuade the Government and the CEGB to adopt a more steady power-station ordering programme. Just as the two turbine-generator makers danced round each other, so did the two large boiler makers, Clarke Chapman and Babcock, and in neither case did the necessary restructuring take place.

Once NEI was formed, further acquisitions were made, the most significant of which was that of Amalgamated Power Engineering in 1981. In this group were W.H. Allen Son & Co., Belliss & Morcom, Crossley Engines, Lee Howl, Allen Gears and Valtek. The product range – diesel engines, steam turbines of up to 30 kW, air and gas compressors, gears, pumps and valves – complemented NEI's existing product ranges. APE stayed as a separate entity renamed NEI Allen.

INTO PROJECT MANAGEMENT

In the 1980s, the biggest contract for NEI came not in the UK but in India. In September 1982, those two formidable leaders, Margaret Thatcher and Indira Gandhi, shook hands on a deal whereby a 1,000-megawatt power station at Rihand, a remote spot in the State of Uttar Pradesh in India, would be built by British companies led by NEI. The deal was worth £340 million, with the UK Government providing £100 million in aid, and most of it would go to NEI. (Margaret Thatcher would have reason to recall the deal when Peter Lockton, the man eventually put in charge of the project, described it as a 1,000-megawatt contraceptive: i.e. if it worked and the lights stayed on, people stayed up; if it did not, people went to bed.) For NEI, it was a dream come true. As we have seen, the CEGB had prevaricated throughout the 1970s and had not placed a new power-station order since 1979. NEI had yet to prove itself as a turnkey project manager, and this was a great opportunity to do so. As Terry (now Sir Terence) Harrison, by this time Chief Executive of NEI, said:

We took Rihand to get into the project management power game.

There was hope that the contract would lead to others in India and China.

Unfortunately, the dream turned into a nightmare. The agreement had been made before the technical and performance criteria had been worked out, and details took more than a year to be finalised. As a result, the company was working against the clock from the beginning of the project. The location of the site made for further horrendous difficulties. It was on unused land nearly 500 miles south-east of Delhi. The nearest large town was Varanasi, about 150 miles away. There was no telephone connection. NEI's 70 to 80 project experts on site, who for a time had to live in tents, could communicate with their base in Newcastle only by way of daily couriers to and from Varanasi, five hours by road. For months there was only one bulldozer on site. The 10,000 civil workers were 'head loaders' carrying soil in baskets on their heads. Cement was carried in the same way, often by women with babies on their hips. NEI supervised the shipping and assembly of 110,000 tonnes of material, involving more than 15 million parts, the heaviest weighing 230 tonnes. Cargoes went through twenty different handling operations between Tyneside and the site, and many components arrived already damaged. The last 40-mile leg of the journey was a long road that crumbled under heavy loads. Three Indian state borders had to be crossed, and lorries were halted and often delayed for days, even weeks, at the checkpoints.

The foundations and underground workings required deep excavations. The rise and fall of the level of Lake Rihand, no less than 20 metres, meant that the cooling-water inlets had to be tunnelled deep enough to guarantee supplies at any season of the year. For most of the year, the contractors suffered from drought and intense heat, but in the July-to-September monsoon season, torrential rain cut road links and the rising lake turned the building site into a sea of mud.

The structure of Rihand was much larger than that of a power station of comparable type and output in Europe because of the high ash content of the coal supplied from the huge open-cast coal deposits. The plant was designed for 48.8 per cent ash, which meant larger boilers, larger precipitators to remove the dust from the exhaust gases and larger pump facilities to transport the ash slurry to the disposal area.

While NEI struggled with all of these difficulties, the project fell behind, and it seemed it would be late in completion. The company tried a number of people in control as the media – including the influential *Financial Times*, as well as the Indian customer, The National Thermal Power Corporation (India's equivalent of the CEGB) – criticised the delays. Salvation came when Peter Lockton was put in charge. He moved to live permanently at the site, and by some miracle the project was completed on time. It had taken 66 months, six months less than it took the CEGB to build the Drax B station in the rather more benign environment of Yorkshire, England.

It was undoubtedly a great achievement and is still considered the most efficient power station in India. Cities supplied included Delhi, Lucknow, Panipat, Kanpur, Agra and Jaipur, some of them nearly 900 kilometres away.

Rihand's first 500-megawatt unit went into commercial operation on 1 January 1990, and the second similar unit a year later. In the first five years of its life, the station averaged a plant load factor of 78 per cent, against the national average of 61 per cent. In 1993, Rihand was the first power station in India to achieve more than 90 per cent generation over two consecutive months. Others, built since, have been modelled on Rihand. Nevertheless, pride was all that NEI could feel, for they reaped no financial benefit. As Harrison said in 1988:

No one has made money in Rihand including subcontractors.

Furthermore, the earlier bad publicity had not been erased, and NEI made the mistake of not taking world journalists to the site to show them what had been achieved. Harrison admitted:

Rihand damaged our reputation.

NO PLANS FOR RATIONALISATION

Looking back from 2002, the question has to be asked: why did Rolls-Royce buy NEI when it has now sold off most of the components parts? Analysts and financial journalists were not very keen on the merger at the time. Nick Garnett wrote in the *Financial Times* the day after it was announced:

Yesterday, both Sir Francis and Mr Harrison said the merger was not a defensive one. But NEI on its own is just a small independent power equipment maker outside the tide of electrical engineering mergers.

Garnett pointed to a number of uncertainties, including the impact on the different partners of each company:

Mitsubishi supplies industrial gas turbines to NEI. But it is a potential competitor on power plant with both Rolls-Royce and NEI.

He noted that the necessary rationalisation of NEI's businesses was being put on hold by Sir Francis Tombs, who said that there were no plans for rationalisation.

   Garnett also wondered whether the merger gave both companies what they really wanted:

From NEI's point of view, Rolls is certainly not the kind of partner other European electrical engineering companies have sought. Mergers in Europe have largely been among similar companies, designed to give them greater bulk.

The Times wrote of the performance of the *Turbinia* of Sir Charles Parsons at the Fleet Review on 26 June 1897: 'Among these [unauthorised vessels] was the now famous *Turbinia*, the fastest vessel in the world. At the cost of a deliberate disregard of authority, she contrived to give herself an effective advertisement by steaming at astonishing speed between the lines [of naval ships] shortly after the Royal procession had passed.'

The power station at Rihand, which NEI undertook to build, was
situated on unused land nearly 500 miles south-east of Delhi.
The nearest large town, Varanasi, was about 150 miles away. The
foundations and underground workings required deep excavations.
The rise and fall of Lake Rihand, no less than 20 metres,
meant that the cooling-water inlets had to be dug deep enough to
guarantee supplies at any season of the year.

The Nanticoke coal-fired power station of Ontario Hydro, equipped with eight NEI Parsons 500-megawatt turbine generators.

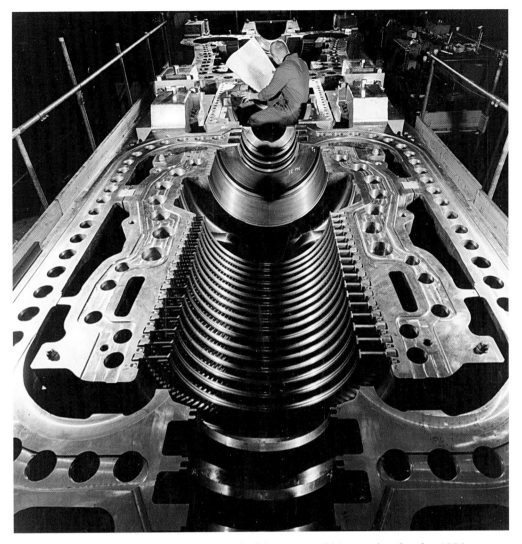

A Parsons steam turbine. A wonderful name and history, but by the 1990s its market share was less than 1 per cent, and Sir Ralph Robins, after putting Parsons up for sale, said, 'We will focus on sectors where we are a major player in the world, which we were not in large steam turbines.'

OPPOSITE TOP: NEI Reyrolle supplied and installed the power switchgear for the Sellindge 2,000-megawatt link, through which power could be transferred between the French and British power grids, matching surplus capacity in one system to high demand in the other.

OPPOSITE BOTTOM: NEI Clarke Chapman developed systems for replenishment at sea extensively used by the Royal Navy and other fleets. Here, the carrier HMS *Invincible* is being refuelled by the replenishment vessel RFA *Fort Victoria*. The system covered the transfer of fuel, ammunition and general stores.

TOP: In addition to supplying virtually all kinds of materials handling equipment, NEI Clarke Chapman developed a worldwide business in port design and management. Bulk unloaders for coal, ore and other materials formed an important part of the product range and are typified by this grabber unloader in Thailand.

BOTTOM: The NEI Clarke Chapman 'Syncrolift' system of dry-docking by shiplift is installed in dockyards throughout the world and is capable of handling any kind of vessel, from small pleasure craft to very large warships and commercial vessels. The Syncrolift installed at Barrow-in-Furness VSEL yard is here seen with the Trident submarine HMS *Vanguard*, whose nuclear propulsion system was supplied by Rolls-Royce of Derby. Syncrolift can launch vessels or can be used to lift them from the water and 'park' them for repair and maintenance, avoiding long-term occupation of a conventional dry-dock.

TOP: NEI's Thompson Defence Systems developed a range of lightweight tactical bridging now extensively used by the Army. The components were made of aluminium and could be used in many configurations, including mounting on a tracked armoured vehicle which could lay sections over an obstacle and use them as a bridge to maintain its advance. The system effectively replaced the long-serving Bailey Bridge and introduced many new variants to meet tactical requirements.

BOTTOM: NEI Nuclear Systems formed a unit to carry out maintenance and repair of reactor plants. Its operations involved intensive training in rigs which exactly simulated the temperatures and limitations of access experienced in reactors. The unit had its roots in Clarke Chapman of Gateshead, which was involved in every significant UK development of nuclear power from Calder Hall in the 1950s to the AGR programme, which included Clarke Chapman nuclear steam generators at Hinkley Point, Hunterston, Heysham and Torness.

Sir Terence Harrison, Chairman of NEI and Chief Executive of
Rolls-Royce after NEI was acquired, worked hard to integrate the
engineering company into Rolls-Royce.

He wondered even more whether the merger was a good move for Rolls-Royce:

From Rolls' point of view, NEI is the first step in a diversification programme; but it offers hardly the most attractive sector into which to diversify, nor the most attractive partner.

He noted that NEI was not a dominant partner in any major product area. It had recently signed deals to take products or technology from Mitsubishi in rail traction, switchgear and gas turbines and from the German company MTU in big diesels. While these deals were commercially logical, they were also a reflection of technological weakness.

In spite of these expressed doubts, Rolls-Royce and NEI tried hard to make the merger work. Terry Harrison, a strong and decisive manager, continued to extract cash from his businesses based in the North-East, and the group as a whole benefited, especially at a time when it was having to invest heavily in the development of the Trent. In 1991, industrial power accounted for 42 per cent of Rolls-Royce's £3.5-billion turnover and made a £73-million profit compared with a £6-million loss for the aerospace division. Lord Tombs told the author in June 2000:

NEI brought in profits and cash at a time when Rolls-Royce needed it, and we didn't pay a high price. NEI's share price was low when we bid initially in 1988 and although this was rejected we did not raise the price when the bid was accepted in 1989.

There were some synergy benefits. Stewart Miller, in his role as Corporate Director of Engineering and Technology, said in 1993:

My job is to see what can be squeezed from each sector to benefit the other.

He could see four levels of technological activity where there were opportunities for synergy between the Aerospace Group and Rolls-Royce Power Engineering (the name given to the former NEI). First, there was the basics, the physical materials and computational tools. Then there was the transfer of component technology – for example, the possibility that the lightweight fan-blades concept might also make modules for a lightweight heat exchanger. Third, there were the subsystems such as the turbo-machinery that the company was developing under its WR21 contract with Westinghouse Electric for a more fuel-efficient propulsion system for the US Navy. And the fourth level was the integration of complete systems.

Miller wondered whether the accumulated engineering experience of the

Rolls-Royce fan blade, stretching back more than two decades and costing tens of millions of pounds to develop, could be applied to the Parsons steam turbine:

In size and shape it's not all that different from the last-stage blade. In fact, the blades are almost the same length – 1,200 mm for the solid steel blades of a 900 MW [megawatt] steam turbine, compared with 1,023 mm for the titanium-skinned hollow fan blades of the Trent 800 turbofan.

And Miller saw opportunities for Rolls-Royce Power Engineering to help the Aerospace Group. Its International Research and Development company possessed 'quite remarkable expertise, particularly with regard to refurbishing materials'. Even before the 1989 merger, IRD was supplying Rolls-Royce with sophisticated welding machinery for blade-tipping and continued to provide machines for welding work on Trent fan blades.

To facilitate technology transfer, Miller set up expert panels in specific technologies to 'brainstorm' the possibilities. The first was for computational fluid dynamics, and this was followed by panels for combustion, materials technology and environmental measurement. These panels reported to the Rolls-Royce Research Board, which in turn reported to the main Rolls-Royce Board.

While synergies were sought and both the Aerospace and Power Engineering Groups struggled to emerge from the recession of the early 1990s, there were some significant successes that suggested that Rolls-Royce had made a good strategic move in buying NEI.

In June 1992, it was announced that a fifteen-year agreement with the giant US corporation Westinghouse had been signed. Terry Harrison said:

The arrangement with Westinghouse takes us into the world market.

The deal would also link Rolls-Royce with Westinghouse's partners, Mitsubishi Heavy Industries in Japan and Fiat Avio in Italy, and pitch against aero-engine competitor GE in the field of power generation. As surplus capacity and the breakdown of protected national power-plant markets encouraged consolidation and cross-border partnerships, Rolls-Royce Power Engineering had chosen the collaborative as opposed to the niche route. GE had already had a wide range of partners, from GEC/Alsthom in Europe to Toshiba and Hitachi in Japan. Siemens in Germany had links with Rolls-Royce's other aero-engine competitor, Pratt & Whitney, while Asea Brown Boveri had acquired the US boiler maker Combustion Engineering and the power-generation interests of Ansaldo and Franco Tosi of Italy. Terry Harrison commented:

We've clearly gone for the broad alliance.

At Parsons, after a very difficult patch that necessitated the reduction of its workforce from 5,000 in 1985 to 2,500 by 1992, two large orders were secured in 1992. It won a £70-million contract from Calcutta Electric at the new coal-fired Budge power station, and it also won an order worth £100 million to supply three 250-megawatt steam turbine generators for stage three of the Pulau Seraya power station in Singapore. Richard Maudslay, Managing Director of the Rolls-Royce Industrial Power Group, was able to say that his business was 'quite well loaded; much better than 12 months ago'.

In October 1993, the Industrial Power Group announced that it had received a £140-million order from the Ministry of Defence for the next generation of bridges to be used by the Army's Royal Engineers. These would be made at Thompson Defence Projects in Wolverhampton. The following month, Parsons Power Generation Systems signed a memorandum of under-standing for two Indian power stations, but it had to wait until March 1995 before that £450-million order was signed. As the *Financial Times* put it:

Parsons, one of the most famous names in UK engineering, was thrown a lifeline yesterday with the news that it has clinched two India power station orders ... Without the projects, Parsons' order book for steam turbines would have run out this summer.

The split of Rolls-Royce, after the merger with NEI, into two groups put civil aero-engines, military aero-engines and repair and overhaul of aero-engines into the Aerospace Group. Nuclear, industrial and marine gas turbines in the former Reyrolle Parsons group and materials handling were put into the Industrial Power Group. Also into the latter went Rolls-Royce Industries Canada Inc.

As we saw in Part Two, Trans-Canada Airlines (TCA) operated Merlin-powered Lancastrians during the Second World War and chose the Merlin to power its Canadair DC-4M North Star airliner, whose maiden flight took place in July 1946. The TCA business was considered important enough for Hives to send Jim (later Sir Denning) Pearson to open an office in Montreal and a spares base at nearby Dorval to support the operation. Shortly after-wards, the Royal Canadian Air Force bought a number of war-surplus Lancastrians and Mustangs, and the Rolls-Royce technicians at Dorval were kept busy bringing the engines of these aircraft up to the latest modification standard.

In 1951, the Royal Canadian Air Force ordered the Lockheed T-33 Shooting Star to be built at Canadair and powered by Rolls-Royce Nene engines in place of the standard Allison J-33. Rolls-Royce Canada was given a contract for the production of 900 Nene Mk 10s. Although most of the engines would come from the UK, a small number were to be built in Canada. The premises at Dorval were not large enough, and the company bought property and buildings that had been used as stables by a local brewery on the Côte de Liesse Road, three-and-a-half miles east of Montreal Airport.

In 1957, Rolls-Royce Canada expanded its business to include repair and overhaul, beginning with support for the Dart powering a number of aircraft including first the Viscount and then the Argosy, CV600/640, F227, Gulfstream I, HP Herald, HS748 and YS11. In 1960, repair and overhaul began on the Tyne, which was being used by Canadair CL-44 and Yukon aircraft. In the following 23 years, 500 Tyne engines went through the plant. The first industrial engines supported by Rolls-Royce Canada were Avons. TransCanada PipeLines bought its first industrial Avon in 1964 to pump natural gas across Canada. However, with all this extra activity, the most important part of Rolls-Royce Canada remained the servicing of the Nene for the T-33. Engines are still being overhauled today, though they are now contracted out to a specialist overhaul business.

The success of Rolls-Royce in winning orders for the Spey to power the Fokker F28, BAC 111 and Gulfstream II and III necessitated a large factory expansion to the Montreal plant in 1967 – the same year in which Rolls-Royce Canada was awarded a contract by the Royal Canadian Air Force to repair and overhaul the GE CT-64 engine that powered the Buffalo. Servicing the Viper, which powered the HS125 business jet, was introduced in 1974. After about 1,000 Viper engines had been serviced in Montreal, this work was transferred to Motores Rolls-Royce Limitada, Brazil, in 1995.

A new test cell was built in 1986, enabling the testing of up to 100,000 lb thrust. This allowed Rolls-Royce Canada to provide full support for the Tay, which powers the Gulfstream IV, Fokker F100 and Boeing B727QF aircraft. By the early 1990s, the large fan engines were in service, and to accommodate them a further 61,000-square-foot extension was added to the plant. Included in the extension was an assembly shop for the RB 211, and a new engine washline, inspection and process facility was opened within the extension in 1993. Support for the Adour used in the US Navy T-45 Goshawk trainers also began in 1993.

When Rolls-Royce decided to develop an industrial Trent at the same time as an aero version – the first time this parallel development had been pursued – a new subsidiary, Rolls-Royce Gas Turbine Engines Canada Inc., was set up near Rolls-Royce Canada on the Côte de Liesse Road to carry through this design and development. Also in 1995, Rolls-Royce Canada signed an exclusive contract for the support in North America of the BMW Rolls-Royce BR710 engine which powers the Gulfstream V and Canadair Global Express aircraft. This was followed two years later by its appointment as the authorised maintenance centre by the Allison Engine Company (acquired by Rolls-Royce in 1995) for the support of the AE 3007, which powers the Cessna Citation X business jet and the Embraer EMB-145 regional jet. In the same year, Rolls-Royce Canada was given responsibility for worldwide production, assembly and testing of all Rolls-Royce's large industrial gas turbines – the 17 MW industrial Avon, the 28 MW industrial RB 211 and the 50 MW industrial Trent.

While this expansion was taking place, Rolls-Royce Canada continued to run Bristol Aerospace, which Rolls-Royce had acquired when it bought the Bristol Aeroplane Company in 1966. Based in Winnipeg, Manitoba, Bristol Aerospace employed 960 people by the mid-1990s and was engaged in maintenance contracts with the Canadian armed forces, production of rockets for the US National Aeronautic and Space Administration (NASA) and the manufacture of missiles and military targets, which were exported to a number of countries. Bristol Aerospace also achieved considerable success with a helicopter cable-cutting device.

After the merger with NEI, Rolls-Royce Canada also became responsible for NEI's interests in Canada, for Parsons Canada and Ferranti Packard Transformers, with plants in Trois Rivières (Quebec), St Catherine's (Ontario), Buffalo (New York) and Mexico.

'WE WILL FOCUS ON SECTORS WHERE WE ARE A MAJOR PLAYER'

In spite of these limited successes, by the mid-1990s Rolls-Royce could see that its Industrial Power Group was not going to provide the growth it had sought in its diversification strategy. NEI had not been a world player and had been unable to invest sufficiently in the 1980s to challenge its best competitors. Large steam turbines and boilers, which accounted for about 30 per cent of NEI, had not fitted into Rolls-Royce's overall plan. The power-generation market had proved to be very tough in the early 1990s and was dominated by big international groups.

Because of the rationalisation at the end of the 1980s, NEI's share of markets was dwarfed by such giants as ABB (formed after Asea of Sweden merged with Brown Boveri of Switzerland), GEC-Alsthom (a merger of the power equipment and some other interests of GEC of the UK with almost the whole of Alsthom of France), Siemens of West Germany, GE of the USA, and Mitsubishi, Toshiba and Hitachi of Japan.

Rolls-Royce had a market share in steam turbines of under 1 per cent. To add to the difficulties, prices were falling at 10 to 15 per cent a year due to the increasing globalisation of competition following the deregulation of electricity generation in many countries. Furthermore, demand for power equipment shifted from big coal-fired 400-megawatt steam-turbine plants run by large utilities to smaller stations up to 150 megawatts. Orders for nuclear plants requiring steam turbines dried up completely. There were orders for steam turbines, notably in coal-rich countries like China and India, but price pressure made it very difficult for suppliers to provide them at a profit.

To make matters worse, supplying large turbines to such countries often meant taking responsibility for the whole power-station construction contract, including local subcontractors. This was a high-risk, low-return business best left to giants such as Siemens who could spread the risk over many contracts. Sir Ralph Robins summed up the situation:

The market for large steam-power generation equipment has changed radically over the last few years and it is increasingly unlikely that Rolls-Royce can develop a leading global position in this sector of the market.

In July 1996, Rolls-Royce put the turbine power-generation business, i.e. the old Parsons, up for sale. In 1995, the steam-turbine business had lost £30 million on a turnover of £280 million. While many expressed regret at the possible demise of one of the most famous names in UK engineering, others were more realistic. Steve Thomas, a researcher at the Science Policy Research Unit at Sussex University, said:

Parsons has been a drag on Rolls-Royce for some time.

City and industrial analysts praised the move, saying that it would allow Rolls-Royce to concentrate on its core strengths, while Sir Ralph Robins said that it was more important to secure Britain's industrial future than to dwell on the past, adding:

Our prime responsibility is to ensure that the industrial future of this country is maintained. That means going forward in world markets with Rolls-Royce products … We will focus on sectors where we are a major player in the world, which we were not in large steam turbines.

Rolls-Royce had already signalled its intentions by appointing its youngest Board member, John Rose, Managing Director of the Aerospace Group, to replace Harrison as Chief Executive of the whole group, and he immediately started work on the process of disposing of Parsons. He had earlier under-taken research which had shown that some of the contracts Parsons had entered into were going to result in Rolls-Royce sustaining large losses and had recommended to the Board that Parsons be sold.

The sector on which he wanted to concentrate was smaller turbines, including electric power generation units up to 150 megawatts, where the synergies with aero-engines were greatest and contracting risks were minimised.

In April 1997, it was announced that Siemens had agreed to buy most of Parsons Power Generation Systems. It would pay £30 million and take on 800 of the 1,700 employed at the Newcastle plant. It was buying the service and maintenance activities rather than the power-station building operation.

In 1996, further rationalisation took place when Bristol Aerospace in Canada was put up for sale, and in June 1997 it was announced that Magellan Aerospace, a Canadian holding company with interests in several North American aircraft-components businesses, had paid 63 million Canadian dollars for the business.

In September 1998, the Reyrolle part of the former NEI went when the electrical transmission and distribution interests were sold to the Austrian engineering group VA Tech and one of its subsidiaries, who paid £137.5 million, cash. At the same time, Rolls-Royce announced that it would also sell the materials-handling business.

By this time, there was very little left of the original NEI. Rolls-Royce had returned to its core business, saying:

Rolls-Royce continues to follow consistent strategies to develop leading positions in growing markets. The company has developed a broad and competitive product range focused upon the civil aerospace, defence and energy markets, where its world-leading gas turbine technology confers a competitive advantage.

One NEI company that Rolls-Royce retained and still retains is Syncrolift, based in Miami. Founded in the 1950s, Syncrolift has installed ship-lifts and transfer systems for 220 customers in 66 countries. The range of vessels that can be lifted and transferred varies from 100 to over 100,000 tons.

But long before Rolls-Royce was deciding to concentrate on its core business, it was coping with a severe cyclical downturn exacerbated by a war in a very sensitive area of the world. It is to this that we shall now turn.

CHAPTER THREE

RECESSION

IT'S WAR AGAIN
'WE ARE SIMPLY IN TOO MANY PLACES'
GE SECURE BA ORDER
ANY GOOD NEWS?
'A DECISION FOR DECADES AHEAD'
INDUSTRIA DE TURBO PROPULSORES

IT'S WAR AGAIN

Nineteen-eighty-eight had been the year when it seemed as though world peace had broken out. Relations between East and West improved, the rapprochement between China and the Soviet Union continued, the Soviet Union talked of withdrawal from Afghanistan, and Iran accepted the UN proposal to end its war with Iraq.

The biggest surprise was the ending of the Iran–Iraq war. After rejecting many mediation attempts, Ayatollah Khomeini suddenly announced on 18 July 1988 that Iran accepted the UN peace proposal. The war had lasted eight years and had cost both sides dearly. It was estimated that 1 million people had been killed, 1.7 million wounded and 1.5 million turned into refugees. In financial terms, the cost was estimated at a staggering $400 billion.

The events in 1988 were surpassed in 1989, the year in which, in retrospect, the Cold War that had threatened the world for over 40 years effectively came to an end.

The post-Second World War blueprint for Europe had been sealed by Winston Churchill, Franklin Roosevelt and Joseph Stalin at the Yalta Conference in February 1945. In May 1945, Berlin fell to Soviet troops, and the Communist Soviet Union dominated Eastern Europe from the end of the War using, where necessary, military force to crush any protest (Hungary in 1956, Czechoslovakia in 1968). To prevent an ever-growing exodus of East

Germans to the increasingly prosperous West Germany, the Berlin Wall was erected in 1961.

By 1988, the desire for change became overwhelming, prompted by the introduction in the Soviet Union itself of *perestroika* (restructuring) and *glasnost* (openness) by the new Soviet president, Mikhail Gorbachev. The gradual loosening of the iron grip of dictatorship in the Soviet Union was bound to arouse the pent-up demand for more liberty and independence in the regions of the USSR as well as in the satellite countries of Eastern Europe.

In the June elections in Poland, the hitherto illegal trades union Solidarity won an overwhelming majority. In Hungary, the Communist Party renounced Marxism and changed its name. In the autumn of 1989, as a result of mass demonstrations, the Communist governments of East Germany, Czechoslovakia, Romania and Bulgaria all fell. The exodus to the West had grown throughout the year, and in early November, after the East German president, Erich Honecker, had been ousted, hundreds of thousands of East Germans swarmed through the Berlin Wall.

The Cold War was over. The Soviet Union was facing reality: Communism had failed. The Soviet economy was in a dreadful state, and if it were to be repaired the high percentage of gross domestic product being poured into the arms race with the USA had to stop. The implications for world peace were good, but, as we shall see in Chapter Six, there would need to be an adjustment in the expectations of defence contractors such as Rolls-Royce.

Nineteen-ninety was the year when war broke out again. Iraq, freed from its war with Iran, invaded Kuwait. The Iraqi president, Saddam Hussein, had been threatening Kuwait for months about its disregard for OPEC quotas and for its extraction of oil from the Rumaila oil field, where Iraq claimed ownership. Few thought that Hussein would go as far as invasion, but, in the early hours of 2 August, Iraqi troops and tanks swept into Kuwait and took control of the sheikhdom. Kuwait's royal family escaped to Saudi Arabia.

The reaction from the West was swift. President Bush condemned the 'naked aggression' and imposed economic sanctions. He also froze both Iraq's and Kuwait's assets held in the USA. Japan, Britain, France and other European countries did the same. The UN Security Council unanimously condemned Iraq's action and ordered it to withdraw its troops. Within days, the Security Council approved a broad trade embargo. Fears of all-out war mounted when Saudi Arabia requested US military protection of its oil fields. (If Hussein had seized those as well, he would have controlled 39.5 per cent of the world's oil reserves.) However, President Bush flew to Finland in early September to meet President Mikhail Gorbachev to confirm that both the US and the USSR would work together to force Iraq's withdrawal from Kuwait. The message to all potential protagonists was clear – the two superpowers were on the same side.

All attempts during the autumn of 1990 to persuade Iraq to withdraw failed, and on 29 November the United Nations Security Council voted overwhelmingly to authorise the use of force to drive Iraqi troops out of Kuwait if they did not withdraw by 15 January 1991. The USA had needed four months to build up sufficient forces to defend Saudi Arabia and force Iraq to withdraw from Kuwait. In August, the USA had immediately sent to Saudi Arabia elements of its Rapid Deployment Force. These included the 82nd Airborne Division, US Marine Corps forces and US Air Force units. US Navy units were also deployed in the Persian Gulf. However, the US ground forces were only lightly equipped, and even with Saudi Arabian and other Arab forces they would probably not have been able to hold off an all-out Iraqi attack. Nevertheless, it was sufficient to deter Saddam Hussein from attempting to attack Saudi Arabia.

The USA had learnt the lessons of the Vietnam War, and they were not going to become involved in an unlimited war. They built up sufficient forces to win and win quickly – 450,000 US, 14,000 UK and 10,000 French personnel, as well as 65,700 Saudi Arabian military personnel and several Egyptian divisions. Against these forces, Iraq could put about one million men into the field, mostly in the army. This gave the Iraqis numerical superiority, but in the air and at sea the US and Allied Forces had a clear advantage.

In the event, the war was short – Hussein did not withdraw his troops on 15 January, and air strikes began on 17 January – and successful in that the Iraqis were driven out of Kuwait. Many believe that the USA and its allies should have pressed on to Baghdad and deposed Saddam Hussein, but the UN Security Council resolution sanctioned only the expulsion of Iraqi forces from Kuwait, and once that had been achieved the US generals called a halt to hostilities. Some also felt that although Saddam Hussein was clearly not an ideal ruler, at least he was a known quantity and a balance to the power of Iran. Furthermore, the USA and its allies would have risked losing friends in other Middle Eastern countries if UN troops had invaded Iraq. We saw in 2001 how Osama bin Laden was apparently turned into an implacable enemy of the USA because of the presence of US troops in Saudi Arabia.

'WE ARE SIMPLY IN TOO MANY PLACES'

The effect of all this caused the numbers of air travellers to plummet. The airlines lost $2 billion in 1990, and predictions for 1991 were even more dire. Several airlines collapsed. Eastern Airlines had already gone in 1989, Continental and Braniff both filed for Chapter II bankruptcy protection, and in Britain Air Europe went bankrupt in March 1991. Later in the year, Midway Airlines and the once-famous and dominant Pan American Airways ceased operations.

On 8 November 1990, Sir Ralph Robins, recently appointed Chief Executive of the Rolls-Royce Group, told his Board that the recession and the high cost of fuel was hitting airlines. Now, as in the early 1970s and 1980s, they were only ordering in emergencies. Build requirements for 1991 and 1992 would probably reduce and then increase in 1993. Rolls-Royce would need to smoothe the programme. Boeing would help by taking early delivery of engines in 1991 and 1992, and Rolls-Royce thought it might be sensible to build Tays in 1992 for delivery in 1993, taking the commercial risk itself. Because of the recession, profits would be very tight for the next two years as the company was heavily committed to research and development spending.

To emphasise the current difficulties, Lord King, Chairman of British Airways, said on 2 November 1990 that, although profits had risen 23.6 per cent in the first half of the year, he did 'not expect a positive contribution in the second half'. That was 'corporate speak' meaning that he expected a loss.

To add to the world's woes, the recession that had begun in 1990 worsened in 1991, and though many thought it might be coming to an end in late 1991 – Chancellor of the Exchequer Norman Lamont mistakenly talked of the 'green shoots of spring' – it persisted well into 1992. The effect on the aircraft industry was nearly catastrophic. *Aviation Weekly & Space Technology* wrote after the Farnborough Air Show in September 1992:

The world-wide aerospace/defence industry faces continuing uncertainty and challenges as the expected recovery from global recession remains elusive, effects of the Gulf War on civil aviation linger and the thaw in the Cold War progresses unabated.

Markets for aircraft manufacturers and therefore for their suppliers, including Rolls-Royce, were declining, leading to sharper, even almost destructive, competition. As orders dried up, rows of unsold airliners appeared in desert storage parks in south-western USA. Guinness Peat Aviation was forced to abandon its public flotation.

There was no help from the military market. The end of the Cold War and the collapse of the Soviet Union as a military threat gave governments in the West the opportunity to cut their defence budgets. Europe's leading military aircraft programme, the four-nation (Britain, Germany, Italy and Spain) European Fighter Aircraft, was put in jeopardy in late 1992 when Germany, reeling under the costs of reunification, refused to carry on supporting the costs. The project was saved by a restructuring round a simpler specification and relaunched under the name Eurofighter 2000.

Naturally, Rolls-Royce was not unaffected, and the first area to feel the pinch was the military engine group in Bristol. This was mainly as a result of cuts in defence spending by the Ministry of Defence, notably a cutting of orders for Tornado fighter aircraft, which used the RB 199.

Paul Betts had pointed out in the *Financial Times* on 12 July 1990:

The 'peace dividend' of détente is turning into a 'peace debit' for the world's three principal aero-engine manufacturers ... Lord Tombs confirmed that there would be a 'pinchback' at the company's military engine operations at Bristol ... Colin Green, director of the group's military engines division, puts the issue even more bluntly. The Government's decision to cancel 33 Tornado aircraft is 'a heavy blow to the military engine group and the Bristol facility.'

Some may have expected that the Gulf War would have brought a large increase in orders for military engines and spares for Rolls-Royce. The company was certainly heavily involved, as we shall see in Chapter Six, but wars, unless they last a long time, actually bring a reduction in military aircraft activity as aircraft fly only specific missions from A to B and back, rather than spending time on more diverse practice activities. The *Financial Times* said:

The outlook looks even bleaker for defence companies since the Gulf War has done little to alter the underlying trend of long-term reductions in government defence expenditure.

Although the Rolls-Royce results for 1990 were excellent – a turnover of £3.57 billion (up 24 per cent), profits of £124 million and an order book of £5.7 billion – by the time they were announced in the spring of 1991, Chairman Lord Tombs was warning that 1991 would be a 'difficult year'. There were 'early signs' of postponements of engine deliveries, and even order cancellations. Tombs told shareholders:

Our inflation rate is falling, but remains higher than that of our competitors, and the strong pound creates serious problems for exporters like ourselves.

Sir Ralph Robins added:

We have to win orders worth £5 million a day just to tick over. We have to face enormous competition to win orders to survive. The margins are very narrow and our unit costs have to become much lower to match the competition.

The knock-on effect of the Gulf War and the slump of 20 per cent in world air travel on airframe and engine manufacturers was severe. In theory, Boeing and Airbus Industrie were sitting on large order books – $200 billion and $72 billion respectively – but these were misleading as deliveries stretched out to the mid- to late 1990s, and, with orders being cancelled left and right, what did they mean anyway?

And, of course, Rolls-Royce was severely affected. In January 1991, it announced cuts of 1,500 jobs at its civil-engine factories in Derby, and the cuts continued throughout the year so that the total number employed by the end of the year had fallen from 64,200 at the end of 1990 to 57,100. The results for the year showed turnover down from £3.76 billion to £3.51 billion, and profits down from £134 million to £24 million.

Robins told the Rolls-Royce Board on 7 February 1991 that he had taken the opportunity the previous week to discuss the civil-aviation scene with the chairmen of most US and some international airlines. It was clear that the industry was suffering profoundly from the fear of terrorism, and transatlantic traffic was down no less than 60 per cent, US domestic traffic by 30 per cent and transpacific operations by some 20 per cent. It was hardly surprising that orders were being deferred and inventories reduced as much as possible.

In May 1991, Rolls-Royce announced further job cuts and the closure of its Leavesden and Coventry plants. Robins said:

We have sites all over the country. We must reduce the number ... The same thing is happening at British Aerospace. We are simply in too many places.

Leavesden's activities would be transferred to Bristol and the Parkside aero-engine component facility in Coventry transferred to nearby Ansty.

The immediate gloom was given expression at the Paris Air Show in June 1991 where Bernard Attali, Chairman of Air France, said that the Gulf War had triggered 'the worst crisis in the airline industry since the Second World War'.

Paul Betts wrote in the *Financial Times*:

Airlines' profits have been savaged. Even strong carriers such as BA, American Airlines and Lufthansa, are operating under severe strain. Airlines lost a total of $2 billion in the first quarter of this year when traffic collapsed by around 25 per cent ... The industry does not expect any sustained recovery until later this year or early next year.

And worse was to come the following year when Rolls-Royce's small profit was replaced by a loss of £202 million, due to substantial provisions of £268 million to cover the cost of lay-offs and other special items. More redundancies followed in 1993, with a further reduction in the workforce in the Aerospace Group of 3,600 and 2,400 in the Industrial Power Group. There were also plant closures.

In the midst of these difficulties, Chairman Lord Tombs retired in October 1992 and was succeeded by Sir Ralph Robins. Robins had joined Rolls-Royce as a graduate apprentice in 1955, spending his first three years as a section leader in the technical services department on the Conway. During the 1960s, he had worked in the development office under Tom Metcalfe and Lindsay Dawson before moving to work as a senior staff officer (now called a programme manager) under Managing Director David Huddie. His next appointment was Executive Assistant to David Huddie, and, while Huddie was spending most of his time in the USA working with Lockheed on the RB 211 for the TriStar, Robins moved to marketing and product support in the USA, before returning to the UK in 1973 to become Managing Director of the Industrial and Marine Division at Ansty. In 1976, he was appointed Commercial Director of the Aero Division in Derby and, in 1978, Commercial Director for the whole of Rolls-Royce. When Chairman Bill Duncan died in 1984, Robins was appointed Managing Director of the whole group, and, as we have seen, he became Chief Executive of Rolls-Royce plc in 1989.

Robins forecast that conditions in the airline industry would take a long time to improve, saying:

In the early 1980s the civil business fell but the defence business remained strong. Now, both sides are down. We don't know what the bottom for the defence will be. We are waiting for the Ministry of Defence to announce their future defence plans.

In spite of these dire conditions, Robins insisted that Rolls-Royce's fundamental strategy remain unaltered.

It is very straightforward. It is to become the leading supplier of high-integrity power systems. That is our mission. It's a long-term strategy which simply doesn't happen overnight. We are reacting to changed market forces and being more rigorous in the analysis and restructuring of all our business processes. Our aim is to take out all non-value-added activities in what we do. We started with our manufacturing processes three years ago. We are now extending this approach to our business and management processes.

In the short term, to add to its woes, Rolls-Royce lost out to GE in the battle to win the engine order for BA's new 777s, which it ordered from Boeing in August 1991.

GE SECURE BA ORDER

We have already seen how Rolls-Royce beat GE to the BA order for 747-400s in 1986. The next crucial BA order was for the Boeing 777, the major new aircraft of the early 1990s. As the *Financial Times* said, it was 'hard to overstate the significance of the order. BA's stringent technical standards [are] renowned throughout the industry.'

The fight to secure the order was fierce, and the situation became complicated by BA's decision to put its engine-overhaul company in Cardiff up for sale. Rolls-Royce bid for the business, British Airways Engine Overhaul Limited, but at a lower price than the £272 million offered by GE. This was about 20 per cent of BA's total market capitalisation and represented a huge earnings multiple on the £11-million pre-tax profits made by the business in the previous year. GE also agreed to continue to overhaul BA's engines at a price below the cost of BA doing the services itself.

In the event, GE won the engine order, and a BA spokesman said that the engine deal alone 'was offered on such attractive terms that the company could not resist'.

Sir Ralph Robins said:

It is disappointing because we had reasonably hoped to win the 777 order. It was an extremely competitive contest and we bid down to a level which we thought was prudent. I can only assume that the competition went below that level.

Everyone assumed that BA had been influenced by GE's offer for the engine-overhaul business. *Flight International* restricted itself to putting 'BA Opts for 777/GE90 Combination' and 'GE Buys BA Engine Overhaul Centre' next to each other on the same page. However, Richard Needham, Minister for Trade at the time, wrote later in his book *Battling for Peace*:

[I went] to see Colin Marshall, John King and David Burnside, respectively managing director, chairman and public relations director at British Airways. They informed us that they had just done a deal with General Electric, who in return for an engine order had taken over all their servicing facilities in South Wales.

In his autobiography *Jack*, Jack Welch, former chairman of GE, wrote:

We had engine shops located around the world. We acquired a large shop in Wales from British Airways in 1991 as part of a deal to sell BA our new GE-90 engines. It was an unprofitable operation that primarily serviced and overhauled Rolls-Royce engines, and BA wanted out of it.

That GE squeezed its margins severely was given credence by the remarks later in the year by Brian Rowe, head of GE's aero-engine industry:

We've got to stop killing ourselves. We've got to co-operate on programmes when we can and the door remains open for Rolls-Royce ... We are now having to make deals on spare parts. That's how tough it is. We must find various ways of working together.

Not only was the loss of the order itself extremely disappointing, it also meant that Rolls-Royce's efforts to win orders elsewhere would be hampered. BA's stringent technical standards, renowned throughout the industry, would help GE win orders elsewhere. Indeed, the first such knock-on effect was seen when All Nippon Airways, which had been expected to specify the Trent for its 777s, chose the Pratt & Whitney engine. Japan Airlines and Korean Airlines orders were also lost by Rolls-Royce. All-Nippon Vice-President Kenzo Yoshikawa told *The Times*:

We tend to feel better about an engine if it is being used by many other carriers, especially the main airline in the country that is making it.

In October, All Nippon Airways, the Japanese carrier, cited BA's rejection of the Trent as one of the reasons for selecting Pratt & Whitney engines for its 777 fleet. And Air India unexpectedly switched a 747 engine order from Rolls-Royce to Pratt & Whitney.

Robins remained calm:

We must keep our nerve. The BA decision was a big disappointment but not a killer. You can't read the whole market on two or three early 777 decisions.

He pointed out that Rolls-Royce had increased its market share in the previous decade from 10 to 20 per cent by making a broad product range and was currently enjoying a firm order book of £7.4 billion.

The bad news continued into 1992. When the *Financial Times* correspondent Paul Betts visited the GE engine plant in Cincinnati in January, Brian Rowe told him:

You've come on a bad day. We are laying off 1,500 of our people.

Rolls-Royce's fight against recession was not helped by political, and consequent economic, events in Britain. The last general election had been in the late spring of 1987, and the new Prime Minister, John Major, had to call another by the spring of 1992. As the Conservatives were well behind Labour in opinion polls throughout 1991, he held on until the last possible minute and, to many people's surprise, managed to win, albeit with a much reduced majority.

As always when an election result flouts the opinions of the pundits and appears to be the opposite of what the opinion polls were predicting, many reasons were put forward for the surprise result. In this case, it was either Labour's mishandling of the taxation issue – Shadow Chancellor John Smith put forward increased tax proposals that, although aimed mainly at the rich, went far enough down the income scale for the Conservatives to exploit 'Labour's tax bombshell' – or it was a distasteful, triumphalist rally held by Labour in Sheffield a week before polling day. As far as Rupert Murdoch's *Sun* newspaper was concerned, 'It Was Us Wot Won It' – its campaign of vilification of Labour Leader Neil Kinnock had obviously done the trick. Perhaps the truth was that the country was not quite ready to abandon 'nurse' in what were, undoubtedly for many, very hard times and still trusted the Tories more in handling the economy than Labour.

If that held true in April 1992, by the end of September that year the Conservatives' supposed skill in economic affairs suffered a blow from which it did not recover for the rest of the decade. Taking the UK into the Exchange Rate Mechanism (ERM) had not been universally popular in the Conservative Party, and it was something of a gamble when Major put continued membership of the ERM at the centre of his economic strategy after the election. The foreign exchange markets already knew that the UK had joined the ERM at too high a rate for sterling, but when in July 1992 the UK began its six-month presidency of the EU, the divisions within the Conservative Party, even in the Cabinet, were brought more sharply to their attention. The UK's economy was crying out for lower interest rates, but, within the ERM, the country was stuck with trying to hold sterling at too high a rate – especially against the Deutschmark, which was being held up by high German interest rates made necessary by Germany unification and the German Government's inflationary decision to convert East German marks to West German marks at parity.

Fortunately, there was a way out of the dilemma of high interest rates and continued recession or lower interest rates and a collapse of sterling out of the ERM. The pound was not alone in struggling, and therefore the obvious solution was a co-ordinated realignment of European currencies against the Deutschmark. Incredibly, Chancellor Norman Lamont rejected this solution at a meeting of European finance ministers under his chairmanship in Bath in August 1992. Instead, he tried to bully the Bundesbank President, Helmut Schlesinger, into cutting German interest rates. This merely showed an ignorance of German politics and the decision-making process of the Bundesbank; Schlesinger could not make a unilateral decision even if he wanted to. All Lamont succeeded in doing was to make an enemy of Schlesinger.

The failure of the Bath meeting increased the pressure on sterling and on the other weak member of the ERM, the Italian Lira. Major decided to tough it out, and at a CBI dinner on 10 September he said that the Government would not be 'driven off their virtuous pursuit of low inflation by market problems or political pressures'. He added:

The soft option, the devaluer's option, the inflationary option, would be a betrayal of our future.

And he asserted that devaluation would not work. It would bring 'rising import prices, rising inflation and a long-term deterioration in Britain's competitiveness which would offset any short-term gain'.

The following weekend, the Italians devalued and the Germans agreed to a small cut in interest rates. Pressured by the UK to do more, Schlesinger implied to journalists that he thought there should be a 'more complete realignment' of currencies. That was it; the pressure on sterling became intense. On the morning of Wednesday 16 September (Black or Golden Wednesday, depending on your point of view), the Bank of England was forced to spend billions of pounds to try to hold up sterling. At the same time, interest rates were raised from 10 to 12 per cent, and at a lunch-time meeting of John Major and some senior ministers it was decided to raise them even further, to 15 per cent. This last raise, due to take place the next day, was never implemented, because, at 7 o'clock in the evening, Norman Lamont emerged from the Treasury looking shell-shocked and announced that Britain's membership of the ERM had been suspended. [It is a dilemma for the chartists of interest rates – did they rise to 15 per cent or only to 12 per cent? The chairman of one beleaguered public company said to the author when he heard they were going up to 15 per cent, 'I might as well call in the receivers.' It was a good job he didn't, because he sold the company for over £100 million four years later.]

This apparent debacle was extremely damaging to the Conservative Government, but the results – a sharp devaluation of sterling and a reduction in interest rates (they were down to 6 per cent by early 1993) – were exactly what the British economy needed, and almost from that moment it started to revive. In the City, the *Financial Times* 100 index rose over 100 points and carried on rising for the next seven years. From Rolls-Royce's point of view, the best outcome was a virtual 25 per cent devaluation of sterling against the US dollar, from about $2 to the pound to $1.50.

ANY GOOD NEWS?

They were, of course, talking their own book, but both Boeing and Airbus produced forecasts that showed a healthy future for air travel and consequently for the sale of aircraft. In February 1991, Boeing produced a forecast that expected the sale of 9,000 airliners between February 1991 and 2005. This was slightly lower than its forecast a year earlier, but it was still a large number. Later in the year, Airbus Industrie produced a broadly similar forecast. The Gulf War had brought a nasty short-term glitch, but that was what it was, a glitch, and growth would resume in line with the growth in world GDP. It always had in the past, and it would in the future.

For Rolls-Royce itself, orders were hard to come by, but there were some successes. In May 1990, it had won a $600-million contract to re-engine the entire Boeing 727-100 fleet of United Parcel Service (UPS). The deal, including options, was for 280 engines for 80 aircraft. Rolls-Royce had adopted a different approach from its competitors in tendering for re-engine contracts. The airlines were being forced to re-engine their older jets to meet new pollution and noise requirements, and, while its competitors were offering so-called 'hush-kits', Rolls-Royce was offering new engines. This enabled them to offer not only lower pollution and noise levels but also fuel-economy improvements, greater payload, increased range and lower maintenance costs.

As we saw in Part Two, the Boeing 727 was in its day the most successful passenger and freight airliner ever built. More than 1,800 were built between 1962 and the late 1980s. When new, the 727-100s, built in the 1960s, were considered state of the art, but by 1990 they were inefficient and noisy and, to comply with new regulations, required extensive modification. Many were retired and their sale value fell to less than $1 million. Nevertheless, UPS was prepared to spend $400 million on their fleet, and the biggest part of this investment was the installation of three Rolls-Royce Tay 651-54 turbofans, the same engine that had been so successful on one of the quietest and most efficient new passenger jets, the Fokker F100. The Tay was, of course, a development of the Spey, itself a scaled-down derivative of the RB 141, the AR963 derivative of which was offered originally by Rolls-Royce and Allison over 30 years earlier for the original Boeing 727.

Why did UPS re-engine their 727s when everyone else was beginning to think about scrapping them? It was because they saw no cost-effective replacement. A new aircraft of equivalent capacity would cost $35 million and have to be modified from passenger configuration. The package-carrying version of the 727-100 was just what UPS wanted. It was an inexpensive airframe that would have an almost unlimited life thanks to the much lower flying hours per year, 600 to 700, compared with the 3,000 hours of the average passenger airliner. Whereas the passenger aircraft would need a heavy airframe overhaul every seven or eight years, UPS's aircraft would fly for much longer without such expensive overhauls. Furthermore, UPS would benefit from the quieter Tay. Whereas airlines fly most of their passengers by day and hush-kits would meet the daytime noise regulations, the freight and package carriers – UPS, DHL and FedEx – fly by night and have to meet more stringent noise regulations. Hush-kits might not cope.

In June 1991, Rolls-Royce won another large order for the Tay when Gulfstream bought a further 300 Tay 611 engines to power its Gulfstream IV. This brought the number of Tay engines ordered and operated by Gulfstream since its launch in 1983 to 684.

In September 1991, Rolls-Royce won an order from Thai Airways International, who specified the Trent for their 777s, and in December it was announced by Emirates, the United Arab Emirates airline, that it would buy 36 Trent 877 and 884 engines in a deal worth $500 million. This was a significant breakthrough with an airline that had traditionally been a GE customer. This was quickly followed by a $900-million order from UPS for RB 211-535 engines to power twenty Boeing 757s. UPS's first 25 Boeing 757s were powered by Pratt & Whitney engines. UPS's comment was succinct:

The industry is very competitive. Rolls-Royce gave us a better deal.

It would have been the two orders for the Trent that were most pleasing to Rolls-Royce. As the *Wall Street Journal* wrote:

The competition to get the engine on the Boeing 777, due to enter service in 1995, has been particularly intense. Rolls-Royce suffered a devastating blow when it lost longtime customer British Airways to GE. Shortly afterward, All Nippon Airways, citing the British Airways decision, opted for Pratt & Whitney instead of its earlier favourite, Rolls-Royce.

Rolls-Royce has since recovered winning its first order for 777 engines from Thai Airways International. Thursday's Emirates order brought some momentum. 'It looks like they could still do very well with the Trent despite the loss of British Airways', said Ed Wright, an aerospace analyst with Barclays de Zoete Wedd.

UPS also said:

The RB211-535 is noted for its reliable, quiet, fuel-efficient operation.

This was all very significant for Rolls-Royce. Any airline that had bought a TriStar had automatically become a Rolls-Royce customer. However, on the Boeing 747, Rolls-Royce had only been an option, and success had only been achieved in the British Commonwealth – with British Airways, Qantas, Air New Zealand, Cathay Pacific and South African Airways. Now, the Trent was selling outside those confines not only to former GE and Pratt & Whitney customers but to airlines with whom Rolls-Royce had never done business.

Indeed, in a year when civil-aircraft orders reduced sharply, the Rolls-Royce share of new engine orders in 1991 could be seen as very encouraging. Their market share increased from 20 per cent in 1990 to 23 per cent, with a 38 per cent share where a Rolls-Royce engine was on offer. There was some compensation for the loss of the BA 777 order in that Rolls-Royce took 40 per cent of the domestic US new business. *Lex* in the *Financial Times* echoed this view in March 1992:

The story that came out of Rolls-Royce yesterday was certainly not that of a defensive company humiliated at the hands of British Airways. Chairman Lord Tombs is a wily old bird, of course, and employed unusual openness in his effort to show that last year's widely publicised order setback was in contrast to progress elsewhere. Even so, it is hard not to be impressed by his forecast that civil engine deliveries next year will be more than double the number achieved in 1987, by the steady growth in Rolls's market share, and by the relentless if inescapable attack on costs.

In April 1992, Cathay Pacific showed its continuing faith in Rolls-Royce by placing firm orders for eleven Trent-powered Boeing 777s with an option on another eleven. This brought Rolls-Royce's share on the 777 to 28 per cent. In the same month, cabinet approval in Thailand was received for Thai International to increase its order from six to eight Trent-powered 777s.

As the hours of testing on the Trent 700 built up, confidence grew in its performance. Frank Turner, civil engines director, told *Flight International* in July 1992:

We've got around 500 hours' running experience under our belts. The first Trent 700 for the Airbus A330 goes to test this month and we expect to get the first one on the aircraft in early August. We're going full-steam ahead on the 700 certification programme and we've done all the ingestion tests successfully. [The Trent 600 had not been successful and only Air Europe chose it for their MD-11s. When Air Europe collapsed, the Trent 600 programme was abandoned.]

Turner admitted that there was 'a bit of a weight problem' but claimed that the engine was still much lighter than its competitors. He added:

We're attacking the weight problem with some material changes in the engine, mostly on the main structural elements which were originally made on the conservative side.

The reputation for reliability of the RB 211, and therefore of its derivatives, continued to grow and was enhanced by the announcement that an RB 211-524B had made history when it was finally removed from a Delta Airline TriStar after more than five years and over 24,000 flying hours, a world record for service. And nearly 100 RB 211-524G/H engines on Boeing 747-400 aircraft exceeded 10,000 hours on the wing, setting new standards for the industry. Ten thousand hours was the equivalent of five million miles or 200 round-the-world trips. In the twenty years since the RB 211-22B first entered service in 1972, the RB 211 family had surpassed 50 million flying hours.

In spite of all the gloom and doom and his announcement of a £184-million loss for 1992, Sir Ralph Robins was able to tell shareholders in early

1993 that by the end of 1992 the Trent had been selected for approximately 40 per cent of all Airbus A330 aircraft ordered and more than a quarter of all Boeing 777s. The RB 211-535 had been selected by several new operators of the Boeing 757, including the Civil Aviation Administration of China. The Russian-built Tupolev 204 airliner, powered by two -535 turbofans, made its first appearance at the Farnborough Air Show. It was the first Russian modern airliner to be powered by engines manufactured in the West.

We have already seen how UPS bought the Rolls-Royce Tay to re-engine its 727s, and Tay orders were also won through Fokker F100 sales in China, Korea, South America and Britain. Success continued for the engine on the Gulfstream G-IV. The V-2500 engine, produced by the consortium International Aero Engines in which Rolls-Royce had a 30 per cent shareholding, won an order worth over $16 billion from United Airlines to power up to 100 A320 aircraft, while new versions of the engine were certificated to power A320, A321 and MD-90 aircraft. Also in 1992, the 1,900lb thrust Williams-Rolls FJ44 turbofan received its certification, and production-engine deliveries for the Cessna Citation jet began in early 1993.

The Williams-Rolls FJ44 resulted from an approach to Rolls-Royce by Dr Sam B. Williams, who had spotted the need for a small, more efficient low-cost aircraft powered by engines employing the same design and manufacturing principles as his small turbines, which he had been supplying to the US military since the 1950s.

He founded Williams International in 1954 after graduating from Purdue University and working for a short time at the Chrysler Corporation on the development of a turbine-powered car. The US military were soon impressed with his work because he seemed to have the answer to their need for a small, lightweight, reliable jet engine to power a new family of air-launched cruise missiles. His engines subsequently powered almost every cruise missile in NATO's forces.

Williams's contra-thinking meant that he rejected the generally held view that small engines were less efficient and more complex than large ones, saying:

My philosophy has been that you can do just about anything with a small engine that you can do with a large one. And the noise is reduced because of the smaller size ... When you cut a dimension by half you cut the weight to one eighth but the thrust to only a quarter. Accordingly you have some room to work with. As you come down in size, you can simplify and make parts more rugged and still have them smaller and lighter. We often use integral rotors and stators. They are single-piece castings. In the compression end we use single-piece machined rotors. A scaled-down large engine might have 12,000 to 20,000 parts. We have 600. The cost is reduced accordingly.

A partnership agreement with Rolls-Royce was signed in 1989, but the companies had been in contact for many years before that. Williams said:

We introduced the design to Rolls-Royce more than five years ago. They have been a very good influence on the engine. Their knowledge and experience with durability of critical components and materials has been very effective. And we will be using their excellent test facility for altitude and other certification testing.

As well as for the engineering expertise, Williams was almost certainly attracted to a partnership with Rolls-Royce by Rolls-Royce's existing marketing organisation and high reputation in the civil-engine field. He also needed Rolls-Royce's worldwide customer support base.

Even in the generally depressed market, Rolls-Royce was selling many more engines than a few years earlier. In March 1993, the company won business from another US airline when US Air, the sixth largest carrier in the USA, converted options into firm orders for RB 211-535E4 engines to power fifteen Boeing 757-200 aircraft. As Robins pointed out:

Until 1989 we were selling about 100–150 engines a year. It's now around 400 a year because we can offer products to power many more different airliners than in the past ... We have captured about 22–23 per cent of the civil aero-engine market compared with 26–28 per cent each for GE and Pratt & Whitney ... The fact there is a short-term turbulence in the market should not divert us from our long-term aims. I don't see a change in the world's desire to travel by air. The opportunity for us is clearly still there.

He would say later, after the atrocity of 11 September 2001 in New York, that the first year of each decade was a jinxed one for Rolls-Royce. In 1961, when Pratt & Whitney won the battle to power the 727 instead of Rolls-Royce and Allison with the Spey derivative, the company was forced to lay off some of its workforce. In 1971 ... well, we all know what happened in 1971. In 1981, the worldwide recession brought on by the sharp oil price-rise following the fall of the Shah affected the aerospace industry very badly and almost drove Rolls-Royce into the arms of GE. The year 1991, with the Gulf War and the world recession following the binge of the 1980s, brought heavy pain again. However, the world economy always recovered and the growth of air travel with it. Robins was confident it would do so again.

Nevertheless, there was no relief from the short-term pain. At the Rolls-Royce Board meeting in June 1993, directors were told that:

The whole airline and commercial aerospace manufacturing industry is struggling as the commercial losses continue. This is leading to difficulties in relationships as each side seeks to gain relief through pricing concessions, delayed payments and any other schemes that might protect their balance sheets. Increasingly aggressive demands are being made by long term customers and partners. Our ability to be responsive is limited. To date, we have handled matters satisfactorily but expect future difficulties in relationships.

John Sandford, President of Rolls-Royce Inc. and a Board member of Rolls-Royce plc, said the mood of the industry in the USA was 'angry'. The major airlines continued to make heavy losses, which meant a very aggressive market-place for all suppliers. It was a tough, tense period requiring Rolls-Royce to handle problems carefully, balancing the interests of the company with its customers and suppliers, both in the short and longer terms.

And at the July meeting, the directors heard that:

BA, Qantas and US Air have all requested permission to freely exchange past RR contracts. This is part of a campaign designed to 'cherry pick' between the best price, warranty and guarantees. As yet, we have not agreed to the request on the grounds that it could be anti-trust. Relationship difficulties are anticipated as BA could regard this as unco-operative.

By the autumn of 1993, the overall situation was little easier. This was the order situation:

Airbus A330

	GE CF6-80E1	Pratt & Whitney PW4000	Rolls-Royce Trent 700
Air Inter (France)	15		
Cathay Pacific			10
Euralair (France)		2	
Garuda (Indonesia)			9
ILFC	4	3	5*
LTU (Germany)		5	
Lufttrafik (Germany)		1	
Malaysia		10	
Northwest		16	
Thai International		8	
TWA			20
Total	19	45	44*

* Where an engine decision has been taken.

Boeing 777

	GE GE90	Pratt & Whitney PW4084	Rolls-Royce Trent 800
All Nippon		15	
British Airways	15		
Cathay Pacific			11
China Southern	6		
Continental	5		
Emirates			7
Euralair	2		
ILFC	6		
Lauda (Austria)	4		
Thai International			8
United		34	
Total	38	49	26

Rolls-Royce was holding its own, but none of the three engine manufacturers was being overwhelmed with orders. Meanwhile, the investment costs were very heavy. Keith Hodgkinson, aerospace analyst at the London office of the American investment house Shearson Lehman, said:

They have been caught in the classic pincers, with research and development costs running very high at a time when cash-flow is inhibited by poor trading conditions.

Rolls-Royce helped its cash position by launching a rights issue to bolster its balance sheet by £307 million. Robins said:

Life has become very tough. We haven't had any serious surprises with the Trent 800, but the market is the big worry. I can't see any recovery before 1995 or 1996. Nevertheless, the high rate of R&D was exactly what we predicted and it is now peaking.

Rolls-Royce was also helped from the end of 1992, and increasingly through 1993, by the strengthening of the dollar against the pound. As a big exporter, especially into a market where the dollar was the means of exchange, Rolls-Royce benefited from a strong dollar and conversely was harmed by a weak one. The US currency had been particularly weak in the early-1990s recession, and Rolls-Royce had suffered accordingly, bearing a £10-million drop in profits in the first half of 1992 as a result. Britain's ejection from the ERM in September brought an immediate 12 per cent fall against the dollar, and the slide continued. It was welcome relief. As Rolls-Royce said, 'We build in pounds and sell in dollars.'

The other weapons that Rolls-Royce used besides restructuring and extra finance were joint ventures and risk-and-revenue sharing agreements. By mid-1993, over 20 per cent of the development of the Trent was being carried out in Europe, Japan and South Africa. There was also a broad array of alliances. The International Aero Engines consortium had been put together in the mid-1980s. In the early 1990s came the BMW/Rolls-Royce joint venture – which, claimed Robins, 'killed Pratt & Whitney-MTU in the market-place' – and the Industria de Turbo Propulsores subsidiary in Spain. There were also non-equity partnerships in Indonesia, Korea and Japan. Robins added:

We need collaborative relationships to go on developing a wide range of products – no one is big enough to go on doing that on their own – and also to ensure market access. We will see the smaller players disappear into some sort of relationship with the bigger players.

In May 1991, Rolls-Royce was able to announce an extremely significant joint venture, this time with BMW, the German motor-car and aero-engine manufacturer, to build a new series of engines, the BR700, with power between 12,000 and 22,000 lb thrust. These engines would be aimed at large business jets and short-range regional airliners, a market where the Tay had achieved dominance. Rolls-Royce took 49.5 per cent of the company called BMW Rolls-Royce Aero Engines (BRR), while BMW took the other 50.5 per cent.

'A DECISION FOR DECADES AHEAD'

On St Valentine's Day 1990, the merchant bank Morgan Grenfell had approached Rolls-Royce with a proposal: the German car manufacturer BMW was looking for an alliance in the aero-engine field and wondered if Rolls-Royce would be interested. John McLaren of Morgan Grenfell and Hans Jörg-Hafner of BMW talked to John Rose, Director of Corporate Operations at the time, who quickly saw the potential benefits to Rolls-Royce. Sir Ralph Robins was also soon convinced and authorised discussions to continue. Rose led a team from Rolls-Royce, in which Charles Coltman, Rolls-Royce's Director of Strategic Planning, was a key figure, and a deal was signed with BMW within three months.

BMW's association with aircraft aero-engines went back a long way. Indeed, the firm began its life as an aero-engine manufacturer in 1917, and the trademark that was to protect all the company's products and which became so famous represented an aeroplane propeller on a white and blue background. Between the wars, BMW built its reputation for producing fine aero-engines as well as distinctive motorcycles and motor cars, most notably the R32 motorcycle and the 328 motor-car series. (When they bought the Eisenach Vehicle Factory in the 1920s, they even made the Austin Seven under licence for a time.)

In the air, BMW engines powered the Dornier flying boat, the 'Whale', which was flown round the world in 1932 by Wolfgang von Gronau. He noted in his log that 'Our BMW's purred along nicely.'

At the Treaty of Versailles in 1919, Germany was banned from producing aero-engines for five years. When the ban was lifted (BMW got around the ban by manufacturing in Russia), BMW began to build in Germany again, at first concentrating on water-cooled in-line engines. However, following the trend of air-cooled radial engines, it took a licence from Pratt & Whitney to build the Model 132, which it continued to manufacture throughout the 1930s and the Second World War, powering most famously the Junkers JU52. During the Second World War, the company was, of course, a key military equipment supplier.

It provided the turbojet engine, the BMW 003E-2, unusual in that it had an axial rather than a centrifugal compressor (we read about the difference in Part Two – Dr Griffith would have been proud of them), for the Heinkel He162 Salamander aircraft. Designed in 1944, the Salamander was a wooden-airframed jet fighter and was also know as the *Volksjäger* or 'people's fighter'. The aircraft flew adequately in the hands of experienced pilots, but flown by inexperienced members of the Hitler Youth, by this time being used increasingly in combat duties, its stability problems made it little better than a suicide missile. By the end of the War, some 275 had been built, and 500 were still on the production line. The single dorsally mounted BMW 003E-2 also powered the Arado AR234 Blitz bomber and variants of the Messer-schmitt ME262.

Most of BMW's plant was virtually destroyed by May 1945 when the War in Europe ended. And the Allies decided to dismantle and break up what had not been already destroyed by bombing. Hermann Ostrich, the 003 designer, was snapped up by France's SNECMA and worked on the Atar engines that powered early French jet fighters for many years.

Professor Munzberg, who had worked on the jet engine in the team around von Oheim – the German engineer who had done so much pioneering work on the jet engine – also went to SNECMA and stayed there until the 1960s, by which time he was Director of Engineering, before moving to Munich University as a full-time professor.

The future at BMW looked bleak. However, one or two rays of sunshine began to appear. As Horst Mönnich, the author of *The BMW Story*, put it:

Fritz Fiedler, the creator of the 328 and the last technical director, had been refused entry into the works as a former baron of the war economy. So he did not waste too much time humming and hawing when an offer reached him from the Bristol Aeroplane Company to do there what could not be done in Germany – to prepare the design and series production of a large car. The offer came within the framework of 'reparations' as well as 'old friendship'. The former head of the BMW licensee for Britain, Frazer-Nash, none other than Aldington, had been appointed to head Bristol Aerospace. Immediately deciding to build sports cars and so put Britain in the lead in post-war Europe, he had struck a kind of secret deal with Donath. [Donath was formerly works manager at the BMW aero-engine works in Spandau.]

As a result, a faithful copy of the BMW 327 Coupé came off the Bristol Aeroplane production line in spring 1947 with the name 'the Bristol 400'.

Gradually, BMW picked itself up, first with motorcycles then with cars. Nevertheless, at the end of the 1950s the company faced bankruptcy. It was saved by the Quandt family, which had built up a significant shareholding. One solution was to allow Daimler-Benz to rescue the company by taking it over, a solution seriously considered but finally rejected by Herbert Quandt. Its aero-engine subsidiary, BMW Power Plant Production Co. Ltd., also negotiated with various companies including General Electric in the USA, MAN in Germany and Bristol Siddeley in the UK. Mönnich wrote:

Pavel and Wilcke [confidant and legal adviser respectively to Herbert Quandt] had also negotiated with Bristol Siddeley, the third possible partner in the field of jet engines. There had been mutual visits to London and Munich, and discussions about solutions which amounted to Bristol, with its long attachment to BMW, considering taking up 25 per cent of the share capital to be raised in BMW AG. Throughout May 1960, the Bonn-based Bristol delegate rang Wilcke in Munich almost every day. Yet by 1 June (the deadline for submitting tenders) there was no proposal on the table which the supervisory board might still discuss.

BMW came to an agreement with MAN, and the Federal Defense Ministry issued the contract for manufacturing under licence General Electric's J79 engine for the Starfighter. It had also manufactured some Rolls-Royce Tyne engines under licence.

However, it was in cars not in aero-engines that BMW became a world force. In 1962, it seemed unlikely. Turnover was a mere 300 million Deutschmarks. [At that time, there were 12 Deutschmarks to the pound. Thus the turnover was £25 million, perhaps £400 million in today's terms.] But growth in the 1960s was strong, if not as spectacular as in subsequent years. By 1968, turnover reached one billion Deutschmarks, and on 1 January 1969 a key appointment was made. Eberhard von Kuenheim became chairman of the company's management board.

But this is the story of Rolls-Royce, not BMW. Suffice it to say that under von Kuenheim BMW expanded and expanded, selling cars of almost unrivalled engineering quality and style that by the end of the 1980s were the envy of the motor industry in every corner of the world. When von Kuenheim took control of BMW in 1969, the company employed 23,000 people, and the turnover was just over one billion Deutschmarks. By the beginning of the 1990s, the workforce had expanded to 74,000 and sales to 30 billion Deutschmarks. By then, BMW was not content to be tied to motor cars exclusively. BMW stands for Bavarian Motor Works not Bavarian Car Works. Von Kuenheim said:

From time immemorial, we have never been frightened of changing course – from aero engines to motor cycles, from motor cycles back to aero engines, and via motor cycles to cars. Let's make it clear – we won't be going across into making shoes. We shall remain loyal to our technological domain. I admit we would have gladly bought back MTU from MAN, but Daimler had the option to buy.

At the time, the management at Daimler-Benz seemed intent on building the German equivalent of General Motors, and the mood throughout Germany industry, encouraged by the fee-enhancing ambitions of the banks, was for diversification and expansion across as broad a front as possible. [Currently, the buzz-words are 'focus' and 'core business', but 'diversification' will be back on the agenda by the end of the decade.] The management at BMW were probably affected to some extent by this atmosphere.

Just before Rolls-Royce and BMW signed their agreement, MTU caused some fluttering in the dovecotes by breaking off its 25-year relationship with GE and transferring its allegiance to Pratt & Whitney. GE responded by launching a $1.15-billion lawsuit against MTU and its parent, Daimler-Benz, accusing them of fraud, misappropriation of trade secrets, misrepresentation, breach of contract and breach of fiduciary duty.

This falling-out highlighted the dangers inherent in collaborative arrangements. If the dominant partner was too open, it risked giving away previous know-how. If it was too closed, it risked alienating its partner. Boeing always went to great lengths to protect its proprietary technology. In the mid-1980s, Boeing signed up the industry divisions of Mitsubishi, Fuji and Kawasaki, the Japanese companies, as 25 per cent partners in the development of the 7J7 airliner. One hundred and twenty Japanese engineers worked at the Seattle plant, but they were denied access to key areas because Boeing feared a steady seepage of technological expertise in manufacturing, wing design and logistics.

GE's problem seemed to be that it had been too open. Its 24-page suit, filed in a New York court, maintained that GE gave MTU highly sensitive and detailed design specifications for the thermodynamics, size, thrust-ratios, component configuration, advanced materials and fuel efficiency of their new GE90 engine. It said that MTU was now in a position to build a competitor to the GE90 without the research costs. Martin Menrath, currently a Board member at Rolls-Royce Deutschland and formerly an employee at MTU, thought it extremely unlikely that MTU would have acquired such a capability from GE.

Nevertheless, MTU certainly harboured the ambition to manufacture a complete engine of its own. MTU, standing for Motoren and Turbinen Union, had grown out of the aero-engine interests of BMW and MAN, which had merged when MAN bought those of BMW. When Daimler-Benz took a 50 per cent stake (later increased to 100 per cent), these aero-engine interests were renamed MTU.

MTU's strategy was to find a European partner to develop engines for the military market and an American partner to develop engines for the civil market. In the 1970s, Pratt & Whitney was still number one in the civil aero-engine field, and, after making the LP turbines for the PW2037, MTU signed a strategic agreement with Pratt & Whitney. By the end of the 1980s, the two companies were developing a regional aircraft engine, the RTF180.

In the meantime, BMW looked for further expansion to the aero-engine business. Von Kuenheim said:

In the car business, we are not big enough to ensure we can continue to stay a significant force, even with 1.4 or 1.5 per cent of the world market ... We are a small, but important group, and we are preparing to expand into other product areas which are in line with our business ... Nowadays, more than 750 million passengers take off every year in one of more than 7,500 passenger jets currently being used all over the world ... It has been calculated that in the next 15 years air traffic will more than double again.

Von Kuenheim maintained that BMW could contribute 'significant experience in cost control' and felt that Rolls-Royce could teach BMW something about zero-defect production, an objective he said had always been important to him. When questioned about the decision to invest in something new in the middle of a recession, he took the same view as Sir Ralph Robins, saying:

Short-term setbacks are not a reason to give up. Our decision to re-enter the aero-engine business is a decision for decades ahead. Everything costs money, so fundamentally it doesn't matter whether you're developing an aircraft engine or a car engine.

BMW was not arrogant enough to feel it could enter the aero-engine business on its own. Some work had been done by a small team under the renowned engineer Professor Günther Kappler, looking into the possibilities of small gas-turbine engines in cars. Menrath remembers that an Allison Model 250 engine was borrowed from the German Air Force. And, on the subject of aero-engines, Kappler talked to Menrath about the Rolls-Royce Tay engine. There would need to be a successor, and maybe a family of engines round a common core would be the way forward. A number of discussions were held with other aero-engine manufacturers, and Rolls-Royce was chosen as the desirable partner. The timing was impeccable.

Rolls-Royce had just committed itself to the development of the Trent family of engines, a commitment that would stretch its resources to the utmost. Nevertheless, the company knew it needed a replacement for the Tay and that MTU was preparing to launch an engine in the Tay class and expected to gain German Government funding. Negotiations between Rolls-Royce and BMW moved quickly, and by July shareholders' approval for BMW Rolls-Royce GmbH had been achieved. As well as collaborating with Rolls-Royce on new engines, BMW would join the two Japanese companies and Hispano-Suiza as risk-and-revenue partners on the Trent. Its share would be 5 per cent. BMW also bought 2.9 per cent of Rolls-Royce plc, though Rolls-Royce did not take a stake in the German company.

As ever in the aero-engine world, there was competition in the range where BMW Rolls-Royce was hoping to be successful. The 80-to-130-seat regional jet market was estimated to be between 2,000 and 3,000 aircraft in the years from the mid-1990s to the year 2009. The resulting engine market would be for 6,500 engines. At the Farnborough Air Show of 1990, there were no fewer than eight engine manufacturers offering their products, but by the time of the Paris Air Show in June 1991 the number had reduced to three – BMW Rolls-Royce and Pratt & Whitney/MTU, both offering brand new engines, and SNECMA, possibly teamed with GE, offering a new engine based on the core of its existing military M88. There were three airframe possibilities: Deutsche Aerospace (DASA) teamed with Aerospatiale and Alenia, which was planning a family of new aircraft in the 80-to-130-seat range; Fokker, with a stretched and shortened version of the Fokker F100; and British Aerospace, with a 130-seat twin-engined derivative of the BAe 146 called the NRA (New Regional Aircraft). [It is interesting that the two eventual clear winners of the regional jet market, Bombardier and Embraer, did not seem to be in the frame at this point.]

BMW Rolls-Royce was early into the contest. Indeed, by the Paris Air Show of 1991, it was the only company that had actually launched something – the core of a planned family of engines covering large business jets as well as regional aircraft. What would the contributions of the two partners be?

While BMW would bring a great deal of knowledge in materials, systems and design, Rolls-Royce would bring the lion's share of the propulsion know-how. The BR700 concept was to build a core that would be common to all engines in the 13,000 to 23,000 lb thrust class. Two variants were planned, the BR710, up to 16,000 lb, aimed at large business jets, and the BR715 for regional airliners, providing power from 15,000 to 23,000 lb. The core would be designed to be as simple, and easy to maintain, as possible and would have a ten-stage high-pressure compressor driven by a two-stage high-pressure turbine. The low-pressure system would be adjusted to the thrust requirement. In the lower thrust version, a two-stage low-pressure turbine would drive the fan, while in the larger engine a three-stage low-pressure turbine would drive a two-stage booster as well as the fan.

Reg Moore, head of BR700 engineering, said:

When the company was founded we decided, with the support of our two shareholders, to create a family of engines and looked at various compressors and turbines. The result was a core design around which we could put any one of three low-pressure systems. This gives us a range of reliable, high-performance, low-risk engines which deliver what the customer wants. These can be produced using a proven core, thus obviating the higher risks associated with developing new engines.

BMW talked of German Government aid but said it was not essential. For its part, MTU made it clear that such aid was central to its investment plants. As for the German Government itself, faced with two claimants, it decided that it would not give support to either. (By this time, it was realising the enormous short-term cost of German reunification.) As a result, MTU decided not to proceed with the development of its engine, and BMW Rolls-Royce had won an important early victory. [Development work on Pratt & Whitney/MTU's RTF180 did continue, and after several steps it eventually became the PW6000.]

The joint venture purchased Klockner Humboldt and Deutz Luftfahrt-technik, formerly Motorenfabrik Oberursel, a company near Frankfurt specialising in small gas turbines and greatly experienced in the maintenance, repair and overhaul of engines for civil and military aircraft. The factory had been built 100 years earlier, opened in 1892 and initially manufactured farm implements. During the First World War, it built military aircraft for Anthony Fokker, the Dutchman who had come from Java in the Dutch East Indies. During the war, Fokker built more than 40 types of aircraft for the German High Command. Manfred von Richthofen, the Red Baron, visited the factory to make sure that the engine going into his aircraft was powerful and reliable.

In his biography *Fokker: The Creative Years*, A.R. Weyl paints a picture of a

In May 1990, Rolls-Royce won a $600-million contract to re-engine the entire 727-100 fleet of United Parcel Service. It was important for UPS, which did most of its flying at night, to have quiet engines.

The Williams-Rolls FJ44 engine resulted from an approach to
Rolls-Royce by Dr Sam B. Williams, who had founded Williams
International in 1954. He had spotted the need for a small,
more efficient low-cost aircraft, powered by engines employing the
same design and manufacturing principles as his small turbines,
which he had been supplying to the US military since the 1950s.
He was attracted not only to Rolls-Royce's technological expertise
but also to its worldwide marketing and support operations.

TOP: BMW began life as an aero-engine manufacturer in 1917. In the 1920s and 1930s, it also gained a reputation for building distinctive motorcycles, such as the R32, and, having made the Austin 7 under licence as its first motor car, went on to make sports cars such as the 328 pictured here.

BOTTOM: BMW provided the turbojet engine, the BMW 003E-2, unusual in that it had an axial rather than a centrifugal compressor, for the Heinkel He162 Salamander aircraft. The BMW 003E-2 also powered the Arado AR234 Blitz bomber and variants of the Messerschmitt ME262.

LEFT: Eberhard von Kuenheim, the brilliant engineer and manager who took BMW from a turnover of 300 million Deutschmarks in 1969 to 30 billion Deutschmarks in the early 1990s. He said of BMW's joint venture with Rolls-Royce, 'There is enormous respect in Munich for Rolls-Royce and especially for its Chairman, Sir Ralph Robins.'

RIGHT: Bernd Pischetsrieder, now at the head of VW, was in charge of new developments at BMW in the early 1990s and was also a great supporter of the Rolls-Royce/BMW collaboration. His uncle, Alec Issigonis, created Britain's famous Mini in the early 1960s.

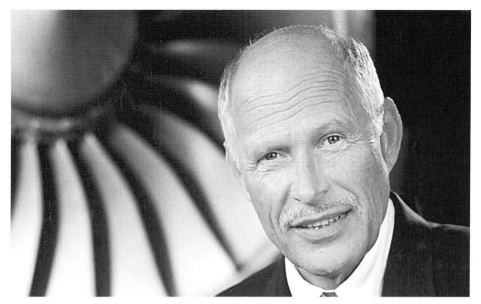

TOP: Professor Günter Kappler, the distinguished German engineer, who put together a team in the mid-1980s to look at the possibility of a small gas turbine in the motor car. This led on to work on a family of engines to succeed the Rolls-Royce Tay engine.

BOTTOM: The BR710 engine. By the end of 1994, BMW Rolls-Royce had received firm orders for 260 BR710s, a testimony to the reputation of the two companies.

Powered by two BR710 turbofans, the Bombardier Global Express
would be able to fly eight passengers and a crew of four at
Mach 0.8 for 6,500 nautical miles, enabling it to link cities such as
New York and Tokyo non-stop.

OPPOSITE TOP: Gulfstream gave BMW Rolls-Royce the launch order
for the BR710 for its GV when it ordered 200 engines plus
200 options at the Farnborough Air Show in 1992, only two-and-
a-half years after BMW and Rolls-Royce started discussing a
joint-venture company.

OPPOSITE BOTTOM: The BR715 engine was chosen for the
MD-95, renamed the Boeing 717 after Boeing bought
McDonnell Douglas in 1997.

TOP: An advertisement for Rolls-Royce used in Spain, showing a Trent engine and the words *La fuerta de España, La potenzia de Rolls-Royce* ('The strength of Spain, The power of Rolls-Royce').

BOTTOM: The King of Spain visiting the ITP facilities in Ajalvir, near Madrid. Also in the photograph, from left to right, are: Ignacio Sánchez-Galán, general manager at the time; Jorge Sendagorta, president of SENER; Bob Crabtree of Rolls-Royce, and Adolfo de la Peña, president of ITP at the time.

serial entrepreneur. He had immense guts, plenty of charm and, according to Weyl, few business ethics:

Fokker was delighted to find himself for once in a seller's market [at the outbreak of the First World War in August 1914]. He was only too willing to sell to anybody: had the Allies come for his aeroplanes he would have sold to them just as readily. For cash, of course.

In fact, German aircraft manufacturers were informed that all aviation material was subject to requisition by the German Army. Fokker built up his aircraft interests on the back of military orders and bought rotary engines from the Oberursel factory. To protect his position, he acquired the company in 1916. Weyl points out that some of the engines from the factory were proving unreliable, so it was not surprising that the Red Baron wanted to make an inspection.

The plant continued to make aero-engines during the 1930s and 1940s and, after the Second World War, built Orpheus and Gnome engines under licence from the Bristol Aeroplane Company. In the 1970s and 1980s, it manufactured parts for the Panavia Tornado, most particularly its own-design auxiliary power unit, as well as gearboxes and small gas turbines for drones.

Phil Wilkins, who was appointed as Director of Production and Procurement of the new BMW Rolls-Royce company in August 1990, remembered that when von Kuenheim came to visit the factory, the driver sent to pick him up at Frankfurt airport was surprised that von Kuenheim knew the back roads to Oberursel when they were confronted by a traffic jam on the autobahn. When questioned about this later by Wilkins, von Kuenheim said:

I have visited Frau Quandt at Bad Homberg a number of times. You see, everyone has a boss.

As BMW and Rolls-Royce came together, they discovered that KHD Luft-fahrttechnik was effectively for sale as the company had suffered a setback in losing the contract to supply the auxiliary power unit for Eurofighter to Allied Signal's German subsidiary. The factory was restructured and modernised, and by September 1990 the joint company's first engine, the BR700, was selected for the Gulfstream's new aircraft, the G-V.

During 1991 and the early part of 1992, discussions took place that might have led to the merging of BMW Rolls-Royce with MTU. The talks, supported by the German Government, were aimed at avoiding the two companies competing with their turbofan engines in the regional-airline market. While BMW Rolls-Royce was developing the BR700, MTU was working with Pratt & Whitney on the RTF180. Both were chasing DASA hard to be the launch engine on their Regioliner. However, in April 1992 the talks between BMW Rolls-Royce and MTU broke down with the two sides unable to agree on who would take leadership on a joint programme.

There were some considerable problems in getting the new venture off the ground. A report to the Rolls-Royce Board in April 1993 highlighted some of the problems, noting that:

A full BMW Rolls-Royce esprit de corps is not yet in place, but the background cultures are being progressively combined towards that objective. This is not helped by the necessary geographical dispersion at this stage in the BR700 programme. Consolidation at Dahlewitz from next year will bring many benefits, but the move itself is a formidable task.

Programme discipline and ownership has been noticeably lacking, but procedures and commitment have already begun to improve.

It had been clear from the formation of the company that a new facility would be required. An office north of Munich, another at the Rolls-Royce plant in Hucknall, Nottinghamshire, and the plant at Oberursel near Frankfurt would not be conducive to an efficient operation.

The new factory at Dahlewitz, 30 kilometres south-east of Berlin in the State of Brandenberg, which made a significant contribution in funding, took two years to build and equip. A number of possible locations had been considered, and Phil Wilkins remembered charging around Germany with Bernd Pischetsrieder, then in charge of new developments at BMW, in Pischetsrieder's BMW 850. First they looked at Moosburg in Bavaria, then at Wackersdorf, also in Bavaria, then at a plant in Kassel before their search turned to an area near Berlin. In the years immediately following reunification, BMW would have felt morally obliged to consider locating a new plant in the former Eastern Germany. The first location near Berlin that was looked at was an existing factory at Ludwigsfelde that had manufactured Russian Mil 8 helicopters. However, the factory lacked modern facilities and had paid scant attention to pollution. As MTU was also showing interest in the plant, Rolls-Royce BMW was not unhappy when MTU bid higher.

Once the new factory was built at Dahlewitz, its responsibilities became the testing and development of engines and also the assembly of the complete engines wherever the components were made. The factory at Oberursel, still employing 1,000 people, continued to manufacture engine parts as well as carrying out repair and overhaul, especially for the German Air Force.

Discussions with Gulfstream established the need for a new engine to power their new Gulfstream G-V, and the BR710 was seen as appropriate. The engine would have a 48-inch fan diameter and would deliver 14,750 lb thrust at take-off, with a capability of growth to 18,000 lb with the same core and fan. A later version, to be called the BR715, would also have the same core but a larger fan and would have a take-off thrust up to 22,000 lb.

At the Farnborough Air Show in 1992, Gulfstream gave BMW Rolls-Royce the launch order for which they were hoping – 200 engines firm and options on another 200. Up to this point, Gulfstream had pursued a conservative policy of using well-proven engines with more power than was needed for their aircraft. In this way, they could be confident in promising their customers reliability and long life on the wing. For example, Gulfstream I had used the Rolls-Royce Dart, Gulfstreams II and III, the Rolls-Royce Spey, and Gulfstream IV, the Tay – effectively a Spey plus fan. Buying the as yet unproven BR710 was a very unusual step for Gulfstream and said a lot about the trust that had been built up by Rolls-Royce.

Following the Gulfstream order, it was announced in March 1993 that the Canadian Bombardier Group had selected the BR710 to power its Canadair Global Express business aircraft. It was reported to the Board that:

This was finally won against strong competition from Pratt & Whitney/MTU.

Bombardier had been built up over the previous 30 years by Chairman and Chief Executive Laurent Beaudoin. Trained as an accountant, he had taken over at the head of the company when he was 27 and when it only manufactured his father-in-law's invention, the Ski-Doo snowmobile. Within ten years, Bombardier dominated the North American snowmobile market. When the oil crisis of 1973 damaged the industry, Beaudoin diversified into public-transport equipment, and within twenty years Bombardier had become a leader in that field, with major contracts for subway cars from Montreal and New York.

Beaudoin had always been interested in aviation and, with the major markets for snowmobiles many hundreds of miles in the north, had become a regular user of business aircraft. In 1986, he bought Canadair from the Canadian Government and quickly followed up to try to make Bombardier a leader in the regional- and business-jet market by purchasing Short Brothers of Belfast, Learjet of Wichita, Kansas, and de Havilland in Toronto.

After all this whirlwind activity, the *Financial Times* wrote on 28 January 1992:

Bombardier has successfully turned three ugly ducklings of aerospace around and must now repeat the process at DHC [de Havilland Canada]. The timing at least seems favourable. The workforce has given the deal an enthusiastic welcome, and the commercial aircraft market seems finally to be climbing out of its Gulf War tailspin.

By the early 1990s, its Canadair Regional Jet and Dash 8 family of turboprops were operating throughout the world. Now he was planning to add a new aircraft, Global Express, to Bombardier's line of business jets, the Learjet 31A, 45 and 60 and the new-generation Canadair Challenger 604.

Powered by two BR710 turbofans, the Global Express would be able to fly eight passengers and a crew of four at Mach 0.8 for 6,500 nautical miles, which would enable it to link cities such as New York and Tokyo non-stop.

The Gulfstream V had already guaranteed a range of 6,500 miles. The BR710s, which replaced the Rolls-Royce Tay Mk 611-801s in the Gulfstream IV, would contribute to a 15 per cent reduction in specific fuel consumption. The net result was an improvement of no less than 57 per cent in range over the G-IV.

BMW Rolls-Royce had been considering new engines in the range below 15,000 lb thrust, but when, in 1995, Rolls-Royce purchased the Allison Engine Company, it was decided that BMW Rolls-Royce would concentrate on the 15,000 to 22,000 lb range and leave the smaller engines to Allison. Sir Ralph Robins told his Board on 22 December 1994 that in his discussions with Bernd Pischetsrieder, at that time President of BMW and Chairman of the BRR Shareholders Committee, Pischetsrieder was 'fully supportive of the Rolls-Royce purchase of Allison and understood the interaction between Allison and BMW Rolls-Royce'.

By the end of 1994, BMW Rolls-Royce had received firm orders for 260 BR710s – 200 from Gulfstream and 60 from Bombardier – and the 18,500 lb thrust BR715 had been selected by McDonnell Douglas as the exclusive power plant for its MD-95 regional aircraft, with a possible 1,400 engines required over the aircraft's lifetime.

John Sandford was a main Board director of Rolls-Royce in the early 1990s and, because of his experiences of the US aircraft industry where he had been President of Gulfstream, was closely involved in the marketing of the BMW Rolls-Royce engines. He wrote later:

Getting the first aircraft customer to commit to a new civil-engine application has always been tough. When compared to a derivative engine, for both the buyer and the seller the risks are significantly greater. With a 'clean sheet of paper engine,' meeting the specification performance and reliability requirements can be extremely challenging and all too frequently a new engine runs into teething problems during development, followed by delivery schedule difficulties and then they often have service introduction troubles. When such risks are combined with the unknowns of a start-up company, to be created on a green-field site in former East Germany, finding that first customer just has to be considered much tougher. Furthermore, because we were starting from scratch, there was little that the marketing team could show to the potential customers that would convince them that they should risk their aircraft and program investment success on our being able to do what we said we could and do it on time.

That the partnership included the well-known and respected names, BMW and Rolls-Royce (BMW-RR or BRR), probably mitigated some concerns, but challenges remained with issues such as: would the right engineers and managers relocate and could the know-how, experience and technology be smoothly transferred, on time, to the new team? To put this in perspective it should be recalled that it took ten years before a launch customer signed up for what became the world's most successful CFM-56 engine. It is built by General Electric (GE) and Snecma, the long-established French company. A further factor was that the CFM-56 wasn't a brand-new design; rather it was derived from the best sections of two different engines that the partners had developed for their respective militaries.

During my tenure at RR the successful market launch of the Trent engine was absolutely crucial to the future of the Corporation. However, within the Company ... the concurrent successful launch of the BRR engines was also a very high priority. Remarkably, in spite of the major hurdles coupled with aggressive competition from firmly established and highly respected US engine companies, we won the first three applications competitions, within five years from the joint venture getting underway. The launch included both the BR-710 and 715 engines. That it all took place this quickly is remarkable in itself.

In the event, the MD-95 suffered a difficult birth, as McDonnell Douglas struggled to secure a big launch order. It could have expected that Scandinavian Airlines System (SAS) would have replaced its MDC DC-9s with the new MDC aircraft, but SAS opted for Boeing 737s instead.

Eventually, McDonnell Douglas secured an order for 50 aircraft from Valujet, almost certainly at a very competitive price – Airbus executives were rumoured to have blanched at the price Valujet was prepared to pay for the A319. Valujet had only paid $5 million for its existing DC-9-30s and made it clear it would only take on new aircraft if the price was right. When Boeing took over McDonnell Douglas in 1997, it renamed the MD-95 the Boeing 717, and by early 1999 prospects for the aircraft seemed to be improving. *Flight International* wrote in January 1999:

BMW Rolls-Royce is gearing up to double the production rate of its BR700-series engines over the next two years as prospects for the Boeing 717 programme finally begin to improve. The 717 – the only airframe application to date for BMW Rolls-Royce's BR715 turbofan – attracted letters of intent from two new customers in December, potentially taking the firm order book to 115 aircraft, plus 100 options.

BMW Rolls-Royce Chairman, Dr Klaus Nittinger, said:

We need two to three more substantial 717 orders to have the full breakthrough. Once you are above the 250–300 aircraft threshold, I think you can say you have achieved successful penetration. When you have the evidence that the market is accepting the product, then the growth comes automatically.

In May 1999, BMW Rolls-Royce announced it was investing further in the plant at Dahlewitz to enable annual engine production to increase from 220 to 300 by the year 2000.

BMW Rolls-Royce was on target to gain type approval for the BR710 and certification by August 1996. The BR710 would fly in a prototype Gulfstream V in November 1995, and deliveries to Gulfstream customers would begin in 1996 and to Canadair customers in 1997. Certification for the large BR715 was planned for the end of 1997, with MD-95 deliveries to McDonnell Douglas customers beginning in 1998. This was a huge improvement on the original plan, which envisioned delivery of an engine by the turn of the century.

Apart from working to secure further orders, the main task of the years 1997 and 1998 was the production of the BR710 for Gulfstream and Bombardier. As we have seen, once Boeing had taken over McDonnell Douglas and renamed the MD-95 the Boeing 717, attention turned to new prospects not only for the BR710 but for the BR715. By the middle of 1999, the BR715 entered service in the Boeing 717-200 with launch customer AirTran Airways, who had taken over the operations of Valujet after that airline had collapsed following a tragic accident in Florida.

By that time, BMW Rolls-Royce had accumulated orders for more than 900 engines, and production of both BR710s and BR715s was being stepped up. Deliveries, 100 in 1998, would be 200 in 1999, with production expected to rise to 260 in 2000. Nittinger said:

It's a big challenge. Boeing intends to produce five aircraft a month so we have to supply 10 engines a month. We can adapt to up to 15 engines a month, and, if needed, we have the ability to assemble engines in Derby because they have the capability and have worked on the V2500 which is a similar engine in some respects.

After overcoming initial problems with containment and turbine-blade cracks, the engine had already earned a reputation with Boeing as a trouble-free and fuel-miserly performer.

At this point, the majority of the orders were for the BR710: 400 for Gulfstream V, 160 for Global Express and 88 for the British Aerospace Nimrod MRA4 maritime-patrol-aircraft programme. Incredible though it may seem, this aircraft, in one form or another, had been flying for over 50 years: first as the Comet I, powered by the de Havilland Ghost, then the Comets II, III and IV, powered by the Rolls-Royce Avon, then as the Nimrod, powered by the Rolls-Royce Spey, and finally as the Nimrod MRA4, powered by the BMW Rolls-Royce BR710.

In October 1999, it was announced that Rolls-Royce would take full operational control of BMW Rolls-Royce. At the same time, BMW bought 90 million shares in Rolls-Royce plc, raising its stake from 2 to 8 per cent. Rolls-Royce planned to issue a further 33.3 million shares to BMW, which would take its stake to 10.1 per cent.

Denying that BMW was losing interest in the aeronautical sector, a spokesman said:

We effectively exchanged our 50.5 per cent stake in the joint venture company BMW Rolls-Royce for a 10 per cent stake in Rolls-Royce plc. It was a repositioning not an exit. Our engines are better positioned within the Rolls-Royce group. It is not necessary that we have to do the operating.

It is impossible to divorce BMW's desire to sell its stake in BMW Rolls-Royce to Rolls-Royce from its decision at the same time to sell Rover, its motor-car subsidiary in the UK. BMW had bought Rover from British Aerospace in the early 1990s but had not been able to stem the losses the British company had been making for many years. Apart from the archaic practices, both in management and on the shop floor, there was a branding confusion. By the 1990s, BMW had deservedly acquired a reputation for producing sporty, desirable, superbly engineered and reliable motor cars. By contrast, Rover had acquired an equally deserved reputation for producing dull and unreliable motor cars. If a potential purchaser wanted to buy a car from BMW or a BMW subsidiary, why should he buy a Rover rather than the real thing?

By 1999, Rover was losing £800 million a year, a sum serious enough to hurt not only BMW's current trading but also its balance sheet. The Quandt family said, enough! We do not want or need these loss-making subsidiaries. Under the circumstances, BMW Rolls-Royce, even though it had achieved its planned targets, which included the understanding that it would not make a profit until the new millennium, was deemed ripe for sale too. It had not been supported by the whole of the BMW top management. For example, Wolfgang Reizle, the *Vorstand* of Engineering, made his view pretty clear by never visiting the plant at Dahlewitz.

BMW Rolls-Royce would now be called Rolls-Royce Deutschland GmbH.

Rolls-Royce expected the new subsidiary to take on an expanded role. Chief Executive John Rose said that the company could take on a significant share of the development work for the planned Trent 900 for the Airbus A3XX, having already designed the high-pressure compressor for the smaller Trent 500 set to power the latest versions of the A340. He went on to say that the aim was to apply Rolls-Royce Deutschland's capabilities 'to programmes other than those for which the company was established'. He confirmed that it would be responsible for systems integration of two-shaft civil aero-engines in the 13,000 to 23,000 lb thrust bracket, and added:

We hope that in the future we may be able to extend this responsibility to higher thrust engines.

There was some uncertainty at Dahlewitz, and Rolls-Royce made every effort to make it clear that the plant would be responsible for the group's two-shaft engines in the 15,000 to 22,000 lb thrust range. Research and development would continue with the same intensity as before, and other projects, such as the work on the Trent 900, would be carried out. The top management structure remained in place, with Klaus Nittinger continuing as Chairman, Duncan Forbes running engineering and Neil Ansell, operations. It was not until the end of 2000 that Nittinger left, and, while Forbes continued to run engineering, Ansell took over projects while Menrath took on operations.

Production increased so that 265 BR710s and 715s were delivered in 2001, and the BR710 won the competition to engine the Global 5000. Rolls-Royce Deutschland also became one of the six partners (the others being SNECMA, MTU, Fiat Avio, ITP and Techspace Aero of Belgium) involved in developing the engine for the A400 Military Transport aircraft, the replacement for the long-serving Transall. This is seen as a very important project and increasingly so as the war against terrorists in far-flung places following the tragedy of 11 September 2001 has highlighted the German Air Force's lack of capability to move forces and equipment in large numbers quickly. At 28.4 per cent, Rolls-Royce Deutschland's share of this project is substantial.

At the beginning of January 2002, Rolls-Royce Deutschland also won an important contract within the Rolls-Royce group when it took over the engineering support in service of all the Rolls-Royce Spey, Tay and Dart engines.

In 2002, Rolls-Royce could look back at the decade of its joint venture and feel considerable satisfaction. It had been able to invest in the two new, and already successful, engines at a time when its own financial resources were at full stretch developing the Trent. If we look at the two German-based aero-engine manufacturers, Rolls-Royce Deutschland can now provide the complete propulsion system, whereas MTU is still effectively a component supplier with no direct route to market.

Eberhard von Kuenheim had no doubts. Asked by the author in July 2000 whether he felt the co-operation between the two companies had been a success, he said:

Undoubtedly. There is enormous respect in Munich for Rolls-Royce and especially for its Chairman, Sir Ralph Robins. Here in Germany, there are many engineers at the head of our companies. Engineering is a highly respected profession. In England, the structure of society is such that engineers do not have the same position. But Sir Ralph has made it. He is there at the top of one of your greatest companies. When I go round a factory with him he can pick up pieces of the engine and talk in detail to those working on the engine. He is highly respected here in Munich.

Sir Ralph Robins and Rolls-Royce are also highly respected in the State of Brandenberg. The company is Brandenberg's largest investor and provides no less than 20 per cent of its exports.

INDUSTRIA DE TURBO PROPULSORES

While Rolls-Royce was busy making its joint venture with BMW successful, it also worked hard to establish an equally successful joint venture in Spain.

The foundations of Industria de Turbo Propulsores (ITP) go back to the company SENER, one of Spain's leading engineering companies and a company in which the family Sendagorta is a majority shareholder. SENER was founded by Enrique Sendagorta, a naval architect, in 1956. Shortly afterwards he was joined by his brother, José Manuel, an aeronautical engineer who had been involved in both jet and rocket propulsion. José Manuel, known as Manu, had worked with Gregorio Millan, another aeronautical engineer who in turn had worked with the famous Theodore von Karman in Paris after the Second World War. Other members of this team were Jacobo Valdes (later to become Chairman of ITP) and Carlos Sancher Tarita. They worked together on rocket propulsion and gas turbines.

By the 1960s, SENER was involved in nuclear and chemical plants as well as marine engineering and in 1967 secured its first significant space contract when it built a rocket-launching plant. The company diversified further into civil engineering, process and power plants, shipbuilding and the space industry. By the 1980s, it felt it should be in another leading technology area, defence, and became involved in both the production of laser-guided bombs for the Spanish Air Force and the development of jet engines.

Although Spain had produced piston aero-engines in the 1920s, it had little experience in the gas-turbine field. SENER was offered subcontract work from General Electric in the early 1980s but felt that this was too restrictive, and when Spain began discussions with Britain, France, Germany and Italy on a new European fighter aircraft in 1984, both SENER and the Spanish airframe manufacturer CASA wanted to be involved. As we shall see in Chapter Seven, the consortium that agreed, after much discussion, to develop the European Fighter Aircraft (EFA) was made up of the UK and Germany with a 33 per cent share each, Italy with 21 per cent and Spain with 13 per cent. France went its own way following disagreements over the specification of the aircraft. As the official ten-year history of ITP put it:

1986 was a hectic year … The Ministers of Defence for the EFA programme … signed the Memorandum of Agreement. The air forces of the participating countries established the operational requirements, as did the national representatives in the EFA Management Committee, as well as the four engine manufacturers [Rolls-Royce, MTU, Fiat and SENER] and the Eurojet consortium was created for this purpose. Thus in February 1987 NEFMA, an administrative agency in Munich, became operational, with a Spanish managing director.

To pursue its involvement, SENER and the Ministry of Industry (INI) set up the company ITP in 1989. They discussed possible engine partnerships, but the preferred technical partner was Rolls-Royce. The Spanish shareholders were SENER, CASA, Bazan (a group of Spanish shipyards) and a Spanish bank. The Spanish interests held 55 per cent of the shares and Rolls-Royce 45 per cent. Later, the bank would sell its shares so that the Spanish interests held 53.2 per cent and Rolls-Royce 46.8 per cent.

At this point, ITP had only twelve employees in offices in Madrid and Bilbao. If the company was to participate fully in the EFA programme, it needed a plant for development work, production and assembly. Land was bought in Zamudio Technology Park near Bilbao and a factory built and opened in June 1991. The first engine parts manufactured by ITP were delivered to Rolls-Royce in December 1991.

In June 1990, ITP also bought CASA's Aviation Engine Maintenance Centre in Ajalvir, near Madrid, and took over the aircraft maintenance and repair operations. The first models of the EJ200 assembled in Ajalvir were also delivered in December 1991.

ITP's early involvement in the development phase of the EFA engine, the EJ200, was in two main areas – major isogrid structures (casings), of which the nozzle and turbine exhaust diffuser were the most important, and dressings, including pipes, cables and external accessories. This programme, especially with regard to the nozzle, presented a tremendous challenge for the Spanish engineers with their limited experience of gas turbines.

As well as work on the EJ200, which, as we shall see, suffered some delays following German reunification and consequent doubts on the efficacy of the programme by the German Government, ITP decided to diversify into civil-engine programmes as well as the maintenance and overhaul of engines, initially for the Spanish Air Force but later also for civil aircraft. ITP also wanted to work more closely on Rolls-Royce programmes, and in 1992 negotiated a 2.5 per cent risk-and-revenue-sharing contract with Rolls-Royce on the Trent programme. This contract, involving design and assembly on low-pressure (LP) turbines was a significant step forward for ITP. This is how the ITP history put it:

From the end of 1993 and regularly from 1994 onwards, new and advanced designs were worked on in collaboration with Rolls-Royce, in the Advanced Low Pressure System, in the aerodynamic design of two phases of the British company's WR21 turbine, and various engineering projects for the Trent 700 and 800 engines, which are installed in the Airbus-330 and the Boeing 777 respectively. However ITP wanted more. The technical ambition also to design rotary parts culminated in an agreement for work on the low pressure turbine of the BR715 engine.

The CQC 103 Quality Certificate had been granted to the Zamudio plant by Rolls-Royce at the end of 1993, and in 1994 the ISO 9001 Quality Certificate was granted first to Zamudio and then to Ajalvir, and the CQC 103 Certificate was also granted to Ajalvir by Rolls-Royce. In November of that year, ITP signed a contract with the Royal Air Force for the maintenance of its Tucano aircraft fleet.

As we shall see, Rolls-Royce took over the Allison Engine Company in Indianapolis in 1995, though negotiations were effectively completed in 1994 and in December 1994 ITP had begun working with Allison on their 601K industrial turbine. At the same time, given the need to maintain profitability, ITP talked to other aero-engine manufacturers besides Rolls-Royce and its subsidiary Allison, and in October 1996 signed an agreement with General Electric to participate in their LM2500 turbine programme. It also began work with SNECMA, MTU and Fiat on the M138 project in June 1997.

The following month it signed a partnership agreement with Allied Signal on the TF50 industrial turbine and, in September, signed a contract with CASA for maintenance on its Garrett TPE 331 engines.

On the development side, ITP was making giant strides and was most proud of its work on the thrust-vectoring nozzle. As it said itself:

Of all the activities of ITP, the thrust-vectoring nozzle is the model which has had the most repercussions at international level. It is the logical continuation of the work for EJ200. It is a combination of an original idea, design and build, and brought ITP international renown as a centre of excellence.

Its next great success was the design, development and manufacture of low-pressure turbines. After success on the Allison A601K, Rolls-Royce gave ITP responsibility for the design of the LP Turbine on the Trent 500, the engine for the Airbus A340-500/600 which we shall read about later. By 1998, Rolls-Royce was considering the signing of an agreement with ITP for the design and manufacture of all its LP turbines in civil engines over 35,000 lb thrust. This was to be the main industrial plant of ITP's engineering and manufacturing activities. ITP would be to Rolls-Royce what SNECMA is to GE and MTU to Pratt & Whitney.

Meanwhile, again to maintain its profitability, ITP scoured the world for maintenance contracts to keep its Ajalvir plant busy. Cutbacks in defence spending following the end of the Cold War had reduced the potential for military maintenance contracts. Assembly and development work on the EJ200 helped, especially after 1994, but the plant was filled only by bringing in work from overseas – Argentina, Brazil, Colombia, Ecuador, Angola, Morocco, Jordan, Holland and the UK.

To increase its share in the maintenance market, ITP made its first acquisition, buying 60 per cent of Industria de Turborreactores (ITR) in Queretaro in Mexico from the Mexican company CINTRA. The company was mainly involved in the maintenance of Pratt & Whitney JT8 engines in DC-9s and Boeing 727s.

By 2002, ITP was well established and had been consistently profitable. It was originally conceived as an operation to participate in military programmes, but Bob Crabtree, Rolls-Royce's representative on the ITP Board since its conception, had gradually persuaded his fellow Board members that the company should participate in civil programmes. As Fernando Pombo, a senior partner in the leading Spanish law firm Gómez-Acebo & Pombo, put it:

It was a big switch when we started to look at the civil market. It seemed risky. However, from the beginning Bob Crabtree wanted us to consider it. There was plenty of discussion, but now, here we are – ITP is a serious partner on several Trent programmes.

Both Pombo and Mike Steele – the Rolls-Royce executive appointed by Crabtree to work on the spot in Spain to look after Rolls-Royce's investment in ITP – noted that there had been considerable difficulty in the early 1990s persuading Rolls-Royce plants in the UK, which were not working at full capacity because of the recession, to let work go to the plants in Spain. Nevertheless, thanks to tact and persistence, transfers had gradually been made, and by the end of the decade ITP operations were centres of excellence comparable with any Rolls-Royce plant anywhere in the world.

THE ALLISON ENGINE COMPANY

THE BRICKYARD

RECORDS SHOW THAT THE Allison family settled in Indiana in 1840 and became involved in various businesses, including river boating, wholesale groceries and textiles. Their most interesting business, set up at the end of the nineteenth century, was the Allison Coupon Company. The idea was successful enough for the coupons to be used as part of the pay for workmen building the Panama Canal between 1904 and 1914, and in 1922 General Motors Acceptance Corporation used them for their customers taking out motor-car loans.

Nineteen-hundred-and-four, the year that Royce built his first motor car and met the Hon. C.S. Rolls, brought the Allison family's first involvement in motor cars when Jim Allison joined Carl Fisher and Percy Avery in setting up the Concentrated Acetylene Company, later renamed the Prest-O-Lite Company.

Fisher had opened one of the first motor-car garages in the area and was building a network of car sales franchises. He listened as Avery spoke enthusiastically about marketing compressed acetylene for use in powering motor-car headlights. Up to that time, cars were using the unreliable and messy calcium-carbide acetylene generator to power them.

Further involvement in the motor-car industry came through the organisation of a 24-hour race in Indianapolis, and after the staging of a successful race a group of enthusiasts developed the idea of a specially designed banked track, paved with bricks, two-and-a-half miles long. It took four years to build, and in 1909 Allison and Fisher were joined by Frank Wheeler and Arthur Newby in setting up the Motor Speedway. On Memorial Day, 30 May 1911, the first Indianapolis Speedway 500-mile International Sweepstakes Race was held at what became known as the 'Brickyard'.

Prest-O-Lite continued to prosper in downtown Indianapolis and in 1915, following an explosion at the plant, moved to a site close to the Speedway. Meanwhile, the outbreak of war in Europe in 1914 reduced the number of entries in the annual race. Nevertheless, on 14 September 1915, Allison, Fisher, Wheeler and Newby were joined by Theodore Myers and founded the Indianapolis Speedway Team Company. This was the precursor of the Allison Engine Company.

Cars were purchased and race teams formed. As the races continued, Allison became frustrated by the distance between the track and the car-servicing operation three miles away and in 1916 constructed a small building close to the track to house his machine shop, on the site of what later became known as Allison Plant No. 1. In January 1917, the team, now twenty strong, moved in, and the company was renamed the Allison Speedway Team Company. Norman Gilman moved from National Motors and became chief engineer. A solid engineering business was established as other teams turned to the company for special parts and servicing.

Allison himself was a perfectionist with the same approach as Royce, saying to his workmen:

I want you to remember that this is not just another machine shop. Whatever leaves this shop over my name must be the finest work possible.

On 23 February 1917, the company changed its name again, to the Allison Engine Company, reflecting its work in addition to that on racing cars. And its general skills were soon in further demand as the USA joined the European war on 17 April 1917. Allison instructed Gilman to find war orders, saying:

Take any jobs you like, especially the ones other fellows can't do, anything that will help get us started. Don't figure costs or wait to quote prices. We'll take care of that later.

One of their jobs was to make parts for the newly designed Liberty V-12 aircraft engine, and at the end of 1917 the company learnt that the US Navy was planning to buy aircraft capable of transatlantic flight that would need Liberty engines equipped with reduction gearing.

Maurice Olley, the brilliant Rolls-Royce engineer about whom we read in Part One, had been sent to the USA with Rolls-Royce Managing Director Claude Johnson to help set up the production of Rolls-Royce Eagle engines. He was loaned to the Liberty project and worked with Al Moorhouse of Packard to design an epicyclic reduction gear. Gilman most probably involved himself in this work and prepared a proposal for the US Navy.

On New Year's Day 1918, Gilman flew to Washington and secured a contract for 250 epicyclic-geared Liberty V-12 engines. When the war ended in November 1918, the company was employing 350 draughtsmen, engineers and skilled machinists.

After the war, the Indianapolis 500-mile Sweepstake Race was resumed, and the Allison team won the first post-war race with a modified Peugeot. This was probably one of the Peugeot racers that won the 1913 Grand Prix and which influenced the Mercedes Grand Prix racers. Royce got hold of one of the Peugeots, and then, as we saw in Part One, a Grand Prix Mercedes was taken to Derby after the outbreak of war. However, Allison felt that the future of this company lay beyond the development of racing cars, and he sold his race team and cars to concentrate on wider engineering. This led to a further change of company name in 1921 to the Allison Engineering Company.

During the 1920s, Allison's mainstay was the upgrading, overhaul and modernising of 2,000 to 3,000 Liberty 12-As for the US Government, but it also manufactured a number of aviation-related products, notably the Roots-type superchargers. It also, at the US Navy's request, began work in 1927 to produce a two-cycle, in-line, water-cooled, six-cylinder diesel engine to replace the 2,500 lb, 600 bhp German Maybach engines powering the Navy's rigid airships. It was hoped that the Allison diesel would develop 900 bhp and weigh less than 3,000 lb. As it happened, this project attracted the attention of Charles 'Boss' Kettering of General Motors, who was also working on the development of a diesel engine. He visited Allison's plant regularly. Allison was also building prototype high-speed superchargers for General Electric – a useful prelude to their manufacturing superchargers for their own V-1710 engine.

GENERAL MOTORS TO THE RESCUE

The years 1928 and 1929 brought a period of turmoil to the company. On 4 August 1928, Jim Allison died from bronchial pneumonia at the age of only 55, and control of the estate was left in the hands of executors who wanted to keep the business in Indianapolis. Eddie Rickenbacker, who features elsewhere in Part Two of this story of Rolls-Royce, had already expressed interest to Allison in buying his company. He had been a racing driver before the war and indeed had captained the Prest-O-Lite team and, as we know, had been perhaps the best-known US fighter pilot of the First World War. In 1927, he had approached Jim Allison, by this time partially retired and living in Florida, with a view to buying the Allison Engineering Company. Allison wanted to retain a share in his company to provide an interest when he returned to Indianapolis during the summer and suggested that Rickenbacker buy the Speedway. This is how Rickenbacker recalls the events in his autobiography:

I knew that Jim Allison had partially retired, and I went to Indianapolis to ask him to sell me the company.

'Well, Eddie, I'll tell you,' he said, 'it's true I spend most of my time in Florida these days, but when I do come home for the summer I like to have a desk I can put my feet on. But I have a better idea, one tailor-made for you. Why don't you take over the Speedway?'

The Speedway had been built by four men – Allison, Carl G Fisher, Frank H Wheeler and Arthur C Newby. 'The way it stands now' Allison said, 'Frank Wheeler is dead, Art Newby is no longer interested and Carl Fisher is spending his time developing Miami Beach. I'd like to see it in younger, capable hands.'

I told Jim quite truthfully that I had never thought about buying the Speedway, but I began to think about it at that moment. I went out and took a look at the property. When the Speedway had been built in 1909, it had been far out in the country and its 320 acres had been acquired for $72,000. But now it was practically surrounded by the city, and its real-estate value alone had multiplied many times.

Allison gave me a price of $700,000 and a thirty-day option. I had a survey made, which verified my belief that the price was fair. The more I thought of it, the more enthusiastic I became. Owning and operating the Indianapolis Speedway, home of the world's greatest automotive event, would be a thrill in itself.

Allison had strongly hinted that, if I did not take it over, it would probably be sold to real-estate speculators. The Speedway would be razed and the land subdivided. To someone who had been as close to the Speedway as I had been for so many years, such an idea was unthinkable. Fleeting nostalgic scenes of color and excitement raced through my mind, beginning with the very first '500' in 1911. That was when, as a 20 year-old amateur from the dirt tracks of Iowa, I had relieved Lee Frayer in his Red Wing Special.

He succeeded in raising the required $700,000, but when Allison died he realised he could possibly now buy the engineering company.

Daniel D. Whitney, who has researched and written a detailed account of the Allison V-1710 engine, *Vees for Victory*, wrote of this episode:

Wright Aeronautical, the leading engine maker of the time, was somewhat interested.

After looking [it] over they decided there was not a sufficiently good profit record to justify operating the business, so they would only take the people and patents. Consolidated Aircraft also took a look, and came to a similar conclusion. Through his associations, Rickenbacker was kept informed of the discounted prices being offered by the few bidders and kept raising his bid accordingly. He finally bid $5,000 more than the previous highest bidder, and the Allison Engineering Company was his, for a price of $90,000. Though he did not have the money, Rickenbacker managed to get a loan from an Indianapolis bank. In addition, he optioned the land around the company's Speedway facility for future expansion.

According to Rickenbacker's autobiography, after acquiring the company he realised that he had neither the time to run it properly, nor the money or credit that would be required for proper expansion over the next few years. Still, during his months of ownership he claims to have been the one to arrange with the Navy to build the prototype GV-1710-A, though more specific records give May 7 1929 as the date when Norm Gilman and his staff began to sketch and design the VG-1710, as it was known at Allison at the time. It is entirely possible that Rickenbacker did have conversations with Navy personnel that encouraged Gilman that such an engine might find a buyer, but the timing suggests they could not have been conclusive.

Rickenbacker further relates that, at that time, the Fisher Brothers Investment Trust was buying into the aviation industry and they agreed to take the Allison Engineering Company 'off his hands'. Effective January 1 1929 the Allison Engineering Company was purchased by the Fisher Brothers, who also happened to be sitting on the General Motors Board; Eddie Rickenbacker was named president of the Fisher operation.

General Motors was also pondering further involvement in the air engine business and had been impressed by Allison's reputation and skills. Kettering had noted that Allison's diesel development was ahead of that of General Motors. At the Executive Committee meeting of 3 May 1929, it was proposed and approved:

General Motors Corporation Appropriation: $800,000 Purchase of Allison Engineering Company.

Of this sum, $600,000 was to cover the price paid by Fisher and $200,000 was for required additions during the rest of the year.

Whitney notes that:

It is curious that Rickenbacker could purchase the Allison Engineering Company, 'Lock-Stock-and-Barrel' for $90,000 and four months later sell it to the Fisher Brothers for $500,000! A going engineering and manufacturing enterprise of Allison's size should have brought, on the open market, a figure nearer to $500,000 than $90,000! As confirmation, the Allison Engineering Company Balance Sheet of

January 31 1929 shows a net worth of $492,866.88. One might conclude that events surrounding Mr Allison's scandalous divorce from his long-time wife, and the subsequent marriage to his secretary Miss Lucille Musset, which occurred only five days before his death, were factors.

Allison's estate was estimated at between three and six million dollars, which legally was to go to his new bride, for there was no will. Two days following his death his first wife filed a $2 million suit claiming 'alienation of affections' against the new Mrs Allison. Ultimately, his 80 year old mother, Mrs Myra J Allison received most of the $3 million estate.

Evidently the executors (long-time friends of both Rickenbacker and Jim Allison) did not care to see the new wife profiting from the tragedy, and by the expedient of requiring the firm to stay in Indianapolis, caused the firm to be heavily discounted in the eyes of the other bidders. Rickenbacker was in the right place at the right time, and had the inside track.

He certainly thought everyone should be pleased with the outcome. He wrote later:

General Motors decided to go into the aviation industry, and the Fishers turned the Allison Company over to General Motors for the same price they paid me for it, including a liberal commission. General Motors poured millions into the development of the company before selling the first Allison engine. It eventually sold eighty thousand of them; the Allison engine powered the P-38 and the P-51 [until the Rolls-Royce Merlin replaced it], among others during World War II. In 1928, however, such an investment was far out of my reach.

As it was we all came out ahead. I had the Speedway, General Motors had Allison and the nation had a superb workhorse engine that powered thousands of planes for use in war and peace.

In retrospect, it was a fortunate time for a small company to be swallowed by a very large one. In the autumn of 1929, the long American boom of the 1920s came to an end as prices on Wall Street crashed, the general world economic situation deteriorated rapidly and years of depression ensued. Allison was fortunate, not only to have the giant General Motors to protect it but in its connections with the US military, both Navy and Army. Norman Gilman was appointed President and General Manager of the Allison Engineering Company, which retained its name. He had conceived the idea of developing a 1,000-horsepower liquid-cooled engine and, in 1930, secured an order from the Navy for a 750-horsepower liquid-cooled engine. It was rapidly designed and built, and was delivered in March 1932. The US Navy then ordered similar engines to replace the Maybach engines in the airships USS *Los Angeles*, *Akron* and *Macon*. These were reversible engines.

Unfortunately, on the day the engines for the *Macon* were to be shipped, news arrived that the *Macon* had crashed in the Pacific Ocean, and the US Navy stopped further airship development.

It was at this time when Rolls-Royce and Allison first did business together that Allison sold to Rolls-Royce some bearing components for experimental evaluation.

THE V-1710

Luckily for Allison, the US Army had also become interested in their liquid-cooled project and gave the company an order for a 750-horsepower engine with the remit to keep developing the engine until 1,000-horsepower was reached.

Allison achieved 750-horsepower but struggled to improve on it. By 1936, the company concluded that a brand new design was needed, and, in only three months between early March and mid-June, a new engine was designed, built and delivered to Wright Field, Dayton, Ohio – the US equivalent of Farnborough and Boscombe Down. After a 140-hour qualification test had been successfully completed, a crack developed in one of the cylinder heads. This part was redesigned, and in April 1937 the new engine completed its 150-hour type test. The engine, called the Allison V-1710, became the USA's first 1,000-horsepower aircraft engine.

The first V-1710 flight was made in a Consolidated A-11A aircraft, and, after a 300-hour flight test, another V-1710 was installed in the Curtiss-Wright XP-37. The next development was the Curtiss P-40 which, with the V-1710, won the Army Air Force's fighter competition in 1939 with a speed 40 mph faster than the previous top US fighter speed. As a result, Allison received its production order, and, in spite of the fact that it was verbal and for less than 1,000 engines, General Motors approved the construction of a new Allison production plant. Their faith was justified as orders came in from Britain, France and China. Production began in February 1940, and by December 1941, in spite of many production difficulties, 3,500 engines had been shipped and the production rate had reached the planned 1,000 per month. The Japanese attack on Pearl Harbor on 7 December 1941, and the outbreak of war between the USA and both Japan and Germany, brought further pressure for increased production.

There was also pressure for increased performance, and many new and improved models of the engine were developed. At the same time, production of the sleeve bearings, which Allison had pioneered, was stepped up, as every aircraft engine used by US forces in the Second World War used these bearings. Total wartime production reached ten million. Production peak for the engines at the rate of 3,000 engines a month was reached in 1943, by which time the workforce had expanded to over 23,000. By the end of the War, Allison had built 70,000 liquid-cooled engines to power Curtiss P-40 Warhawks, a very reliable warhorse, Bell P-39 Aircobras, many of which went to help the Russian war effort, magnificently effective Lockheed P-38 Lightnings, the good low-level North American P-51 and A-36 Mustangs, and the upgraded Aircobra, the P-63 Kingcobra. (As we know from Part Two, the Rolls-Royce Merlin replaced the Allison V-1710 in the P-51, due to the Merlin's high-altitude capability, and made it the Allies' best all-round fighter.) Power development meant that the 1710 engine, which had delivered 1,000 hp in 1937, was delivering 1,600 hp at take-off and a combat rating of 2,000 hp by the end of the War.

Eddie Rickenbacker wrote in *US News and World Report* in 1965:

From 1940 to 1945 Allison turned out 70,000 engines – 60 per cent of all of the engines supplied for US fighter aircraft during the war! [This is something of an exaggeration, yet it gives a fair idea of the prominence of Allison as a supplier of US military aircraft engines.]

The pressure on space was such that the US Government paid for a new plant to be built. Edward B. Newill, who was appointed General Manager in 1943, was to say later in 1979 when interviewed by R.T. King in an oral-history research project at Indiana University:

Practically all materials were basically short. One rather interesting point is that when we were building a two-million square-foot plant to enlarge our production, we could not get the steel for the structural portion of the building, so that building, as of today, has wooden beams, struts, braces and so on. That's a nuisance because the wood insists on warping, and each year Allison has to have a specialist in this respect come in and retune those structures to keep them straight. [The plant is still being fully utilised, nearly 60 years after it was built.]

Towards the end of the War, Allison also became involved in the development of the gas-turbine engine, the jet, which, as we have seen, had been so successfully pioneered by Frank Whittle, with its further development and production taken up by Rolls-Royce. Allison delivered its first jet engine in February 1945 and was moving towards volume production when Japan sued for peace in August 1945.

Edward Newill told King in his interview in 1979 how Allison became involved in jet-engine manufacture:

I was at Wright Field one day on a wholly different errand, and a Colonel MacNamara reached me by telephone from another office and asked me to drop by his office, which I did. Our production of piston engines was declining sharply at that time, so this must have been on the order of 1944 or 1945. 1944 I believe. When I got to Colonel MacNamara's office, he closed his door and made sure nobody was within earshot, and he said, 'Can Allison manufacture jet engines?' I said, 'Well, Orv,' his name was Orville, 'I never saw a jet engine nor the design of one, but if anybody can make them, we can make them.' And he said, 'Well, General Electric is beginning to build some J-33 engines. We need a lot of them, and with Allison's declining piston engine production we're considering Allison to build jet engines.' So I said, 'That's fine. Could we get two or three of these engines to put in a test cell and operate them and learn something about them?' And he said, 'There's never one of them been built.' And so I said, 'How about giving me three sets of drawings so that we can at least study the paper work?' He says, 'The drawings aren't finished.' So I said, 'Orv, are you kidding me, or what's going on here?' And he said, 'I was never more serious in my life, and we want you to build jet engines, and we want a lot of them. I'd like to have you back in this office one week from today with a bid on what it will cost you to get into this jet engine business and what the price of the engine is going to be.' So I said, 'Well, Orv, what can you tell me about the engine? Do you know what it weighs?' He says, 'Yes, I do know what it's going to weigh.' And he gave me a figure. He also had a small drawing showing half of a cross section and half of an external view of this J-33 engine. He says, 'I can give you a copy of that, but that's absolutely all I can give you.' So I took the copy, of course, and the next morning had a meeting of our staff, as soon as I got back into Indianapolis, and we discussed what we could do to meet his request of a quotation of building this engine at a price and with a promised delivery date, and what it would cost to revise our [power] plant to get into it. Well, we had changed the piston engines enough to have a pretty good idea of what it would cost to go from one type of a model to another type of the same model. And so we did a 'guesstimate' of what that cost would be. We didn't know a thing about the parts of the jet engine that we were going to be asked to build, so finally I said, 'Well, we know what the weight of the engine is; it can't cost more than $20 a pound, so that's the price.' So, adding the preparation costs in as a burden cost over and above the engine manufacturing cost, we said to each other, 'Well, why do we wait for a week from now … I'll go back to Wright Field tomorrow morning and give them this quotation?' Which we did. And we came within about four percent of what the cost of it actually turned out to be after we had built two or three hundred of the engines.

It is impossible to write about Allison and the V-1710 engine during the Second World War without mentioning the Mustang P-51 and the replacement of the Allison engine with the Rolls-Royce Merlin. In *The Magic of a Name: The Rolls-Royce Story: The First Forty Years*, published by Icon Books in 2000, the full story of Ronnie Harker's testing the P-51 at Duxford is told.

103

He recommended that the RAF and the USAAF use P-51s with Merlin engines, and they both took his advice. As a result, there has been a tendency, especially in Britain, to assume that the Rolls-Royce Merlin was a better engine than the Allison V-1710 *in every respect*. Daniel Whitney analyses both engines in great detail in his book, *Vees for Victory*. He makes the point that there were many configurations of engine within the overall types, Merlin and V-1710, and concludes his chapter on the subject with these words:

The Allison V-1710 and the Rolls-Royce V-1650 liquid-cooled V-12 aircraft engines were really very many different engines. The active production period for each extended for nearly 15 years. A large number of variations of the engines were built to meet the needs of military tacticians related to the key roles both engines played during the war. Both engines were needed, and while one particular model or another was preferred for a given mission, not every airplane, and not every engine, should be expected to perform every mission with equal superiority or effectiveness.

The V-1710 was designed to be a two-stage supercharged engine, albeit with the first stage being a turbosupercharger [and was used as such in the P-38 Lightning and P-63 Kingcobra]. When pressed into service as a single-stage power plant it should not be a surprise that it would be 'altitude' limited. Power ratings were quite similar once the U.S. military allowed WER [War Emergency] ratings; the V-1710 was able to equal or exceed comparable Merlin performance.

Although the V-1710 had a four year headstart in design and testing, the Government funded Merlin benefited from the experienced Rolls-Royce development team. They had the engine ready and with it the Battle of Britain was won. At that point in time, the V-1710 had just gone into series production. Furthermore, Rolls-Royce was able to grow the capabilities of the engine with their masterful arrangement of superchargers and aftercooling to provide a compact two-stage engine that was able to establish air superiority over both Europe and Japan. Allison was able to match this performance, but was never able to get its most advanced engines into production combat aircraft during the war.

Edward Newill said:

There was only one competitive, liquid-cooled in-line engine manufactured in the United States in these sizes and for these fighter engine applications, and that was the Rolls-Royce engine which Packard manufactured. The Packard engine was an excellent engine, and for certain applications it exceeded the performance of the Allison engine. For certain other applications the Allison engine exceeded the Packard engine.

When King asked Newill whether Allison benefited from captured enemy engines, Newill said, 'Not to any extent, no.' He went on to say:

I don't remember any instance of where we had a foreign-built engine except some Rolls engines, because we were developing a co-operative arrangement with Rolls which continues to this day, whereby we did engineering work for each other. We made parts for each other. And that has been quite a valuable partnership ... We learned a great deal from the Rolls engineers. They were splendid engineers and, of course, had been building high-performance engines longer than we had. So we got a great deal from Rolls.

INTO JETS

The post-war era was the jet age, and although initially Allison's production of jet engines was reduced, the company was given the responsibility for continuing the development of the J-33 turbojet engine. The brief was to achieve increased power and dependability. In September 1946, Allison also received contracts for further development and manufacture of the J-35 axial-flow jet engine. Both the J-33 and J-35 gradually improved in power and reliability and powered the USA's new military aircraft: the Lockheed F-80 and its trainer version, the TF-80 Shooting Star, the Republic F-84 Thunderjet, Grumman F9F-3 Panther, Northrop F-89A Scorpion, North American FJ-1 Fury, Northrop RB-35B Flying Wing, Martin P4M-1 Mercator and North American AJ-1.

In a competitive world, records brought useful publicity. In 1947, a Lockheed Shooting Star brought the world's air-speed record back to the USA for the first time in more than twenty years with a speed of 623.8 mph, and later this record was twice broken by an Allison-powered Douglas D-558, a Navy research aircraft, with speeds of 640.7 mph and 650.6 mph.

As we saw in Part Two, a Rolls-Royce Derwent-powered Gloster Meteor F Mk 4-EE549, flown by Group Captain E.M. Donaldson, had set a new world air-speed record of 615.81 mph on 7 September 1946.

In 1948, the J-33 became the first turbojet engine to be certified for commercial-airline use in the USA.

In the meantime, the contract for supplying the V-1710, now fitted with two-stage supercharging, for the P-82 Twin Mustang was completed, and production of the engine ceased. With spare capacity, Allison searched for new products to fill their plants.

The employment graph at Allison encapsulated the problem faced by all munitions suppliers during a period of conflict. The workforce builds up rapidly while the war is being fought and declines just as sharply when it is over and the orders dry up. In 1939, fewer than 2,000 were employed at the Indianapolis complex. By early 1940, when the first V-1710 was delivered from Plant 3, employment had risen to 3,000. By December 1941, when Pearl Harbor was attacked, it was nearly 13,000. By early 1943, when the first V-1710 was delivered from Plant 5, employment was approaching 20,000. It peaked at about 23,000 at the end of 1943, and then fell almost as precipitately as it had risen – to 16,000 on D-Day in June 1944, to 10,000 on VE Day in May 1945, to under 8,000 on VJ Day in August 1945 and on down to a low of about 5,000 in early 1946.

Plant 3, the original production plant, was converted and tooled for the manufacture of automotive shock absorbers, hydraulic lifts, diesel blowers and transmissions. Although the shock-absorber production was discontinued, Allison became a major supplier of principal parts for the diesel locomotives built by General Motors' Electro-Motive Division in LaGrange, Illinois. The company's experience in gearing on the V-1710 engine was also put to use in a transmission development programme. This led to production programmes for General Patton tanks and heavy-duty commercial vehicles including buses manufactured by General Motors' Truck and Coach Division.

Newill said later:

Well, toward the end of World War II the US Army ordnance department decided they needed a new set of heavy-duty vehicles, tanks, personnel carriers, amphibious vehicles and so on, primarily tanks. So they approached us to see if we would develop these transmissions. It was purely an engineering product at first ... We had one that was built for about 250 horsepower engines, one for 400–500 horsepower and one for 1400 horsepower. The first two prospered, the last didn't go very far, although we did complete the development. But we borrowed some General Motors people who knew the transmission field, and have now built a very substantial business. It was substantial before I retired in 1960 and much more so now [1979].

In the jet field, Allison concentrated on the military. As Newill put it when asked about whether the company tried to compete in the civil turbojet field:

Well, we made a lame effort, and that had to do primarily with the corporation policy with which we agreed. I didn't, personally, much favour trying to make a living for the rest of my life building engines for commercial aircraft, because it's an in-and-out business. It's either a feast or famine. And that doesn't appeal to most manufacturers. So, we had a policy and stated this openly to the air force and other governmental officials, the Secretary of Defense, and the Secretary of the Air Force that 'we'll build for you anything you're willing to pay for, but you pay for whatever we build.' That was not the policy to get the commercial aircraft business, because primarily Pratt and Whitney and General Electric were both willing to enter this as a business and to take the risk and pay the price of developing new engines and having them available for whatever commercial applications there were. We, frankly, weren't. We weren't willing to pay the very high price of developing a new engine with the possibility of selling it commercially. So that's the basic reason that Allison has not prospered in the jet engine field.

However, Allison did compete in the turboprop-engine field. It developed a turboprop, the 501D3 (the 501 was the company designation for the military T56), for the military transport aircraft, the Hercules C130, manufactured by Lockheed. The US Government effectively paid the development costs.

Allison also received a contract to develop an axial-flow turboprop engine, the T38, along with the T40 in December 1945. The T38 powered four aircraft: a Boeing B-17 test bed, a Convair 240 test bed, the supersonic McDonnell XF-88B propeller test bed and a Piasecki YH-16A. Only one of each of these aircraft was built. However, in operating these test aircraft, the T38 evolved into a configuration that set the standard for many subsequent Allison turboprops, including the T56.

On the pure-jet engine front, Allison did benefit from the Korean War in the early 1950s. Newill said:

We had developed a higher rated engine which we sold to Douglas for one of their bombers and that gave us some good business for two or three years, but not continuously.

Allison's success with its 3,750 hp turboprop engine in the Hercules led Lockheed to choose the engine for its new airliner, the Electra. This aircraft was designed in the mid-1950s in response to the request from the president of American Airlines, C.R. Smith, for a turboprop aircraft that would cruise easily at speeds of more than 400 mph, operate profitably on flights as short as 100 miles and as long as 2,700 miles, carry at least 65 passengers and take off fast enough and land slowly enough to operate in and out of any of the USA's 100 major airports, large and small – particularly those that would not be able to handle the forthcoming pure jets. In other words, American was looking for the most versatile aircraft ever designed, and all the manufacturers were interested. The British Vickers offered a stretched version of the already successful Viscount. Douglas, already busy on its pure jet, DC-8, nevertheless put forward a turboprop proposal. But it was Lockheed that won the day with an aircraft initially called the L-188, but named, like many other Lockheed aircraft, after a star: the Electra.

The story of the Electra is worth telling briefly, not only because Allison provided the engines but also because of its effect on Lockheed in the civil market, which became important in the Rolls-Royce story when the TriStar and RB 211 engine came to the fore in the late 1960s.

There was no doubt that the Electra was a heavily tested aircraft. Bob Gross, the chairman of Lockheed, apparently said to his engineers:

It is going to be the most thoroughly tested airliner in aviation history.

And the engineers took him at his word. It was analysed and tested – on drawing boards, in wind tunnels, on computers and in laboratories. Three full-scale mock-ups were built, as well as a mock-up of metal for checking structural tolerance, fabricated parts and actual operation of the complicated control systems. The engineers put a one-sixteenth scale model through 60,000 wind-tunnel tests at speeds of more than 400 mph and put the main landing gear through 270,000 simulated flights involving every load from an empty aircraft to one carrying 95 passengers plus full cargo, baggage and maximum fuel capacity.

Nothing was left to chance, and, although Lockheed had already accumulated 250,000 flight hours with Allison engines on the C130, the engineers put four engines on a Super Constellation airliner and flew it for another 3,370 hours. When the Electra received its certification, both ground and flight tests had reached 350,000 engine hours.

By the time the first aircraft were built, Lockheed had spent $50 million on development and were confident they had designed and manufactured the best and safest aircraft in their history. Construction of the prototype began in December 1955, and Lockheed had secured two firm orders: 35 for American Airlines and 40 for Eastern Airlines. The eventual order book was 180 aircraft for 14 airlines. The first test flight was on 6 December 1957, and the aircraft entered service in 1958. All went well until there were two fatal crashes: one at Buffalo, Texas, and one at Tell City in Indiana.

In trying to analyse what had gone wrong with the Electra to cause the disastrous crashes, the initial solution offered by the Lockheed engineers was 'whirl mode'. Whirl mode was not new and had developed occasionally in piston-engine aircraft, but it was always contained without spreading to the wing area. For some reason it had spread to the wing area in the Electra. As Robert Serling pointed out in his book, *The Electra Story*, published by Doubleday in 1963:

It is a tribute to the common sense, judgement and faith of airline passengers that they do not panic like frightened children after a bad crash ... No US airliner ever built has been immune from accidents, including those caused by some weakness or defect in the plane itself. This statement applies to every commercial transport from the beloved DC-3 to the modern jets introduced in the late fifties and early sixties. Yet passengers have not cancelled reservations in Constellations after a 'Connie' crash. They have not refused to fly in a DC-6 because a DC-6 had just gone down. There was no rush away from the Viscount in 1960 after one lost a wing over Chase, Maryland, in a thunderstorm. Even temporarily mysterious, unsolved accidents seem to bother the professionals more than the laymen. The then unexplained crash of a Boeing 707 shortly after taking off from New York's Idlewild Airport on March 1 1962, had no effect on 707 load factors. Neither did the rash of landing-gear difficulties encountered by Boeings in 1960, nor a spate of hydraulic failures suffered by DC-8s in the summer of 1961. As a matter of fact, passenger reaction in the latter incidents significantly was far calmer than some Congressional reaction which in certain cases approached the hysterical … Yet it is remarkable that accidents, with two exceptions, resulted in no more than an imperceptible and very temporary drop in air travel. The first exception occurred in the 1946–48 period, when the airlines suffered noticeable drops in load factors, unusually sharp declines attributed directly to several fatal crashes in the United States alone. The load factors remained depressed for a considerable time, until public confidence was restored gradually.

But the second exception was the Lockheed Electra after Tell City, and for the first time in commercial-aviation history a crash generated fear and prejudice toward an individual airliner.

And then the rumours and the sick jokes started. A disc jockey in Miami said to his audience, 'Did you hear about the guy who said to the ticket agent, "I'd like a ticket on the next Electra flight to New York"? And the agent replied, "We don't sell Electra tickets, we sell chances."'

Bookings and load factors fell. Northwest's went down from over 70 per cent to 56 per cent. National's fell to 49 per cent, and Western's also fell from 77 per cent to under 50. However, the Electra was a fine aircraft and fought back. By the middle of 1961, airlines were flying it with confidence, and load factors had recovered.

Unfortunately, that was not the end of the tragic story of the two accidents. By spring 1962, $55 million of lawsuits had been filed against Lockheed, Allison, Braniff and Northwest. Lockheed had said originally that the accidents were 'state of the art' and no one was to blame. Robert Gross, the chairman, had told the house subcommittee investigating the Electra in November 1960:

I know it is disturbing to many people and perhaps to you how highly competent and old-line aircraft companies can turn out planes which after a few months of service experience difficulties. The art of aircraft design has grown rapidly and in spurts from the days of the earliest rudimentary machines to the present-day planes requiring hundreds of thousands of man-hours, of engineering design, wind-tunnel testing and flying.

New and complicated problems arise with each generation of aircraft, requiring an ever-increasing volume of analyses and tests to assure safety. Sometimes, however, it is just not possible to foresee the almost infinite variety of combinations of circumstances that can affect an airplane in flight.

The two Electra accidents in Texas and Indiana resulted from conditions that were not disclosed in the thousands of tests to which the Electra was subjected. They were unpredictable within the then-existing state of the art. It is some consolation to realise that the state of the art has advanced as the result of our findings.

However, faced with the barrage of lawsuits, Lockheed abandoned this stance and blamed Allison. In April 1962, Lockheed claimed that the whirl mode had been triggered by a fatigue break in the propeller reduction gearbox. Allison responded by claiming that the engine damage was caused by violent loads originating outside the power plants. The first court case ended with the jury awarding the family of one of the crash victims $250,000 (the family had claimed $500,000) and found Lockheed and Allison equally responsible. It held that both companies were jointly involved in the engine-mounting design and found negligence in the overall design of the aircraft and its power plants, in engine/airframe compatibility and in the flight testing. This set a precedent for the rest of the lawsuit actions.

During this period, there was also a crash in Boston involving an Electra, which was initially attributed to power loss due to bird ingestion by the engines. However, as this case dragged on through the courts in the 1960s, a pilot, listening to lawyers discussing the case against the airframe and engine manufacturers, asked to see the maintenance record of the crashed aircraft. He showed that it was faulty maintenance that caused the accident. The co-pilot's seat had a fault that could cause it to slide backwards. In the take-off in the Winthrop Bay crash, this is what had happened when the aircraft yawed initially when birds had affected one of the engines. The pilot's foot had come off the rudder pedal, causing the aircraft to yaw again. More seriously it had caused him to pull back the stick, thereby putting the aircraft's nose in the air and causing a stall. When all this was put to the jury, they found Eastern Airlines, not Lockheed or Allison, responsible for the crash.

Both Allison and Lockheed recovered from the trauma of the Electra crashes, though Lockheed was wary of the civil market until it found the military market just as tough and returned to the civil market with the TriStar at the end of the 1960s. Even then, the Electra haunted them. Lloyd Frisbee, the chief engineer and TriStar programme manager at Lockheed, told the author in 1998 that because of the problems on the Electra Lockheed was forced to spend millions of dollars on structural tests for the TriStar.

During the 1950s, Rolls-Royce and Allison proposed an engine for the US Government's TFX multi-role fighter (later designated F-111) based on Rolls-Royce turbofan technology. This competition was won by Pratt & Whitney. Another great opportunity for a successful collaborative venture between Rolls-Royce and Allison in the 1960s was to manufacture an engine for Boeing's 727. We have already seen that Boeing had judged the market for this size of aircraft perfectly and that orders were flooding in. Allison submitted the AR963G, effectively a Rolls-Royce Spey engine. In 1961, Boeing offered the 727 with this engine, and the lead airline for the aircraft, United Airlines, accepted it. However, Eddie Rickenbacker, by this time the president of Eastern Airlines, rejected it. We saw in Part Two that Rickenbacker may have had personal reasons for doing so, but, in any case, in the 1960s when the USA was concerned about its balance-of-payments position, it was not difficult to persuade airlines and aircraft manufacturers that they should buy American components if they possibly could.

Boeing persuaded Pratt & Whitney to develop a military engine for commercial use, and the result, the JT8D, became the most successful fan-jet in commercial aviation history, powering the 727, 737, DC-9 and MD-80 series (until being displaced by the CFM56 in the late 1990s).

During the 1960s, Allison collaborated closely with Rolls-Royce on production of an engine called the TF41: effectively a Rolls-Royce Spey with a bigger compressor system on the front end. The TF41 powered the LTV (Ling Temco Vought) A-7, a single-engine fighter-bomber that became one of the most used aircraft in the Vietnam War; over 1,500 were built. Robert McNamara, the US Secretary of State for Defense, wanted a third engine manufacturer involved in supplying the US military. As the war in Vietnam escalated, General Electric and Pratt & Whitney were struggling to cope with demand. Mike Hudson, currently Vice-Chairman of Rolls-Royce North America, remembered that although, in theory, all the parts should have been manufactured in the US, many were made by Rolls-Royce and shipped over. There was some discussion about the turbine blades that Allison had been casting; Rolls-Royce insisted that they were forged.

Rolls-Royce also talked to Allison and its parent, General Motors, about collaboration on the new and revolutionary RB 211. Allison was in favour, and the decision reached Board level at General Motors. However, the Board decided that the investment on a non-mainstream General Motors product was too large, and the mooted partnership was abandoned.

During the 1970s, deregulation of trucking in the USA led to an explosion in demand for trucks, and Allison used a significant proportion of its capacity for the manufacture of diesel engines. Its owner, General Motors, felt that the company was not really capable of competing in the civil-airline business and refused to authorise funding for a new civil product. On the aero-engine front, Allison was sustained during the 1970s by the production of Model 250 helicopter engines, many used in oil exploration (following the OPEC oil price hikes of 1973/4, there was a period of frantic exploration in the USA and its surrounding water), and by production of the T56 turboprop engines for the E2, C2, P3 and C130. By 1983, over 12,000 T56 engines had been sold in over 60 countries.

The Model 250 free-turbine helicopter engine was developed under US

Army contract beginning in 1958, with a first run in April 1959. Over the next 40 years, 28,000 engines were built in four series with fleet hours exceeding 150 million.

A NEW HOME

Allison had reached a low ebb by the early 1980s when Garrett, a subsidiary of Signal Oil, made an offer for the company. The investment bank Morgan Stanley told General Motors that the offer was too low and suggested that they recruit someone to run Allison who had experience of making gas-turbine engines. The result was the hiring of Blake Wallace, a relatively unusual selection as the leader of an aerospace business, which in many cases were run by accountants, lawyers or marketeers. Wallace, like the current chairman of Rolls-Royce, was an engineer. He had worked at Pratt & Whitney, Garrett Air Research and General Electric, where he was manager of advanced technical plans and programmes. He and Hudson put together a strategic plan to revive the company.

Three divisions were created – large engines, small engines and marine engines – and a policy set in place: first, to protect Allison's markets in the turboprop, helicopter and industrial marine markets; second, to re-enter the civil air-transport market, and third, to compete in the fighter-engine business. They also sought closer ties with Rolls-Royce, suggesting that the two companies try and repeat their success with the TF41. Discussions took place with Gordon Lewis, Director of Engineering in the Military Engine Group at Bristol, Alan Newton, Director of Engineering in the Civil Engine Group in Derby, and Stewart Miller, chief engineer on the RB 211-535 at the time.

One attempt at collaboration was based on Allison's interest in the turbo-prop area. Allison requested that Rolls-Royce consider co-operation on developing the Model 578 with contra-rotation prop fans, but Rolls-Royce refused due to heavy workload on other projects. Allison turned to Pratt & Whitney, setting up a 50:50 joint venture to develop the engine. Somewhat later, discussions took place about co-operation on an Allison programme with the Swedish company SAAB on the development of a high-speed turbo-prop. In the end, these ventures did not prove successful as the public had decided that the turboprop was yesterday's engine. Rolls-Royce had obviously made a shrewd decision to decline investing in these joint development programmes.

Areas looked at included business-jet engines, new large-turbofan engines and regional-airline engines. The large-turbofan project, which later became the Trent programme, and business-jet and regional-airline engines were selected for co-operative ventures. Allison designed and built one of the early versions of the high-pressure compressor for the large engine, and Rolls-Royce carried out configuration definition and design work on a small turbofan, designated the RB 580 and based on the core from the T406, the V-22 Osprey engine. However, shortly after the first set of Trent compressor hardware had been fabricated and the small-engine configuration established, General Motors decided not to commit to the full investment in the large engine.

Another collaborative programme was the development of an 8,000 lb-thrust engine for the Embraer small airliner being built in Brazil. Robins, conscious of the importance of not diluting the company's focus on the Trent programme and concerned about the restructuring that was taking place at that time at Embraer, pulled Rolls-Royce out of this collaboration.

However, contacts with Rolls-Royce were maintained, and when Rolls-Royce was struggling with the compressor on the V-2500 engine (see Chapter One) Allison was asked for its help, which led to its contribution to the development of the compressor used on the Trent engine.

By the early 1990s, the new top management at General Motors – the president, Lloyd Reuss, and the chairman, Bob Stemple – in reviewing their business decided that Allison, with its focus on gas turbines, was not a core business to them and that its $1-billion turnover at that time was really too small to fit into the automobile manufacturer's operation with a total turnover of $129 billion. Other subsidiaries – EDS, the computer services company, and Hughes, the aircraft-component and satellite-and-missile manufacturer – were not in the automobile business either, but they were larger than Allison and structured as stand-alone businesses with separate Boards.

At this point, some of Allison's major projects, especially supplying engines for the Brazilian Embraer and the V-22 Osprey engine, were at a critical stage of development, and the whole helicopter programme was under review.

The Allison management team did not favour being acquired by either GE or Pratt & Whitney, suspecting that within a short time most of the manufacturing would be transferred to the plants of the parent company. A request for offers was issued in early 1992, and offers came from Rolls-Royce, Pratt & Whitney, GE and Allied Signal, but all of them had unacceptable contingencies attached to them. Rolls-Royce offered $300 million, but General Motors turned it down, expressing concern about the possibility of the regulatory authorities vetoing a takeover from a non-US company because of Allison's defence contracts. Backed by the investment group Clayton, Dubilier & Rice, Blake Wallace and Mike Hudson offered General Motors $500 million, but that too was turned down. For the remainder of 1992, Wallace and Hudson explored ways to raise money for a management buy-out and talked to a number of companies in Europe, including Rolls-Royce, BTR (now merged with Siebe and called Invensys), ABB and Fiat. Finally, in the autumn of 1993, they, with Clayton, Dubilier & Rice, offered General Motors $325 million, and in December 1993 this was accepted.

The code name used by Rolls-Royce in contemplating the acquisition of Allison was Project Sioux, and in May 1993 John Rose, Managing Director of the Aerospace Group at that time, made a presentation to the Rolls-Royce Board on the objectives, commercial logic, regulatory issues, business valuation, shareholder-value enhancement and organisational structure outline associated with a bid. Rose believed Allison was now expecting an approach from Rolls-Royce 'on a wider basis than a series of joint ventures' where, anyway, 'it was Rolls-Royce's view that the full potential for cost savings could not be achieved'. In the view of Sir Ralph Robins, Allison's long-term future as an independent company was in doubt, and he supported the full takeover approach.

Consequently, Rolls-Royce was watching all this activity with interest and came to the conclusion that Clayton, Dubilier & Rice would soon want to take its profit and move on. The shorter the time that they held their investment, the better the return on capital when they sold it. Both Rolls-Royce and Pratt & Whitney stayed close to the financiers, and Pratt & Whitney came close enough to purchasing Allison to carry out a due diligence exercise with the management. However, Clayton, Dubilier & Rice became concerned that an attempted purchase by Pratt & Whitney could be blocked by anti-trust problems, and in 1994 they began to favour an acquisition by Rolls-Royce, especially as they appreciated that Rolls-Royce wanted to invest in the USA and would be most unlikely to remove work from the Allison plant.

Rolls-Royce sent in a team to assess Allison's prospects. The report sent to the Board in October made these positive assessments:

There was a solid on-going military programme supplying the C130 and the P-3 multiple helicopter. There were also significant future military programmes – the V-22, the Comanche helicopter and the updated C-130J. There were 25,000 Allison engines in service providing a robust spares stream. There were sales approaching $100 million in industrial power products. There were two new engines with good long-term potential, the 7500 lb thrust AE3007 and the turboprop AE2100. The margins on mature engines and spares were good. The Department of Defence was a good customer, and there were some high quality technology contracts including a potential 25 per cent share in GE future military programmes.

The team also saw great opportunities for integration and rationalisation with Rolls-Royce in several areas – including repair and overhaul, product support, manufacturing, technology, engineering and procurement – and with Rolls-Royce Inc.

In 1904, the same year that the Hon. C.S. Rolls met Henry Royce,
Jim Allison joined two partners to set up the Concentrated Acetylene
Company. This was the precursor to the Allison Engine Company.

Allison was one of a number of US manufacturers involved in the
production of Liberty engines. However, Allison's true success story with
the Liberty came with the invention of the steel-backed bronze bearing.

OPPOSITE TOP: On Memorial Day, 30 May 1911, the first Indianapolis
Speedway 500-mile International Sweepstakes Race was held at
what became known as the 'Brickyard'.

OPPOSITE BOTTOM: After the First World War, racing resumed at the
'Brickyard', and the Allison team won the first post-war race in
a modified Peugeot.

The magnificently effective Lockheed P-38 Lightning, perhaps the Allison V-1710 engine's most successful application. It was called *Der Gabelschwanz Teufel* (The Fork-tailed Devil) by the Germans. Allison produced 29,862 engines for the P-38.

Known as both a brilliant engineer and a gentleman, Ed Newill (left) was transferred from General Motors' Frigidaire plant in Dayton to Indianapolis to organise Allison production in the Second World War. He led the conversion from the production of piston engines to turbine engines and to transmissions. Under him, the Allison engineers invented the hydromatic transmission. Here, he is with Jimmy Doolittle, who led the famous Doolittle raid on Japan after the attack on Pearl Harbor and who later called on Allison as part of his task of liaising with suppliers on behalf of USAAF. Doolittle had also won the Schneider Trophy for the USA in 1925 in a Curtiss 3RC-2.

An early P-51 Mustang, powered by the Allison V-1710. This engine was later replaced in the P-51 by the then more highly developed Merlin 60 engine, the two-speed, two-stage intercooled supercharging of which gave the Mustang, as the British called the P-51, a phenomenal high-altitude performance.

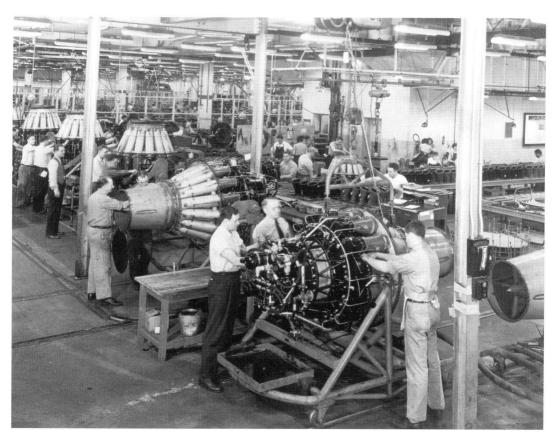

The J-33 was one of the many derivatives of the Whittle W2. It was engineered originally by General Electric but was built by Allison, who went on to produce 15,525.

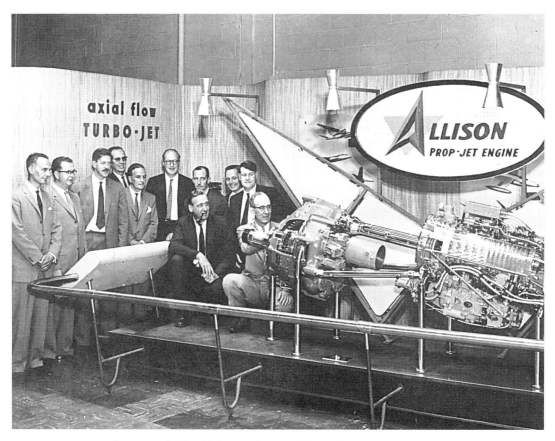

Rolls-Royce had collaborated with Allison for many years before
Rolls-Royce finally acquired the company in 1995. Here,
in 1959, Ed Newill, the Allison General Manager, is showing the
Allison prop-jet engine to a group of Rolls-Royce engineers
including Rex Nicholson, Norman Priestley, Peter Braybrook,
Trevor Salt and Roy Speed.

OPPOSITE TOP: Allison's understanding of gearboxes mounted on
shafts, gleaned from its wartime experience, combined with its
new understanding of gas turbines, yielded a series of turboprop
engines that culminated in the historic T56. It has been in
continuous production since 1953, with over 16,000 engines built.

OPPOSITE BOTTOM: The C130 Hercules, a most noble workhorse
employed in tactical airlift in over 60 countries. Powered for many
years by the Allison T56, it is now fitted with the
Rolls-Royce AE 2100.

TOP: Also powered by the Allison T56, the Electra was Lockheed's chosen aircraft for its re-entry into the civil market. In spite of being one of the most thoroughly tested aircraft in aviation history, it suffered some catastrophic accidents. Fortunately, there was never any question of these being caused by engine failure.

BOTTOM: At the request of Defense Secretary, Robert McNamara, Allison and Rolls-Royce collaborated to produce an Americanised version of the Rolls-Royce Spey, which was called the TF41. It powered the LTV A-7, a single-engine fighter bomber that became one of the most heavily used aircraft in the Vietnam War.

The helicopter engine, the Model 250, has been produced by Allison since the 1950s, powering over 130 different aircraft types. There are still 17,000 engines flying in over 140 countries. Here, the Model 250-C40B powers a Bell 430 intermediate twin.

Mike Hudson, recently retired as vice-chairman of Rolls-Royce North America, worked hard to make sure that Allison was acquired by Rolls-Royce. After the acquisition, he said: '[Sir Ralph Robins] gave [us] his personal assurance that Rolls-Royce intended to stay in Indianapolis, that Allison would retain its identity and that his vision was for Allison to continue to grow.' He is seen here with the engines produced at Indianapolis. Top row, left to right: T800, Model 501, Model 250; bottom row, left to right: AE 1107, AE 3007, AE 2100.

OPPOSITE: The T406 (BOTTOM) was specifically designed for the tilt-rotor V-22 (TOP), which required the engine to operate in conditions ranging from full nose-up to full nose-forward. The engine was certified both for military use in an aircraft-carrier environment and for civilian use.

The regional-jet market expanded rapidly in the mid-1990s, and
the Brazilian Embraer company benefited accordingly. Its
EMB-145, powered by the AE 3007, was a striking success.

Powered by the Rolls-Royce AE 3007-C, the Cessna Citation X set no
fewer than eight world air-speed records in 2000.

Jim Guyette, President of Rolls-Royce North America Inc., was persuaded out of retirement in 1997 following a successful career in civil aviation that had culminated in a spell as chief operating officer at United Airlines. His responsibilities include Rolls-Royce's plant in Indianapolis.

More specifically, a base in the USA would be helpful in trying to get the RB 211-535 on to the Lockheed C5, either new-build or re-engine, and on to the Boeing B-52 as a re-engine, and in trying to get the RTM322 on to the McDonnell Douglas AH64 and the Medium Lift Helicopter. US corporate citizenship would improve prospects in the military market, which would be helpful in the promotion of the EJ200 and ASTOVL (Advanced Short Take-Off/Vertical Landing) aircraft. Also, Allison's access to US research and development programmes from DoD, NASA and DARPA (Defense Advanced Research Project Agency), when coupled with Rolls-Royce's expertise, would provide increased capability for the Indianapolis facility and to the US Government.

There were three main reasons why Rolls-Royce should buy Allison. It would:

- broaden the Rolls-Royce business base
- enable Rolls-Royce to contribute to US Defense and enhance Allison's US research and development programmes
- position Rolls-Royce to expand its US sales.

As for the price paid, it was justified on the income that would come from spares for the T56 which powered the C130 Hercules, apart from other extras already mentioned.

Due diligence was carried out through the summer and autumn of 1994, and John Sandford, Managing Director of the Aerospace Group, told the Board in September that there had been full Cherokee (the code name had changed for the new bid) co-operation and response to Rolls-Royce's detailed enquiries. He said:

Whilst, not unexpectedly, there were some hazards, there had been no surprises. There was also some good news – military business would give Rolls-Royce the chance to improve performance and margins. Nothing had been found to change the basis of Rolls-Royce's initial strategic assessment.

The Chairman, Sir Ralph Robins, emphasised that the rationale for the acquisition was driven by three principal factors:

- the need for Rolls-Royce to preserve and develop its contribution to the US Defense programmes, which was not sustainable without a strong US presence
- the respective product ranges were interlocking
- the benefit of two new engine developments that had largely already been paid for and which were capable of successful exploitation.

The deal was struck, and on 21 November 1994 it was announced that

Rolls-Royce had acquired Allison for $525 million [at that time equivalent to £320 million]. To finance it, Rolls-Royce launched a £300-million placing and open offer. In spite of this, the Rolls-Royce share price advanced slightly as analysts assessed the long-term benefits. Apart from broadening Rolls-Royce's range of engines, especially at the lower-thrust end, the acquisition would provide Rolls-Royce with a manufacturing base in the USA, which was seen as important to boost Rolls-Royce's chances of involvement in future US Defense programmes. Robins said:

Getting on new programmes such as ASTOVL and JAST [Joint Advanced Strike Technology] will require a constituency in the US.

Many observers felt that one of the most promising military markets was large turboprop engines, where Allison had a virtual monopoly, while their other strong market position, helicopter engines, would also have strong growth prospects given the swing in defence budgets towards rapid response and surveillance.

At the Board meeting held on 24 November, Robins was able to report that:

City reaction to the Company's announcement had been good. Whilst there have been some comments on the price, the strategy had been fully understood. [Press comment was generally favourable. Even the usually hard-to-please *Lex* in the *Financial Times* said: 'Rolls-Royce's proposed acquisition of Allison Engine makes sound industrial and commercial sense. It takes the UK company into new niches within the defence market – for example large turbo-prop engines and small engines used by light helicopters – and broadens its offering in civil markets. The deal appears to make financial sense as well.'] In Indianapolis the announcement had also been well received. At a series of meetings with the workforce and Union representatives the atmosphere had been positive and co-operative. The local Mayor was wholly supportive, the local Senators were on side and Congressman Burton, who had expressed reservations about the deal as a foreign takeover, had also been persuaded of the advantages and had become supportive … In the UK, the Chairman had briefed Michael Heseltine [the Secretary of State for Defence]. His reaction was constrained by the need for the matter to be submitted to the OFT [Office of Fair Trading]. The Ministry of Defence seemed to be supportive of the deal and its relevance to the FLA [Future Large Aircraft] programme had been noted. At British Aerospace, Chairman Dick Evans had understood Rolls-Royce's position.

John Sandford confirmed that a very positive attitude had been expressed by Allison senior management. Both GE and Allied Signal, who had joint ventures with Allison, seemed prepared to maintain their relationships.

Robins also reported that both Bernd Pischetsrieder and Eberhard von

Kuenheim understood the reasons for the deal, but that 'the situation as it affected BMW Rolls-Royce would need to be carefully managed'.

The one possible snag that could jeopardise the deal was US security. Section 721 of the Defense Production Act (more commonly known as Exon-Florio, after the names of its two authors: former Senator Jim Exon and former Congressman Jim Florio) was enacted by the US Congress in 1988. The Exon-Florio provision granted the President of the United States broad authority to review all 'mergers, acquisitions, and takeovers that could result in foreign control of persons engaged in interstate commerce in the United States'. Following review, the President was authorised to block a transaction if he determined that it presented a threat to 'national security' and that no other provision of law was adequate to deal with the national security concern.

The administration of the statute was delegated to the Committee on Foreign Investment in the United States (CFIUS). The process of reviewing any given acquisition involved several steps. Upon receiving notice of a proposed acquisition by a foreign investor, CFIUS conducted a 30-day review to determine whether the transaction presented national security considerations that warranted a full-scale investigation. If CFIUS found that the transaction did not pose such concerns, the process ended there. However, if CFIUS found that it did pose concerns, the review process continued with a 45-day investigation, culminating in a recommendation to the President as to whether he should block the acquisition.

Notice under Exon-Florio was voluntary, but as Rolls-Royce's legal advisers in Washington, Kaye Scholer, pointed out:

A foreign investor who seeks to avoid CFIUS review by failing to provide notice of a transaction does so at his peril. Acquisitions for which CFIUS does not receive notice remain *forever* open to executive branch scrutiny and potential divestment orders.

While 'national security' was not defined specifically, in the preamble to the regulations CFIUS noted:

Generally speaking, transactions that involve products, services and technologies that are important to US national defense requirements will usually be deemed significant with respect to the national security.

Without doubt, Allison fell into that category. A measurable level of Allison's business was on 'highly classified', fully funded US Government programmes, including Allison's leading-edge work on advanced technology demonstrators under the Pentagon's Integrated High Performance Turbine Engine Technology programme and also its proprietary Lamilloy blade-cooling technology.

Nor was Rolls-Royce helped by amendments made to the Exon-Florio provision in the Defense Authorization Act for Fiscal Year 1993, which stated that any amendments require a full 45-day formal investigation of any case in which an entity 'controlled by or acting on behalf of a foreign government' is engaged in an acquisition that could affect national security. The British Government still held one 'golden' share in Rolls-Royce.

In their advice to Rolls-Royce, the law firm of Kaye Scholer concluded:

Since 1988, several hundred transactions have been submitted to CFIUS for review. Some, albeit a few, have been subjected to the formal 45-day investigation, and in one instance – involving the purchase by the China National Aero-Technology Import and Export Corporation, a Chinese government-owned company, of MAMCO Manufacturing Inc., a Seattle-based aircraft part manufacturer – the President actually invoked his authority to compel foreign divestment under Exon-Florio. [A few others had been withdrawn and the acquisition process terminated when it appeared they would be rejected in a full CFIUS review.]

The fact that only one acquisition has been blocked since the Exon-Florio amendment was enacted – and few acquisitions subjected to formal investigation – has led some to conclude that Exon-Florio is a 'paper tiger'. The reality is quite different. The Exon-Florio process ensures close scrutiny of foreign acquisitions. Investigations are avoided through careful planning, and through the structuring of foreign transactions to address national security concerns. In some cases, significant constraints may be imposed on the foreign interest's oversight and control of the US interest, particularly where the US interest is engaged in the performance of classified contracts. For all of these reasons, it is prudent for all parties to consider the Exon-Florio process when a merger, acquisition or a joint venture is contemplated that involves a foreign interest.

In other words: Rolls-Royce, if you want to buy Allison, take the Exon-Florio amendment very seriously. And take it seriously they did. When Rolls-Royce appeared before the committee – and there were 26 departments and sub-departments involved – Charles Coltman, Director of Strategy for Rolls-Royce, made sure he was the only Briton and that every other witness for Allison was an American. Rolls-Royce set up a two-tier company arrangement with former high-ranking military personnel such as Rear Admiral Riley Mixson and Major General Ray Franklin on the Board of the primary company (later, General Ronald Fogleman was also added), and a separate Board with outside directors was responsible for what was known as Allison Advanced Development Corporation (AADC), a separate company established as a wholly owned subsidiary of Allison.

With the negotiations led by Larry Garrett, a lawyer and former Secretary of the US Navy, this tiered 'Chinese wall' approach was accepted by the

CFIUS committee, and the acquisition was given the go-ahead on 23 March 1995. However, there was no slackening in the protection of Allison technology, as is made clear by this memo from John Rose, then Managing Director of the Aerospace Group, on 7 April 1995:

ALLISON – SPECIAL SECURITY AGREEMENT

Now that the acquisition of Allison is complete, the various US Government Agencies will be paying particular attention to ensure that Allison and Rolls-Royce comply with the controls established to protect US technology.

The terms of the Special Security Agreement between Allison and Rolls-Royce are still being finalised. It will include a Visitation Policy and a Technology Control plan. The draft policy requires formal notification and approval seven days in advance, of all visits between employees of Allison and Rolls-Royce and its subsidiary companies, with the exception of the Allison Inside Directors i.e. P. Heiden/J. W. Sandford. In addition, Allison employees must log all telephone, fax and letter and social communications, although prior approval is not required.

It is vital that Rolls-Royce are seen to act to the spirit and letter of these requirements, particularly at this time. Failure to do so may result in further tightening of these already burdensome restrictions.

Visit approval is for specific single visits, and is in addition to the long standing requirements for visitors to hold the appropriate level of HMG/NATO security clearance. Confirmation of, or queries concerning, clearance levels may be made with the Security Department, Bristol or the Chief Security Adviser in Derby.

All visits to Indianapolis must be approved within the business group and endorsed by P. Heiden prior to travel.

Now that the acquisition of Allison was complete, the Board appointed J. George Mikelsons as its new Chairman, an appointment cleared by the US Government Agencies. The Chairman of his own airline, American Trans Air, Mikelsons had lived a truly remarkable life. Born in Riga in Latvia in 1937 with a highly talented violinist for a father, he had been forced to flee to Germany in 1944 with his mother, leaving his father behind. He told the author in September 2001 that he could vividly recall searching among dead bodies in the bombed cities of Germany for scraps of food.

When the War was over, and with Germany split into four zones and occupied by the USA, Britain, France and the Soviet Union, Mikelsons and his mother moved from camp to camp within the British sector, hoping to find Mikelsons senior but not even knowing whether he was alive. In the meantime, the father had come to Germany to look for his wife and son. Fortunately, he met a colonel who was an accomplished pianist, and they struck a deal. As the colonel toured the British Zone playing concerts to the troops, Mikelsons could accompany him on the violin. That way they might find mother and son – which is exactly what happened.

The reunited family spent four years in 'displaced persons' camps waiting to return to Latvia, and when in 1949 it became clear that the Soviet Union did not want such people back, up popped the Colonel again and helped them to emigrate to Australia, a country long on resources but short on people. Unfortunately, in the late 1940s and throughout the 1950s, Australia's priorities did not lie in building up orchestras, and Mikelsons senior was not able to use his skills as a violinist. The family had to wait until 1959 for their next stroke of luck. That year, the conductor of a visiting orchestra from Indianapolis was so struck by the skills of an Australian violinist who played with them that he asked him who had taught him. When he told the conductor it was Mikelsons, the conductor persuaded Mikelsons to come to Indianapolis to teach his other violinists. By this time, our George Mikelsons was 22 and, having told his father that in spite of his inherited musical talent he did not want to become a professional musician, showed a longing to fly. His father backed him, and after he had learned to fly he joined a flying club as a pilot. In the days before deregulation, the only way flights could be offered at lower-than-regulation prices was through joining one of the flying clubs.

After years of flying for the club, Mikelsons started his own flying club, American Trans Air, in 1973 with a $50,000 loan and one Boeing 720. After five years, he was able to buy a second 720. Then came airline deregulation, though Mikelsons waited until 1981 before applying for a certificate to operate charter flights. Five years later, he took American Trans Air into scheduled services, and it was in the mid-1980s that he first came into contact with Roll-Royce. Boeing had taken back some Lockheed TriStars from Delta Airlines in exchange for some new Boeing aircraft and offered them to Mikelsons at a good price. Mikelsons checked with Rolls-Royce that the engines would be all right, and, to his surprise, the company advised him to be very careful. The engines were early RB 211-22s, and Delta had only ever used them for internal US flights. Rolls-Royce knew that Mikelsons was going to use them for transatlantic flights and advised Mikelsons not to buy the aircraft before Rolls-Royce engineers had looked at the engines. In the end, he bought the aircraft, no doubt at an even lower price, and bought re-conditioned engines from Rolls-Royce. He was eternally grateful to Rolls-Royce, and, indeed, in 2002 American Trans Air still operates fifteen TriStars, all with RB 211s, and a number of RB 211-535E4-powered Boeing 757s.

Apart from his closeness to Rolls-Royce, George Mikelsons was a very acceptable Chairman to the US authorities, as American Trans Air had long been close to the American military, having carried more troops in recent years than any other airline. For his part, Mikelsons has no doubt that Rolls-Royce, with its 'enormous corporate integrity, will be good for Allison, and that in its turn Allison will be very good for Rolls-Royce in the USA'.

Mike Hudson echoed these sentiments, saying:

That the acquisition went so well is a tribute to Rolls-Royce's stature in the world's business community and in the eyes of the government, and its reputation for being a people-oriented company. But they put a lot of effort into it. Rolls-Royce Chairman, Sir Ralph Robins, came to Indianapolis and met with employees, and then with the local politicians and civic leaders. He gave them his personal assurance that Rolls-Royce intended to stay in Indianapolis, that Allison would retain its identity and that his vision was for Allison to continue to grow. So we had someone who came in like a statesman, someone who could talk about the long-term future of the business and someone who thoroughly understands the business. That is the sort of philosophy that we can relate to and that our customers appreciate.

EMBRAER TO THE FORE

In the seven years that Rolls-Royce has owned Allison, the merits of the purchase have become evident from the big increase in sales and deliveries, and the big bonus has been the success in selling the AE 3007 to the Brazilian company Embraer to power its series of regional aircraft. In the reasons-to-buy presentations made to the Board when the acquisition was being considered, first in the early 1990s and then again in 1994, this engine was not seen as a strong reason for purchase.

We have already seen how Allison wanted to enter the civil market in the 1980s and how it began a joint venture with Rolls-Royce on an engine called the RB 580. Essentially, this would have the T406 engine as its core, and Allison hoped they could sell it to Rolls-Royce, who would then add a low-pressure spool and take it to a 7,000 to 10,000 lb-thrust turbofan. The targets were the Embraer aircraft and the Short Brothers FJX, a 50-seat regional aircraft. Unfortunately for Allison, the Canadian company Bombardier bought Short Brothers and cancelled the aircraft. In the meantime, the Brazilian company hit financial turbulence, and Sir Ralph Robins decided that Rolls-Royce's priorities should be with the Trent family of engines.

In spite of these difficulties, Allison decided they would repackage the engine and develop the first turbofan the company had designed by itself. They called it the GMA 3007 and, keeping close to Embraer, put it forward in competitive programmes two or three times as Embraer struggled with its finances. In the meantime, Allison successfully sold a version of the engine, the GMA 3007C, to Cessna to power their new Citation X. The Citation became the launch aircraft for the engine and carried out all the flight testing in 1991 and 1992.

At the same time as Allison was trying to sell the GMA 3007 to Embraer, it decided to enter the competition to power the new regional aircraft being developed by SAAB, the SAAB 2000. Al Novick, Commercial Director of Allison at the time, flew to Linköping in Sweden in December 1988 to talk to

SAAB. He recalled later that the Chairman of SAAB thought he was from Allis-Chalmers, the agricultural-equipment manufacturers. Novick offered the T56 and, in competing with GE, who were putting forward their GE38, offered to supply the nacelle as well. The Swedes accepted Allison's bid, and an agreement was signed on the propitious 4 July 1989. It was Allison's first contract on a civil transport aircraft since it sold Lockheed its 501D3 turboprop to power the Electra at the end of the 1950s.

They were not sure whether SAAB was right to go for the turboprop or Embraer with the turbofan, but Allison decided to go for supplying both. It was the first company to build a common core for both turboprop and turbofan. Al Novick would say later:

We would classify it as a model development programme, in part because we started with a core that had 50,000 hours of development running on it. We were developing a turbofan at the same time as two other programmes were developing the core. It made it really quite painless for us.

As it turned out, Allison was well rewarded for its persistence with Embraer because its turbofan approach won out over the turboprop approach of SAAB, who built only 64 SAAB 2000s.

Relations with Embraer cooled a little during the Clayton, Dubilier & Rice ownership of Allison because of Embraer's respect for General Motors, but close harmony was restored following Rolls-Royce's purchase in 1994, ratified in 1995. In early 1995, Al Novick, along with Colin Green (who had been sent by Rolls-Royce to oversee the merging of Allison and Rolls-Royce), visited Embraer in Brazil; a deal was struck, and the Embraer was launched with the AE 3007. The aircraft was certificated at the end of 1996, and the first deliveries made to Continental Express in December 1996.

Since that time, the sales increase for jet-powered regional aircraft has taken off, aided initially by the American public turning against turboprop aircraft after an American Eagle ATR72, powered by Pratt & Whitney turboprop engines, crashed on a flight from Indianapolis to Chicago. In June 1997, *Flight International* was writing:

It has been bubbling away for years, but the regional jet market is finally exploding into action. More than a dozen regional jet types are either under intense study, in developments or in production. The increased tempo has sent the engine makers into a flurry of activity, and the cut-throat power struggle is every bit as competitive as anything the industry has seen in the high-thrust bracket … The same engines [the GE CF34-8C and the SNECMA/Pratt & Whitney SPW14] are pitted against Allison's AE30XX for another potential 70-seater project, Embraer's EMB-70. Allison is thought to be firmly in the driving seat if the Brazilian manufacturer opts to go ahead with either its 70-seat or 30-seat regional jets, as its AE3007 is in production for the EMB-145. Allison is also busy developing a high thrust 42kN version, dubbed the A1, for a hot-and-high variant of the -145.

Founded by Brazil's air force in 1969, Embraer – Empresa Brasileira de Aeronáutica S.A. in São José dos Campos in the State of São Paulo – had invested heavily in development and engineering, winning a reputation for quality with customers in 37 countries. Its Brasilia 30-seat passenger turbo-prop and Tucano military trainer became leaders in their markets. However, with the Brazilian Government apparently ever willing to bail it out, costs ran out of control, leading to mounting losses that reached $337 million in 1994. At this point, the company was privatised, and Maurício Botelho was brought in to run the company from Bozano Simenson, the Rio de Janeiro investment bank that led and advised Embraer's majority owners. Botelho stemmed the losses by cutting costs and focused the company on its markets, saying:

Everything in the space between the shareholders and the market is mutable. With less than 100 customers, you have to concentrate entirely on what they want.

Among his priorities was a speedy completion of the EMB-145 programme. Conceived in 1989, at the same time as its competitor the CRJ of Bombardier, Embraer's slower development gave the CRJ three years' run at the market before the EMB-145 was certified in 1996. Nevertheless, the EMB-145 had been a striking success. At the Paris Air Show in June 1997, it picked up 42 firm orders and 25 options from American Airlines' regional subsidiary, American Eagle, as well as a further 25 firm orders from Continental Express, the regional arm of Continental Airlines. This followed a contract for an initial 25 firm orders and 175 options signed the previous autumn.

In total, by July 1997 Embraer had secured 132 firm orders and 194 options, worth about $5 billion in total, for the EMB-145. The company promoted it as a 'jet for turboprop costs'. Allison, as the exclusive power-plant supplier, was very happy with all this.

And the future looked bright. Bob Booth of Aviation Management Services in Miami said:

People prefer jets [as opposed to turboprops]. Fifty-seaters are becoming very significant. There are many routes that don't justify a 100-seater, where 50-seaters can do two or three flights a day. On business routes frequency is everything and two flights a day are much more than twice as good as one.

The AE 3007C version of the engine, rated at 7,000 lb thrust, was certificated by the US Federal Aviation Administration for the Cessna Citation X in February 1995 and for the EMB-145 in mid-1996, and Allison received a further boost for the engine in 1995 when the AE 3007H version was selected by the US Defense Department for its Tier II Plus unmanned-aerial-vehicle programme led by Teledyne Ryan Aeronautical. The requirement called for long-endurance flying at altitudes up to 70,000 feet.

The superb performance of the Citation X and its Rolls-Royce AE 3007C engines was proved by the serial record breaker Steve Fossett, who, by mid-October 2000, was the proud possessor of eight world air-speed records, all achieved in the Citation X. The most dramatic was his 41 hours, 13 minutes and 11 seconds round-the-world record for medium-sized aircraft, which he set in February 2000. It lopped no less than six-and-a-half hours off the previous record set in 1988 by Edward Kaiser in a Hawker 800.

Fossett had to make six fuel stops, and these provided the drama and biggest threat to his record attempt. The first problem arose in Agadir, Morocco – the centre of a somewhat more serious crisis 90 years earlier – where the fuelling company wanted cash not a credit card. A much more costly delay occurred in India where the procedure is to re-file the flight plan after refuelling and customs clearance. China went smoothly, and on their final stop at Midway (also better known as being the turning point of the Pacific War in World War Two) they were rewarded for their meticulous research work. They landed just before midnight to avoid a nesting colony of more than 800,000 albatross, which fly and feed their young during the day. By arriving in the middle of the night, Fossett avoided both the birds and other airline traffic. They were able to stop on the runway, where a fuel truck was waiting. In 10 minutes, he had taken on 1,600 gallons of fuel, and his total time on the ground was just 18 minutes, 44 seconds.

The Citation X's top speed is Mach 0.92 and its service ceiling 51,000 feet. Fossett cruised at 45,000 feet and mostly at 0.889 Mach, sacrificing a little speed for range. In spite of all the aircraft's records, Cessna felt some improvements could be made and talked to Rolls-Royce about some changes to improve performance. As a result, the current Citation X has a 5 per cent greater thrust from its Rolls-Royce AE 3007C engines. This means that take-off rolls will be shorter, allowing operators access to many more airports. It will also allow Cessna to add 400lb to the aircraft's maximum weight, enabling them to make previously optional equipment standard.

In September 1997, Embraer launched its 37-seat EMB-135, saying it would invest $100 million in the programme and that it hoped to sell 500 within ten years. Allison won a competition involving Allied Signal's AS108 and Pratt & Whitney's PW308 to win the position as sole engine supplier with its AE 3007-A3. Certification for the EMB-135 was scheduled for May 1999 with deliveries beginning in July that year. The orders soon rolled in for the $12-million aircraft. By September 1998, commitments had been received for over half the 500 Embraer expected to sell.

All the engine makers were predicting a bright future for this segment of the market. Allison, Allied Signal and GE all expected markets of around 4,000 regional jets with fewer than 100 seats over the next twenty years. What none was sure about was whether the majority would be in the 30-to-50-seat or the 70-to-100-seat area. Allison saw the bigger potential in the smaller aircraft, although Ken Roberts, regional-market analyst at Allison, expressed some caution, saying:

We still firmly believe in the 30-seater, but the shift is predicated on the operating costs happening the way many expect them to.

He expected a demand for more than 1,800 30-seaters between 1998 and 2017, of which '60–70 per cent will be jets'.

Allied Signal agreed, saying:

Our opinion has changed in the 30/35-seat jet market. We originally saw a demand for maybe 500 to 700 but now we have a view that there will be between 1,400 and 1,500 because they are effective in replacing turboprops.

GE agreed too but felt it could not easily justify the cost of developing an engine for this market. GE's small-commercial-turbofan department general manager, Frank Klaus, said:

We would love to have an engine in that market because we think there is great potential. We have prospective customers coming to us and saying 'we want a GE engine' but we don't have one to take off the shelf. We'd have to develop one. We've studied it and we don't have an answer.

To give substance to these optimistic predictions, Embraer received a massive $2-billion order in September 1998 from American Eagle for 75 ERJ-135s (Embraer had changed the EMB prefix to ERJ) with another 75 options. For the newly formed Rolls-Royce Allison, it meant 500 million dollars' worth of orders for its AE 3007. And to emphasise the point, Embraer announced its first profit for a decade for the year 1998. Its sales had increased from $746 million in 1997 to $1.31 billion, and it had turned a $29.6-million loss into a $102.9-million profit.

And the good news continued. When Embraer developed a new regional jet, the ERJ-140, in its family, Rolls-Royce Allison became sole supplier. In September 2000, Embraer announced orders for 93 of this new aircraft, mainly from American Eagle. In June 2001, American Airlines' subcontractors – Trans States Airlines and Chautauqua Airlines – bought 60 ERJ-140s. Mike Terrett said:

The AE-3007 is now one of our fastest-growing engine programmes. Firm orders and options now total 1,600.

Rolls-Royce could feel very satisfied with its acquisition of Allison in 1994/5. There had been some amalgamation problems, and the early days of the AE 3007 had not run entirely smoothly. The engine suffered some serious bearing problems, significant enough for the Chairman, Sir Ralph Robins, to take a personal interest in finding a solution. It was fortunate that Rolls-Royce's reputation for sorting problems was in place to protect Allison, which until the late 1990s had little experience of the civil-airline market and therefore no reputation to fall back on.

Gordon Bethune, President of Continental, had said of a planned visit from Sir Ralph Robins, 'Look forward to seeing him, tell him to bring his tool kit.' But by 2001, Rolls-Royce could look at the Allison range of engines and their applications and have warm feelings about the future. In the turbofan sector, the AE 3007 was powering the Cessna Citation X, the Embraer ERJ-135, -140 and -145, and Northrop Grumman's Ryan-Aeronautical-Center Global Hawk, while the F120 from AADC in conjunction with GE was a contender for the Joint Strike Fighter (which we shall read more about in Chapter Six). In the turboshaft segment, the AE 1107C powered the Bell Boeing V-22 Osprey, and the Model 250 – first developed, as we saw, at the end of the 1950s – powered the Northrop Grumman/Schweizer VTUAV, the MD Helicopters MD-500, MD-520N NOTAR, MD-530 and MD-600N, as well as the Bell 206 Jetranger, Bell 407 and Bell 430. Finally in turboprops, the AE 2100 powered the Lockheed C130J, the Lockheed/Alenia C27J, the ShinMaywa US-1A Kai and the SAAB 2000, while the T56 – with its origins in the T38 first developed as long ago as 1945 – powered the Northrop Grumman E-2C+, the Lockheed Martin C130A-H, the P-3C Orion and the E-2C Hawkeye. Lastly, the Model 250 powered the Tradewind Turbines Bonanza, the O&N Aircraft Cessna P210, the BN Group Turbine Islander, and the AerMacchi SF-260TP and MT290T Predigio.

And we must not forget that the Allison industrial and marine engine family came from the A501, which was developed into an engine to power destroyers and cruisers in the US Navy. There are now over 300 in service. The mechanical drive version is the sole power plant for the Boeing Jetfoil, many of which were built under licence by Kawasaki Heavy Industries in Japan.

Add to all of this the benefits of having a base in what would always be Rolls-Royce's biggest market in both the civil and military fields, and the acquisition did indeed, as *Lex* in the *Financial Times* said at the time, make industrial, commercial and financial sense.

CHAPTER FIVE

'THE NAME IS SYNONYMOUS WITH THE BEST'

'YOU CANNOT GET A ROLLS-ROYCE PRICE FOR A HOLE'
SHAREHOLDER VALUE
'IF IT ISN'T HURTING, IT ISN'T WORKING'
FOR SALE
THE BENTLEY BOYS
FAST CAR, FAST SERVICE

'YOU CANNOT GET A ROLLS-ROYCE PRICE FOR A HOLE'

FOR THE FIRST TIME in the history of this business we have put together a ten-year plan, starting in 1988.

This was said in 1987 by Peter Ward, the new Chief Executive of Rolls-Royce Motor Cars. Just as Rolls-Royce plc was beginning a new era as an independent company and making strategic plans to build a world-class family of aero-engines, in the motor-car world great changes were taking place at the Rolls-Royce division of Vickers.

In Part Two, we saw how the Motor Car Division was split off in 1973 from the core company making aero-engines. It was then floated on the London Stock Exchange separately at a valuation of £33 million [about £500 million in 2002 terms] and was, at the time, the highest-value privatisation. Sealed bids from interested parties had not reached £30 million.

Eventually, a new model, the Silver Spirit, to replace the Silver Shadow which had been launched in 1965, was brought to the market in 1980. David Plastow, Chief Executive, was to say later that he felt the Board meeting in 1976, at which they debated whether to introduce this model, was the most crucial of his career. At the time, following the fuel crisis of 1973/4, voices were raised for caution and a postponement of any new model. However, courage won the day.

The Silver Spirit was based on the Silver Shadow II base unit, using the same engine and drive train but with a revised rear suspension and mineral-oil hydraulics (first used on the Corniche and the Camargue). Fritz Feller had succeeded John Blatchley as the chief designer. The styling was more angular than the Shadow, and the Spirit appeared much larger although it was only three inches longer and two inches wider. The main difference giving this appearance of extra size was the increase of 30 per cent in the glass area. At the same time, the Silver Spur replaced the Silver Wraith II and the Bentley Mulsanne replaced the T2 series. Modifications were also made to the Flying Lady mascot, the Spirit of Ecstasy. Safety laws were affecting bonnet mascots, or 'hood ornaments' as they were called in the USA. These were accommodated by the creation of a retractable Spirit of Ecstasy, which withdrew into the radiator shell if struck.

By the end of the 1970s, Rolls-Royce Motor Cars needed more money to expand, and a fellow engineering company, Vickers, whose defence and aerospace businesses had been nationalised, needed new products and management. A merger was arranged, though the idea won few plaudits. Even Plastow, who became managing director of the new Vickers group, said:

To be realistic there is no conventional synergy in the deal. We are taking two small engineering companies, and putting them together to make a sizeable one in international terms. In the end we will insulate ourselves from the business cycles and troughs.

Having said this, however, the group was immediately hit by the trough of the early-1980s recession, caused by another large hike in the price of oil. Rolls-Royce's sales fell by 25 per cent in 1982, prompting some radical changes at the factory at Crewe.

And 1983 was another disastrous year, when directors forecast production of 3,400 cars but only 1,500 were produced. For the first time ever, dealers were panicked into discounting. It had always been the marketing policy to have a waiting list for the cars. About 2,800 workers went on strike for five weeks, and, as the *Financial Times* reported, observers were taken aback by the 'sullenness outside the factory gates and the animosity bubbling to the surface in every conversation'.

One senior shop steward said:

There's a true class system which operates right through the plant. George Fenn [the managing director] is an absolute gentleman, but we hardly ever see him down in the factory.

And, even more worrying, as the recession eased from 1983 onwards, many of the company chairmen who had given up their Rolls-Royce did not return to the fold. Overall sales stalled at 2,400, well below the 3,300 achieved in the late 1970s. The company would have to change, sweep away its outdated personnel and factory practices and become much more market-oriented.

At the top, the old management was replaced. Plastow said later:

Clearly, I am indictable. I had presumed that all the people I left in place were going to be able to cope. I had not forecast the economic difficulties. They were a great bunch of men but they had all got to their late 50s and their departure was necessary.

In came younger men, mostly from the world of mass production. Peter Ward, the new managing director, had been marketing director at Peugeot Talbot and, before that, sales director at the BL subsidiary, Unipart. Mike Dunn, the new engineering director, came from product development at Ford; Ken Lea, the production director, came from the same job at Leyland Vehicles, while Malcolm Hart, the sales and marketing director, came from the job of franchising director at Austin Rover.

The new team put in new practices both on the shop floor and in marketing. The workforce was cut from 6,000 to 4,000, but those that were left were briefed at regular monthly meetings, and by 1987 the shop floor was linked to dealers' showrooms. Demand and production would at last be dovetailed. Dick Perry had run the division before Ward took over as managing director. A long-serving Rolls-Royce man, Perry had run the Mulliner Park Ward coachworks before Plastow had brought him to Crewe in 1982. He had immediately seen that the factory, with its fourteen trades unions, was being throttled by demarcation disputes and equally antiquated management practices. Although a piece-rate pay system was in operation, there was no way of checking whether the work had really been done. Piece-work needed the sort of organised workflow that had never existed in the Crewe factory. Workers who could not meet targets because of organisational chaos in the supply of components to the shop floor either did not receive their bonus or browbeat the management into giving it to them anyway.

There was virtually no stock control. If a worker needed an item, he would probably take it from someone else's bench or possibly make it himself – 62 per cent of the 80,000 components were manufactured in-house, including even nuts and bolts. This was partly due to Rolls-Royce not moving with the times but also partly because some suppliers were not interested in producing small quantities at competitive prices. By the mid-1980s, many changes had been made. Stock control was ensured by keeping components in a wire cage to which access could be gained only by use of an authorised plastic card. A £750,000 computer-controlled machine had been installed that made many parts previously manufactured manually and singly. Plenty more remained to be done. As Bob McClintock, machine-shop manager, pointed out:

Walk down the machine-shop and you can see banks of 30 Cincinnati drilling machines, manned by individuals who are drilling individual holes. Each requires its own setting. This is silly. You cannot get a Rolls-Royce price for a hole.

On the other hand, there were certain items for which you could demand a Rolls-Royce price and which were not changed. For example, most of the thousand hides used for the upholstery each week came from Denmark. They cost 40 per cent more than British ones, but they were half as likely to have been spiked by cows rubbing against barbed-wire fences. Each Spirit of Ecstasy, or 'flying lady' mascot, was still made from a wax model originally sculpted in 1911. However, each one, in the hand-finishing, was made slightly different and polished using crushed cherry stones. Those made for the Middle East had the lady kneeling. And of course, the fine line on the wheel discs was still painted on with a potter's wheel. Until the Silver Spirit, the fine lining on the bodywork was also still drawn by hand – from stem to stem!

Attacking factory costs was essential. The other essential need, of course, was to increase sales, and Peter Ward and his team brought techniques and practices that would have been considered totally alien to previous generations of Rolls-Royce salesmen. Potential customers were identified and targeted. As well as 'Old Money', Rolls-Royce now looked at 'Glitzerama', or what would now be called Celebs or Slebs. [There is a subtle difference here between Celebs – those such as 'Posh and Becks', who have achieved something in the public eye – and Slebs – those who have not, but for some reason hold a fascination for the media, such as Tara Palmer-Tomkinson.]

Rolls-Royce appointed a new advertising agency, Brookes & Vernons, which targeted 'new money' and the self-made millionaire – 'Do not be bashful about owning a Rolls-Royce. See it as the fulfilment of all your efforts.' Ward cut the dealer network from 72 to 38 and advertised second-hand Rolls-Royces to combat discounting. He went to New York, and, after being told by the Manhattan showroom executives that the local limit was 35 cars a year, appointed a young dealer who had been trading in 'grey-market' Rolls-Royces from Canada. In the following twelve months, he sold 175 cars.

One of Ward's greatest achievements was to revive the Bentley. In the early 1980s, scarcely distinguishable from the Rolls-Royce, it accounted for only 4 per cent of sales. He said:

Any marketing man worth half his salt would have been blind not to see that we had a name, in Bentley, that has unbelievable recall in history.

Reverting to the glorious days of the 1920s, the wire-mesh grille was fitted as standard to the cheapest model, the Bentley Eight. The Bentley Eight, launched in July 1984, was close to being a loss leader. With precisely the same engineering as a Rolls-Royce, its price was £49,500, about £6,000 cheaper than any other car sold by the company. As Ward said:

We had to put a limit on volume. It was a very, very tight margin car. Very close to break-even.

However, it brought in new customers, while the Bentley Mulsanne Turbo – with a maximum speed of 150 mph, the fastest luxury car in the world – selling for £85,000 and the Continental convertible at over £100,000 brought in the profits. For comparison, Rolls-Royce prices ranged from £73,000 for a Silver Spirit to £207,000 for a Phantom VI.

By the mid-1980s, the Bentley was selling almost as well as the Rolls-Royce, and in 1990, for the first time, Bentley sales outstripped Rolls-Royce worldwide: 1,714 to 1,601. In Britain – the largest market – Bentley enjoyed 60 per cent of Rolls-Royce Motors sales. By this time, the price of the Bentley Eight had been raised to a more comfortable £79,811, while the Turbo R, at £108,994 was £4,249 more expensive than the comparable Rolls-Royce Silver Spirit II. Even so, it outsold the Silver Spirit by 945 to 782.

In 1990, Rolls-Royce Motor Cars introduced its first completely new design since the Silver Spirit was launched in 1980. The Bentley Continental R had grown from a concept car shown at the 1985 Geneva Motor Show and was initially called 'Project 90'. William Woollard, presenter at that time of *Top Gear* on BBC television, said:

Biggles would have loved it.

Ward was delighted, saying:

We knew by then that the name Bentley had extraordinary recall. Project 90 told us that we could create a Bentley grand tourer. The instant boardroom reaction was 'Let's build it'. We were caught up in the euphoria but it didn't take long to realise that we already had an expanded range and that we could take our time.

As had become the tradition at Rolls-Royce, the new car was given an Asian country as a code name. In Part Two, we saw how the Silver Shadow had been called 'Tibet', and 'Burma' with a larger engine, while the Silver Cloud was called 'Siam'. The Bentley Continental R started life as 'Nepal'. Six Nepals were manufactured, and four were completed and tested for a year. Heat trials were carried out in Death Valley, California, and track trials in

131

southern Italy. Low-temperature trials were carried out at the Arctic Falls test centre in northern Sweden, and the car, weighing two-and-a-half tonnes, was driven around on a frozen lake, though only after an 18-tonne bulldozer had tested the ice. Avon designed tyres exclusively for the car.

However, there were some internal disagreements on styling. On two points, the modernists clashed with the traditionalists. The first was over whether the bonnet should have the symbolic Bentley 'winged B' as an upright mascot as well as in flat-badge form. A compromise was agreed whereby the shape was inscribed in the middle of the new alloy wheels.

People became more animated about the angle of the radiator. The traditionalists wanted it to lean slightly forward while the modernists wanted it to rake backwards. The modernists won. Nevertheless, the Bentley grille remained and was squatter. The car was as long as a Rolls-Royce but seemed to be lower. This was really a design illusion created by the 'power bulges' that swept from bonnet to boot to become a disguised spoiler at the back. With the shallow-angle rear window above and huge tyres below, the Bentley Continental R felt closer to the ground. In fact, a Rolls-Royce was only one inch taller.

The result was a beautiful, automatic-ride-control (ARC) motor car that would go from 0 to 60 mph in 6.5 seconds and leave a Jaguar XJR-S at the lights. At £160,000, it did cost a little more than the Jaguar or even the £111,999 Ferrari Testarossa and £129,950 Aston Martin Virage. Marketing Director, Malcolm Hart said:

When you are in the £125,000 to £250,000 band, price is not the significant factor.

While the Bentley Continental R was being developed during the second half of the 1980s, improvements were carried out on the existing range. The year 1987 saw the introduction of several improvements to the Silver Spirit range. From its introduction in 1980, fuel injection had been standard on cars exported to the USA and Japan. Australia followed in 1986, and fuel injection became standard for all markets in 1987. The 1987 engine complied with all European emission control standards. At the same time, the number of engine components was reduced by 40 per cent, and the engine produced greater power and better fuel economy. Anti-locking (ABS) brakes were fitted for all markets except the United States. Improvements were also made to the inside of the car.

Further significant changes were made for the 1989 Rolls-Royce and Bentley models, the most obvious being a change in the Bentley's frontal appearance. All the Bentley saloons – the Eight, the Mulsanne S and the Turbo R – were given twin, seven-inch, round headlights. This was the main change, but there were some other smaller ones, all designed to give the Bentley a markedly different appearance from the Silver Spirit. Other improvements were made to the whole range including the Silver Spirit, Silver Spur, Corniche II and Bentley Continental convertibles. And at the Frankfurt Motor Show in October 1989, the Silver Spirit II and the Silver Spur II were launched.

As Martin Bennett wrote:

These series II cars set new standards of ride comfort, even for Rolls-Royce, with the introduction of a computer activated automatic ride control system developed over a four year period in the Experimental Department at Crewe.

SHAREHOLDER VALUE

The improving fortunes of Rolls-Royce Motor Cars Ltd. within the Vickers group invited speculation that predators might be attracted to the idea of adding the world's most prestigious car range to their stable. The first to take action was Sir Ron Brierley, the New Zealand entrepreneur who had thrived during the long bull market of the 1980s successfully buying into and selling out of unwary companies.

Born in Wellington, New Zealand, in 1937, Brierley began his career as a Sun Insurance office boy and became interested in investment through reading a racing tip-sheet. In 1961, at the age of 24, he founded Brierley Investments Ltd. He originally bought a stake in a British company in 1967, but his first large investment in the UK was in 1985 when he bought 50 per cent of the motor distributor TKM. He also bought stakes in Budgens supermarkets, paper maker William Somerville and brewer Scottish & Newcastle. By 1990, Brierley Investments Ltd.'s assets were valued at £3.2 billion, 41 per cent of them in the UK or USA. Unmarried and quiet, Brierley made investments that could be unusual but which were never made without careful study.

In Brierley's view, Vickers was a mishmash of ordinary businesses with one jewel – Rolls-Royce. People struggled to see the logic of Vickers buying the Italian luxury-boat builder Cantieri Riva SpA for £9.1 million in January 1990. Riva was eventually sold to Stellican, a London investment company, in July 1998 for a rumoured price of about £4 million. Rolls-Royce alone would be worth half the market capitalisation of Vickers, and Brierley wanted it to be floated separately. So convinced was he that this would happen or that a break-up bid would be made for Vickers that he spent £80 million building a 17.25 per cent stake during 1989 and early 1990 via his Industrial Equity Pacific company (IEP). Others thought a bid unlikely, pointing to the uncertainty of Vickers' defence-related businesses following the collapse of communism in Russia and Eastern Europe as well as the uncertainty surrounding use of the Rolls-Royce name, held under licence by Vickers from Rolls-Royce plc.

Stuart Mitchell, the managing director of IEP, held talks with Sir David Plastow and said that Plastow had not ruled out an 'unbundling' of Vickers. He quoted Plastow as saying:

We have thought it out [i.e. the possibility of a demerger] and if we thought it would enhance shareholder value we would do it.

On 16 January 1990, Plastow was stung into writing to shareholders saying that the uncertainty created by the presence of 'a large destabilising overseas holding' was not helpful to Vickers when the UK Government had still to make a decision about the replacement of the British Army's Chieftain tank. When asked about the letter, Plastow said:

We have not been rattled in the classic sense of the word. But we do not intend to sit back and see creeping control. We are just trying to inform shareholders of the position. This is not Rambo Plastow.

Plastow had met Brierley three times. The first meeting, in November 1988, had been very friendly, and the conversation had ended with them talking about cricket. The next, in late 1989, had been less friendly, with Brierley critical of what he saw as Vickers' 'expensive' £108-million purchase of alloy maker Ross Catherall. He also suggested that Rolls-Royce Motor Cars Ltd. should be sold to 'realise shareholder value', prompting Plastow to reply sharply:

Don't tell me how to break up a business.

Plastow told Brierley that he was quite willing to ditch businesses that did not fit, but that Rolls-Royce, with sales growth of 5 to 7 per cent per year, did not come into that category. He cited the fact that, after saying that Vickers' lithographic-printing-plate arm was a core business, he had sold it to DuPont because it had 'peaked'. He also thought that his £9-million purchase of the Italian luxury-power-boat maker Cantieri Riva was a master stroke. Others thought the money might have been better invested in developing a new Rolls-Royce or Bentley.

Throughout these discussions with Brierley, Plastow pointed out that Vickers did not own the 'Rolls-Royce' marque and that any new owner would have to gain approval from Rolls-Royce plc before it could use the name on the motor cars. While negotiating with Brierley, Plastow met Sir Ralph Robins and suggested that Rolls-Royce plc might like to take a stake in Vickers. Robins discussed the idea with the Chairman, Lord Tombs, but Tombs was not in favour of such a relationship.

Two months later, in March 1990, Vickers paid £163.5 million for Cosworth Engineering, the specialist manufacturer of high-performance engines. Cosworth had come from Michael Green's Carlton Communications, which had acquired it with its purchase of UEI, the digital processing and engineering company.

About 70 per cent of Cosworth's sales were to the Ford Motor Company, which it supplied with engines for the Sierra Cosworth. It also supplied engines to several Formula One teams. Plastow claimed that Cosworth would contribute to Rolls-Royce's expertise in combustion technology and that he would consider putting Cosworth engines into Rolls-Royces and Bentleys at some point in the future.

The deal would be contingent on shareholder approval and also shareholder rejection of Brierley's proposal that Rolls-Royce should be floated off as an independent company.

These two issues were settled at Vickers' AGM on 26 April 1990. Brierley's resolution was defeated by a margin of 67 to 33 per cent, and the acquisition of Cosworth was approved by 64 per cent.

Having seen off Brierley, Plastow now had to see how he could cope with the recession that blew through the world in the early 1990s. Would his prediction made at the time of the merger, that 'we will insulate ourselves from the business cycles and troughs', prove to be correct?

'IF IT ISN'T HURTING, IT ISN'T WORKING'

The long upswing in business came to an abrupt halt in 1990. It had been signalled in the autumn of 1987 by a severe correction on the stock markets of the world, ending a bull market that had begun in 1982.

The foundations for this bull market were laid as far back as 1975 when Wall Street underwent its financial revolution and abandoned fixed rates of commission for its brokers. Other restrictions regulating the financial markets in New York were also removed. The removal of restrictions killed off many small brokerage firms and led to the rise of massive firms that handle everything from buying and selling shares to financing company takeovers. Ten years later, the City in London followed suit as Margaret Thatcher, having tackled the restrictive practices of the trades unions, turned her attention to those operating in the City. A 24-hour market was developing in the world's financial markets, and London was in danger of missing out. (By the early 1980s, more shares in ICI, Britain's largest manufacturer, were being traded in New York than London, thanks to lower charges.) Gordon (now Lord) Borrie, of the Office of Fair Trading, threatened to take the Stock Exchange to court when Cecil (now Lord) Parkinson, Secretary of State for Trade and Industry, persuaded Sir Nicholas Goodison, the chairman of the Stock Exchange, to make changes. The same revolution as in New York was under way, but was known in London as 'Big Bang'. While all this was going on, the world's economy rose from the shock of the first oil crisis in the mid-1970s, dipped again with the second oil crisis in 1979/80, and then rose strongly again as the 1980s progressed. Feeding off this growth, and also helping to fuel it, was a sharp and continuing rise in all the world's major stock markets. In London, for example, the horrendous bear market that had taken the *Financial Times* 30-share index down from a peak of 532 in May 1972 to its nadir of 146 on 6 January 1975 was given its final shake-out after the collapse of the Burmah Oil Company just before Christmas. The FT-30 (now largely replaced in most people's minds by the more broadly based *Financial Times* 100-share index, known as the 'Footsie') rose sharply throughout the rest of 1975, then moved largely sideways until it took off again in the early 1980s. By 1986/7, the markets had long since become divorced from economic reality. *Business* (a joint-venture magazine of the *Financial Times* and Condé Nast) said that markets reached a point 'at which reason and experience in the form of historical evidence and the cycles of economic activity are discounted and a peculiarly optimistic psychology captures the market. Once it had taken hold, many of the players came to believe that the market had to continue going up and up.' This delusion seems to take hold in every bull market, as we have just seen in 1999–2000.

But it was not only people in the City and Wall Street who were making money. There were many private shareholders in the USA, and, though not as many in the UK, even in Britain many people experienced the feel-good factor through the ownership of shares in unit trusts and were encouraged through the Government's privatisation of British Telecom, British Airways, British Gas and others. They also expected that their pensions would be fatter thanks to booming share prices. Furthermore, their one big investment, the house they lived in, was leaping up in value too. The icing on the cake came from privatisation of the state-run monopolies that had been nationalised 40 years earlier and benefited everyone – the City, which made fat fees and good instant profits, the people, who effectively received a series of free lunches, and the Government, who took the credit.

Then, in the autumn of 1987, clouds appeared. The world economy was clearly beginning to overheat, and the German and US monetary authorities engaged in a public argument about the correct level of interest rates. Just as in 1929 after stocks around the world had risen higher and higher – BANG! It had all stopped. First New York, then Tokyo and Hong Kong, then London, then New York again, then Hong Kong, Tokyo and Sydney, then London, Paris and Frankfurt all turned into screaming, yelling pits of hysteria as the markets lost a year's gains in 24 hours. To exacerbate the situation, the hurricane in Britain three days before prevented many dealers from reaching their screens.

It was only twelve years or 3,000 trading days since the FT-30 Index had stood at 147. Now it had lost 183.7 in a single day. If anyone thought that was difficult to cope with, the Dow-Jones fell by over 500 points, and it was only five years or 1,250 trading days since that index had been around 600. But that, of course, was part of the reason. The indexes had risen a long way, and once punters wanted to cash in some of their profits there could only be one result. Black Monday, 19 October 1987, was so called after Black Monday on Wall Street in October 1929, which had itself been named after the Black Friday of 24 September 1869 when a group of punters tried to corner the gold market, causing a panic that led to a crash and a depression.

So many records were broken on this Black Monday – biggest one-day fall, biggest volume, more deals on the New York Stock Exchange that day than in the whole of 1950 and so on – that everyone ran out of superlatives; certainly, no one thought it was particularly superlative. Being the nuclear age, John Phelan, Chairman of the New York Stock Exchange, described it as 'the closest to meltdown I'd ever want to get'.

It was serious. By the middle of Tuesday in New York as the Dow was plunging again – by then it had lost 800 points in less than five days' trading – the New York Stock Exchange was in touch with the White House and considering the suspension of trading. At that moment, the market rallied, and although it might only be a dead-cat bounce it was at least a bounce and removed the pressure for a moment. If New York had suspended trading, the effect on prices in London would have been catastrophic, as that would have been the only escape hatch. The Hong Kong Exchange did suspend trading, and that exerted extra pressure elsewhere, especially in Sydney.

The crisis passed. Indeed, in retrospect the so-called 'Crash' of 1987 seems like a pause in the bull market that began in the early 1980s and was still in place in the late 1990s. But it was giving a warning. The world economy was growing too fast, and it was given another push by the collapse of communism in Eastern Europe and the reunification of Germany. To ease this reunification, the West German Government poured money into the former Eastern Germany, adding a notch or two to growth which was already unsustainable.

It had to stop, and the result in the early 1990s was a recession, mild in most parts of the world but severe in Britain. The Crash of 1987 had been telling the world something, but for a time it was not clear what. The consumer boom that had built up round the world in the 1980s did not lose its momentum overnight, and most of 1988 was another good year, especially in Britain. The Chancellor of the Exchequer, Nigel (now Lord) Lawson, had read his economic-history books and knew that what turned the Wall Street Crash of 1929 into the world depression of the 1930s was the tightening of credit everywhere and the mistaken attempt to balance budgets. He and others were determined that should not happen this time and lowered interest rates to maintain liquidity in the financial system. Unfortunately, he overdid it. Most British consumers are not directly affected by the stock market, and, though the Crash made dramatic headlines and hurt a few large private investors, the mass of people went on spending, confident that their main asset – the house they lived in – was still worth far more than they paid for it. The house-price spiral was given a final upward twist when Lawson announced the end of double tax relief on mortgages for unmarried couples living together. However, the new law would not apply until August, and the early summer of 1988 witnessed the final frenzy of house purchase at what, in retrospect, came to be seen as silly prices. What those who were buying failed to notice was that the interest-rate cycle had turned.

After reducing interest rates at the end of 1987 and in the early part of 1988, Lawson realised that the British economy was overheating badly. The mature, some would say sclerotic, British economy could only grow at about 3 per cent before it hit restraints and ran into inflation and balance-of-payments problems. Lawson took a long time to realise that the economy was growing much faster than this. (One of the Thatcher Government's public-expenditure economies had been to cut down on the Whitehall department supplying statistics on the economy, and these were taking a long time to become available. It proved to be a very expensive 'economy'.) However, by early summer 1988 the overheating was obvious as the inflation rate turned upwards and the balance-of-payments deficit ballooned alarmingly.

Lawson should probably have raised taxes in his 1988 Budget instead of reducing them, but the real problem was the amount of liquidity in the economy. He tackled this by raising interest rates. The only problem was that a national economy is a big ship, and big ships take a long time to stop and turn round. People did not realise the implications – in all fairness, nor did most businessmen, financial commentators or politicians. The balance of payments got worse, and interest rates went up again until they eventually reached 15 per cent. This meant that most people were paying 18 to 20 per cent on their overdrafts, loans and mortgages. It may have taken some time to stop the ship, but stop it certainly did and with some very nasty, related and self-feeding consequences.

Not only had house prices risen very sharply but the financing of them had become very easy – 90, 95 or even 100 per cent loans had become available. On a £100,000 mortgage, 10 per cent was £833 a month – quite a lot of money but manageable if both partners were earning £1,500 per month each. The sums looked different by the end of 1989 when the repayments had moved up to £1,600 a month and one of the jobs was looking a little shaky. If the worst happened and one of the partners lost his or her job (and high interest rates also bring recessions), the couple would have to sell the house and move to something cheaper. And it was only then that the real calamity of the house-price spiral hit home. The house that had been bought for £110,000 with a £100,000 mortgage could not be sold: certainly not at £110,000, nor at £100,000, nor even at £90,000 or £80,000. It could perhaps be 'given away' at £70,000. The couple faced disaster. They could not keep up the mortgage payments, but if they sold the house they owed the mortgage company £30,000. John Major, who took over from Nigel Lawson as Chancellor when Thatcher determined he should take the blame for this fiasco, said:

If it isn't hurting, it isn't working.

For many it was hurting all right, Rolls-Royce Motor Cars among them.

After the boom years of the 1980s – accompanied, it had to be said, by some ostentatious and conspicuous consumption – the recession years of the early 1990s hit Rolls-Royce Motor Cars doubly hard. First, many people could not – or more important, felt they should not – afford luxury cars; and second, in the 'caring' 1990s, it was not politic to be seen driving a brand new luxury car. By this time, break-even was probably sales of around 3,000 cars a year – a number exceeded throughout most of the 1980s, and, indeed, in 1990 itself 3,300 cars were produced and sold. However, in the next two years sales plunged.

Sales worldwide fell 48.3 per cent to 1,723 cars – the lowest since 1968 – from the 3,333 in 1990. Sales in the UK halved to 513 from 1,007, while in the USA they fell 65.2 per cent to 400 from 1,149. Radical restructuring was essential to bring the break-even figure down to around 2,000 cars a year. The UK workforce was cut by more than a third to just over 3,000, and a new labour agreement was pushed through, removing many restrictive practices that had disappeared in the rest of the car industry years earlier. The seven trades unions at Crewe agreed to act as a single union, and the number of union representatives was cut from 110 to 40.

By the end of 1991, the old stories about takeover resurfaced, prompting Vickers to say that:

As a result of the very much lower sales volume, Vickers is again reviewing the many options for its car business.

Vickers went on to say that the possible sale of all or part of the Rolls-Royce and Bentley car operation had 'attracted considerable interest from a number of international companies'. It had been involved in discussions with BMW about technology links, distribution support and the sale of part or all of the equity. Technology discussions had also taken place with Porsche on engine development and talks about suspension levelling systems with Citroën. In February 1992, it was announced that BMW would supply airbag systems and that discussions were taking place about co-operation on the development and supply of other component systems such as electric seat mechanisms and electronic automatic-gearbox controls.

Losses in 1991 and 1992 totalled no less than £100 million, but in July 1993, with two updated cars – the Silver Spirit III and the Silver Spur III – the company announced that production would be increased by 25 per cent. Helped by Britain's withdrawal (seen as humiliating at the time) from the European Exchange Rate Mechanism in September 1992, with a consequent decline in the value of the pound sterling, Rolls-Royce Motor Cars made renewed efforts to secure overseas sales. Along with a continued recovery in world markets, especially in the UK and the USA, sales gradually recovered.

Sales had bottomed at 1,360 cars in 1993 after 1,378 in 1992, but in the first quarter of 1994 they rose 9.3 per cent. At the end of 1994, Rolls-Royce Motor Cars announced that it had reached an agreement with BMW whereby the German company would supply technology and components for a new model, most notably a modern V12 engine to replace Rolls-Royce's V8 power unit. Both Mercedes and BMW had been engaged in discussions for more than a year to supply engines, and finally BMW had won, so that the engine was now added to the electronic systems which BMW already supplied, as well as the body panels from its subsidiary, Rover.

Colin (now Sir Colin) Chandler, who had become Chief Executive of Vickers in 1992, called on Sir Ralph Robins to elicit his views on whether Rolls-Royce Motors should install a Mercedes engine in the cars. Sir Ralph told him that as it was their company obviously they could do so, but if they did, Rolls-Royce plc would withdraw their right to call the car a Rolls-Royce. Chandler was angry at what he saw as interference with his running of the company. Nevertheless, BMW received the contract for the engines, and Ward relinquished his position as managing director of Rolls-Royce Motor Cars.

FOR SALE

Having survived the stomach-churning recession of the early 1990s, Vickers found the courage and the finance to develop a new model and, at the same time, to modernise the factory at Crewe.

The Silver Seraph – *seraph* is defined in the Oxford Dictionary as 'a celestial being of the highest order, associated especially with light, ardour and purity' – was launched in the spring of 1998 from a modernised factory. Following an investment of £40 million, the maze of eighteen separate compartments had been removed. The groups of workers, previously separated and concentrating on one component of the car, were now part of an open-plan factory and could feel involved in the total assembly operation as they worked on Rolls-Royce's first ever conveyor-system production line. Gordon Dawson, who joined the company in 1938, disputes that this was the first moving assembly line, maintaining that one existed in the Derby works before the war:

In the recent publicity about the Seraph car, reference is made to 'Rolls-Royce's first moving production line' just installed. While this may be the first at Crewe, there was a mobile assembly line in Nightingale Road in 1938. It must of course be remembered that in 1938 the company only built chassis with the bodies being fitted at various coach-builders.

The line was situated at the back of the main office block running parallel with this for about half to two-thirds its length. It consisted of a series of four-wheeled trolleys which could be hooked on to the back of the one in front by a six-foot towing bar. This could also be used manually to manoeuvre the trolley when empty through a steerable front bogey.

An empty trolley had a bare chassis frame loaded on to it and was hooked to the one in front at the end of the line while the trolley chain was pulled forward by a rope and windlass. When the chassis on the first trolley was completed to appropriate stage of assembly, the trolley was disconnected, the chassis removed for completion of assembly and test and the trolley returned to the end of the line.

Along one side of the line were racks containing parts, assemblies and tools appropriate to the station. I cannot honestly remember how many trolleys were on the line at one time – about ten, I guess.

The line disappeared in 1939 when car production was stopped and the space turned over to aero production.

Back in 1998, Tony Gott – project director for the Seraph and its sister, the Bentley Arnage (named after the corner at the end of the famous Mulsanne straight at Le Mans) – said:

People were proud to work here but somehow found the company difficult to work in. By reorganising the whole process, we have opened it out, got people's involvement with the product and made sure that management and workers interact.

Graham Morris, recruited as the new managing director of Rolls-Royce after holding senior posts at Rover and Audi, claimed that productivity improvements had been such that the man-hours required to assemble a car had been brought down from 730 to 400.

For the first time, engines had been brought in from outside. BMW supplied its V12 for the Seraph and its V8 for the Arnage, and at the same time also supplied a number of engine-related components such as management systems and the air conditioning. But, while Vickers had decided to eliminate engine manufacture, it approved the investment in a body-welding shop. The bodies produced proved to be cheaper than those bought from Pressed Steel and also 65 per cent more rigid.

There were a number of critics of this new approach, some claiming that the Seraph and Arnage were merely 'expensive models of the BMW 7 series'.

By 1997, sales had reached 1,918 cars, and the official company forecast was for them to grow by about 10 per cent a year for the next three years, taking them to about 2,600 by early in the next century.

Speculation about the future of Rolls-Royce Motors was heightened by comments made by Bernd Pischetsrieder, BMW's Chief Executive, at BMW's press dinner on 2 November 1995, when he said that Rolls-Royce would be a natural extension of BMW's brand portfolio. Rover had expanded BMW's range of cheaper vehicles, and there was room for a niche, low-volume, luxury brand above BMW's price ceiling.

In January 1997, Vickers again denied that Rolls-Royce was for sale, but in October, following a leak in the *Sunday Times,* it announced that it was indeed putting the company up for auction. 'Dry your eyes', said *Lex* in the *Financial Times*:

Many will be sad to see another part of Britain's industrial heritage falling under foreign control. But Rolls-Royce Motor Cars should be better as part of an international car company than with a loose engineering conglomerate.

Having recovered so successfully from the early-1990s recession, why should Vickers choose such a moment to sell Rolls-Royce? After all, it had denied vehemently reports in the *Financial Times* in January 1997 that talks were taking place with BMW which would lead to the German company buying the car division of Vickers. A spokesman for Vickers had said that the division remained a core activity that stood to reap the benefits of a new BMW-engined model due to be launched before the end of the decade and added:

We would hardly have invested £75 million in research and development in the past two years if we were going to sell before taking the rewards of that effort.

The cost of keeping the company going through the recession – the claimed losses were £100 million – had frightened the Vickers Board. Furthermore, they appreciated that the investment required to keep Rolls-Royce and Bentley as the best two cars in the world would be enormous. Both Mercedes and BMW had announced plans to manufacture luxury cars with all that

that implied for the relatively tiny Rolls-Royce. As if to emphasise the point that only the biggest and strongest would survive in the twenty-first century, the German company Daimler-Benz and the American company Chrysler announced in the spring of 1998 that they were going to join hands in a £56-billion merger. Sir Colin Chandler, who had succeeded Sir David Plastow as Chairman of Vickers, hoped to find a purchaser for Rolls-Royce for £300–£400 million and invited bids. As the *Financial Times* pointed out:

Vickers is selling at the right time. Having sunk about £200 million in new models, it can offer the buyer the glory of next year's launch while skipping the final expense of getting the cars to market.

Clearly, all the major European, Japanese and American motor manufacturers could be interested, but most quickly ruled themselves out.

An early and unexpected distraction came in the form of a hostile bid from Mayflower Corporation, the car components group, for the whole of Vickers. Mayflower said it would sell Vickers' defence arm and keep the other three divisions: Rolls-Royce, Cosworth engines and propulsion technology. It implied that it enjoyed BMW's support. This brought an angry response from Bernd Pischetsrieder, who said:

We have nothing to do with this Mayflower bid. It is embarrassing for us that somebody gives the impression that he has our support. We have no interest to support that at all.

Pischetsrieder also warned that it would terminate its contract to supply engines to Rolls-Royce if Mayflower's bid for Vickers was successful. This was enough to frighten off Mayflower, whose largest customer was Rover, a BMW subsidiary.

VW soon made up its mind. On 14 November 1997, the company announced it would compete with BMW for control of Rolls-Royce Motor Cars.

Why would two of the world's leading car manufacturers, with high perceived product status of their own, be interested in buying another car manufacturer whose annual sales, even in good times, barely exceeded 3,000 and in bad times plunged to half that, thanks to the 'fat cat' image?

There were probably two main reasons. The first was the undoubted prestige value of the brand. Though many would say that by 1997 the Rolls-Royces and Bentleys coming out of Crewe were not technologically the 'best cars in the world', as had been claimed since before the First World War, nevertheless they still carried a certain cachet in markets around the world. Car makers were still prepared to pay a premium for prestige brands, as we saw when Ford paid £1.6 billion for Jaguar in 1989.

The second reason was the transformation of the production facilities at Crewe so that the plant was capable of turning out much higher numbers than the 2,000 to 3,000 Vickers was ever likely to sell. If, for example, the eventual purchaser wanted to develop a baby Bentley with a sales target of 8,000 to 10,000 cars a year, the new Crewe production facility could probably cope.

Vickers' shareholders were relieved when VW came on to the scene, as the reaction of BMW to Mayflower's bid for Vickers had made them fear that BMW's supply contracts with Rolls-Royce were in effect a stranglehold that would deter other companies from entering the auction. VW's interest improved the chances of a higher price. Vickers emphasised that the contracts with BMW did allow for an orderly adaptation for the new cars if BMW decided it did not wish to continue the technology agreements with a new owner.

While BMW and VW prepared to do battle, some remained convinced that Mercedes-Benz could yet enter the fray. It was said that Rolls-Royce engineers favoured Mercedes because of its experience in luxury cars and its strong distribution network, especially in Asia. It would also remove the competition of the Mercedes-Benz Maybach, the name revived from the past that Mercedes-Benz was going to use for its new luxury cars. (Wilhelm Maybach, 1846–1929, was the chief designer of the first Mercedes automobiles, and cars with the Maybach marque were produced from 1922 to 1939.)

Also dragged into the fray was Rolls-Royce plc, the original Rolls-Royce company, now largely an aero-engine manufacturer. On 5 January 1998, Vickers, seeking to keep the auction field as wide open as possible, said that it had been told by legal advisers that Rolls-Royce plc had no veto powers over the use of the Rolls-Royce name if Rolls-Royce was sold to a third party.

Sir Colin Chandler, who had become Chairman of Vickers in 1997, said:

There are a number of credible purchasers. Vickers has created today's value in Rolls-Royce Motor Cars and we alone will be responsible for determining which of them should be the future owner of the business.

In reply, Rolls-Royce plc said it was surprised by the statement and that the agreement of 1973 had never been previously challenged, adding:

We believe the ownership of the name and the marques rest with us. Our prime goal is to protect our name. We're not there to exploit the name but to protect it.

Vickers went further, requesting the European Commission to remove the veto powers from Rolls-Royce plc on the grounds that they were anti-competitive and discriminatory under European law. In response, Rolls-Royce plc said its rights were enforceable and it would make early efforts to protect them.

Rolls-Royce plc's view was this:

Rolls-Royce was the second best known marque worldwide and was synonymous with quality. The marque allowed the company great access to business and political decision takers and was therefore a fundamental trading asset. The maintenance of the image of excellence had to be the first priority if this advantage was to continue. The use of the name did have value but maintaining the marque was more important than any potential franchise income. Nothing else, apart from cars, had ever been allowed to use the name and arguably it would be better for the car to become history rather than the marque be devalued.

Of the possible bidders, BMW was seen by Rolls-Royce plc as the best qualified to maintain the image of the marque. BMW already enjoyed a quality image and fully understood how to promote and protect a marque. It also enjoyed cordial relations with Rolls-Royce plc through the aero-engine joint venture.

Also in January 1998, another potential bidder appeared on the scene. It was effectively a group of 'high-rollers' led by barrister Michael Shrimpton. Shrimpton claimed he had been contacted by investors with a net worth of about £1 billion, some of whom were apparently prepared to invest nine-figure sums [presumably that's at least £100,000,000] in order to keep Rolls-Royce Motor Cars British. Shrimpton said:

There is an element of the 1966 world cup about it.

Clearly, there was a dash of xenophobia in it too.

In late March, the bidding opened. Mercedes-Benz had fallen by the way-side, Jürgen Schrempp, its chairman, saying, 'We are definitely not going to buy it.' However, on Tuesday 24 March, VW submitted its bid. The next day, BMW also put in a bid. A third bid came from Kevin Morley, a former Rover director who had been working with a group of Rolls-Royce enthusiasts, and a fourth bid came from Doughty Hanson, the venture capital group. The chances of these last two succeeding were thought to be very slim. Graham Morris, Chief Executive of Rolls-Royce Motor Cars (Peter Ward had 'resigned' after the Vickers Board had overruled his agreement with Mercedes that they would supply engines), said that Rolls-Royce had always favoured being bought by another motor-car manufacturer.

The auction was over quickly. On Monday 30 March, Vickers announced that it had accepted a bid of £340 million from BMW (VW had apparently bid £310 million) and that it had granted BMW exclusivity for a month while it carried out its due diligence. Chandler and Pischetsrieder shook hands on the deal. Responding to chatter that VW would be prepared to bid more,

Pischetsrieder said that BMW would terminate engine supplies if another bidder were successful.

He also outlined plans to reshape Rolls-Royce's Board with the inclusion of four non-executive directors. One would be an independent 'diplomat' to help maintain Rolls-Royce's British image. He added:

We should follow British traditions. The company will remain British in the future. It will have even less BMW about it than it does today.

At the same time, he pledged increased investment on new models, and higher output and employment, saying:

We have done a lot of intellectual work in advance. We have a few surprises in the future for Crewe.

VW did not delay in coming back with a higher bid. It delivered it on the day BMW's successful bid was announced. While acknowledging that BMW had been granted a month's exclusivity, VW said:

We will wait for a month and then see.

Before BMW's exclusivity period had expired, it was leaked from VW's headquarters in Wolfsburg that the VW Board had given Chief Executive Ferdinand Piech authority to offer more money for Rolls-Royce Motors, and, indeed, in early May the German company delivered a new offer of £430 million.

Piech flew in the VW private jet to Northolt airport on 7 May where he met Andrew John, commercial director of Vickers (Chandler was out of the country), in the Winston Churchill lounge. Helping to convince Vickers that it should recommend the deal to its shareholders was VW's willingness to drop some of the conditions of its earlier bid. Most importantly, it decided to step into the deal Vickers had agreed with BMW. It also took upon itself the risk that Rolls-Royce plc might not be willing to transfer the right to use the Rolls-Royce name. The Vickers Board had no choice but to recommend this much higher offer to its shareholders.

With Rolls-Royce plc still holding to its line that it would not allow VW to use the brand name Rolls-Royce, Sir Colin Chandler attacked the company openly, saying:

Rolls-Royce plc is quite deliberately interfering in a process in which we are striving to get best value for our shareholders. We have saved the car marque. We have restored it to health and Rolls-Royce plc has had a zero role in this. When it comes to

TOP: With a maximum speed of 150 mph, the Bentley Turbo R was
the fastest luxury car in the world. More importantly, it had phenomenal,
yet effortless, acceleration. One motoring magazine described
it as 'Crewe's missile'.

BOTTOM: William Woollard, presenter of *Top Gear* on BBC Television,
said of the Bentley Continental R, 'Biggles would have loved it.'
This automatic-ride-control motor car would go from 0 to 60 mph in
6.5 seconds – faster than a Jaguar XJR-S.

TOP: The early-1990s recession inflicted great damage on
Rolls-Royce Motor Cars, but in 1993, with two new cars – the
Silver Spirit III and Silver Spur III – production was increased
by 25 per cent.

BOTTOM: A 'celestial being of the highest order', the Silver Seraph
was launched in spring 1998 from a modernised Crewe factory.

TOP: The Bentley Arnage, also launched in 1998, was named after the corner at the end of the famous Mulsanne straight at Le Mans.

BOTTOM: After VW had bought Rolls-Royce Motor Cars, it decided to enter a Bentley into the Le Mans 24-hour race to try to recapture the glory days of the 1920s. The EXP Speed 8, pictured here, was essentially British apart from its Audi V8 engine. In the 2001 Le Mans race, it came third – a remarkable achievement.

Sir Ralph Robins, Bernd Pischetsrieder (then of BMW,
now of VW) and Ferdinand Piech of VW shake hands on the deal
whereby VW will make Bentleys, and BMW Rolls-Royces.

preserving the trade mark I believe there is no difference between major auto companies such as BMW and VW taking the business over. We cannot see why they are so predisposed to BMW.

VW kept up the pressure by signing a letter of intent before the crucial Vickers shareholders' Extraordinary General Meeting in early June, saying that it would buy the Cosworth Engine Company for £120 million. [You will remember that Vickers had paid £163 million for it in 1990.]

Cosworth had played an interesting cameo role in the whole Vickers/Rolls-Royce/BMW/VW saga. BMW had made it clear to Vickers that it had no interest in buying Cosworth. There were two main reasons. One was that the Rolls-Royce Seraph and Bentley Arnage cars were already engineered to take Munich-built engines. The other was that it had no use for the racing-engine technology for which Cosworth was world famous. BMW had already decided to launch itself into the glamorous and powerful publicity world of Formula One, but it wanted to gain the kudos with its own engines developed in-house. [The wisdom of this approach could be appreciated by the end of 2001 after a season in which the BMW-Williams team won three Grands Prix and the straight-line speed of their cars, powered by BMW engines, was greater than those of any other team, including Ferrari and McLaren.]

On the other hand, when the VW team from Wolfsburg visited the Cosworth plants in Northampton, Wellingborough and Worcester, they realised how useful Cosworth could be. Cosworth had developed a complete turnkey-engine capability for road as well as race engines. The company also possessed, virtually ready to go, its own V8 engine capable of powering a new generation of sporting Bentleys, as well as a V10 equally capable, after further tooling and other investment, of powering any Rolls-Royce model.

VW also discovered how Cosworth could help the image of its Audi and VW brands in the all-important North American market. As well as supplying engines for Formula One cars, Cosworth also supplied about half the engines for Indy Car racing, a favourite sport of middle America. The only problem was that Cosworth's biggest customer was Ford – perhaps VW's biggest competitor throughout the world.

Rolls-Royce plc's interest was not just confined to protecting the Rolls-Royce marque. Chairman Sir Ralph Robins met Bernd Pischetsrieder to discuss the situation, and they decided there were two possibilities. Either they should make a joint bid for the whole of Vickers, or the brands of Rolls-Royce and Bentley would have to be split, as Robins was not going to allow VW to use the Rolls-Royce name.

They met on Wednesday 27 May and, with their advisers, pursued the purchase option for the rest of the week. These discussions culminated in an all-day meeting on Sunday at the offices of Freshfields, Rolls-Royce's legal advisers. Unfortunately, although the teams worked through until midnight, they could not reach final agreement, and the proposed bid for Vickers was called off.

Robins said later:

In retrospect, we did not allow enough time to iron out the details of such a complex bid.

Pischetsrieder told the author in June 2001:

I think it may have been my fault. I listened too much to the lawyers.

BMW had said its offer was final and did not raise it. Consequently, at an Extraordinary General Meeting at the Royal Horticultural Hall, Vincent Square, in London on Friday 5 June 1998, Vickers shareholders voted to reject the BMW offer and – after an intervention by Michael Shrimpton, the barrister representing a newly-formed company, Crewe Motors, which caused an hour's adjournment – voted in favour of accepting the offer from Volkswagen. Helping their cause, Volkswagen also offered to pay a generous £120 million for Vickers' specialist engine maker, Cosworth. The unknown remained the Rolls-Royce brand name. As *Lex* in the *Financial Times* put it:

Also to be added to the bill will be the pound of flesh that aero engine group Rolls-Royce plc may extract for VW's use of the brand it owns. Since the sale is unconditional, VW is very much at the British company's mercy, unless it wants to end up with just the Bentley brand for its considerable trouble.

This was perceptive of *Lex*, for on 28 July 1998 it was announced that under a tripartite agreement reached between VW, BMW and Rolls-Royce plc, BMW had paid Rolls-Royce £40 million for the right to manufacture and sell Rolls-Royce cars from 2003 onwards. VW would make and sell them until then but thereafter would only be able to use the Bentley name.

Bernd Pischetsrieder, the BMW chairman, said that a brand new Rolls-Royce would be built 'somewhere in England – not Britain, I mean England'. (After much speculation that it might be Derby or Oxford, it was announced on 30 May 2000 that it would be in Sussex on the Goodwood Estate.)

Everyone seemed reasonably happy, Sir Ralph Robins had achieved what he had always wanted – production of the Rolls-Royce motor car by a world-class design and engineering company in whom he had great faith, and therefore the crucial protection of the Rolls-Royce brand name.

Bernd Pischetsrieder had acquired the right to sell and manufacture Rolls-

Royce motor cars and had paid £40 million for the use of the name, not £340 million as he had bid originally for the whole motor-car division. He could also start from a greenfield site. *Lex* described the deal as 'a nifty piece of overtaking on the inside by BMW' and continued:

It leaves Volkswagen, which crushed BMW's bid, bereft of a tantalising part of the business – the Rolls-Royce brand – while giving BMW an important part of its goal on the cheap.

And finally, VW was probably not entirely unhappy. BMW would continue to supply engines, and VW would not therefore have to re-engineer the Silver Seraph and its Bentley counterpart to take its own engines, which would have been an expensive exercise. VW could concentrate on expanding the Bentley range to give a volume of cars much higher than had ever come out of Crewe before.

Ferdinand Piech claimed that taking over the Bentley brand name plus the facilities to increase production to 10,000 cars a year was all he had ever wanted. He could put Bentley alongside the recently acquired Lamborghini and offer a range of luxury models in addition to the successful Audi, Skoda and Seat, as well as VW's own brands.

And, of course, Sir Colin Chandler was happy. He had taken a lot of flak over his decision to sell a British crown jewel to the Germans. [The author went to the EGM in June 1998, and he was certainly given a hard time there as xenophobia was given free rein.] At the end of it all, he said from the Vickers head office:

Rolls-Royce nearly bankrupted this company in the early 1990s and I vowed not to let it happen again. The sale to VW means we have been able to pay our investors an 80p special dividend, the equivalent of 11 years of dividend payments all at once. By my book, that is not bad going.

When criticised for letting Rolls-Royce fall into foreign hands, he replied:

There is always going to be a lot of emotion attached to something like Rolls-Royce. But if you look at the end result, we got a very good price – £479 million. That's as good as best City estimates.

He could have added that no credible bid came from a British company. He did say:

Rolls-Royce needed the backing of a large automotive company to underpin its future.

And, of course, by 1998 there were no large British automotive companies left.

However, not everyone was happy. Graham Morris, Chief Executive of Rolls-Royce Motors, resigned, feeling that he could not stay after failing to deliver on his promise that Rolls-Royces and Bentleys would continue to be manufactured at Crewe. Eric Barrass, President of the Rolls-Royce Enthusiasts Club which boasted 9,000 members, said:

One really feels that this is the end of the line, that there will be no more Rolls as we know them. And the cars have been identified in the past on the engineering of Sir Henry Royce and his successors. If you take that ingredient out of the car it's difficult to see, in philosophic terms, how you can describe it as a Rolls-Royce.

It's degrading – it's an insult to a great name when people start kicking it around among themselves and saying: 'How much can we make out of this, or that or the other?'

Another group that was not happy was one formed of Rolls-Royce enthusiasts, led by Professor Donald Longmoor, a retired surgeon, called the Rolls-Royce Acquisition Consortium. Longmoor had initially worked with Shrimpton but found his approach 'erratic', saying, 'He's delightful, but potty.' Longmoor's group formed Heritage Motoring Limited and appeared to have raised £500 million to outbid VW. The newly formed company hired the well-known London law firm, Gouldens, who wrote to Sir Colin Chandler on 2 July, saying:

Our client has instructed us to offer ... the sum of £500,000,000 ... payable in full in cash at completion for the entire issued share capital of Rolls-Royce Motors Holdings Limited.

Gouldens appreciated that the offer had come very late in the day (Vickers was due to complete the transaction with VW the very next day, 3 July) but said that:

[A]t the extraordinary general meeting of Vickers plc held on 4 June 1998 Sir Colin Chandler specifically confirmed to the meeting that if any offer for Rolls-Royce higher than VW's offer were received that offer would have the opportunity of being put to the shareholders in Vickers plc. With this in mind, our client would greatly appreciate your urgent response to this offer.

Chandler's response was to complete the transaction with VW the next day.

Was he right to ignore the Heritage Motoring offer? Strictly speaking, from the purely short-term financial interests of the Vickers shareholders, he was possibly throwing away £70 million. 'Possibly' because there was no guarantee that Heritage Motoring would have completed, whereas, within 24 hours, VW did so. Furthermore, buying a motor-car manufacturer is one thing, making it financially viable with attractive new products and guaranteeing its long-term future, quite another. Not only did VW clearly possess the financial resources to make the required investment, probably at least another £1 billion within five years on top of its £430 million, it also possessed the necessary design, development and manufacturing skills to turn the investment into the reality of thousands of top-quality motor cars rolling off the production line. Heritage Motors could not guarantee the extra £1 billion, and it clearly did not possess the design, development and manufacturing resources in any depth.

One person who could at least be happy with the uncanny accuracy of his prediction was *Financial Times* journalist Stuart Marshall, who had written in *Car* magazine all the way back in November 1980:

A lot of Rolls-Royce people can't see their sort of car surviving conditions like those [the high costs of developing new models and rising fuel prices]. The word is that 1998 – or close to it – is likely to be the end [of the company's independence].

Perceptive indeed!

Another who seemed happy was Lord Montagu, whose father, as we saw in Part One, had been the lover of Eleanor Thornton, the model for the Spirit of Ecstasy. Montagu told the French newspaper *Le Monde*:

BMW has the old and good traditions, the culture of excellence and the technical expertise appropriate to such a jewel.

The potential conflict of interest at Cosworth was solved by VW selling Cosworth Racing, the motor-sport division, to Ford. This was a great relief to Ford, who had built up a relationship over 30 years with Cosworth both in Formula One and Indy Car racing.

On a handshake, I've promised the first car to one of our established customers. He has a large collection, including a Silver Ghost. [Actually, he has several.] I've promised delivery on January 1, 2003. It's not only in my hands, but that is our target.

That's what Karl-Heinz Kalbfell, director of Project Rolls-Royce within BMW, said in March 2000. He was talking of a brand new Rolls-Royce – part radical, part traditional – that had been designed in great security in a white building opposite Hyde Park in Bayswater which had once been a branch of Barclays Bank. Three full-scale models were put before the BMW Board in December 1999, and the Board chose a model by Merrick Djordevic

151

of Pasadena Art Center College of Design, who had been working at Designworks, BMW's Californian studio. Kalbfell said of the design:

Above all we wanted authenticity. Rolls-Royce is a national monument and we are defining its tradition for the future. We must not only reflect on the past but describe Rolls-Royce in modern terms. It is one of the strongest marques in the world – the name is synonymous with the best. Have no fear that anything else but a Rolls-Royce will come out. It is timeless and classical.

On performance, Kalbfell said:

Our aim is to give the new Rolls-Royce enough torque so it is faster away from the lights than a Porsche 911 Turbo. The Porsche can pass the Rolls-Royce when they get up to cruising speed, that's fine, this is the difference. We don't want to produce a slow car but it won't be too sporty. The owners will be able to take the performance for granted.

Meantime, VW were not sitting back. They announced that they would pro-duce a new baby Bentley, with the production beginning in 2003 and building to an annual output of 9,000 cars. They expected the USA and UK to take 25 per cent each, Europe 30 per cent and the rest of the world 20 per cent. At £85,000, the new model would be considerably cheaper than the Bentley Arnage, whose price started at £150,000. VW brought in Durk van Braekel, who had worked on Skoda's Octavia and Fabia models, to lead the design team.

Tony Gott, who had succeeded Graham Morris as Chief Executive at Crewe, said:

It's the first time a brand has shifted down in the market to compete with Mercedes. It should be a sector-changing event.

He added that the new car would use 'slightly more' components sourced from outside the UK but that this was the consequence of working with 'a global company with global sourcing with the major automotive suppliers based in Germany'.

Perhaps noticing that BMW had been slow to take full control of Rover, VW appointed two German directors in key positions on the Rolls-Royce and Bentley Motor Cars Ltd. Board. Hans-Georg Melching became finance director and Hans-Joachim Rothenpieler, engineering director.

THE BENTLEY BOYS

To stake a claim on their future as a builder of sporty new Bentleys designed for a broader and younger age group, VW backed the idea of entering two

Bentleys into the 2001 Le Mans 24-hour race. By this time, VW had committed close to £1 billion to Bentley – £470 million on the purchase and another £500 million in planned investment. Of this, £10 million a year was allocated for the racing programme. This was nowhere near the annual £100 million that a Formula One team could spend, but it was still £10 million out of the advertising budget. As Michael Harvey put it in the *Financial Times* on the day of the 2001 Le Mans race:

The Le Mans programme has to deliver. For the young, it has to confirm that Bentley is sexy, technically competent, sporty (crucially) and relevant.

How did the lads at Crewe persuade Ferdinand Piech that racing a Bentley at Le Mans again was a sound commercial idea and not just boys with big toys spending rich daddy's money? According to *Autocar*, it was a bit like pushing at an open door:

It started, as so many things at Bentley do, with Dr Ferdinand Piech. A day or two after his Volkswagen Group purchased the venerable luxury car company of Crewe, Piech called in to meet its senior managers. He spoke winningly of his aspirations for Bentley, and when he called for questions, there was a forest of hands. One question had been bothering Bentley bosses for roughly 70 years: would the marque race again at Le Mans? There was a ripple of excitement when Piech answered.

Yes, he replied without hesitation, one day Bentley will race again at Le Mans.

In spite of this commitment, Bentley at Crewe still had to convince their German masters that they could build a car that would do *well* at Le Mans. There was plenty of downside potential if they performed badly.

They put together a car that, apart from the Audi V8 engine, was essentially British. The body, chassis and suspension were all built by Audi-owned Racing Technology Norfolk (RTN), formerly TOMS Toyota, builders of the open-cockpit Audi sports-racers as well. The EXP8 transmission was by Xtrac; the brakes came from AP Racing. RTN were building a closed-cockpit car, and Bentley worked with them to make it their own. Chief Executive Tony Gott said:

We accepted and developed the closed car in the same way any company commissions a new design. The task was to align a promising proposal unmistakably with Bentley values.

By May 2000, the plans for Bentley EXP8 were ready, and the Crewe team had worked out how to align the EXP8's technology with Bentley's road-going products. It was time to go back to Piech and remind him of his promise. Tony Gott said:

153

Our task was to convince the big bosses, Dr Piech and Dr Buchelhofer [Audi chairman], that the whole thing was a good idea. So last August, in time for their regular visit and well before the world knew a Bentley Le Mans effort was even a possibility, we brought the car here to Crewe and set it up in time for their regular visit. They knew we were going to do it but didn't know precisely what to expect. The car carried the full Bentley livery, and looked fantastic. Piech and Buchelhofer saw the potential and gave us the go-ahead.

Marketing director Adrian Hallmark put the Le Mans entry into its historical context:

Bentley has been a sister to Rolls-Royce for 70 years and our job is to re-establish its roots as an independent company. A lot of that goes back to Bentley's Le Mans wins in the '20s and early '30s. That's not to say we're racing this year just for the sake of what happened 70 years ago, but people understand from the history that racing suits our marque values.

And what a history it is!

Andrew Frankel captured the essence of it in the *Daily Telegraph* of 16 June 2001, the day of the race:

Le Mans, June 21, 1930: Bentley is out to win the famed 24-hour race for the fourth time running. Between it and victory stands a Mercedes SSK driven by Rudolf Caracciola, Germany's greatest driver until the Schumacher era. The strategy is simple: Sir Henry 'Tim' Birkin will run his 4.5-litre Blower Bentley on pure benzole to provide power to match the pace of the supercharged 7.0-litre SSK, despite knowing that such a move means the engine is almost certain to break.

The less stressed Speed Six Bentleys will run behind, waiting to mop up should Birkin break the Mercedes. He sets about his task at once, to lie second behind the Mercedes by the third lap.

On the long Mulsanne Straight, he inches up on his rival despite a tyre throwing a tread under the strain. Undaunted, he approaches the Mulsanne hairpin at more than 125mph while the Mercedes occupies all of the narrow strip of road ahead. But there's always the grass – and Birkin has two of his three remaining tyre treads on it as he pulls off the overtaking manoeuvre of the decade.

Caracciola, as he later graciously concedes, never even sees the Bentley coming. On the third lap Birkin sets a new outright track record before first a tyre and then, later in the race, the engine give up. By then however, the job is done. The Mercedes is broken and Woolf Barnato's Speed Six claims Bentley's fifth and final win at Le Mans.

The 'Bentley Boys', as they became known, were the stuff of legend in the otherwise drab years of the 1920s, when for many, in Europe if not the USA, unemployment was a constant threat. Perhaps twenty qualified to be considered as one of the gang. They included the caustic wit George 'Titch' Duller, a professional jockey who raced cars for the sport of it, and the tall, tough John Duff, who was a successful motor trader and took Bentley to the first Le Mans race in 1923. With Bentley's professional race-driver-cum-engineer Frank 'Sunshine' Clement, they finished fourth, but they won the following year. Duff changed careers, becoming a horse-riding stuntman in Hollywood. Clement himself was no ordinary mechanic. He came from a family of wealthy jewellers and was a founder member of the British Racing Drivers Club. Then there was Clive 'Gallo' Gallop, who had owned a racing Peugeot while still at Harrow and who went on to fight as a Lieutenant-Colonel in the legendary RFC56 Squadron during the First World War. Another daredevil was Glen Kidston, who had been a submarine officer in the First World War. He won Bentley's fourth successive Le Mans in 1930 alongside Woolf 'Babe' Barnato and was tragically killed two years later in an aeroplane crash in South Africa after setting air records to Cape Town.

And there were foreigners in the gang, most notably Jean Chassagne, known as 'Chass' or 'Petit-Jean'. His most famous exploit was in the 1928 race (won, of course, by Bentley) when he saved the day by running with two jacks to rescue Tim Birkin, shouting 'Maintenant, c'est à moi!' Birkin himself was perhaps the best driver of them all, though a manic depressive – right up one minute, right down the next.

And there were others – 'Snitch' Callingham, 'Scrap' Thistlethwaite, the Baron d'Erlanger, Dick Watney, Berris Harcourt-Wood, the brothers Jack and Clive Dunfee, not to mention Jack Barclay, who went on to open the eponymous showroom in Berkeley Square. Number 28 Berkeley Square was the home of one of the most famous of the Bentley Boys: Dr J. Dudley 'Benjy' Benjafield, a leading bacteriologist of his day and known to his chums in the team as the bald-headed chemist. In her autobiography *Spreading My Wings*, Diana Barnato-Walker – daughter of Woolf Barnato, and a famous wartime ATA pilot who flew 260 different Spitfires – tells the story of how she was allowed to stay up late when father had some of the Boys to dinner, and how one night, as Benjy was about to fall asleep in his soup, she leant forward and tapped his bald head with a spoon. He later presented her with a scarf for saving him from drowning. [Diana Barnato-Walker went to the 2001 Le Mans race to help celebrate the return of Bentley.]

Benjy Benjafield won the 1927 Le Mans for Bentley, driving with Sammy Davis, sports editor of *Autocar*. The 1927 race was famous for the crash at the White House Corner, which knocked out two Bentleys and damaged the third – the one driven by Benjafield and Davis. In spite of serious damage, including a bent chassis, this Bentley went on to win, and at the party at the Savoy to celebrate was driven up the steps into the hotel. Many parties were held at Benjy's house at 28 Berkeley Square, and the house was later turned into Morton's Club by Ferrari driver Peter Morton.

Most famous of all was Woolf 'Babe' Barnato who owned a magnificent house in Surrey. At one of his many parties, Brooklands-style racing pits were constructed along the quarter mile to the house. Arriving in their Bentleys, the Boys, accompanied of course by the Bentley Girls, roared into the pits for their champagne. Barnato was not only a great driver, he was also a scratch golfer and county cricketer, and bred successful racehorses; he was the man who raced and beat the Blue Train from Saint Raphael, near Cannes, to Calais, a feat which brought him a rebuke from the RAC. He won the Le Mans race every time he entered – 1928, 1929 and 1930 – driving successively with Bernard Rubin, Sir Henry 'Tim' Birkin and Glen Kidston. Barnato helped Bentley with its financial difficulties, but, as we saw in Part One, even his wealth was diminished by the world depression of the early 1930s; he felt he could no longer support the company, and it passed into the hands of the receiver and on to Rolls-Royce in 1931.

Rolls-Royce did continue to support Bentley in its racing activities in the 1930s, notably with Eddie Hall (about whom we read in Part One), and at Le Mans through to the 1950s and also with the Embiricos Bentley referred to earlier in Part One.

As VW poured money into the factory at Crewe and prepared to launch the new Bentley in 2003, the future of the Rolls-Royce motor car in England lay on the Earl of March's estate in Goodwood in Sussex, where permission was received to build a greenfield factory capable of producing a thousand cars a year. The entire structure of the new Rolls-Royce, code-named RR/01, an extruded aluminium 'skeleton' with aluminium panels, will come from BMW's Dingolfing plant in Germany. A dedicated engine is being developed with a thus far unidentified 'outside partner'. Final assembly will take place at Goodwood.

Goodwood had been favoured by BMW because of its link with the 'golden' age of motor racing and because the surrounding area was home to a large pool of skilled workers in the yacht-making and Formula One businesses. There was also the 30-acre disused gravel pit on the Earl of March's estate opposite the race circuit. As well as carrying out final assembly, the complex would be home to a 30-strong design team, a research and development laboratory, engine test cells and offices for the new Rolls-Royce motor car company's worldwide sales operation. The Goodwood circuit could also be used for chassis testing.

FAST CAR, FAST SERVICE

It is not only in the field of luxury cars that aero-engine maker, Rolls-Royce, has an involvement. High-performance engines, on the ground or in the air, work at the extreme – whether in design, the materials used, the technology, the torque, the temperature or the speed.

In Formula One racing, the car is put under enormous strain, not only through the chassis and suspension but above all through the engine. Listen to that high-pitched scream as the engines push out over 17,000 revs and you can imagine the tolerances to which the engine must be working. Formula One is highly competitive, with hundreds of millions of pounds spent each year to win both the Drivers' and Constructors' Championship. The teams work at the edge of motor-racing technology.

Unlike aero-engines, where reliability and durability come before performance (important though performance is), Formula One engines are built for maximum power from minimum fuel for the length of a race. After the race, the engine is scrapped or at least completely rebuilt. The teams push the technology to the limit or frequently beyond it. On one such occasion, McLaren, long one of the leading Formula One teams, found that they were going over the limit and were in serious trouble just before the first race of the season.

The season was 1996 and the first race, in early March, was in Adelaide, Australia. The teams test constantly through January and February in preparation for the season, and in this case McLaren were testing in Estoril, Portugal, in the final two weeks before the race when it became clear they had serious problems. In less than an hour of testing, five of their six engines blew up.

The problem seemed to be in the pistons, which were made from a high-strength alloy called RR58, a material developed and patented by Rolls-Royce primarily for use in aero-engines. Ron Dennis, who runs the McLaren race team, knew Sir Ralph Robins and asked for his help. He explained that while McLaren employed experienced specialists as did their engine manufacturer Ilmore, based in Northampton, they were of necessity lean teams without the staff necessary to carry out major fault analysis. Rolls-Royce are staffed, of course, to carry out such analysis in depth; the need for reliability and safety demands it. Robins responded immediately – as a man who races his own Bentley, he takes an interest in all motor sport. [There was some banter about payment. Dennis talked about 'goodwill'; Robins said he preferred folding stuff he could count.]

On the Tuesday morning, with Practice Day – in Adelaide on the other side of the world – ten days away, the engineers from McLaren and Ilmore arrived in Derby and talked to the Rolls-Royce team allocated to the task of solving the problem. Dr Julia King put together the Rolls-Royce team led by Dr Mike Hicks, Head of Materials, and Steve Williams. The first thing the Rolls-Royce team did was to subject the pistons to detailed analysis, and this was time well spent, for when the stress analysis results came through the next day the area of fatigue had been identified at the top of a gudgeon-pin boss. A crack was appearing and causing piston failure.

The Rolls-Royce and McLaren teams needed to strengthen this area, and drawings were summoned from the Ilmore factory in Northampton. By Thursday morning, four new designs were available, and by Thursday afternoon the preferred solution, which would give 30 per cent less stress than the original design in the critical area, had been agreed. The design was sent to McLaren, who made slight modifications to make the manufacturing process easier.

The next problem was the worry that the fault had not been primarily a design one but the result of a poor batch of material. This concern made McLaren reluctant to use their existing supply of RR58 alloy. On the Saturday – six days to go, though in reality, with the flight time and time difference, only four days to go – McLaren asked Rolls-Royce if they could find some RR58. Rolls-Royce hunted across their plants and eventually found some of the alloy at their wide-chord-fan manufacturing base in Barnoldswick, ten miles north of Burnley in Lancashire (where, you will remember from Part One, Rolls-Royce had done most of its early work on the jet engine during the Second World War).

The material was despatched from Barnoldswick and picked up halfway to Northampton by McLaren. By Sunday evening, the redesigned pistons had been made and were running on test. The tests were run all night, and the engines were still running on the Monday morning without any breakdown. On the Wednesday, the cars and the engines were flown out to Australia.

The Rolls-Royce team could feel great satisfaction. As Steve Williams said:

The nice thing about a project like this was that it was all or nothing, there was no middle ground. When you are doing life assessment work on aero engine parts it can be years before you know if one design has been better than another or indeed if you have a problem. With this job the solution either worked or it didn't. It was a big team and we worked all-out but we needed to in order to pull it off. It made watching the race on television pretty exciting knowing that you had been part of making it happen.

And did McLaren win the race? No, though the engines did not blow up. Did they win the Constructors' or Drivers' Championship in 1996? No. Williams Renault ruled the roost in 1996 and 1997. But 1998 and 1999 were the years when McLaren did win the Constructors' Championship and their driver, Mika Hakkinen, won the Drivers' Championship.

Goodwill? McLaren provided tickets for the Rolls-Royce team at the British Grand Prix at Silverstone.

Folding stuff? Sir Ralph got it.

CHAPTER SIX

THE TRENT FAMILY

'THE TRENT PROGRAMME IS WELL ADVANCED'
AIRBUS INDUSTRIE
'THE SUN IS SHINING'
'WE'RE CASHING IN ON THE DESIGN HERITAGE'
NEW LABOUR
MAKING OUR CUSTOMERS OUR PARTNERS
A VERY LARGE AIRCRAFT

'THE TRENT PROGRAMME IS WELL ADVANCED'

WE LEFT THE CIVIL-AIRCRAFT business in Chapter Three still in recession. John Sandford, President of Rolls-Royce Inc., had described to the Rolls-Royce Board in June 1993 how the mood of the industry in the USA was 'angry' and the pressure on suppliers intense. Nevertheless, there were signs of an improvement in general business and consumer confidence throughout the world, an essential prerequisite to more air travel and therefore more orders for aircraft and aero-engines.

Where was Rolls-Royce with its new Trent engine at this point? Launched in 1988, the Trent ran for the first time in 1990, was scheduled to fly early in 1994 and to enter service in 1995. Designed to meet the needs of large airliners for the rest of the 1990s and well into the next century, it had already been ordered for the wide-bodied Airbus A330 and Boeing 777 twin-engined jets. We have already seen how Rolls-Royce increased the thrust of the Trent to cope with the demands of both Airbus and Boeing for extra range with higher payloads. The airlines were also demanding increased take-off thrust so that they could begin their cruise at high altitude. This would mean not only lower fuel consumption but also an increased possibility of securing operating slots at busy times of the day.

By mid-1993, the Trent 700 had been ordered by Cathay Pacific, Trans World Airlines, Garuda and the International Lease Finance Corporation to power their A330s. The engine would enter service at 72,000 lb thrust, but its thrust was expected to increase to 78,000 lb as the aircraft weight grew.

The thrust demands of the Boeing 777 were greater than those of the A330. Initially, the 777 would cover domestic and regional operations, known as the A market. But by the end of the decade, it would be required to cover the routes from Europe to the West Coast of the USA – the B market – and, at a later date, the longest transpacific routes – the C market. This would mean thrust levels into the 80,000 lb-plus area. The Trent 700's fan diameter of 97.4 inches would not be sufficient, and so Rolls-Royce had developed the Trent 800 with a fan diameter of 110 inches.

The Trent 800 had the same HP system and IP turbine as the Trent 700 but an increased-capacity IP compressor and a five-stage LP turbine. The engine had a higher pressure ratio of 40:1 at take-off and ran hotter than the 700, and as a result the material of the stage 5 and 6 HP-compressor discs had to be changed from titanium to a nickel-base steel alloy and the IP turbine blade to a new third-generation single crystal material. At the higher pressure ratio, its optimum HP turbine capacity was 3 per cent larger than for the 700. To achieve this, the HP nozzle guide vanes and HP turbine blades were skewed.

The Trent 800 was scheduled to enter service in 1996, certificated at 84,000 lb thrust, though initially it would be derated to 75,000 lb for the A-market 777s. By mid-1993, Thai, Emirates and Cathay Pacific had selected the Trent 800 for their 777s.

The Trent 700 and 800 were the lightest engines on offer for the A330 and 777 respectively. Weight saving had been achieved by using hollow wide-chord fan blades that were superplastically formed and diffusion-bonded, and by the use of aluminium isogrid casing. This aluminium-isogrid, Kevlar-wrapped containment system was no less than 380 lb lighter than the steel containment system used on the RB 211-524G engine.

Reliability and safety had always been of paramount importance to everyone in the airline industry, but with the new wide-bodied, twin-engine airliners it became, if possible, even more important. The airlines demanded that the A330 and 777 have clearance for 180-minute ETOPS (extended-range twin-engine operations). This permitted twin-engined aircraft to operate up to 180 minutes of single-engined flying time distant from an airfield, but only where service experience had demonstrated an in-flight shutdown rate better than 0.02 per 1,000 hours, i.e. one shutdown in 50,000 engine hours. ETOPS was an airworthiness requirement of both the Federation Aviation Authority (FAA) and Civil Aviation Authority (CAA) for twin-engined aircraft.

The RB 211-535E4 achieved 180-minutes ETOPS approval on the Boeing 757 in 1990 and the -524H on the 767 in March 1993. The Trent would build on techniques for reliability developed on the RB 211-535E4 and -524H which were now embedded in the Project Derwent process. It would also be subjected to a 3,000-flight-cycle ETOPS bench test using airline maintenance methods before the engine went into service. Boeing would conduct a programme of 1,000 flights with the 777 before the aircraft entered service, with the aim of providing ETOPS approval before the start of airline operations in order to compete with the A340 which, as a four-engined aircraft, did not require ETOPS approval.

Jeff Pearson, chief project engineer on the 777 in the earlier 1990s, said in December 1993:

The Trent development programme is well advanced. Pre-production engines have run more than 1,700 hours and over 5,000 cycles ... Along with the airlines, we also included the engine manufacturers in the 'Working Together' programme (devised by Boeing for developing the 777).

Phil Condit, the general manager of the 777 project, and later President of Boeing, said:

In the past, Rolls-Royce would have designed the propulsion system but for the Trent 800 we have co-designed the system under the 'working together' programme. By working together, on a complete propulsion system, we will have one that is even more reliable and easier to service. The contributions of Rolls-Royce offer an excellent example of the teaming concept in propulsion systems.

If Rolls-Royce saw a bright and sunny future for its Trent family of engines, good old *Lex* in the *Financial Times* was its usual dour and pessimistic self, writing in February 1994:

The current contest to produce the world's most powerful aero engine seems to be driven by machismo. While very high thrust engines are required for new wide-body twin-engined jets, the recent tests of the GE90 and Rolls-Royce's Trent produce 25 per cent more power than such aircraft currently require. At present only the Airbus A330 and the Boeing 777 need these engines, yet GE, Pratt & Whitney and Rolls have all invested hundreds of millions in this technology while orders have been scarce. All three have to compete on power and price for what business there is. In that context, Rolls' loss of the engine order for Japan Airlines' new Boeing 777s is disappointing but unsurprising. JAL can hardly afford to spend lavishly and, since the two other Japanese airlines have already specified Pratt engines for their 777 fleets, JAL has an incentive to share maintained facilities. Rolls may be leading the race for orders on the Airbus 330, but is lagging badly with the more significant Boeing 777s. That has stretched out the pay-back period for the Trent. Perhaps even more significantly, the market may not grow rapidly enough to justify the investment in three such engines. With orders unlikely to pick up for at least two years, competition will intensify.

What are the advantages of a 'family of engines?'

The adaptability of the Trent's three-shaft design is one of its most important advantages. The three-shaft design allows each engine module to be scaled up or down, and matched to suit performance and thrust requirements while maintaining proven combustion/turbine temperatures during take-off and climb. Engine maintenance costs are linked to the hottest parts of the engine, so maintaining even temperatures reduces maintenance costs. Furthermore, particular combinations of modules can create a range of cores tailored to drive two fans with different diameters – 95.5 and 110 inches.

Combined with the largest-capacity IP and HP compressors, the larger fan gives the Trent 800 a thrust-range from 75,000 lb to 100,000 lb, catering for all sizes of Boeing 777. At the same time, a scaled-down core with a smaller fan in the Trent 500 provides a thrust range of 53,000–62,000 lb for the Airbus A340-500/600. Such combinations mean that the Trent 700 and 800 share a 6:1 bypass ratio (i.e. the front fan driving seven times the flow of air used by the hot core), and the Trent 500 has a bypass ratio of 6.8:1 – a very long way from Rolls-Royce's first turbofan, the Conway, with a bypass ratio of only 0.3:1.

Also in the family are the Trent 900 with the larger fan, rated at 67,000–84,000 lb, suitable for the heavyweight versions of the Airbus 380, and the Trent 500 with a different fan, rated at 63,000–68,000 lb, suitable for the heavyweight versions of the 747 and 767.

To summarise, with thrust capabilities from 50,000 lb to 100,000 lb, the Trent family provides an engine for every latest-generation wide-bodied aircraft. And the design allows them to be made from short, simple modules which can be easily removed, split and rebuilt. Scaling and mixing the same range of parts means high commonality, especially for casings, nacelles and accessories. Common design also reduces training time.

The 700 was the first Trent into production, entering service on the Airbus A330 in March 1995. It has not been necessary to increase the thrust, as the A330 variants have weighed little more than the original aircraft.

The Trent 800 has been faced with stronger challenges as Boeing have increased the weight of the 777. Extended-range versions weigh up to 660,000 lb, compared with 545,000 lb for the first 777 in service. Rolls-Royce developed the Trent 8014, which produced over 100,000 lb thrust using new blade aerodynamics but without an increase in fan diameter or number of core stages. The most revolutionary development was the new scimitar-shaped or 'swept' fan blades which formed part of the Trent 900.

These latest fan designs are fabricated using external titanium-alloy panels and a central titanium-alloy membrane sheet. The key diffusion-bonding operation takes place in a clean-room complex to provide the appropriate environment for bond quality. The diffusion-bond heat treatment selectively joins this fabrication by atomic transfer. Next, the diffusion-bonded pack is inflated with an inert gas between precision-machined dies to form the internal Warren Girder core by superplastic forming, while at the same time producing the external aerodynamic shape. The manufacturing process is completed by numerical control machining and surface-processing operations.

The result of all this is a blade that is about 15 per cent lighter than earlier wide-chord fan blades and much lighter than those in competing big engines. It is also more economical to make than earlier fan blades and more resistant to bird-strike.

The first full-scale test of the swept fan was carried out in January 1995. It allowed the Trent 8014, with its 110-inch-diameter swept wide-chord fan, though rated at 104,000 lb thrust, to achieve 110,000 lb. The swept fan would bring much greater thrust without any increase in engine diameter.

AIRBUS INDUSTRIE

Immediately after the Second World War, there was no European aircraft industry. The former French and German aircraft factories lay in ruins. In Britain, the factories were geared to produce bombers and fighters which, but for a few exceptions, no one wanted any more, while in the USA the airframe manufacturers were quickly turning the technology acquired producing transport aircraft into airliners such as the Constellation, the DC-4 and the DC-6.

As we saw in Part Two of this history, the British, prompted by the Brabazon Committee, made a valiant effort to become a world player in civil-aircraft manufacture. The Vickers Viscount was a success, and the de Havilland Comet showed immense promise before its tragic accidents. However, by the time the Comet's problems had been solved, the American Boeing 707 and the Douglas DC-8 had stolen the market. Neither the Viscount's successor, the Vanguard, nor the VC10, BAC 111 or Trident sold in sufficient numbers, and Britain's challenge faded. Over in Europe, a number of airframe manufacturers tried to compete, and no fewer than ten different turbine-powered airliners were offered. But too often they were competing with each other, as well as the Americans. For example the Caravelle, the Trident and the BAC 111 were all short-range aircraft carrying about the same number of passengers. Total sales of all three aircraft amounted to 625, the number required for *one* to break even; instead, sales were split between two countries and three manufacturers.

Jean Pierson, Managing Director of Airbus Industrie from 1985 until 1998, said of the position at the end of the 1960s:

From the point of view of technology, the Europeans were capable, and comparable with the United States. But the Europeans competed against each other and fragmented the market in Europe. This internal competition prevented them having a great success in exporting aerospace goods while, at the same time, the US had a huge domestic market, which provided a good base for exports. People in Europe also realised at that time that the amount of money needed to develop new projects was becoming so high that, nationally speaking, it was quite impossible to pursue this policy.

The answer was co-operation, and by the early 1960s, with encouragement from their respective governments, the manufacturers were talking to each other.

If the British, French and Germans came together, it would not be the first example of co-operation since the war. The British and French had already begun work on developing the Concorde supersonic airliner, and the French and Germans were already working together on the Transall military transport aircraft.

In September 1967, Britain, France and Germany signed a Memorandum of Understanding to launch the opening phase for the development of a 300-seat wide-body aircraft called the European Airbus. It was to be a short-to-medium-range twin-engined aircraft to be called the A300, with 37.5 per cent of the work to be carried out in France, 37.5 per cent in Germany and 25 per cent in Britain. Sud Aviation of France would be the lead company. Hawker Siddeley, which had been working with the French companies Breguet and Nord Aviation on an aircraft called the HBN 100, was chosen as the lead British company and was therefore obliged to break off its relations with Breguet and Nord, and work instead with Sud Aviation. The British Government insisted that no prototype should be built until at least 75 firm orders had been received.

After much discussion on how to run the project, Sud Aviation was given the lead on the airframe and Rolls-Royce the lead on the engine. They also decided to form a limited company. As Henri Ziegler, Airbus Industrie's first general manager, said:

I knew it was essential to have the industrial partners as members of a legally established corporation, with a board, a chairman and a president. Otherwise, no one was responsible.

The French Government had originally refused to countenance a European Airbus project. It was something of a personal triumph for Ziegler that he was able to persuade the Government to change its mind, stating that he would not agree to work on Concorde unless the Government reconsider.

As the first general manager of Airbus Industrie was a Frenchman, it was decided that the chairman should either be British or German. An obvious choice was Franz-Josef Strauss, the German politician who had made aviation his speciality. Ziegler said at the time:

He played a vital political and financial role to convince the Germans that Airbus was an important programme, and that they should make all efforts for it to go ahead.

There was considerable debate in Germany as to whether they wanted to be involved in co-operative aerospace projects. (As we shall see, Eurofighter nearly foundered when the Germans threatened to pull out of the project in the early 1990s.) Fortunately, Strauss was not only the federal Minister of Defence but also Prime Minister of the State of Bavaria, where many of the German aircraft manufacturers were located.

In 1965, five German aircraft manufacturers – Bolkow, HFB, VFW (formed two years earlier to bring together Weser, Focke-Wulf and Heinkel), Messerschmitt and Dornier – formed the Studiengruppe Airbus to act as an interlocutor with the British and French firms.

Roger Beteille was appointed technical director in July 1967 and worked closely with the German engineer Felix Kracht to iron out many of the early technical problems. On the British side, the chairman of Hawker Siddeley, Sir Arnold Hall (later to be chairman of Rolls-Royce for a short interregnum between Sir William Duncan and Sir Francis Tombs), kept up the British interest.

Two big problems emerged in the late 1960s. The A300 being planned was perceived by many – most importantly, three of the most likely first custo- mers, Air France, Lufthansa and British European Airways – as being too large. Second, Rolls-Royce, who were of course pushing hard to have their new large engine, the RB 207, as the sole engine on the aircraft, began to run into problems in the development of the RB 211, which they had sold to Lockheed for the L.1011, the TriStar.

The choice of engine had been contentious. The French favoured the Pratt & Whitney JT9D which Boeing had chosen for their new wide-bodied 747. An agreement had already been signed for this engine to be made under licence by SNECMA and Bristol Siddeley Engines. As we saw in Part Two, Rolls-Royce could not countenance Bristol making the JT9 to compete with the RB 211, and it was partly, perhaps mainly, for this reason that Rolls-Royce bought Bristol in 1966. This made Rolls-Royce virtually the only aero-engine manufac- turer in Britain, and the British Government insisted on the choice of a Rolls- Royce engine as a condition for its participation in the Airbus programme.

The shrewd Beteille, noting these developments, set up a team to design a scaled-down version of the A300. Instead of 300 passengers, this version would carry 250. It could also be powered by an engine smaller than Rolls- Royce's planned 47,500 lb-thrust RB 207. Any of the three engines with a

42,000 lb thrust being offered by Rolls-Royce (the RB 211), GE (the CF6-50) or Pratt & Whitney (the JT9D-15) would be acceptable.

This proposal by Beteille had a number of advantages. A choice of engine would make the A300 acceptable to a wider range of customers and, as the engines were not being developed exclusively for the A300, development costs would be much lower.

Beteille's new design, originally the A250 but eventually the A300B, was accepted in May 1969. Beteille was not only a great builder of consensus, he also possessed marketing flair. He it was who insisted that the language of Airbus consortium should be English, saying:

My decision that English should be the language of Airbus was related to the same rule that I applied all along – the customer is king. All airlines in the world use what I might call west coast American aircraft slang. That had to be the language.

As well as using English as the Airbus language, the Airbus accounts were drawn up in the currency of the aerospace business worldwide: US dollars. For a French company to be allowed to do this required special dispensation from the French Government.

The next problem was the withdrawal of the British Government from the project. In the late 1960s – indeed throughout the 1960s and the whole of the 1970s, for that matter – the British economy was performing extremely badly compared with its competitors in Europe, the USA and Japan. British governments faced crisis after crisis and struggled with constant difficult choices between investment in industry and expenditure on social needs such as education and healthcare. Concorde's budgets had consistently overrun, and there were plenty of voices calling for no more involvement in joint European aerospace ventures.

In March 1969, Harold Wilson's Labour Government, by this time deeply unpopular, pulled out of the Airbus project on the grounds that the aircraft did not meet BEA's requirements and that the project was unlikely to be economic. Undeterred, the French and Germans decided to proceed without Britain. Responsibility for the airframe was shared between Sud Aviation (which merged with Nord Aviation in 1970 to form Aerospatiale), and the Deutsche Airbus consortium. (This consortium was made up of MBB and VFW, which would merge later, and Dornier.) GE and Pratt & Whitney were invited to compete for the engine, and the GE CF6 was chosen largely because GE were prepared to share much of the development work with the French engine manufacturer SNECMA, and also because the whole GE CF6 propulsion system was already flying on the DC-10. Furthermore, GE had developed an engine, the CF6-50, to power the long-range DC-10-30 which was suitable for the Airbus aircraft.

Sir Arnold Hall, outraged by the British Government's decision, kept Hawker Siddeley in the game by negotiating a private arrangement to manufacture the Airbus wings. Although the French were annoyed by the British Government's withdrawal, they acknowledged that British aircraft-wing technology was the best in Europe. It would also have added to the cost to find another manufacturer for the wings.

When the British Government withdrew, the French and Germans each took 50 per cent of the project and, in December 1970, when the Spanish company CASA became a partner, each gave up 2.1 per cent to give CASA a 4.2 per cent shareholding. (The British eventually came back in with a 20 per cent share in 1978.)

The maiden flight of the A300B1 took place at Toulouse on 28 October 1972. Sales took a little longer. In fact, the next few years, punctuated by the first oil crisis, were described as a 'marketing desert', and orders only began to come through after the appointment of Bernard Lathière as president in 1975. There were worries that the consortium might not survive, and black jokes such as 'Don't forget to catch the last train from Toulouse to Germany!' began to circulate.

After a number of almost-signed deals and as embarrassing lines of white tails queued up on the airfield at Toulouse, Airbus finally made a breakthrough in the all-important US market in 1977, when Frank Borman, former astronaut and by this time chairman and president of Eastern Airlines, signed a lease on four A300B4s for six months. The trial period went so well that in March 1978 Borman ordered 23 more, with a further nine on option.

Others gradually followed – SAS in December 1977, Iran Air in March 1978, Olympic Airways in June 1978, Swissair and Pakistan International in July 1978, Philippine Airlines and Alitalia in November 1978, and Iberia in December 1978. Nineteen-seventy-nine brought in Garuda, Malaysia, Air Afrique, KLM, Laker Airways, Cruzeiro, Egyptair and Singapore Airlines. It also brought orders for the second member of the Airbus family, the A310, from Swissair, Lufthansa, KLM, Air Afrique, Martinair, Air France, British Caledonian, Sabena and Inex Adria. The SAS order was significant because the airline insisted on having Pratt & Whitney engines. This brought Pratt & Whitney on to Airbus for the first time and left Rolls-Royce as the only engine supplier out in the cold.

However, Rolls-Royce came close at the beginning of the 1980s when Libya wanted to buy Airbus 300s and 310s. Because of their relations, or lack of them, with the USA, they were not able to buy GE or Pratt & Whitney engines, and Rolls-Royce were approached to see if they would supply. Unfortunately, the RB 211 with its larger fan than either the GE CF6 or the Pratt & Whitney JT9 did not comply with the ground clearance regulation and a pylon modification would be required. Libya was prepared to pay for the modification, but the order still foundered as some of the cockpit instrumentation was also made in the USA. Yet again, Rolls-Royce's attempts to get on Airbus were stalled.

The big story of the 1980s was the development of the A320. Initially, there was a debate about whether to develop the 150-seat, single-aisle A320 or the larger A330/340. Roger Beteille recalled:

When we had to decide between the A320 or the A330/340, the Germans, under pressure from Lufthansa, were in favour of going for the A340, while the French, perhaps not completely unconnected with their part in building the CFM56, were in favour of the A320. As far as I was concerned, there were two elements, one being the market needs, which were for a 320 earlier than a 340, and secondly, for the technical reason that, having to make a significant step forward in technology, like fly-by-wire, it was considerably easier and less risky to enter in this field with a smaller aircraft than with a big, long-range aircraft. There were some divergent ideas within Airbus but the final decision to go for the A320 was a smooth one.

Jean Pierson recalled that British Aerospace were in favour of proceeding first with the A320.

Further debate took place over how much new technology to build into the A320. Beteille argued successfully against producing a 'Boeing 737 look-alike', and Airbus bravely tackled the new high-tech possibilities, including fly-through computer systems, sidestick controls, gust-load alleviation and increased amounts of composite materials in the primary structure. Most significantly, the A320 also had a larger cabin diameter and industry-standard-LD3 container cargo capabilities. Rod Eddington, the chief executive of British Airways, told the author in February 2002:

This fly-by-wire decision by Airbus was absolutely critical in their success. Boeing were derogatory about it at first but soon had to concede that they were right.

The planned in-service date was March 1988, and only one suitable engine, the CFM6-A1 with 25,000 lb thrust, had been certified by that date. As we have seen, Rolls-Royce had concentrated its efforts on the USA since the late 1960s and had not powered an Airbus aircraft. It now saw a chance for its new consortium engine, the V-2500. As we saw in Chapter One, the International Aero Engines consortium, in which Rolls-Royce had a 30 per cent stake, claimed that the V-2500 was technically superior to the CFM56, but early development problems meant that CFM continued to win most of the early A320 orders. We saw how IAE won a prestigious contract from Lufthansa only to suffer the humiliation of losing it as the German airline fretted about the consortium's development of the engine. (Lufthansa would return to IAE for engines to power its A321s.)

The A321, a stretched version of the A320, was launched in November 1989, Jean Pierson seeing it as the counter-attack against the Boeing 757 in Europe. Typical seating was 186 – 16 in first class, 170 in economy – compared with 150 in the A320. In the meantime, the much larger A330 and A340 were launched in June 1987 and were targeted at the same market as the future Boeing 777, the McDonnell Douglas MD-11 and, to a certain extent, the 747. The twin-engined, medium-to-long-haul A330 aimed to seat 335 passengers in two classes, while the four-engine, long-range A340 expected to carry 295 passengers in three classes.

The two models had first been conceived in the 1970s. The A340's origins can be traced back to the proposed four-engined A300B11 derivative of the short-fuselage B10, later launched as the A310. Powered by the then newly developed CFM56, the long-range 200-seat A300B11 was conceived as a new-generation replacement for the Boeing 707 and Douglas DC-8. An enlarged A300, the B9, which would eventually evolve into the A330, had also been under study since the early 1970s.

As we have seen, there was much debate as to whether to go for a big twin-engined or a four-engined aircraft. The world's airlines were divided on the issue. Adam Brown, marketing vice-president of Airbus in the 1980s, remembered that 'North American operators were clearly in favour of a twin, while the Asians wanted a quad. In Europe opinion was split between the two.' He added:

The majority of potential customers were in favour of a quad despite the fact, in certain conditions, it is more costly to operate than a twin. They liked that it could be ferried with one engine out, and could 'fly anywhere' – remember ETOPS hadn't begun then … Customer interest meant that we planned to do the quad first and so initially it was called the A330 and the twin the A340. Then our salesmen came back and said the airlines would never get their brains around a twin having a '4' in its name and the quad not, so we reversed the designations.

As is often the case, the range requirement grew. Initially, customers seemed happy with 6,000 nautical miles (nm) or 11,100 kilometres (km). By the launch in 1987, this had grown to 6,600 nm (12,200 km), and by the time the A340-300 was in production the range had increased to 7,300 nm (13,900 km). Brown said in 1997:

Customers now tell us that passengers don't mind being on an airliner for 18–19 hours and the A340-500 will be able to fly 8,500 nm (15,700 km) non-stop.

As we have seen in Chapter One, at the end of 1986 IAE approached Airbus with an ultra-high-bypass 'Superfan' development of the V-2500, which incorporated a gearbox-driven, variable-pitch, ducted fan added to the front of the V-2500 core. Airbus adopted this engine for the A340 as it offered the required thrust (30,000 lb plus) as well as claimed fuel-consumption savings of almost 20 per cent when compared with a similar-thrust turbofan.

Lufthansa were the first to commit to this aircraft with the IAE engine when it ordered fifteen, with fifteen options, in January 1987. Unfortunately, in February 1987 IAE were forced to cancel the Superfan, saying:

It is felt premature to launch in the light of the technical programme risks of meeting the spring 1992 service entry.

Airbus were forced to revert to the less powerful and less efficient, but also less risky, CFM56-5. Sir Ralph Robins was alternating with Art Wegner as chairman of IAE and distinctly remembers how 'colourful' Jean Pierson's turn of phrase was when Robins had to ring to tell him that he felt IAE could not develop the superfan in line with the promises made by the salesman and would not therefore be proceeding.

Before the launch of Boeing's 777, Airbus's main competitor in the long-haul market was McDonnell Douglas's MD-11, and talks were held in the late 1980s about the possibility of a co-operative venture. Again, pressure came from Germany, which could see a lower outlay of money and easier entry into the lucrative US market if Airbus could combine with McDonnell Douglas against Boeing. These foundered (Jean Pierson would say later, 'it was a waste of my time'), and McDonnell Douglas seemed to put itself in a strong position when it beat Airbus to an order from Singapore Airlines for twenty MD-11s in 1990. However, in 1991 the airline cancelled its order when it became clear the MD-11 would not meet its exacting performance requirements. Singapore opted for twenty A340-300s instead. Airbus strengthened the A340's wing structure and boosted the range to 7,500 nm (13,900 km) to meet SIA's requirements. Brown commented:

The SIA switch was a marker in the MDC/Airbus battle. It was effectively the end of the MD-11.

At last, Rolls-Royce secured engine orders on an Airbus aircraft when Cathay Pacific ordered ten A330s and specified the Rolls-Royce Trent 700 engine. By the time this aircraft flew for Cathay in September 1994, Rolls-Royce was offering engines for the whole of the Airbus family – replacements for the older A300 and A310 wide-body airliners (provided someone would pay for the pylon modification), future derivatives of the A330 and A340, and the proposed A3XX super-jumbo. Jean Pierson, welcoming the roll-out of the first A330 equipped with a Rolls-Royce power plant, said:

It is high time we saw a made-in-Europe engine on an Airbus aircraft.

But the big breakthrough for Rolls-Royce with Airbus came in 1996 when General Electric effectively threw away their position as one of Airbus's most favoured suppliers. In April 1996, Airbus signed a six-month exclusive study agreement with GE for GE to develop an engine for the new versions of the A340, the -500 and -600. It was expected that Airbus would need to invest $2 billion in developing the aircraft and that GE would have to invest $1 billion to develop the new engine.

After careful study of the market and discussions with focus groups, Airbus decided to develop two new versions of the A340. The first was a 20-frame stretch with a larger wing and higher-thrust engines. This aircraft would provide the best balance of capacity and range. Dubbed the A340-600, the new model would carry about 380 passengers over the same ranges as the A340-300. At the same time, an aircraft slightly larger than the 295-seat A340-300, but still with the -600s bigger wing and engines, would carry 313 passengers over longer ranges. This would be called the A340-500.

Asked by the author in January 2002 how this situation came about, Pierson said:

A new engine was needed for the A340-500 and A340-600 and it could not be the GE/SNECMA CFM56 because that was already at the limit of its capabilities. All three leading engine manufacturers were invited to compete and at the end of this competition we decided to pursue the GE offer. I met the President of General Electric, Jack Welch, in New York and gave him six months to pursue his offer and during that period said that we would not have any conversations on the engine with either Pratt & Whitney or Rolls-Royce.

At the end of the six months, Jack Welch came to Toulouse and we were in agreement on all technical and financial aspects of their engine and their offer. However, Welch, in view of his heavy investment in the engine, said that he wanted an exclusivity deal on the Airbus A340 while at the same time being able to offer the engine to Boeing.

Non, non, non, jamais! I said to him. We cannot tie ourselves exclusively to you giving you the chance to increase your price. I am sorry, but, no. [Jack Welch in his autobiography *Jack*, published in 2001, does not mention this conversation. Indeed, he does not mention Jean Pierson nor even Airbus Industrie.] So we then talked to Pratt & Whitney and Rolls-Royce. I met George David, the Chairman of United Technologies and John Rose, the Chief Executive of Rolls-Royce. Both engines were technically acceptable but again, David started talking [about] exclusivity and even John Rose mentioned it.

In the end we chose Rolls-Royce and gave them not exclusivity but rather a period of privilege of some years before we would discuss an offer from anyone else.

David Hygate, working for Rolls-Royce at Airbus's headquarters in Toulouse at the time, recalled that the competition with Pratt & Whitney became very intense, and through the early months of 1997 the two fought to convince Airbus that they should choose their engines.

Rolls-Royce had offered a re-cored Trent 700, effectively a 600. However, in view of the problems with the earlier 600, Rolls-Royce did not want to call it a 600 and – as it produced 56,000 lb of thrust – named it the Trent 500.

In June 1997 at the Paris Air Show, Airbus announced that it had selected the Rolls-Royce Trent 500. The larger of the two new models, the A340-600, would be 11 metres longer than the A340-300 and would be able to carry 378 passengers, in three classes, some 370 km further – i.e. 13,900 km. The smaller, the A340-500, would have the new wing, engines and increased weights of the -600, with a slightly stretched -300 airframe and about 48 per cent more fuel capacity, allowing it to carry 313 passengers and giving a range of over 15,700 km.

Airbus maintained that its arrangement with Rolls-Royce was not exclusive because it '[allowed] other engine manufacturers to come in at a later date'. However, Pratt & Whitney, which had proposed its PW4500 engine, ruled itself out, insisting that it would need to have a sole-source agreement to justify the investment.

On 1 September 1997, Virgin and Air Canada placed the first orders for the Rolls-Royce Trent-500-powered A340s, and by the end of September seven airlines had placed orders for 100 of the A340 variants, all to be powered by Trent 500s. Rolls-Royce Chief Executive, John Rose, said:

This is the strongest launch we have ever had for a new engine programme. It's tremendous news for the Trent family.

As Airbus committed itself to the programme, it forecast sales of 1,500 aircraft in the category by 2010, and it expected to supply 50 per cent of them.

Development of the Trent 500 went smoothly. It was certificated at 60,000 lb thrust but was derated to 53,000 lb for the long-range A340-500 and to 56,000 lb for the higher-capacity A340-600. Within two years, over $5 billion of orders were won, much of it with new customers, making it one of Rolls-Royce's most successful engine launches in its history. The Trent 500 had the same 97.5-inch fan diameter as the Trent 700 and a reduced-flow core derived from the Trent 800. The reduced core size provided an 8.5:1 bypass ratio, giving low fuel burn and extremely low noise. The fan consisted of 26 titanium wide-chord hollow fan blades with a composite conical spinner. The LP fan was driven by a five-stage LP turbine, an eight-stage IP compressor driven by a single-stage IP turbine, and a six-stage HP compressor driven by a single-stage HP turbine. In the compression system, the eight-stage IP compressor included three variable stator stages to optimise the compressor operating characteristics. These were at the front of the engine in a cooler environment. Both the IP and HP compressors had double casings to separate the gas path from the load-carrying structure. This helped to maintain circular inner casings and to maintain minimal compressor blade tip clearances, which improved efficiency. For overall engine-efficiency improvement, both compressors incorporated viscous-flow-design aerofoils throughout.

For the airlines, the attraction of the Trent 500 was Rolls-Royce's ability to scale proven designs from existing Trent family members while incorporating the latest technology where appropriate. As with all Rolls-Royce's large engines, the Trent 500 was a three-shaft design allowing each shaft to be scaled to operate at an optimum speed, meaning that the engine could be lighter, shorter and stronger.

Ian Kinnear, the programme director, said:

We have specifically designed the Trent 500 to exceed airline expectations for reliability and the team is aiming at the elimination of disruption to airline operation. This will deliver a smooth entry into service and a successful ongoing operation for our customers.

By July 2000, Airbus had secured orders for 129 A340-500/600 aircraft. Kinnear said:

It is by far the fastest ramp-up of a big fan engine production programme we have ever seen. Fortunately we have increased annual production from a few hundred engines 10 years ago to more than 1,000 so we're ready for it.

And Rolls-Royce knew that engine reliability was of the utmost importance. Robert Nuttall, the Trent-500 head of marketing, said that they had sat down with Airbus at the beginning of the programme and decided that the in-flight shutdown (IFSD) rate should be zero from entry into service, adding:

Any other target would be unacceptable. It is important that we deliver because Airbus is relying on us. They have nowhere else to go.

'THE SUN IS SHINING'

On 15 November 1995, John Rose happened to be going to Rolls-Royce's Derby plant from Rolls-Royce's head office in Buckingham Gate in central London to announce that the company was contracting out its information-technology systems. It was a big deal worth £600 million over ten years as 750 Rolls-Royce staff were transferred to General Motors subsidiary, EDS.

On the way there, he received a telephone call which gave him the news that Singapore Airlines had just told Nick Devall, Rolls-Royce's sales director in Singapore, that the Trent 800 had been selected to power the 61 Boeing 777s they had ordered. This was clearly a deal of a somewhat different dimension. When Rose arrived in Derby, he told the workforce:

I want to tell you why the sun is shining in Derby today.

The significance of the order for Rolls-Royce could hardly be exaggerated. As Andrew Lorenz wrote in the *Sunday Times* four days later:

SIA is what the industry calls a 'reference' order – an endorsement of the Trent after exhaustive evaluation by an industry leader. As such, it hugely enhances Rolls's prospects, particularly in Asia, which will double its civil-aviation market share over the next 15 years.

Such press coverage was a welcome change from the headlines in the previous year, when Singapore Airlines had ordered Boeing 747s and Airbus A340s, the 747s to be powered by Pratt & Whitney 4056 engines and A340s by CFM56 engines. Then, the headlines had been 'Rolls Setback' and 'Unhappy Rolls'.

The growth of Singapore Airlines, from a standing start in 1947 to a position as one of the world's leading airlines by the early 1990s, is one of the great stories of the world's airline industry.

In 1947, Malayan Airways, jointly owned by BOAC (British Overseas Aircraft Corporation) and Qantas, began services between Singapore, Kuala Lumpur, Ipoh and Penang using twin-engined Airspeed Consuls. Later in the year, Douglas DC-3s were added to the fleet for flights to Jakarta, Medan, Palembang and Saigon. The following year a service to Bangkok was launched, and in 1949, with an additional three DC-3s, services to North Borneo, Sarawak, Mergui and Rangoon. Growth was steady, if unspectacular, in the 1950s and 1960s as DC-4 Skymasters, Vickers Viscounts, Lockheed Super Constellations, Bristol Britannias, Comet IVs and Fokker F27s were added to the fleet.

With the creation of the Federation of Malaysia in 1963, the airline was bought by the Government, renamed Malaysian Airways Limited and then, in 1967, Malaysia-Singapore Airlines. In that year, services to Perth and Taipei were launched, as also was the Boeing 707-320B fan-jet service to Sydney.

The real turning point came in January 1971 when it was announced that the Malaysia and Singapore governments would set up separate national airlines.

Immediately after the Second World War, Singapore had been returned to civilian rule as a Crown Colony separate from Malaya, which became the Malayan Union. In 1948, a state of emergency was declared in Malaya and Singapore. The Malayan Communist Party, which had been founded in 1930,

175

was proscribed and went underground. During the first half of the 1950s, the Malayan Union and Singapore negotiated its independence from the UK, and in 1957 the Federation of Malaya became independent. In June 1959, Singapore was declared a self-governing state, with Lee Kuan Yew sworn in as Prime Minister. He began to urge support for a merger with the Federation of Malaya, and in a referendum held in September 1962 Singaporeans approved such a merger. In the following year, Malaysia, comprising Malaya, Singapore, Sarawak and Sabah, was proclaimed. Lee Kuan Yew fought to establish a multi-racial society but faced dominance by the Malays, and in July 1965 Tunku Abdul Rahman, the first Prime Minister of the Federation of Malaya and later of the Federation of Malaysia, agreed that Singapore should become a separate State, saying to Lee Kuan Yew:

There is no other way now. I have made up my mind; you go your way, we go our own way. So long as you are in any way connected with us, we will find it difficult to be friends because we are involved in your affairs and you will be involved in ours. Tomorrow, when you are no longer in Malaysia and we are no longer quarrelling either in parliament or in the constituencies, we'll be friends again, and we'll need each other, and we'll co-operate.

On 9 August 1965, Singapore separated from Malaysia. The British Government recognised the new nation the next day, Prime Minister Harold Wilson writing to Lee Kuan Yew, 'You may be sure that we wish you well.'

Lee Kuan Yew wrote later that he was 'prepared to do whatever was needed to make an independent Singapore work', though he did not know that he was 'to spend the rest of his life getting Singapore not just to work but to prosper and flourish'.

Prosper and flourish Singapore did – and Singapore Airlines along with it.

On 30 June 1972, the national airline of Singapore was named Singapore Airlines (SIA). From that moment, the growth of the airline was phenomenal. In July, SIA signed a contract with Boeing for the purchase of two B747-200s and an option on two more. A twice-weekly service to Athens and Zurich, and a thrice-weekly service to Frankfurt and Osaka were launched, while the service to London was increased to five times a week. By April 1973, SIA was flying daily to London.

SIA decided that the only way they could compete with the giants in the industry was by offering better service. They pioneered free drinks and headsets when others were charging for them (just as Japanese carmakers broke into Europe and the USA by offering, as standard, gadgets that indigenous car makers charged as extras). They also offered a choice of meals in economy class. Furthermore, they kept ahead, continually innovating with such services as an in-flight telephone for every passenger and a multiplicity of video channels on their interactive KrisWorld entertainment system. Nor did all this extra service mean initial losses for the airline as it built market share. It had been profitable from day one.

By 1978, SIA was operating a Concorde in conjunction with British Airways and in that year signed a record $900-million deal with Boeing to buy thirteen B747s and six B727s. In May 1983, another huge order was announced when SIA bought six B747-300s, four B757s and six Airbus Industrie A310s, an order worth $1.4 billion. By the end of the 1980s, Singapore Airlines had consolidated its position as South-East Asia's leading airline, and in July 1989 the governments of the UK and Singapore signed an aviation agreement allowing extra flights between the two countries. This gave UK airlines liberal access to the important hub of Changi Airport (opened in July 1981), but it also gave SIA extra capacity and operating flexibility in its services between Asia and Europe.

In February 1989, SIA formed a subsidiary, Tradewinds, later re-named Silk Air, which began its career with a service to Pattaya using a leased MD-87.

Later that year, SIA signed a long-term alliance with Delta Air Lines, thereby improving its position in the important US market.

By 1991, SIA had bought 56 Megatop 747s worth nearly $10 billion, and later that year it bought twenty Airbus A340-300s. On 22 June 1994, it placed another huge $10.3-billion order for 22 Megatop B747s and 30 Airbus A340-300Es.

Singapore Airlines had established itself as one of the world's leading airlines. Over the previous decade it had been awarded nearly 100 service quality awards. In 1994, *Air Transport World* had said:

Singapore Airlines is the measure by which others are judged.

Dr Cheong Choong Kong, Deputy Chairman and Chief Executive of SIA, told the author in the spring of 2002:

We were situated perfectly from a geographical point of view, but we were very open-minded and our philosophy was 'We want a young and modern fleet'. As a result, we became an influential buyer of aircraft and engines.

The first of the Trent-powered Boeing 777s which Singapore Airlines had just ordered would be delivered in 1997, the fiftieth anniversary of the airline's foundation. The company had floated on the Singapore Stock Exchange in 1985. The flotation had coincided with a recession in Singapore and a crisis on the exchange, which closed for three days. The SIA shares, floated at $5, fell back briefly to $4.40 before recovering. [They are now $14, the equivalent of $28 as there has been a one-for-one split.]

SIA's recent financial performance had been outstanding, especially when it was compared with most airlines around the world. Its net profit for the year ending 31 March 1995 increased by 14 per cent to a record $917.5 million.

In 1994, at what turned out to be the last days of the early-1990s recession, though it was not clear at the time that the world economy was about to enjoy six years of growth, Singapore Airlines announced orders for $10 billion of new Boeing and Airbus Industrie aircraft. The managing director, Dr Cheong Choong Kong, said:

We don't think you can really call the future and know when the cycle will turn. There is considerable lead time in the ordering and delivery of aircraft and you have got to plan ahead.

Lorenz in the *Sunday Times* also tracked the tough time Rolls-Royce had been having in the depressed market of the early 1990s against two competitors with infinitely greater resources. He referred to the shattering blow of losing the BA order for 777 engines to GE, writing:

Many believed the move of Britain's flag carrier to buy American sounded the death-knell for Rolls in the market for big engines. The deal killed Rolls's prospects of breaking into the Japanese market through selling the Trent to All Nippon Airways. Some, both inside and outside Rolls, thought it heralded the loss of its independence.

As we have seen, Rolls-Royce hit back after the loss of the BA and Japanese business, winning orders from Thai, Emirates and Cathay Pacific. It lost its customer Saudia, who bought 777s and 747s with GE engines after pressure on the Saudi Government from President Clinton. Even though Rolls-Royce could claim that the Trent was smaller and lighter than its rivals thanks to the unique three-shaft design, in many competitions the greater political and financial clout of its competitors seemed to win through. But not in the case of Singapore Airlines. How did Rolls-Royce do it?

According to Nick Devall, who arrived from Rolls-Royce Inc.'s office in Reston, near Washington, to take over Rolls-Royce sales in South-East Asia in June 1994 – the day, as it happened, that Rolls-Royce lost out in the competition to power the new 747s Singapore Airlines had ordered – it was because they established a clear and simple strategy and stuck to it.

There were four main points to the strategy.

First, the Rolls-Royce team had to sell Rolls-Royce as a whole to the airline. Not only would it provide the best engines, it would provide the most dedicated support once they were in service. Furthermore, this was a new, international Rolls-Royce, established and selling throughout the world (the

TOP: Henri Ziegler, the first general manager of the Airbus consortium, insisted on forming it into a limited company, saying: 'I knew it was essential to have the industrial partners as members of a legally established corporation, with a board, a chairman and a president. Otherwise, no one was responsible.' Here, Ziegler (in glasses) is signing the documents setting up the corporation with Franz-Josef Strauss, the first chairman.

BOTTOM: Roger Beteille, appointed technical director of Airbus in 1967, could see that Rolls-Royce was going to find it difficult to develop the 47,500 lb-thrust RB 207 as well as the 42,000 lb RB 211 for the Lockheed TriStar. He therefore designed a smaller version of the A300 that could be powered by either Rolls-Royce's RB 211, GE's CF6-50 or Pratt and Whitney's JT9D-15. Here, Beteille (standing) is with Frank Borman, Chairman of Eastern Airlines (centre), and Bernard Lathière, President of Airbus, as they sign the agreement for Eastern Airlines' purchase of four A300 B4s.

A Rolls-Royce Trent 700 on the test bed in Derby. The programme
to develop this engine benefited from the Trent 600 programme,
which was eventually abandoned when Air Europe collapsed and
with it the launch order on the MD-11.

OPPOSITE TOP: The maiden flight over the Pyrenees of the A330,
powered by Rolls-Royce Trent 700s.

OPPOSITE BOTTOM: A Cathay Pacific A330, powered by Rolls-Royce
Trent 700s, coming in to land at Hong Kong airport.

Developed after Rolls-Royce won a 'period of privilege' in
providing the engines for Airbus's A340-500 and -600 (OPPOSITE),
the Trent 500 (ABOVE) was effectively a re-cored Trent 700.
By September 1997, seven airlines had ordered 100 of the A340
variants, prompting Rolls-Royce Chief Executive, John Rose,
to say: 'This is the strongest launch we have ever had for a new
engine programme. It's tremendous news for the Trent family.'

LEFT: Jean Pierson, Managing Director of Airbus from 1985 until 1998, said, when the A330 powered by the Rolls-Royce Trent 700 was rolled out: 'It is high time we saw a made-in-Europe engine on an Airbus aircraft.'

RIGHT: Noël Forgeard, the current Chief Executive of Airbus.

Mike Howse, Director of Engineering and Technology at Rolls-Royce,
with Alain Garcia of Airbus Industrie (on his right), discussing the A340,
Airbus's answer to the Boeing 777.

A Trent 800 on the wing of a Singapore Airlines Boeing 777.
Chew Choon Seng, Commercial Director of SIA, said:
'The selection process was intensive and thorough. We have
a reputation for being a real pain.'

TOP: Joe Pillay, Chairman of Singapore Airlines when SIA selected the Trent 800 for its Boeing 777s, said: 'Both the engineering and the sums pointed to Rolls-Royce.'

BOTTOM: Dr Cheong Choong Kong, Deputy Chairman and Chief Executive of Singapore Airlines, and John Rose, Chief Executive of Rolls-Royce, at the delivery of the first Trent engines to power SIA's Boeing 777s.

ABOVE AND OPPOSITE: American, Delta and Emirates all reached the same conclusion as Singapore Airlines that the Rolls-Royce Trent 800 was the engine for their Boeing 777s. Emirates' Managing Director, Maurice Flanagan, said: 'We are glad to see our choice has been confirmed by airlines which have the greatest respect in our business – British Airways, Singapore, Cathay, Malaysia, American and Delta.'

TOP: Gordon Bethune, President of Continental Airlines, looking forward to the visit of Sir Ralph Robins.

BOTTOM: Richard Turner, Group Marketing Director of Rolls-Royce throughout the successful 1990s.

purchase of Allison was announced in the autumn of 1994). This was not a company from the heart of the British Empire expecting favourable treatment from its former colonies. And there was to be no knocking of the competition. Pratt & Whitney had been a long-term, valued and well-liked supplier to Singapore Airlines.

Second, Rolls-Royce made it clear it would give Singapore Airlines a great commercial deal, as good, if not better, than any its competitors might offer.

Third, it would convince the airline that the aircraft would have very good residual value.

Fourth, and perhaps most important, they would convince the airline that the Trent was the best available engine whether they chose the Airbus A330 or the Boeing 777.

The competition began in October in 1994 with a technical briefing to the airframe competitors, Airbus and Boeing, and the engine contenders, Rolls-Royce, GE and Pratt & Whitney. Dr Cheong Choong Kong, Singapore Airlines' Managing Director, said that the airline was planning to bring forward its decision to acquire between ten and twenty new wide-body, twin-engine aircraft both for expansion and the replacement of older aircraft. At this stage, the potential order appeared to be worth about $200 million, and Rolls-Royce was working towards the possibility of a decision being made in December.

However, the timescale became stretched, first into the spring of 1995, then the summer and finally the autumn. To compensate those working 18 hours a day, day after day, week after week to come up with an acceptable deal, the potential order grew as the general economic climate improved. In the autumn of 1995, as D-Day approached, John Rose asked Joe Pillay, the Chairman of Singapore Airlines, if John Cheffins, now Rolls-Royce's Chief Operating Officer but then Managing Director of Civil Aerospace, could make a final presentation of the Rolls-Royce case to the whole selection team plus the senior management of Singapore Airlines. Rose told Pillay that the Singapore decision was the key decision of the 1990s, just as American Airlines' decision on the 757 had been the key one for the 1980s. Rose wanted Cheffins and his team to be able to sell Rolls-Royce as a company, the Trent 800 as an engine and the whole back-up of the Rolls-Royce organisation, which would provide product support. Pillay granted his wish, and the team duly made the presentation. The team consisted of John Cheffins, who presented Rolls-Royce as a company fully capable of producing and maintaining the engines that SIA required, Phil Hopton, who convinced the SIA selection team that the Trent was the perfect engine for their aircraft, and Tony Woodings, who spelt out the details of the support Rolls-Royce would provide once the engines were delivered. According to Nick Devall, the team, especially Phil Hopton, made a brilliant presentation, exuding confidence in their product. Nevertheless, Pillay and the selection committee gave the Rolls-Royce team a torrid time, inviting them to refute the fact that the Trent was no more than a hybrid of the RB 211-524 and RB 211-535. As it happened, Cheffins only just made the presentation as he had to fulfil a long-standing engagement at a Rolls-Royce award ceremony in Sydney the day before. He hired a Canadair Challenger 600 to fly him to Singapore, but the landing gear failed and the aircraft had to land at Sydney again. He made it to Singapore just in time for the presentation.

Flight International predicted:

For Airbus and Boeing, along with General Electric, Pratt & Whitney and Rolls-Royce, the contest promises to be as bloody as last year's battle. SIA will once again be looking to take full advantage of the depressed market to squeeze and lock in suppliers on future pricing, delivery schedules and after-sales support.

Chew Choon Seng, Commercial Director of SIA, told the author in spring 2002:

The selection process was intensive and thorough. We have a reputation for being a real pain. Both Rolls-Royce and General Electric asked us – Is this just so that you can leverage a better price out of Pratt & Whitney? We told them it was not, the competition would be decided on technical and economic merit.

As far as Chew Choon Seng was concerned, there would be three aspects to the economic merit – the capital cost, the cost of operation and maintenance, and the likely residual value of the aircraft. On the technical front, he reckoned that Rolls-Royce would have a very tough time convincing SIA that its engines were a better prospect than those of Pratt & Whitney, who were offering a variant of the PW4000 which was already giving good service on SIA's B747s, or of GE, whose new GE90 had been specifically designed for the 777. Furthermore, GE were willing to underwrite the enhanced perform-ance capabilities of the GE90. He said:

We thought initially that the Trent was just a derivative of the RB211-524. However, John Cheffins and Phil Hopton put us right on that and convinced us of the advantages of the three-shaft design.

Nevertheless, this was going to be SIA's mainstay product in the first decade of the millennium. As far as they were concerned, it was essential to make the right choice. Chew Choon Seng said:

All three engines had their supporters. There were only shades between them in terms of technical performance. Pratt & Whitney obviously had an advantage as the incumbent supplier. However, the new fleet was going to be of such a size that this advantage would be eroded. Furthermore we were looking, at that time, to place our engineering department in a position where they could bring in outside work. A new engine would help this approach.

Joe Pillay agreed with him:

Both the engineering and the sums pointed to Rolls-Royce. Our engineers, perhaps like most engineers a little conservative, wanted to stay with Pratt & Whitney. They took some convincing but in the end recognised that a change to Rolls-Royce would be good for both them and Pratt & Whitney.

William Tan, who ran the evaluation process, and Mervyn Sirisena, who oversaw the technical appraisal, certainly made sure that every aspect, both commercial and technical, was subjected to the most rigorous due diligence procedures.

The previous year's contest had ended in a draw for the airframe makers with a mixed order for more 747-400s and extended-range A340-300Es. Unfortunately, Rolls-Royce engines were not selected in that order.

Whether Cheffins and the team had done enough would finally be revealed on 14 November 1995. All the interested parties – Airbus, Boeing, GE, Pratt & Whitney and Rolls-Royce – were put in separate, sealed rooms without any means of communication between each other or to the outside world. For Rolls-Royce, Singapore Airlines decreed that the only representative should be Nick Devall, and he had to wait until last.

The results we know: it was the Boeing 777 to be powered by Rolls-Royce Trent-800 engines. The quantity was not the ten to twenty aircraft originally spoken about by Dr Cheong but 77 – 34 firm and 43 options – with up to 157 engines, worth $1.2 billion – then, and still today, the largest single order Rolls-Royce has ever received. (The Singapore Airlines order was for 61 aircraft that would all be powered by Trent 800s. The other sixteen were for Singapore's leasing associate, Singapore Aircraft Leasing Enterprise. The engine decision for these sixteen aircraft had not yet been made.) Devall could hardly grasp the joy of it all and still to this day claims that his overwhelming reaction was, 'Good, I can now go home and spend some time with my family.' Anyway, he was capable of telephoning Rolls-Royce's office in Singapore from Singapore Airlines' office at Changi Airport to tell Tim Jones, Rolls-Royce's South-East Asia regional director, who passed on the good news to the Chairman, Sir Ralph Robins. (Fortuitously, Robins was in Singapore for a Board meeting of Standard Chartered, where he was a non-executive director.) Robins was staying in the Shangri La Hotel, and, as he said, 'The name was appropriate. We had the odd drink that night.' The significance was enormous. Robins added:

SIA is a benchmark airline. Its decision will have an impact everywhere.

When asked by a local reporter how long Rolls-Royce had been working on the deal, Robins replied, 'Twenty-seven years.' The reporter looked quizzical, and Robins repeated, 'I'm telling you, 27 years – ever since we started trying to sell Singapore Airlines the Lockheed Tristar.'

And, of course, though Devall was the man to be given the news, he would be the first to say that he was only the frontman for a team of over one hundred who had worked for months on the campaign.

The *Derby Evening Telegraph* under the banner headline 'Million-Mile Deal Makers', wrote:

Rolls-Royce negotiators from Derby travelled around a million miles to clinch a huge £1.5 billion [a bit up on everyone else's $1.2 billion] order with Singapore Airlines. It is estimated the firm's team made about 60 return trips to the Far East – 16,000 miles every time …

… The work is expected to last well into the next century and takes the Trent's share of the 777 market from 18 per cent to around 33 per cent.

The negotiating team was led by Derby-based Ian Aitken, Rolls-Royce's Aerospace Group vice-president for sales in Asia and the Pacific. He visited the Singapore office around once a month. Sales director Nick Devall spent three out of every four weeks there. Other visitors included the Chairman, Sir Ralph Robins, Aerospace managing director John Rose, finance executives and engineers. John Rose, who had always believed that Rolls-Royce would be successful in winning the order, made no less than nine trips to Singapore in twelve months, usually leaving England on a Saturday to return on a Monday night.

Ian Aitken led the celebrations in Derby with his engineering and sales team, and told journalists who suggested that Rolls-Royce must have cut its price to the bone to see off its rivals, especially the apparently well-entrenched Pratt & Whitney:

It's a very profitable contract for us over time.

Pratt & Whitney's comment was:

Rolls-Royce must have had access to the Queen's coffers to have been able to beat our bid. They must have seen winning this order as do or die.

However, Rolls-Royce knew they had won the order on merit and among all the excitement of the Singapore order came the news that Rolls-Royce had won two other important orders in the same week: a £100 million order from Gulf Air for Trent 700s to power its Airbus A330s and a new order for A330s from Cathay Pacific. To complete a very successful week, Rolls-Royce and Swire, the Hong Kong-based trading company, announced the first of Rolls-Royce's network of joint-venture overhaul facilities, Hong Kong Aero Engine Services Limited (HAESL).

As always, winning the initial order was just the beginning of the whole order process. Indeed, some people believe that an order is not an order until you get a repeat order. Rolls-Royce knew that Singapore Airlines was not only a demanding potential customer when it was tendering to supply but would also be an exacting one once the engines were delivered.

Tim Jones said two years later when the first engines were delivered:

We were euphoric. We were absolutely delighted because this is such a renowned world-class airline – one whose selection criteria and procedures are extremely rigorous. To be chosen in that arena and in those circumstances is a significant achievement. It's a tremendous endorsement of our technical product. We followed through by doing some very thorough and innovative work with an agreed programme of activities to prepare ourselves and the customer for entry into service. The programme steps are jointly owned between people in Singapore Airlines and Rolls-Royce. It's not a matter of them and us. We are partners in this.

Nothing was left to chance. Shortly after the order was announced, Rolls-Royce sent a team of technical experts to Singapore to ensure a 'seamless path of progress toward entry into service'. Singapore Airlines sent engineering specialists to Derby, and a training engine was delivered to the airline's workshops at Changi. As Jones said:

In common with other customers, Singapore Airlines had never had such a big engine in its 'garage'. We delivered them a practice engine very early on so that they could get used to the sheer size and movement. It was very useful in bringing us closer together.

Rolls-Royce sent Steve Davis, who had worked for Rolls-Royce for 27 years, to be the field support manager at Changi. He arrived sixteen months before the first engine and soon realised the professionalism of the Singapore engineers:

They wanted to be able to strip an engine completely and replace the modules by the time the first aircraft arrived – that's unprecedented in my experience.

And how did the engines perform in their first few months? The first four 777s began on the short-haul routes to Penang, Kuala Lumpur and Jakarta and were then moved on to the medium-haul routes such as Melbourne, Madras and Delhi. By the end of 1997, the engines were averaging 240 flying hours, with about 100 take-off-and-landing cycles a month. Eight months after their first flight, not a single delay or cancellation had occurred because of engine problems.

In 2002, Joe Pillay said:

I am no longer with SIA but I talk to my old friends and I have heard no complaints about the Rolls-Royce engines.

After such a triumph, it was an appropriate moment for Rolls-Royce to announce that the managing director of the Aerospace Group, John Rose, would take over as chief executive when Sir Terence Harrison retired on 30 April 1996. It had been a very significant year for Rolls-Royce, one which had included the completion of the acquisition of Allison, a project in which Rose had been closely involved for a number of years, and this highly significant order from Singapore Airlines. Rolls-Royce itself described 1995 as a 'landmark' year.

'WE'RE CASHING IN ON THE DESIGN HERITAGE'

Rolls-Royce could look at itself at the end of 1995 and say, 'We are a very different company from the government-owned business of the early 1980s.' Then, the company's civil-aircraft coverage had been confined to the Boeing 747, the Lockheed L.1011 TriStar (Lockheed decided to cease production in 1980), the Fokker F28 Fellowship and Gulfstream III.

By the end of 1995, engines of the Rolls-Royce group were powering no fewer than 27 aircraft types, as well as civil turboprops and civil helicopters. On the Boeing 777-300, 777-200 and 747-500X/600X, and the Airbus A330-300 and A333-200, were Trents of 68,000–100,000 lb thrust; on the Boeing 747-400 and 767 were RB 211-524s of 50,000–60,000 lb; on the Boeing 757 and the Russian Tupolev Tu-204 were RB 211-535s of 37,400–43,000 lb; on the Airbus A321, A320 and A319, and the McDonnell MD-90 were V-2500s of 22,000–33,000 lb; on the Gulfstream V, Global Express and MD-95 were BR700s of 14,000–23,000 lb; on the Gulfstream G-IV, Fokker F100, Fokker F70 and Boeing 727 were Tays of 13,850–15,400 lb; on the Embraer EMB-145 and the Citation X were Allison AE 3007s of 6,000–12,000 lb; on the Citation Jet, Swearingen SJ30 and Raytheon Premier 1 were FJ44s of 1,900 lb, and on the SAAB 2000 and IPTN N-250 were AE2100s in the 6,000 shp class. Also powering civil turboprops and civil helicopters were Allison Model 250s in the 420–450 shp and the 420–717 shp class.

Rolls-Royce engines were also powering 23 military aircraft as well as light helicopters. On Eurofighter 2000 was the EJ200 in the 20,000 lb class; on the Tornado was the RB 199 in the 9,000–18,000 lb class; on the Harrier, Sea Harrier and AV-8B was the Pegasus up to 23,800 lb; on the BAe Hawk and MDC T-45 Goshawk was the Adour of 5,200–5,990 lb; on the AMX was the Spey of 11,030 lb; on the MB339 was the Viper of 3,750 lb; on the Global Hawk was the AE 3007 of 8,300 lb; on the Nimrod 2000 was the BR710 of 15,000 lb; on SK-60 and the Dark Star was the FJ44 of 1,900 lb; on light turboprops were Model 250s in the 420–450 shp class; on the V-22 Osprey was the T406 of 6,150 shp; on the C130J Hercules was the AE 2100 of 6,000 shp; on the EH101, Apache and NH90 helicopters was the RTM322 in the 2,100–3,000 shp class; on the Sea King was the Gnome of 1,175–1,660 shp; on the Eurocopter Tiger was the MTR390 of 1,274–1,911 shp; on the Comanche and the Bell UH-IHRE was the T800 of 1,300–1,550 shp; on the Lynx was the Gem of 900–1,120 shp, and on light-helicopters were Model 250s of 420–715 shp.

Rolls-Royce had also negotiated many partnerships. As long ago as the 1960s, it had joined Turbomeca to make the Adour, and now expanded that partnership by including Piaggio in Italy to make the RTM322. To make the RB 199, it had joined MTU in Germany and Fiat in Italy. With the same two partners and also ITP in Spain, it was making the EJ200 for Eurofighter. To make the V-2500 engine, it had joined Pratt & Whitney, Japan Aero Engines Consortium, MTU and Fiat to form the International Aero Engines consortium. To make the BR710 and BR715, it had joined BMW in Germany to form BMW-Rolls-Royce GmbH, and, in the USA, it had joined Williams International to form Williams-Rolls Inc. to make the FJ44 and, finally, Allied Signal to form LHTEC to make the T800.

It had also taken on a number of risk-and-revenue-sharing partners on its managed programmes. On the Trent, 24 per cent had been taken on by KHI, IHI, Hispano Suiza, ITP, BMW Rolls-Royce, Denel Aviation, Lucas and Celma. On the RB 211-524G/H8, 1 per cent had been taken on by KHI and IHI, and on the Tay 25 per cent had been taken on by BMW Rolls-Royce, Volvo and Alfa Romeo.

The future was looking pretty good too. Boeing was forecasting that in the coming twenty years to 2015, some 15,900 jetliners would be built, worth about $1,100 billion. About 3,900 would be replacement aircraft so that new aircraft to meet growth would number about 12,000. Rolls-Royce researchers were even more optimistic, forecasting a demand for 18,700 aircraft over the same period, of which 13,000 would be jets and the rest turboprops. Rolls-Royce forecast that just over half the jet-engine market by value would be for the big jet engines for medium-to-long-haul airliners. Rolls-Royce had positioned itself, following the Trent family strategy and its purchase of Allison, to be able to offer an engine for every aircraft – large, medium or small.

The hoped-for knock-on effect of winning the Singapore order was felt in January 1996 when Malaysian Airlines announced it would buy Trent 800s for the fifteen Boeing 777s it was ordering. And in February it was announced that Singapore Aircraft Leasing Enterprise (SALE) had chosen Trent 800s for six Boeing 777s. Dr Cheong Choong Kong said that, although Singapore Airlines held a 50 per cent stake in SALE, the choice of engine would be the prerogative of the airlines leasing the aircraft. There were still a further ten 777s on order where the engines had not been decided.

At this point, every Boeing 777 sold into South-East Asia would be powered by the Trent 800.

The good news was punctuated in March 1996 by the bad news that the Dutch aircraft manufacturer Fokker had gone into liquidation. Rolls-Royce had been supplying 60 to 80 Tay engines annually for Fokker aircraft for a number of years and would lose about $150 million of business as a result. As John Rose said:

It was a good job Fokker didn't go in the early 1990s when sales to them were a very significant part of our business.

For Rolls-Royce, the good news continued into 1997. With the Trent 800, it had reached second place on the Boeing 777 with 32 per cent of the firm orders, still behind Pratt & Whitney but ahead of GE. With the Trent 700, it had also clinched 32 per cent of the Airbus A330 market, again pushing GE into third place. Trent chief engineer Mike Terrett put the success down to the triple-shaft policy, saying:

This engine comes of age with higher thrust. We're cashing in on the design heritage. At this stage, the triple-shaft design allows you to give more thrust with only a little increase in weight. The original design was over-engineered. The RB211-22B, for example, had a huge amount of weight that could be taken out. But, because of that, we didn't get huge bending deflections, and that's one of the main features which gave us confidence in the long term.

As we have seen, for the first time on any Boeing wide-body aircraft, the Rolls-Royce engine was lighter than the competition. As Terrett said:

With the -524 we were heavier, with the -700 we achieved parity and with the 800 we are lighter, roughly 30 per cent lighter in the case of the GE90 and maybe 1360 kg per shipset over the PW4084. The fan is probably a third of our weight advantage. The fan diameter was increased from the 700's 98" to 110" on the 800 for straightforward thrust reasons. The 700 fan would probably have gone to 80,000 lb thrust if we had chosen to, but we'd have had to make some radical changes to strengthen the blades for bird strikes and so on.

A major benefit of the three-shaft design was the simplicity of the uncooled IP turbine. Rotating at 70 per cent of the speed of the high-pressure turbine, it was running at half the stress and at cooler temperatures. Furthermore, the Trent 800 benefited enormously from work done on the Trent 700. The 700 programme preceded that of the 800 by twelve months, and lessons were learnt and absorbed.

Rod Eddington, Chief Executive of British Airways, certainly agreed with this. He told the author in February 2002:

When I was at Cathay we experienced a few problems with the Trent 700, the gearbox I think, but Rolls-Royce put them right, and the Trent 800 has been superb.

The majority of systems were common, with significant changes to only four line-replaceable units out of 70. For example, the air system was common to both Trents and similar to the RB 211, although, in the 800, carbon seals were used to control leakage of oil into the bearing chambers, as opposed to labyrinth seals on the 700.

One significant difference was the thrust reverser. The 700 suffered some problems with the tertiary lock system that had been introduced late on in the engine's development after the accident on a Lauda Airways aircraft. The Boeing-designed system used translating cowls on the 800, as opposed to four tilting buckets on the 700.

Giving credence to Rolls-Royce's view of the superiority of the three-shaft approach was the comment of the Emirates Group managing director, Maurice Flanagan, when asked in the summer of 1997 why Emirates was becoming an all-Rolls-Royce-powered airline:

When we concluded in the course of expansion that we needed bigger aircraft than the A300 and A310, the options were the A330, A340, MD-11 or, just coming to the market six or seven years ago, the Boeing 777.

We built a computer model and ran through it the different airframes and combinations of engines available for those aircraft on the basis of guarantees we had received at that stage from the manufacturers, and we looked to see which produced the best bottom line. We made no assumptions as far as the aircraft were concerned about market appeal.

We also tossed into that comparison the anticipated traffic, using the same aircraft types that we were operating as a benchmark. The best bottom line on those terms was produced by the Boeing 777 with the Trent 800 engine. We then had to consider what the appeal of those different airframes would be to passengers. When you looked at that, the 777 went even further ahead. So that's why we went that way.

Iftikhar Mir, Emirates' senior general manager of engineering, added that the development of the RB 211 had won a reputation and credibility in the market-place. Like the RB 211, the Trent was 'a three-shaft engine, which provides a most efficient matching of rotating assemblies performing at optimum speeds'. He also felt that the engine had advantages because of its shortness and lightness.

Choosing the Trent for their A330 fleet, Flanagan said:

The Trent produced the best economics that encapsulates all the factors you consider about an engine, the total package. That was the reason for putting the Trent on the A330-200. Also, we have already got it on the 777, which is a help as there is a degree of commonality that we would be stupid to ignore.

The total package available for the Trent on the A330-200, the engine itself and the supporting arrangements by Rolls-Royce, placed it ahead of the competition. We picked the Trent for both aircraft, after, and I must stress this, a most meticulous, comprehensive and objective study.

To make Rolls-Royce feel really good, he added:

We are glad to see our choice has been confirmed by airlines which have the greatest respect in our business – British Airways, Singapore, Cathay, Malaysia, American and Delta. Although we are a small airline we do have a reputation for knowing our job, and other airlines do watch us.

Once the Emirates were flying 777s with the Trent 800, Mir had only praise, saying:

We are very satisfied with the performance of the engine. Our pilots like its thrust, rate of climb, indication systems, all sorts of performance parameters and the ability to reduce power and still perform very well. And, of course by reducing power you increase the life of an engine as the deterioration is less.

Our first experience of Rolls-Royce has been on our 777s. The product support which we have received over the past year or so has been good. Any problems are resolved with great dedication and effort. Rolls-Royce has positioned representatives here in Dubai and we have frequent conference calls with their Derby base to resolve any outstanding issues. The response is always prompt. One of the fears an operator has in entering into a one-engine situation is that product support could deteriorate because of lack of competition. But having received such response on our Trent 800s we did not hesitate in selecting the Trent 700 on our A330s.

By 2000, Emirates was carrying five million passengers and was flying 30 aircraft to 47 destinations, a far cry from an airline fifteen years earlier which was flying two aircraft on three routes.

NEW LABOUR

In 1997, the long eighteen-year rule by Conservative governments came to an end when the Labour Party, led by Tony Blair, who became Prime Minister, and Gordon Brown, who became Chancellor of the Exchequer, swept into power with a massive majority. 'Triumph' trumpeted *The Guardian*, 'Massacre' shouted the *Daily Mail*, and 'Landslide' moaned the *Daily Telegraph*. Labour's 419 MPs was a record for the Party, while the Tories' 165 was their lowest number since 1906. Whereas in 1992 many had been surprised by the Tories' success in clinging on to power, everyone had long expected the Labour victory of 1997. The MORI voting-intention poll had shown the Tories and Labour neck-and-neck in the first quarter of 1992, and the Tories five points ahead in the second quarter, the period covering the general election. Following the fiasco of the withdrawal from the ERM in September 1992, the Tories fell twelve points behind at the end of the year and never recovered. Their nadir was a 34-point deficit in the fourth quarter of 1994, but even by the first quarter of 1997, as Prime Minister John Major hung on grimly to the last possible minute before calling an election, the deficit was still 22 points. The fact was, the Party had blown its economic credibility in 1992 and, although both Norman Lamont and Kenneth Clarke proved capable Chancellors of the Exchequer and the British economy performed increasingly well as the 1990s wore on, the electorate were not prepared to forget. The situation was not helped by a series of financial and sexual scandals involving MPs and even senior ministers. David Mellor, Secretary of State for National Heritage and lover of Chelsea, got himself into a frightful mess over an extra-marital affair. The *Sun* newspaper had a field day with Mellor doing all sorts of unmentionable things in his Chelsea strip.

Jonathan Aitken, who had proved so helpful to Rolls-Royce in the Euro-fighter saga with Germany (see next chapter) and whose name had been mentioned as a possible future leader of the Party, was found guilty of perjury and sent to prison. Others, such as Neil Hamilton, became embroiled in a scandal as to whether they had taken money from Mohammed Al Fayed. Finally, the Party was clearly completely split over Europe and Britain's attitude to the European Community.

By contrast, the Labour Party of the early and mid-1980s, which had not appealed to the electorate, had been transformed by a small band around Tony Blair, closely and cleverly advised by Peter Mandelson. 'New Labour', as they came to be known, organised themselves for the election of 1997 as though born to it. It was 1945 all over again – away with what the electorate viewed as the self-serving, sleazy, corrupt and incompetent Tories and in with the reforming party of the people. The big difference from 1945 was that 'we're all middle-class now', so New Labour were very careful to promise that there would be no rise in income tax and that they would stick to the Conservative Party's fairly tight public-expenditure plans for the first two years in office.

In 1979, just before the election that brought Margaret Thatcher to power, Labour Prime Minister James (now Lord) Callaghan said:

There are times, perhaps once every 30 years, when there is a sea-change in politics. It then does not matter what you say or what you do. There is a shift in what the public wants and what it approves of. I suspect there is now such a sea-change – and it is for Mrs Thatcher.

In 1997, there was a sea-change. The public did not necessarily want 'New Labour', but they definitely wanted something different from their perception of the Conservative Party, which had clearly run out of steam and ideas.

As far as Rolls-Royce was concerned, the company has always been fully aware of the importance of the Government. It was, after all, by far the company's biggest single customer. In this case, Rolls-Royce found it had nothing to fear from a Labour Government. This was not the socialist Government of 1945 hell-bent on redistribution of wealth and with a mandate from the people to take into public ownership the means of production and distribution. Clause 4 of the Labour Party constitution had long been abandoned. Tony Blair and Gordon Brown went out of their way to show how friendly they were towards wealth creators and carried on with privatisations begun under Margaret Thatcher in the 1980s, rather than reverting to the nationalisations of the Labour Government in the 1940s. John Rose, in his capacity as President of the Society of British Aerospace Companies, was successful in persuading the Prime Minister to open the Farnborough Air Show.

By 1997, the upswing in the world economy and therefore in the airline industry was well-established. Orders for Rolls-Royce engines came thick and fast. In June, British Airways ordered the RB 211-524HT 'hybrid engines', in preference to GE's CF6-80C2 and Pratt & Whitney's PW4000, for the fourteen Boeing 747-400s it had ordered in September 1996. The -524HT engine was a modification of the -524H using the core of the Trent 700. Also in June, Rolls-Royce announced it had secured a $700-million order to supply Tay engines to power Gulfstream IV corporate jets. Rolls-Royce had already delivered more than 600 Tays to Gulfstream. The new order would keep deliveries going until 2003 and came as a welcome boost to the Tay programme, which had lost an important customer when Fokker ceased production at the end of 1996. At the same time, the US airline, Continental Express, announced that it would exercise its options on 25 Embraer EMB-145 regional aircraft powered by the AE 3007, and the American Airlines subsidiary, American Eagle, confirmed firm orders for 42 EMB-145s with 25 options.

All these announcements came at the Paris Air Show, where Rolls-Royce was also able to announce the deal with Airbus to supply the Trent 500 for the long-range A340 which we read about earlier.

John Cheffins, Commercial Aero Engines Managing Director, said that this selection by Airbus confirmed the flexibility of the company's unique three-shaft design, adding:

It allows us to design a range of engines with relative ease.

The 56,000 to 62,000 lb-thrust Trent 500 would use an 80 per cent linear-scale Trent 800 core. The 97.5-inch fan would come from the Trent 700, and the resulting bypass ratio of 8.5:1 would compare with the 6:1 of the Trent 700 and 800.

By the end of 1997, the benefits of the 'family' approach were becoming clear as orders for engines in the Trent programme passed the 1,000 level. Since the first Trent 700 went into service on the Airbus A330-200 with Cathay Pacific in March 1995, rated at 72,000 lb thrust, the family had grown to cover a range of thrusts from less than 56,000 lb to more than 100,000 lb. Each year had brought a new milestone. In 1996, the first Trent 800 went into service with Thai Airways International on the Boeing 777-200 with an initial 76,000 lb thrust, and in 1997 deliveries were made for the heavier 777-2001GW version with the highest-thrust-rated engine at 92,000 lb. By the end of 1997, the Trent 8014, with a world-beating thrust of 103,000 lb, was being developed for the planned 777-200X/300X. Adapting the Trent to lower-thrust levels had produced the Trent 500, the only engine offered on the Airbus A340-500/600. All of these engines were using the same basic technology and just two fan diameters. Finally, Rolls-Royce had used the Trent high-pressure core to update the RB 211, the original three-shaft engine designed in the 1960s which was still being sold on the Boeing 747-400.

And the prestigious *Economist* recognised the benefits of this 'family' approach, writing in June 1997, under the heading 'Rolls-Royce Flies High':

Sir Ralph Robins, Rolls-Royce's chairman, rejects accusations of buying market share. [These accusations had been made by GE and Pratt & Whitney after Rolls-Royce secured the Singapore Airlines order.] He says that the British company's advanced technology means it can run off a range of different-sized engines from one basic model, so dodging the huge development costs (upward of $1 billion) normally associated with each new engine. Rolls-Royce, for example, has five variations of its big Trent class engines that can fit ten aircraft, while GE's sole really large engine fits only the Boeing 777.

In November, Air Canada chose Rolls-Royce Trent 700s to power the A330-300s it had ordered in August from Airbus. That order was for nine aircraft with options on a further ten. Announcing the order, Air Canada said it had chosen the Trents because of 'their excellent performance, low fuel burn, low noise and emissions, and ease of maintenance'. This order made Air Canada the ninth customer to order the Trent 700 for the Airbus A330. Six days later, American Airlines named Rolls-Royce as the engine supplier for its 777 fleet. It had ordered eleven 777s but said it could eventually buy 50 and would power them with Trent 800s. Bob Crandall, American's Chairman, said:

We have been very pleased with the performance and reliability of the other Rolls-Royce engines we use.

As we have seen, American was already using Rolls-Royce RB 211-535E4s on its 90 Boeing 757s, and Tay 650s on its 75 Fokker F100s.

American was the second large US carrier to choose the Trent 800. Delta Airlines had already said it would power the 777s it had on option with the engine. Later in November, it was confirmed that Delta would buy ten 777s with firm options on twenty more and rolling options on a further 30.

Three months later, American took its firm order for eleven Boeing 777s to nineteen. The new aircraft, for the 777-200ER increased-weight variant, would allow American to fulfil its stated ambition of tackling the Asian and other international markets by enabling the aircraft to fly non-stop routes of 8,000 miles. The Trent 892 engines would supply 92,000 lb of thrust.

By August 1998, Airbus had achieved 120 commitments from nine customers for the Rolls-Royce Trent-500-powered A340-500/600 aircraft. In that month, Emirates Airlines confirmed an order for six with an option on a further ten. Emirates Chairman, Sheikh Ahmed bin Saeed Al Maktoum, said the aircraft would be used for non-stop flights from Dubai to North America and Australia, adding:

The aircraft's ability to operate from the Middle East with its high temperatures on long-range services with full passenger and cargo loads is very important. Only the A340-500 has the performance to fly non-stop to the US east and west coasts whatever the temperature in Dubai. We are very happy with the 777 [also powered by Rolls-Royce engines] but the offer we had from Airbus was the best. As an airline we will always make a decision on a commercial basis and we will remain a client of both manufacturers in the future.

In September 1998, Rolls-Royce achieved what must have been a very satisfying order when BA announced that its new 777s would be powered by Rolls-Royce Trent engines in preference to General Electric GE90s, which, as we saw, launched the 777 with BA. As the *Financial Times* put it:

BA's decision in the early 1990s to power its first generation of twin-jet 777s with GE engines was a substantial setback to Rolls-Royce and provoked political controversy in the UK. Rolls-Royce initially struggled to convince airlines to buy its engines after its national carrier had rejected them. However, Rolls-Royce fought back, winning orders for 777s from others including Thai Airways International, Singapore Airlines, Malaysian Airlines, American Airlines and Delta. [Meanwhile] BA experienced some problems with the GE90.

BA has always maintained that its decision to buy the GE90 as opposed to the Trent was a purely commercial one. However, as we saw in Chapter Three, Sir Richard Needham felt there may have been other considerations, and Jack Welch, the recently retired Chairman of GE, admitted it in his recent autobiography.

Brian Newman, analyst at stockbroker Henderson Crosthwaite, said, of the 1998 order:

This deal is a major victory for Rolls. Its defeat at the hands of GE seven years ago always looked a strange decision by BA and now all the main members of the Oneworld alliance will have Rolls-powered 777s. Rolls is on course to take 50 per cent of the big-engine market, making it the market leader.

This new order was for sixteen 777s with an option on a further sixteen. The engine selected was the Trent 895 with a thrust of 95,000 lb, which won the competition against Pratt & Whitney's 98,000 lb-thrust PW4098 and GE's 93,000 lb-thrust version of its GE90.

By the end of 1998, Chief Executive John Rose was able to say:

In 1998, the company delivered 500 large civil engines and a further 400 small engines, representing an increase in unit deliveries of nearly 50 per cent over 1997. This compares to an average of 400 civil engine deliveries a year in the first half of the 1990s and 200 civil engines a year in the late 1980s.

A third of all civil aircraft ordered in 1998 will be powered by Rolls-Royce engines. This success has been achieved across the product range, which is the broadest on offer in the industry. Rolls-Royce engines have been chosen by eight of the top ten airlines in the world and by 38 of the top 50. Airline customers continue to choose the Trent engine family for their wide-bodied aircraft. This engine secured 68 per cent of the orders placed in its target market during 1998.

Rolls-Royce has added new civil customers at the rate of more than one every month throughout the 1990s and has done this by establishing the broadest possible range available. At the top of the range, the Trent has had particular success and now has a well-balanced order book covering Asia Pacific, North America and Europe. The Trent 800 has been chosen by every Boeing 777 operator in south-east Asia.

MAKING OUR CUSTOMERS OUR PARTNERS

Until the 1990s, repair and overhaul of its engines was not viewed as a mainstream activity by Rolls-Royce. In effect, the company gave it away. However, realising that they were missing a business opportunity, in 1993 Rolls-Royce set up a separate company, Rolls-Royce Aero Engine Services Limited, pulling together sections involved in repair and overhaul at their plants in Derby, Bristol, Scotland and Ansty. This was a beginning, but to realise the potential fully investment would be needed, and in 1996 a completely new organisation was set up with full IT backing. Gradually, facilities were set up round the world and a number of joint ventures agreed.

In 1997 in Hong Kong, Hong Kong Aero Engine Services Limited (HAESL) was formed, a $120-million 50:50 joint venture between Rolls-Royce and Hong Kong Aircraft Engineering Company (HAECO). At that time, HAESL was the only engine-overhaul facility in the Asia-Pacific region able to handle the Rolls-Royce Trent engine. HAECO already had twenty years' experience of handling Rolls-Royce engines, mainly for Cathay Pacific and Dragonair, but this was chiefly on RB 211s. Its facilities could not cope with the Trent, and by this time more than 300 were on order in the region. A new facility was needed and was built, capable of running engines up to 130,000 lb thrust and also of handling up to 25 engines at any one time.

By the end of 1998, Rolls-Royce had fourteen maintenance facilities across the world. In Fort Worth in Texas, there was a joint venture with American Airlines called Texas Aero Engine Services LLC (TAESL), and an agreement with Singapore Airlines had been signed to set up a facility at Changi airport.

TAESL, a purpose-built operation, was designed to support American Airlines through the repair and overhaul of both Rolls-Royce RB 211-535 engines for American's Boeing 757 aircraft and Rolls-Royce Tay 650-15 engines for its Fokker F100s. It would also be prepared for the Trent 800, which American had ordered for its Boeing 777s, and be set up to cope with the increasing number of maturing Rolls-Royce engines in both North and South America.

In Mexico, Rolls-Royce's Spanish affiliate, Industria de Turbo Propulsores (ITP), took a 60 per cent controlling interest in the aero repair and overhaul company Turborreactores, based in Queretaro.

John Rose said of these joint ventures:

Through this growth strategy we have doubled our share of repair and overhaul of Rolls-Royce civil engines to about 50 per cent and expect this to grow as our new products enter service. This will reflect in growing sales for our repair and overhaul business, which we expect to double over the next five years and to continue growing after that.

As well as the planned repair and overhaul facility, Rolls-Royce also set up International Engine Component Overhaul (IECO) at Changi Airport in a 50:50 joint venture with Singapore Airlines. This would specialise in the refurbishment of high-technology aero-engine nozzle guide vanes as well as compressor stators.

By 2001, this expansion had transformed Rolls-Royce's repair and overhaul business from a $400-million operation in 1993, operating from four sites in the UK plus one in Canada and one in Brazil, to a $1.6-billion business handling sixteen sites throughout the world. It enabled Rolls-Royce to offer Total Care packages, and it began to sign some large deals.

On 3 January 2001, it was announced that Rolls-Royce had won its biggest maintenance contract to date. Worth £600 million, it was to overhaul the engines on British Airways' new fleet of Airbus short-haul aircraft. The twenty-year contract was awarded by International Aero Engines, which, as we know, manufactured the V-2500 engines and in which Rolls-Royce was a significant shareholder. More Total Care packages quickly followed.

On 11 January 2001, Rolls-Royce signed a $1-billion ten-year Fleet Hour Agreement with American Airlines. The agreement involved the provision of comprehensive maintenance, at a set cost calculated on flying hours, for American Airlines' existing fleet of 102 Boeing 757s. Another 23 757s, due to be delivered during 2001, would also be covered by the agreement. John Cheffins, President Civil Aerospace at Rolls-Royce, said:

Fleet hour agreements provide operators with the benefit of aftermarket support [and] predictable costs together with the advantage of a long-term association with engine manufacturers.

Continental Airlines became another to sign up to Rolls-Royce's Total Care customer-support programme when it signed a $360-million maintenance, ten-year support agreement for its fleet of RB 211-535E4B engines on its 41 B757-200s. South African Airlink and South African Airways also signed long-term agreements in 2001, the former for its AE 3007-powered Embraer ERJ-135 regional-jet fleet and the latter for its RB 211-524-powered B747-400s.

On 8 April 2002, it was announced that Rolls-Royce had signed a $530-million Total Care agreement with Cathay Pacific for the maintenance of the Trent 700 engines on the airline's fleet of A330 aircraft. This meant that 40 per cent of all Trent engines in service were covered by Total Care packages.

The Total Care packages comprised more than just repair and overhaul; rather, they promised a wide range of services for through-life engine management. On-line systems included predictive maintenance, giving fleet managers immediate access to real-time engine performance data provided by air-to-ground computer links. Data Systems and Solutions, the joint venture between Rolls-Royce and Science Applications International Corporation, provided systems integration, integrated asset management and maintenance solutions.

Reviewing the past five years and looking to the future, Ian Lloyd, Managing Director, Aero Repair and Overhaul, said in 2001:

Rolls-Royce has a worldwide customer base. It therefore also needs a worldwide MRO [maintenance, repair and overhaul] presence. So, since 1995, where a customer in a strategic location has been reviewing its support activities, we have entered into joint ventures or other partnerships. Where Rolls-Royce did not have a geographical MRO presence, we partnered with a customer that did. In this way we have been able to export quality service and world-class standards to where our customers need them. Making our customers our partners has brought us big rewards. And while we continue to develop our expertise in other engines, our main concern will always be our own. After all, no one knows a Rolls-Royce engine better than Rolls-Royce.

A VERY LARGE AIRCRAFT

The big battle in 1999 between Rolls-Royce, GE and Pratt & Whitney was the fight to see who would be chosen to power Boeing's stretched versions of the 777: the 777-200X and -300X. Whoever won would have to develop the most powerful commercial turbofan engine ever built, one capable of more than 115,000 lb thrust.

As the thrust demand had grown, Rolls-Royce moved beyond its original mooted engine for the aircraft, the Trent 8014, which became an 'orphan' power plant and a *de facto* technology demonstrator. All was not wasted as some of the technology was used in the Trent 500, which by 1999 was in the final stages of its development for the Airbus A340-500/600, the rival to the B777X. To cope with Boeing's demands, Rolls-Royce took the core of the 8014 and scaled it up 2.5 per cent geometrically. It also increased the diameter of the fan from 2.8 to 3 metres, while at the same time introducing the swept blade. The new engine, the Trent 8115, would undergo a test programme that would incorporate a 2,000-cycle extended-range twin-engine operations (ETOPS) phase. Rolls-Royce was determined to have 207 minutes' ETOPS clearance 'out of the box'.

Unfortunately, for Rolls-Royce and Pratt & Whitney, it was announced in July 1999 that Boeing had signed an exclusive agreement whereby all 777Xs would be powered by GE's GE90-115B engine. The agreement was reached after meetings involving Boeing Chief Executive Phil Condit, Boeing commercial president Alan Mulally, General Electric president Jack Welch, GE aircraft engines president James McNerney and Boeing commercial product strategy and development vice-president John Roundhill. Roundhill said later:

It was a tough, tough decision. The bottom line was [that] GE's bid was overall better. This included ability to meet noise requirements – a real driver – a look at the schedule in detail and customer service, but the business proposals were a key part of it.

Nothing was said officially about the 'business proposals', but a contribution of $100 million towards the development of the airframe was a figure doing the rounds. Furthermore, both Boeing and GE acknowledged that the buying power of GECAS, GE's commercial aircraft leasing and financing arm, played a part in the decision.

This is what Jack Welch wrote about it in his autobiography, *Jack*:

One favorite story involved a November meeting in 1997 I had with Boeing Co. chairman Phil Condit. At the time, we were trying to win a billion-dollar-plus contract to supply aircraft engines for Boeing's new long-range 777 jet.

I had been the after-dinner speaker at Bill Gates's annual summit in Seattle. That night I sought out Phil and asked him for a private lunch the next day. The GE and Boeing teams had been working long and hard on the engine selection for the long-range version of the 777. Phil was well briefed on the subject. I made a pitch on why our engine was right for the plane and why GE was the right partner.

Phil listened carefully, asked a few questions, and ended the conversation with some good news.

'Let's leave this luncheon by saying you've got the deal,' he said, 'But you've got to make a promise to me. You won't tell your people they've got it. They will have to continue to negotiate in good faith.'

I agreed. Over the next 60 to 90 days, those negotiating the deal were calling me up, saying we had to give Boeing more price concessions and more help with the development. I was dying each time my guys called to tell me about their latest concessions. Yet there was no way I could let them know of my conversation with Phil.

So they kept giving and giving.

Finally, it came to the last day, and we were getting one more squeeze from Boeing. I couldn't take it anymore. I picked up the phone and called Phil.

'Phil, I'm choking. I can't sit here any longer. I've got to break this commitment.'

'You've gone far enough,' he replied. 'Tell your team to say no. They've got the deal.'

The Boeing 777-200X/300X and the Airbus A3XX were being launched into a strong market. At the Farnborough Air Show in September 2000, no less than 42 billion dollars' worth of orders were announced. Boeing gave news of orders for 133 aircraft valued at nearly $15 billion, while Airbus was able to surpass this with orders for 238 aircraft valued at nearly $19 billion. Among Airbus's orders were the first firm commitments for the A3XX when

Emirates Airlines upgraded its interest in twelve aircraft to a firm commitment.

The proviso was, of course, that the programme went ahead, but Airbus was in no doubt, launching a television campaign in Europe comparing the A3XX favourably with the Seven Wonders of the World. The advertisement pointed out that *its* Wonder would have a casino, shopping mall and bedrooms.

Plans for VLAs (Very Large Aircraft) had been laid as early as the 1990s, despite the aircraft industry going through its worst recession since the early 1980s. In March 1994, Stan Todd, Director of Trent engines at Rolls-Royce, told *Flight International*:

Aircraft makers are diligently studying various concepts for VLAs which, if committed, would be the biggest investment decision the civil-aircraft industry has yet taken. Aircraft considerably larger than today's Boeing 747 are going to be needed in the foreseeable future to meet the predicted growth in air travel with further improvements in operating costs.

Pressure for larger aircraft would come not only from the growth in air travel, predicted at 4 to 5 per cent a year for the next twenty years, but also from the limited ability to add extra flights because of lack of availability of air slots, resistance to the building of new airports in many parts of the world and air-traffic-control limits. GE summed up the situation by saying that airlines wanted 'a huge people-mover to go long distances'.

For the three large-engine manufacturers, the challenge would be developing engines with the required thrust that would also meet environmental regulations, particularly those governing noise. They would also have to decide whether two engines would suffice or whether four would be necessary. Todd said:

A twin-engined VLA is an option in theory, but the required engine size is at least twice the thrust of any engine so far developed. Such an engine is technically possible, but the investment would be huge and the market base would appear to be too limited to support that level of investment in the near future.

The take-off thrust required for a twin-engined VLA would probably have to be 150,000 lb, and the likelihood was therefore that any new VLA would have four engines, or even six.

If the engine makers had to worry about their investment, the financial commitment from the airframe makers was perhaps even greater. As *The Economist* pointed out in June 1995:

As for strategy, the perpetual question for Boeing and Airbus is whether there is room for both companies to prosper in a particular segment of the market. If not, the game is to deter your rival from entering alone, perhaps by pretending that you are about to do so yourself – or offering to collaborate.

Just such a game of bluff and counter-bluff is being played in Boeing's decision on whether to build a 600–800 seater 'super-jumbo'. Should Boeing go it alone and risk ruinous competition from Airbus, or collaborate with the Airbus parent firms?

For now, Boeing is playing poker. It has been talking for 18 months to Airbus's parent companies about collaborating on a super-jumbo. But nobody knows whether there will be a viable market. So far only two carriers – British Airways and Singapore Airlines – look keen to buy. That leaves the two aircraft makers watching warily for the other to make a dash. Mr Condit says that if he thought Airbus was jumping off a cliff with an uncommercial plane, he would not follow. Yet it is hard to see Boeing surrendering the top end of the market to its deadly rival.

By 1996, it was becoming clear that both Boeing and Airbus were going to proceed separately. As for the engine makers, Rolls-Royce stole an early lead on its two rivals by announcing that it would use its existing Trent technology to develop the Trent 900.

The Trent 900 would use the same 110-inch-diameter fan, structure, systems and accessories as the Trent 800, with scaled-down intermediate-pressure (IP) and high-pressure (HP) compressors, a new five-stage low-pressure turbine, and reduced-loading IP and HP turbines. The first Trent 900 core was due to be run in January 1998, with the full-development engine running the following September.

In contrast, GE and Pratt & Whitney said they would join forces – the first time they had collaborated on a civil-aircraft engine project – to develop a brand new engine. Some people expressed concern that Rolls-Royce would not be able to compete with this gigantic alliance. Others were more sanguine, even seeing it as a compliment to Rolls-Royce. Chris Avery, aerospace analyst at Paribas, wrote in his monthly analysis of the aviation industry:

The collaboration of the two US engine manufacturers might not be as much of a disappointment for Rolls-Royce as first thought. It is clear that Rolls's Trent engine has some very attractive features, not the least of which are the relative lack of weight and size. The engine has found favour with Boeing, which has publicly expressed its view that its customers are best served by having a choice when buying its aircraft. Thus it is possible to interpret the Pratt–GE deal as genuinely having been encouraged by Boeing in order to have some competition for the Trent, which might otherwise be the only sensible choice on the aircraft.

In October 1996, the Rolls-Royce Trent project director, Charles Cuddington, gave details of the new Trent 900, emphasising its commonality with the Trent 800 as a major selling point, and adding:

This will meet or exceed all Airbus Industrie's targets with ease. The three-shaft design means we can scale the compressors without affecting the fan. We forecast a market for 900 aircraft of this [747-500/600 and A3XX] type, 800 of them passenger and 100 freighters over a 25-year period.

Furthermore, the Trent 900 would be the first engine that Rolls-Royce put into commercial service using swept-fan aerofoil technology and contra-rotation of the HP compressor. It was planned that a swept fan blade and swept-fan outlet guide vane would be incorporated in the engine, based on technology developed by Rolls-Royce over the preceding ten years with its university partners and QinetiQ, formerly DERA.

The technology relied on using fan-blade sweep to enhance the performance of the rotor blade by improving efficiency and flow capacity, and hence thrust. The relative velocity of the air being pulled into the fan rotor exceeds the speed of sound, producing a shock wave within the rotor blade which in turn reduces the efficiency of the fan. With the swept design, a portion of the blade would be swept rearwards, forcing the shock to be more oblique to the incoming air and resulting in higher efficiency. To protect the blade from stalling, the tip portion would be swept forwards. In the Trent 900, this helped reduce the number of fan blades to 24, compared with 26 on the earlier Trent engines. The swept leading edge would also change the angle of the shock wave on the blade, thereby directing the fan noise more effectively into the intake noise liners and reducing the overall noise level of the engine.

By early 2002, design of the swept fan blade for the Trent 900 was complete and manufacturing development well advanced. First deliveries were planned for the middle of 2002.

In January 1997, Boeing told a surprised world that it was dropping its VLA or super-jumbo, the 747-500X/600X. Boeing's reasons were its heavy commitments following its purchases of first McDonnell Douglas and second Rockwell, as well as indifference from airlines deterred by the $200-million price of the aircraft. Furthermore, the A3XX was a made-to-measure aircraft with more favourable economics. As Boeing commercial vice-president Mike Bair, said:

We could not make a business case for it.

Airbus needed to decide how it would react and was forced to choose between the opportunity to save its huge billion-dollar investment in the A3XX and ploughing its resources into bigger A340s. Its initial reaction was to continue with the A3XX 'as long as market and financial conditions support a decision to go ahead'. Airbus had identified four principal A3XX markets: intra-Asia, transpacific, transatlantic and Europe-Asia. Three of them featured Asia, where Airbus was predicting 5.7 per cent annual traffic growth over the next twenty years and, more significantly, a capacity requirement growing from an average of 243 seats per aircraft to 356 by 2014. By contrast, Europe's was set to grow from 179 to 225 and that of the USA to only 211. John Leahy, vice-president of commercial affairs at Airbus, pointed to the forecast global demand for 13,360 aircraft, worth around $1,000 billion, over the coming twenty years, saying:

One third of this will be for aircraft of more than 400 seats, where Airbus does not now compete. That is why we can't afford not to be there.

Nevertheless, Airbus slowed down the programme in late 1997 because – in the words of Airbus President Jean Pierson – Airbus 'had not achieved the engineering target of producing a step change in operating economics [over the 747]'. Airbus had set a target of achieving a 15 to 20 per cent saving in direct operating cost over those of the 747-400. Adam Brown, Airbus vice-president for forecasting and strategic planning, said that A340 levels of technology and economies of scale would result in direct operating-costs savings of 10 per cent over the 747-400. The target of 15 per cent plus would have to be met by reductions in weight and fuel consumption as well as savings in maintenance costs and costs of ownership.

By 2000, Boeing was back in the market with a competitor to the A3XX. It was called the 747X and would be a full-length double-decker, seating about 500 passengers, compared with a maximum 440 in the 747-400. Boeing President Phil Condit said it would be ready to fly by 2005 or 2006, thereby beating the A3XX to market, adding:

We are assuming that the A3XX will be launched. But we believe we have an aeroplane that meets the requirements of the market. We would be willing to proceed with it should sufficient customer interest develop.

Condit also said that, at 1,300 super-jumbos over twenty years, Airbus was overestimating the market, which he calculated at 400 to 500 aircraft, of which Boeing would win half with the 747X.

At the Farnborough Air Show in July 2000, Airbus was able to announce its first firm order for the A3XX, and, in September, International Lease Finance Corporation ordered five A3XXs, specifying the Trent 900 as the engine. This order was quickly followed by one from Singapore Airlines, who ordered ten A3XXs with fifteen options and, in October, specified Trent 900s to power them. We have already seen how influential Singapore was in the market, and Rolls-Royce could feel pleased not only with the order for 100 engines worth $1.5 billion at list price but with the likely influence on other airlines.

A month later, Qantas ordered twelve A3XXs, and in February 2001 selected the Trent 900 to power them. In December, Virgin Atlantic Airways ordered six A3XXs with six options and also specified Trent 900s. By this time, Airbus had received sufficient commitment to launch the A3XX programme. The aircraft would be called the A380. In January 2001, FedEx became the seventh customer to commit to the A380, taking the order book to 60, while at the same time becoming the first US operator to order the aircraft, as well as the launch customer for the freighter version. Phil Condit had always said that the 747X would only be launched if there were a market. By March 2001, it seemed clear that that market was not going to materialise, and the programme was quietly laid to rest.

Boeing believed Airbus was grossly overestimating the market for an aircraft the size of the A380. Alan Mulally, head of Boeing's commercial aircraft division, said:

There is not a groundswell of orders for big planes ... Airlines walk a fine line. You want the biggest plane you can get but you have to be able to fill it.

Nevertheless, Airbus pressed on and showed airlines how the A380 would help their own profitability. It promised to cut 15 to 20 per cent off the direct operating cost of the B747-400. It pointed out that the A380 would have 35 per cent more seats than the B747-400 – 555 compared with 416. Of these, 232 would be what were called 'profit seats' – i.e. the number that could be sold after breaking even on a flight – compared with 123 on the 747-400. At 8,150 nautical miles, the A380's range would be 10 per cent greater.

Now that it was certain that the A380 would be challenged, the competition to provide the power plant became as fierce as almost all the other aero-engine competitions. As General Electric and Pratt & Whitney had joined forces to offer their Alliance engine, the GP7000, at least there was only one contender that Rolls-Royce had to overcome.

Initially, Rolls-Royce won all the orders, as Singapore Airlines ordered ten A380s with fifteen options, Qantas twelve with twelve options and Virgin Alliance six with six options. However, in May 2001 the GE/Pratt & Whitney Alliance received its first orders for the GP7000 when the engine was specified by Air France, who ordered ten A380s with four options, and FedEx Express, who ordered ten with twenty options. At this stage, Emirates ordered seven A380s with five options, International Lease Finance Corporation (ILFC) five, and Qatar Airways two with two options, though none of them had specified which engine.

A month later, at the Paris Air Show, it was announced that ILFC had signed firm orders for no fewer than 111 aircraft across the Airbus range, including the five previously announced A380-800s and a new commitment to five more A380-800F freighters. The ILFC Chairman, Steven Udvar-Hazy, said:

The order reflects our continued commitment to Airbus's outstanding products and ever-increasing market presence. We foresee further increases in the demand for these aircraft, in particular the A380 both in its passenger and freighter versions.

TRENT ENGINES ENTERING SERVICE

Trent 700-powered A330 – March 1995

Trent 800-powered 777 – April 1996

RB 211-524HT-powered 747 – April 1998

Trent 500-powered A340 – mid-2002

Trent 900-powered A380 – 2006

PROJECTED INCREASE IN SERVICE HOURS OF TRENT-POWERED AIRCRAFT

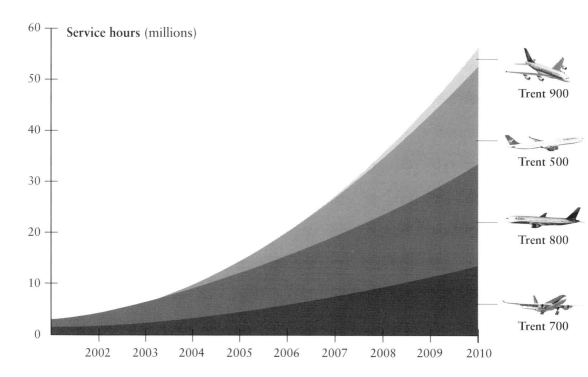

CHAPTER SEVEN

THE MILITARY MARKET

EUROFIGHTER AND THE EJ200
'WHEN THE TIME COMES WE WILL SPEAK'
FREEDOM OF CHOICE
'MORE QUESTIONS THAN ANSWERS'
'THE ENGINES WERE SUPERB'
HELICOPTER ENGINES
FLYING ON
THE LAST OF THE GREAT FIGHTER COMPETITIONS
ALIENS AND STRANGERS

EUROFIGHTER AND THE EJ200

IN THE EARLY 1980s, the air forces of the leading European countries began to consider a replacement for their US-manufactured fighter aircraft as well as the RAF's Tornado ADV (powered by the RB 199 and developed and manufactured jointly by Rolls-Royce, MTU and Fiat Aviazione) and the Jaguar (powered by the Adour and produced jointly by Rolls-Royce and Turbomeca). The initial partners in the venture were the British, French, Germans and Italians, but in 1985 the French left the consortium after a feasibility study showed that they wanted a smaller, lighter aircraft so that a naval version could be produced to replace its LTV F-8P Crusader and Dassault-Breguet Super Etendard. The French also wanted design leadership, 45 to 50 per cent of the work share, control of the new joint industrial company that would be based in France and, finally, control of all export sales. This was totally unacceptable to Britain, West Germany and Italy, and at a meeting in Turin in August 1985 they pulled out of the talks and announced the formation of a tripartite project to design, develop and build the European Fighter Aircraft. They then invited France and Spain to rejoin. Spain accepted, but France decided to go it alone to develop its Dassault-Breguet Rafale.

John (Jack) Gordon, who worked on military aircraft procurement programmes at the Ministry of Defence for over 35 years from 1961 and became General Manager of the NATO Eurofighter and Tornado Management Agency from 1996 until 1999, said of these negotiations:

At the beginning of the 1980s there were two demonstrators, one built by a consortium of British, German and Italian companies and another built by the French. Prior to the Turin meeting, the French had already decided to pursue their own Rafale programme but had not told the German Government. When the Germans found out they were upset and at the Turin meeting, when the French walked out just after midnight, the Germans took the unusual step of reaching agreement, and bringing the Italians with them, before the night was out … Actually, it was an unusual evening altogether. The meeting was expected to end in the early evening and our Italian hosts had arranged for a dinner at a local restaurant.

As the evening wore on phone calls kept going out to the restaurant but by 11 o'clock it was clear that the delegates were not going to make it. An order for something to eat and drink was sent out and eventually a meal of *cold* pizza and chips plus *warm* Pinot Grigio was consumed as the British, German and Italian delegates reached agreement.

While the delegates negotiated in Turin, the British minister responsible, Michael (now Lord) Heseltine, stayed in his office in Whitehall, as did his counterpart in Germany, Manfred Wörner in Bonn. Three-way conversations between Turin, London and Bonn continued throughout the night.

It was fortunate for the EFA project that Heseltine had taken over from John Nott as Secretary of State for Defence. Nott was not an enthusiast for it, as he makes clear in his recently published autobiography, *Here Today, Gone Tomorrow*:

To the distress of the Royal Air Force, I resisted the building of a UK fighter aircraft. For one thing, I did not think, if we were to advance specialisation within NATO, that it was our task to engage with a new fighter in dogfights over Germany – this was for the Germans. We wanted aircraft that could stay in the air for long periods and which had air-flight refuelling, the most sophisticated long-range air-to-air missiles, and better radar. This was to meet the threat from the Backfire bombers out of northern Russia. I wanted to put the perfect case for buying from the Americans the F16 [he must have meant the F-15, a much more able fighter than the F-16], which was a tried and tested aircraft of great sophistication.

… However, I had recently been made responsible for hazarding the parliamentary seats of several Tory MPs in the Thames Estuary by my decision to close Chatham Dockyard; and I was uncomfortably aware that if we did not give some new development work to the aerospace industry, it would wither away quite quickly. Again, many constituencies were involved, mainly in the north of England. I surrendered to the RAF for industrial and political reasons: not because I accepted the rationale for developing a new fighter aircraft, but because of its impact on British industry and politics. I therefore agreed to the building of a demonstrator aircraft, leaving it to my successor to decide on the main programme. Michael Heseltine did so and, as a result, we now have the European fighter aircraft.

Michael (now Lord) Heseltine puts the case for supporting the EFA very clearly in his autobiography, *Life in the Jungle*:

One could never escape the European dilemma. The American space and defence budget is automatically larger than that of the whole of Europe, let alone each individual nation. Almost invariably, when a procurement requirement arose, there would be an existing American system. It worked, was available and was probably cheaper than any equivalent we could produce, given the economies of scale available to the Americans and given that we would have to reincur the research and development costs that the American taxpayer had already borne. But the process of buying American, logically extended, would leave Britain with no research and design capability in the defence field at all. Our military base would rapidly become mere sub-contractors.

The attitude of the ultimate boss was also going to be important. Margaret Thatcher, as Prime Minister, went along with supporting EFA in spite of her propensity to support the USA rather than Europe (as Heseltine was to find out in the Westland affair). However, she wanted to know who was going to be 'Mr Eurofighter' who would personally answer to her when things went wrong. The task fell to Jack Gordon, and, in theory, he should still be at the MoD taking responsibility for the aircraft's production and delivery! Gordon was matched by Colin Green from Rolls-Royce, who led the EJ200 programme, and Garrie Wilcox from British Aerospace (BAe), who had extensive combat aircraft experience, in particular on Lightning and Tornado.

In June 1986, the consortium set up Eurofighter Jagdflugzeug GmbH, owned by BAe of the UK, MBB/Dornier (in 1992, it was renamed Daimler-Benz Aerospace-DASA) of Germany, Aeritalia (later merged with Salenia and renamed Alenia) of Italy and Construcciones Aeronauticas SA (CASA) of Spain.

In September 1986, the Eurojet Turbo GmbH consortium – consisting of Rolls-Royce of the UK, MTU-München of Germany, Fiat-Aviazione of Italy and Sener of Spain – was formed to cover development of the new engine for EFA, with the Rolls-Royce XG-40 experimental engine being used as the basis. The aim of the XG-40 programme was to develop a generic core that could be scaled up or down as required. Once complete, this demonstrator engine had a thrust-to-weight ratio of 10:1, a fan pressure ratio of 3.9:1, an overall pressure ratio of 26:1 and a reheated thrust of 20,000 lb plus. This was close to the design aims of the EJ200 agreed by the European partners at Turin in 1985.

As well as a technology demonstrator, the XG-40 was also used as a cost demonstrator. Rolls-Royce used the engine to discover the likely cost of the sort of parts that would be needed for the EJ200. (It was the same principle that Henry Royce had expounded 70 years earlier – it is cheaper in the long run to work things out in detail before you start cutting metal.) Rolls-Royce developed an 'electronic engine' simulator that was used to de-bug the software for the engine controller. This had become complex in the XG-40. The simulator allowed the engine to be 'virtually' operated over a wide range of conditions, exploring the effects of the different engine sections on fuel consumption and responsiveness before running the actual engine itself. Low fuel consumption at high speed and altitude had been highlighted as an important requirement for the EFA.

The EFA was designed primarily for an air-to-air combat role but also with a capability for ground attack. The programme was managed by the Nato European Fighter Management Agency, known as NEFMA, which gave out contracts to Eurofighter, the four-nation partnership. The customers, who were the air forces of the four nations, agreed the EFA's specification in December 1985 through the European Staff Requirement for Development (ESR-D).

The ESR specified that the 9.75-tonne aircraft, with a 50-square-metre wing and powered by two 90 kN (i.e. about 20,000 lb sea-level thrust) engines, should be extremely agile, and capable of manoeuvres and altitudes more extreme than those possible with previous fighters. Control of the two engines would be by an advanced full-authority digital engine control (FADEC) system, and the aircraft should be capable of rapid acceleration from subsonic to high supersonic speeds and high instantaneous and sustained turn rates. High lift and high angle-of-attack limits were also required at low speed.

The aircraft's required agility and the need to operate in conditions of zero and negative 'g' loading, as well as the necessity to drive aircraft life-support and weapons systems throughout the flight envelope, carried implications for the design of the oil system and engine core. The other companies, as well as Rolls-Royce, had been working on development engines, and the experience and expertise of all four companies was pooled. The resulting engine was similar to XG-40 but with some significant differences. The EJ200 had a higher fan pressure: 4.21:1 compared with 3.9:1. Conversely, its overall pressure, at 25:1, was lower. The higher fan pressure was incorporated to ensure low fuel consumption in the reheat mode for maximum combat duration. The engine core was sized with an eye to built-in stretch, not only to ensure that future EFA role changes could be accommodated, but also to enable other applications and market opportunities to be explored. The high and fast German interceptor mission led to the adoption of a convergent/divergent nozzle to enhance supersonic performance.

Wide-chord aerofoils, benefiting from Rolls-Royce civil-engine experience, would be fitted for their high efficiency. They also gave robust tolerance to foreign object damage (FOD). Three-dimensional transonic-compressor and turbine-aerofoil designs would be incorporated to give high efficiency at low component weight, and powder-metallurgy discs would be used to give high strength and low weight with single-crystal turbine blades conferring long life at high turbine entry temperatures. Turbine blade life was seen as particularly important because of its implications for reducing the life-cycle cost of an engine. The FADEC system mentioned earlier would enable more precise control functions to be adopted, maximising engine performance yet minimising weight and reducing set-up times after engine maintenance work.

The initial development work share split was Rolls-Royce 33 per cent, MTU 33 per cent, Fiat Aviazione 21 per cent and Sener 13 per cent. The design and manufacture of the verification engines was due to be completed by the end of 1988 with testing to run into the middle of 1990. The design and manufacture of full-scale development engines was to be completed by the spring of 1990, with testing completed by early 1994. The flight-test engine programme was scheduled to start in 1991 and run until 1996, and the operational evaluation and service was scheduled to run from the beginning of 1995 and be completed by the middle of 1996. Absolutely key was Rolls-Royce's agreement to help the Spanish to set up and run an engine development and manufacturing company, later called Industria de Turbo Propulsores (ITP), in which, as we saw in Chapter Three, Rolls-Royce took a large equity stake.

John Wragg, Director of Military Engines at Rolls-Royce in 1988, said at the end of that year:

An expression of the confidence of the partners in Eurojet is that not only have they participated willingly in the EJ200 programme but [they] have felt themselves able, contractually, to accept the programme in the terms which have been outlined above. [The partners had accepted a maximum-price contract.] In so doing, Eurojet partners are demonstrating that the EJ200 objectives are both realistic and achievable.

Three samples of the Design Verification Engine (DVE) were manufactured. The first one ran at MTU on 28 November 1988 and achieved 90 per cent of what the consortium was aiming for in the production engines. The second one ran at Fiat shortly afterwards, and the third at Bristol in March 1989.

As the programme moved forward relatively smoothly at the end of the 1980s, two events conspired to interfere not only with relations between the British and German governments but also with the attitude towards funding of the project by the four partners, as their belief in the future need for the aircraft altered in view of the dramatic changes that had taken place.

The first was what Jack Gordon called 'the nose radar dispute'. In a modern jet fighter, the radar is probably the most important and expensive component after the engine, and keen competition to supply the necessary equipment for EFA developed between GEC and Ferranti in the UK and other companies in Germany, Italy and Spain. The Ministry of Defence insisted on an open competition, and it developed into one between Ferranti, heading a consortium which included companies from Italy and Spain, and GEC, who formed an alliance with a German company, AEG. Because GEC said it would allow AEG to lead on its proposed system, which had at its heart the APG-65 system from the US company Hughes, its offer found favour with the German Government. (The German Air Force was already buying the APG-65 system for its Phantoms.) The Ferranti system was new but was based on the successful Blue Vixen system in the Sea Harrier. It was also cheaper than the Hughes, which, according to Gordon, suffered from other disadvantages.

The Ferranti system won the competition, which in an ordinary straight-forward business world would have settled the matter. However, there is never anything straightforward about negotiations between governments, and the German Government objected to the decision. The competition was therefore run again, and not surprisingly Ferranti won again. It was run a third time, and, in spite of the fact that GEC reduced their price, Ferranti won a third time. As both governments dug their heels in, crisis was approaching when Ferranti ran into serious financial problems following a disastrous acquisition in the USA. The situation was so bad that Ferranti was forced into putting itself up for sale. The French company Thompson (now Thales) expressed interest, which alarmed GEC – who promptly bought Ferranti. As a result, GEC dropped their radar bid which was duly awarded to Ferranti, by this time owned by GEC.

Alan Clark, Minister of State at the Ministry of Defence from 1989 to 1992 and writer of notorious diaries, made this entry on Friday 19 January 1990:

Today I dominated the Dept. Repeatedly I sent for Quinlan, Spiers, John Colston. Periodically I talked to Arnold Weinstock [Chief Executive of GEC]. By sheer energy and clarity of thought I put together the deal that saved Ferranti, and its Radar, and thus EFA* in time for us to outface Stoltenberg [Gerhard Stoltenberg, German Defence Minister] when the German delegation come over.

Clark later added the note:

* The Germans were already voicing their misgivings about the European Fighter

The XG-40 Demonstrator Engine, a vital precursor to the development of the EJ200. Seen here with the engine are Mike Neale, Director General Engines (PE) MoD, 1980–87 (front row centre), several other MoD personnel and from Rolls-Royce: Alan Newton, director of engineering (second from left); Brian Ball, manager test measurement (third from left); Stewart Miller, director of advanced engineering (fifth from left); Peter Clark, controller advanced engineering (second from right); and Tony Jarvis, assistant chief engineer, military demonstrators (extreme right).

Colin Green, President of Defence Aerospace, standing in front of the
EJ200, a programme with which he is intimately linked, having signed the
6-billion-Deutschmarks contract as the first *Geschäftsführer* of Eurojet.

OPPOSITE TOP: The Eurofighter 2000 prototype on its maiden flight from
British Aerospace's facility at Warton, Lancashire. At this stage, it was
powered by two RB 199 engines. Later in the programme, these engines
would be replaced by EJ200s developed by the Eurojet consortium of
Rolls-Royce, Fiat Avia, MTU München and Industria de Turbo Propulsores.

OPPOSITE BOTTOM: The engine for Eurofighter, the EJ200, was required to
meet the demands for high reliability, low cost of operation and the
need for extreme agility at both low and very high altitudes, as well as the
need for rapid acceleration from subsonic to supersonic speeds.

In the Gulf War, the Tornado GR1s, powered by Rolls-Royce RB 199s
and referred to as 'mud-movers', attacked the vast Iraqi airfields, flying at
very low levels of less than 200 feet and at speeds up to 550 knots.

OPPOSITE TOP: As Secretary of State for Defence in the first Margaret Thatcher
administration, John Nott wanted to buy the American F-15 fighter.
However, others in Europe saw the case for developing an all-European
fighter.

OPPOSITE BOTTOM: The Jaguar, powered by Rolls-Royce Turbomeca Adour
engines, was fitted with CRV7 air-to-ground rockets produced by
Rolls-Royce's Canadian company, Bristol Aerospace, for use in the Gulf War.

TOP: An RAF Tornado GR1 at Muharraq during the Gulf War. Around the aircraft can be seen Marconi 'Sky Shadow' electronic-countermeasures pods, 500-gallon 'Hindenburger' auxiliary fuel tanks and laser-guided bombs.

BOTTOM: Tornados over an Iraqi airfield during the Gulf War, after inflicting extensive damage.

TOP: A Sea King, powered by the Rolls-Royce Gnome, hovers over a support ship during a supply lift in the Gulf War.

BOTTOM: The Lynx, powered by the Rolls-Royce Gem, gave sterling service during the Gulf War. Here, a Lynx of the Norwegian Coastguard undertakes fishery protection duties.

TOP: The helicopter engine RTM322 was described by a former VH-IB Huey pilot in Vietnam as being capable of saving a combat pilot's life, thanks to its care-free fuel control system with its ability to maintain 100 per cent rotor speed.

BOTTOM: The test flight of the Black Hawk helicopter, also powered by the RTM322. The Black Hawk was used as a flying test bed to check the handling and power characteristics of the engine.

TOP: The RTM322, a collaborative engine between Rolls-Royce and Turbomeca, was chosen to power the Anglo-Italian EH101 helicopter and is here seen in a search-and-rescue winching exercise in Dublin Bay.

BOTTOM: Another success for the RTM322 was the NH90, a collaborative venture between France, Germany, Italy and the Netherlands. One of the key advantages over its competition was the engine's lighter installation, due to the integral inlet particle separator.

In spite of what Bill Paul of Sikorsky told Rolls-Royce's
Gordon Page about the difficulties of displacing GE's T700, the
RTM322 did so when, in July 1997, the British Army chose it
for the Westland/McDonnell Douglas WAH-64D Apache Longbow.

The Eurocopter Tiger was chosen by the French and German armies
and, in its three variants – multi-role, escort and anti-tank – was powered
by the MTU/Turbomeca/Rolls-Royce MTR390 engine.

The Rolls-Royce/Turbomeca Adour engine has powered the most
successful advanced jet trainer and light combat fighter of
the last fifteen years, the Hawk, here seen in its Mk 50 G-Hawk
form flying for the RAF.

The RAF GR7 joint-force Harrier, 40 of which are being upgraded to
GR9A standard with a more powerful Pegasus Mk 107 engine.

During 2000, it looked as though Boeing was ahead of
Lockheed in the competition to win the contract to produce the
Joint Strike Fighter.

On 26 October 2001, Edward 'Pete' Aldridge, US Under-Secretary of Defense, announced that Lockheed had won the contract for the JSF.
Rolls-Royce anticipated $1 billion of business providing the lift systems during the development phase, and much more when full production started.

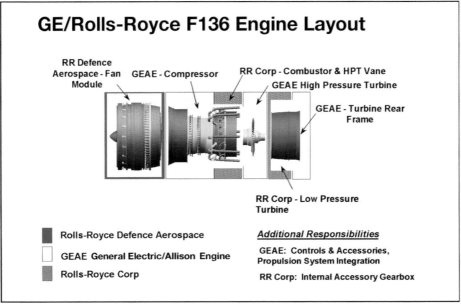

GE/Rolls-Royce F136 Engine Layout

RR Defence Aerospace - Fan Module

GEAE - Compressor

RR Corp - Combustor & HPT Vane

GEAE High Pressure Turbine

GEAE - Turbine Rear Frame

RR Corp - Low Pressure Turbine

Rolls-Royce Defence Aerospace

GEAE General Electric/Allison Engine

Rolls-Royce Corp

Additional Responsibilities

GEAE: Controls & Accessories, Propulsion System Integration

RR Corp: Internal Accessory Gearbox

TOP: Chairman and CEO of Lockheed Martin, Vance Coffman. He gave his unwavering support to the shaft-driven fan concept, from the earliest days of the ASTOVL programme through to the historic win with the F-35.

BOTTOM: Rolls-Royce re-entered the large-combat-engine sector by being contracted to provide 40 per cent of the F136 engine.

Aircraft project. At this time their excuse was that Ferranti (stipulated as the radar contractor) were commercially unviable and this put the project at risk. I encouraged Lord Weinstock to take Ferranti's radar enterprise into GEC, thus totally altering its commercial status.

The next great event brought consequences which were not quite so easily solved.

The ending of the Cold War that had determined the attitudes and actions of all nations for the previous 45 years was so significant, not only for the world in general but also specifically for Rolls-Royce and particularly its defence business, that it is important to spend some time reviewing its history and its final end.

'WHEN THE TIME COMES WE WILL SPEAK'

Nineteen-eighty-nine effectively brought the end of the so-called Cold War, a state of armed readiness which stretched back nearly 45 years and which, of course, was preceded by six horrendous years of 'hot' war.

In the 1930s and during the Second World War, the democracies of Great Britain and the USA were never going to be natural allies of the Communist USSR under the dictatorship of Stalin. However, once war had been declared on Nazi Germany, followed by the Wehrmacht's invasion of the Soviet Union, allies they had to be – at least until Hitler had been defeated.

The three leaders of the Allies, Franklin Roosevelt, Winston Churchill and Joseph Stalin, met together for the first time at Tehran in November 1943. Churchill asked Stalin about his post-war territorial ambitions. Stalin replied:

There is no need to speak at the present time about any Soviet desires but when the time comes we will speak.

The first demonstration of how Stalin viewed post-war Eastern Europe came in the summer of 1944. An offensive had been launched on a broad front by the Russian Army to coincide with the Allies' Normandy landings. The Russian Army advanced westward but stopped on the Vistula just short of Warsaw. As the Russians approached, the Polish resistance in Warsaw rose up ready to proclaim a free Poland. Instead of helping them, the Russians remained where they were and allowed the Nazis to return and crush the Poles. Stalin would not listen to Churchill's pleas to intervene, and 200,000 Poles were slaughtered – 90 per cent of them civilians, including the flower of free Polish resistance. It was an omen of things to come, and, indeed, as early as 1945 there was a dispute about the governance of post-war Poland. The British wanted to install the government in exile in London, while the

Russians wanted the pro-Soviet government that had been set up in Lublin in south-east Poland. Churchill said Britain had gone to war so that Poland should be 'free and sovereign'; it was a matter of 'honour'. Stalin said it was a matter of 'security' and that the USSR had been attacked twice in the last 30 years through the Polish corridor. Stalin largely got his way. In return for a rather ill-defined commitment to 'free' elections, the Soviet–Polish border was moved westward, while, in compensation, the Polish–German border was also moved westward.

As for Germany, it was agreed to divide the country into four zones of occupation – Soviet, American, British and French. The Soviets insisted on vast reparations, while Britain and the USA, learning from the disastrous consequences of the Treaty of Versailles in 1919, tried to resist them. Again, the Allies gave way, and a figure of $20 billion [perhaps $1,000 billion in today's terms] was agreed.

There had been a certain empathy between Roosevelt, Churchill and Stalin, but unfortunately, when Roosevelt died on 13 April 1945, his successor, Harry Truman, who had been kept ill-informed by Roosevelt, lacked the finesse and subtlety of his predecessor, and relations with the Soviet Union soon deteriorated sharply. At the next conference – at Potsdam, close to Berlin – in July 1945, relations scarcely improved, but some horse-trading, with very considerable consequences, was carried out. On reparations, James Byrne, Truman's new secretary of state, suggested that each ally should take from his own zone. If the Soviets would accept this – it would exclude them from the industrial Ruhr valley – the other allies would agree to the new Polish boundaries. It was decided that Italy should be included in the Allies' sphere of influence, while Romania, Bulgaria and Hungary would be in the Soviet sphere. The nature of the regimes was left unclear, but the die had been cast – Europe had been broken up into divisions.

Shortly afterwards, the USA dropped its atomic bombs, first on Hiroshima, then on Nagasaki, and the Japanese surrendered, bringing the war to an end. How did the world look?

Every country, except the USA, was in a much worse condition than in 1939. The defeated nations – Germany, Italy, Japan and their allies – were in a desperate state. But even the victorious nations faced years of hardship. The Soviet Union might have the largest army the world had ever seen, but its country and people had suffered mightily, with up to 25 million people dead, 1,700 towns destroyed, 70,000 villages and hamlets burned down and 100,000 collective farms laid waste.

Looking around at all the devastation was the mighty USA. Many American personnel had died, especially in the defeat of Japan, but the country's economy had prospered. Its gross domestic product had grown from $90 billion in 1939 to $212 billion in 1945. In a word the Americans like to use themselves, their productive capacity had become 'awesome'. Cargo ships were built in three days, bombers assembled in a few hours, and trucks and jeeps rolled off the production line by the thousand.

However, if people admired the USA, they also felt grateful to the Soviet Union, who many felt had borne the brunt of the fight against Nazism, and the virtues of communism seemed attractive to many. Certainly, the capitalist approach had brought nothing but misery for most in the 1930s. Even countries that we now think of as anything but communist, such as France and Italy, were tempted to support the *Maquis* and the *Partigiani*, both of which were associated with the communist struggle against the fascists. Ironically, it was in the Eastern European states that fell in the Soviet sphere of influence that elections produced only minority votes for Soviet puppets. Nevertheless, non-communist politicians in these states were gradually removed. By early 1946, there was no question: the Soviet Union and its satellites were the enemies of the USA and its allies. It was at Westminster College in the small Midwest town of Fulton, Missouri, that Winston Churchill, now no longer Prime Minister but still a world figure, said:

From Stettin in the Baltic to Trieste in the Adriatic, an iron curtain has descended across the continent.

Stalin described the speech as warmongering, and *Pravda* called him racist and likened him to Hitler. The Cold War had broken out, and its first battle took place in Iran – occupied by both the British and the Russians during the war, with the promise that they would withdraw at the end of the war. The British did; the Russians did not. The USA decided to make a stand and took the issue to the United Nations. The Soviet representative, Andrei Gromyko, walked out of the Security Council – the first of many such Soviet walk-outs during the Cold War – but, nevertheless, the Soviets backed down and withdrew their forces.

The centre of conflict moved back to Europe. In early 1947, Britain, under severe economic pressure in the middle of the worst winter anyone could remember, told the USA it was withdrawing its troops from Greece. Realising that Greece would fall to the communists, the American government agreed to take their place. Truman articulated what became known as the Truman Doctrine:

The seeds of totalitarian regimes are nurtured by misery and want. They spread and grow in the evil soil of poverty and strife. They reach their full growth when the hope of a people for a better life has died. We must keep that hope alive ... I believe it must be the policy of the United States to support free peoples who are resisting attempted subjugation by armed minorities or by outside pressures.

Supporting this general principle was the European Recovery Program, or Marshall Plan as it became known, which stated *inter alia* that US policy:

Is directed not against any country or doctrine but against hunger, poverty, desperation and chaos. Its purpose should be the revival of a working economy in the world so as to permit the emergence of political and social conditions in which free institutions can exist.

Although the USA invited all countries in Europe to take part in the programme, including the Soviet Union, Stalin refused and forbade any of his satellites to take part.

The next big flashpoint was Berlin, which, like Germany, was split into four zones, though, significantly, Berlin itself was deep in the Soviet eastern zone of Germany. During 1948, the Russians increasingly blockaded the city and eventually cut off all access from outside. The Soviet Union wanted the Allies out of Berlin altogether. Truman's reaction was:

The abandonment of Berlin would mean the loss of Western Europe.

The British and Americans decided to prevent the Berliners starving, and mounted an airlift which gradually built to a peak of 4,500 tonnes a day. Both Rolls-Royce and Allison were heavily involved in providing the power plants for the aircraft flying to and from Berlin each day. Again, hurt by a counter-blockade of Eastern Germany, the Soviet Union eventually backed down.

In the following year, ten European nations, the USA and Canada came together in a military grouping, the North Atlantic Treaty Organisation (NATO). Its primary aim was mutual defence against Soviet military aggression. In the same year, the need for such an organisation became only too clear when the Soviet Union exploded its first atomic bomb. The Cold War had reached a new, more threatening, level.

Over the next four decades throughout the world, almost every conflict was seen as part of the struggle between the two superpowers and their allies, whether it was the Korean War from 1949 to 1953, the British and French confrontation with Nasser over the Suez Canal in 1956, the erection of the Berlin Wall in 1961, the Cuban crisis of 1962, the Vietnam War from 1954 to 1973 or the Iranian crisis of 1978/9.

FREEDOM OF CHOICE

Finally, as the 1980s progressed it became clearer and clearer that the communist, planned economy with its five-year plans adopted by the Soviet Union and its satellites was not as successful as the unfettered capitalist approach adopted by the USA and its Western allies. The economy of the Soviet Union simply could not afford to keep up the arms race with the USA and support satellite nations throughout Eastern Europe if it was to provide its citizens with a standard of living that even remotely related to that of most people in the West.

The first Russian leader to appreciate this was Mikhail Gorbachev. He faced a US President, Ronald Reagan, who took a far more robust line towards what he memorably described as 'the Evil Empire' than his predecessor, Jimmy Carter. Ironically, it was with Reagan that Gorbachev struck up a rapport, and gradually Reagan realised that Gorbachev meant it when, in countless speeches, he stressed his commitment to arms reductions. The Soviet Union could no longer afford the escalating military game. How would the other Eastern European countries in the Warsaw Pact (the Soviet equivalent to NATO) react without Soviet support?

In December 1988, Gorbachev put them to the test. Soviet forces had put down uprisings in Berlin in 1953, Hungary in 1956 and Czechoslovakia in 1968, but at the United Nations assembly he declared that 'freedom of choice' would have 'no exceptions'. He backed it up with huge troop withdrawals. The unpopular Eastern European regimes would have to face their increasingly restive populations without Russian tanks.

They were soon under pressure. In Hungary, in early January 1989, the parliament voted to allow freedom of association and assembly, and in May Hungarian soldiers began to pull down the barbed-wire fences on the country's border with Austria. In Poland, open elections were held in June. Meanwhile, in the Soviet Union, the first free elections in 75 years were held, and Gorbachev made overtures to Russia's traditional enemy, China.

The East Germany of hard-line Erich Honecker was forced to join the party when Hungary ignored its treaty with East Germany whereby refugees would not be allowed to leave for Austria. On 10 September 1989, the border was opened, and within three days 13,000 East Germans fled west. Gorbachev told Honecker he should introduce reforms as he had in the Soviet Union, and, when the East Germans began to demonstrate, made sure the Russian soldiers stayed in their barracks. Gradually, the East German Government disintegrated, and on 9 November the East Germans streamed through the Berlin Wall into the West. This was the final symbolic collapse of the old Soviet-dominated regime in Eastern Europe. By the end of 1989, the leaders of every Eastern European nation except Bulgaria, which soon followed suit, had been thrown out after popular uprisings.

The Cold War was over. It had cost more than just money – the peoples of Eastern Europe had not been allowed to think for themselves for two generations – but it had also cost a lot of money. One estimate suggested $8 trillion ($8,000,000,000,000) had been spent on nuclear and other weapons. Eduard Shevardnadze, who, alongside Gorbachev, had done much to promote *glasnost* and *perestroika* in the Soviet Union, calculated that as much as 50 per cent of Soviet gross national product was spent on defence, arms and the armed forces.

Now, much of this expenditure could stop, and perhaps some of it could be diverted to improving the lot of the ordinary people. Certainly, governments throughout the world showed a keenness to cut down defence expenditure. This was not, of course, necessarily good news for a defence contractor such as Rolls-Royce.

It was only a year earlier that Michael Donne had written in the *Financial Times*:

The UK aerospace will benefit, to the extent of up to 20,000 jobs over the next 20 years, as a result of the four-nation agreement to build the new European Fighter Aircraft – Eurofighter or EFA – signed earlier this week in Munich.

The £6 billion deal between the UK, West Germany, Italy and Spain covers only the development phases of the new combat aircraft, involving production of eight prototypes, of which two will be two-seaters. The first will fly in 1991, in West Germany, followed by the second aircraft in the UK. However, over the next 20 years, about 800 of the aircraft are likely to be built.

However, as the Berlin Wall came down and the Soviet threat diminished, and as the West German Government began to realise the cost of its pro-gramme for unification with the former East Germany, doubting voices were raised in Germany about continuing with the EFA project. Opponents questioned why Germany, never going to be a world policeman, would now want an air-to-air fighter. Furthermore, if the Russians were no longer going to come streaming through Poland, why did Germany need all this armour? Gordon Waddington, chief engineer on the EJ200 at the time, remembered that his parents took a holiday in Germany and every German with whom they discussed the EFA project became almost apoplectic about the waste of money. They also said that on technological and industrial grounds the loss of the EFA would be made up on civil projects, while supporters claimed cancellation would spell the end of the European aerospace industry, leading to total dependence on the USA.

Undoubtedly, there was a fierce debate within Germany over whether to continue participation, but it was reported to the Rolls-Royce Board in September 1990 that:

Despite press comment that the Germans intended to leave the programme, German officials have initiated discussions on the first steps towards negotiation of a production contract and the Italian Ministry has instructed savings on other programmes in order to fund EFA.

The engine programme continues to go very well with running hours now well ahead of programme ... Discussions are continuing with a number of aircraft contractors on the possible future use of EJ200. These include Volvo, Northrop and Lockheed, who are considering it for future F117A Stealth fighters.

However, a year later in October 1992, it was reported to the Board that:

There has been a serious new development in the EFA situation, with a letter from the German Minister to Jonathan Aitken [Minister of State for Defence Procurement] giving formal notice of his intention to withdraw from the development programme. Payments continue to be made in accordance with the development contract however, and some months of negotiation will follow before any final decision can be taken. The position of Italy and Spain remains unclear. Investigations into a UK-alone programme meeting the existing budget for a 4-nation programme have intensified.

The MTU programme on the digital electronic control unit remains the main hazard to the achievement of EJ200 flight clearance. Alternatives to the existing consortium of manufacturers are being seriously considered.

The German minister responsible, Volke Rühe, investigated the possibility of saving money by developing a slightly smaller aircraft powered by a single engine rather than two engines. This, of course, would actually have increased the *development* costs as the teams would have to start again from scratch. Nor, with the penalty clauses involved, would it have saved the Germans any money. It might have reduced production costs but, at this stage, that part of the programme was a long way into the future and beginning to recede further. Sir Donald Spiers – by this time Controller Aircraft and Head of Profession Defence, Science and Engineering at the Ministry of Defence – told the author in Spring 2002:

As part of wanting this smaller aircraft, Rühe even reopened negotiations with the French [who, as we saw, had left the consortium to make their own smaller aircraft]. He also talked to the Swedes about their Gripen, and looked again at the F-15, F-16, F-18 and Hornet 2000.

Another possibility considered by a German parliamentary working group was the replacement of the EFA by the Russian-built MiG-29 Fulcrum of which West Germany had inherited 24 from the former East German Air Force.

The British press and British ministers began to criticise the Germans in no uncertain terms. Under the headline, 'Aitken Denounces German Minister Over Fighter Jet', *The Times* wrote:

Jonathan Aitken [Defence Procurement Minister] angrily denounced Volke Rühe's call on Tuesday for the four partners, including Britain, to drop the EFA programme and to build a lighter and less sophisticated aircraft to be called EFA 2000. Mr Aitken said that this suggestion was nonsensical, 'The result would be we'd pay more for a less capable aircraft that would lose in combat. You've heard of the film *Top Gun*? Well, with Volke Rühe's EFA 2000 you'd have to rename the film *Bottom Gun*.'

Nevertheless, there was some support for Rühe's idea of abandoning the project. The *Daily Telegraph* wrote on 1 July 1992:

The German military machine has not, it seems, lost the ability to damage our boys' aeroplanes. Yesterday it rattled off a burst of fiscal ammunition and hit the European Fighter Aircraft, causing damage that could well be fatal. British taxpayers can only hope so.

And *The Times* joined in:

The EFA project was widely regarded as an expensive relic of the Cold War. Herr Rühe, a politician with supreme ability to read the public mood, put forward the alternative for Germany of a lighter, cheaper plane whose main role would be to guard Germany's borders. Britain should not dismiss this option too lightly.

However, Defence Secretary of State, Malcolm Rifkind, would have none of it, and on September 1992 told 700 industrialists and ministers, including Ernst Riedl, the German economics minister, at a Society of British Aerospace Companies dinner:

When I am told that the world is transformed into a quiet and tranquil place, I say that we cannot assume what the world will be like in 10 years' time. One goes back to 1931. Who was then anticipating that in two years' time Hitler would be in power, and eight years later the world would be at war? To make the Spitfire took long enough [and, as we saw in Part Two, that was originally developed without any government help but with money provided by Rolls-Royce and Vickers], but to produce EFA takes a damn sight longer.

As Martin Lee, currently director of business strategy and new projects for defence at Rolls-Royce, said:

A lot of work was done on how we could proceed if the Germans pulled out. It was felt that the Italians would probably pull out if the Germans did, and the Spanish had made it clear that they would not increase their share. It would be very difficult – we would lose not only funding but also a large customer – but perhaps not impossible. Fortunately, both Malcolm Rifkind (Secretary of State for Defence), and Jack

Gordon at the Ministry of Defence worked hard to keep the German Government on board as, of course, did DASA who would be carrying out the German share of the production.

The German view that the ending of the Cold War obviated the need for such a fighter was considered illogical by some. As Hugh Harkins wrote in his book, *Eurofighter 2000*:

Much was said at the time of the lack of threat following the break up of the Soviet Union, rendering the requirement for an EFA-class fighter redundant. In fact, the opposite was true, as the break-up of the Soviet Union brought about serious cash problems encouraging the Russians to sell advanced weaponry to any state who could pay for them, regardless of national stability. This combined with the fact that only just over a year previously the United Nations had fought a six week campaign against Iraq that relied extremely heavily on air power should have told even the casual observer that the need for advanced combat aircraft that can match the enemy on an equal or superior basis remained a priority for any air force.

Again, Jonathan Aitken gave full rein to his rhetorical powers, saying:

The motto of the proudest regiment in Britain is 'Who Dares Wins'. If we bought a cheap second rate fighter below the standards of the Russian combat aircraft, the motto of the RAF in the 21st century would be, 'Who Flies Loses'. Russian aircraft [the EFA was originally conceived as a response to the SU27, which in turn was designed to overcome the F-15] are now being sold in increasingly worrying numbers to Iran and other Middle Eastern powers. Countries we regard as potentially hostile or unstable are acquiring Russian built aircraft. We need a fighter capable of winning against the formidable competition it is likely to meet.

Challenged as to whether the fighter was really necessary in a changed world, Aitken responded:

Eurofighter is at the leading edge of advanced technology both in materials and manufacturing techniques as well as design and performance. It will play a vital role in underpinning the broader industrial defence base. If it were cancelled it would almost certainly mean the end of advanced military aircraft development in Britain.

In financial terms alone, it was easy to have sympathy with the Germans. The costs of developing fighter aircraft had escalated to a degree which made people wonder how they could be afforded. A First World War Sopwith Camel cost about £1,000 [£100,000 in today's terms], with development costs of £3,000 [£300,000]. A Second World War Hawker Hurricane cost

£5,000 [£250,000], with development costs of £25,000 [£1.25 million]. Even the post-war Hawker Hunters only cost about £100,000 [£2.5 million]. Each Eurofighter was going to cost £42.4 million, with development costs of more than £10 billion.

While sympathising with the economic difficulties of Germany as it struggled with the costs of reunification, we should not forget that every country was having to cope with a recession in the early 1990s and that all governments were faced with falling tax revenues and increased financial claims from higher unemployment. We saw in Chapter Five how the Government of John Major got itself into a terrible financial tangle in September 1992. The Chancellor of the Exchequer, Norman Lamont, pressed Prime Minister John Major to scrap the project and buy American. However, Rifkind, backed by Michael Heseltine (by this time running the Department of Trade and Industry), won Major's support, and Major, in turn, persuaded Helmut Kohl, the German Chancellor, to back the project in the cause of European co-operation.

MORE QUESTIONS THAN ANSWERS

A compromise was reached, and in December 1992 it was announced that EFA, now to be called Eurofighter 2000, would proceed with all four partners still in place. [EFA first became 'EFA light', then NEFA, i.e. new EFA, and finally 'Eurofighter 2000' because the entry-into-service date had been pushed back to 2000.]

As Group Captain Ned Frith CBE, the British Aerospace director of marketing for Eurofighter 2000, said:

Politics never seem to be far away from expensive defence projects, and following a challenge from the German defence minister, Herr Rühe, on the cost and continuing need for EFA, the defence ministers of the four participating nations met in December 1992. They had before them the results of two studies they had ordered earlier. One showed how price reductions could be made to the existing EFA design without loss of capability and how yet further savings could be affected by a reduction in equipment standard for those nations prepared to accept a small reduction in military capability in some scenarios. This industry study further showed that a smaller, lighter aircraft than EFA would be inadequate against potential threat aircraft and would in fact be more expensive than EFA, bearing in mind the development money already spent or committed on the current programme.

Meanwhile, the study by the four chiefs of defence staff confirmed that a threat from aircraft such as the Sukhoi Su27 Flanker and its developments still had to be countered and this would require an aircraft with a similar level of capability to that of the proposed EFA.

However, savings would have to be made, and the Germans, although they would continue to participate in the development phase, would wait to vote by parliament after the next election in late 1994 on whether they would commit to full production. Deutsche Aerospace (DASA) said through gritted teeth:

There are really more questions than answers for the time being.

The entry-into-service date was postponed from 1996 to 2000, and, in spite of the supposed agreement among the four partners at the end of 1992, Volke Rühe continued to snipe at the project, while squeezing the budget and refusing to provide more funds. By early 1994, with technical problems on top of financial shortfalls causing delays to the aircraft's first flight, the whole project seemed to be in jeopardy once again. Spiers maintained that Jonathan Aitken 'played no small part in ensuring that the Germans stayed with it'.

Flight International wrote in January 1994:

If the beleaguered Eurofighter 2000 does not fly by its planned first-flight date of 15 April, then it will surely be the cruellest month.

Excuses, and patience, for the four-nation Eurofighter 2000 project are running out after two years of missed first-flight deadlines, cost over-runs and technical foul-ups. [The delays were caused mainly by problems with the FCS (flight control system) software, not by any problems with the engines.]

To everyone's relief, except perhaps Volke Rühe, the Eurofighter 2000 made its maiden flight over Manching in Southern Germany on 27 March 1994.

DASA chief test pilot, Peter Weger, who flew the aircraft in Germany, said afterwards that he had:

Never seen such an elegant airplane and such a nice airplane to fly. We will open it up step by step and I think it will be a perfect airplane.

In early May, the second prototype was flown by BAe's director of air operations, Chris Yeo, at Warton in Lancashire, who said:

It's going to be a fighter pilot's aircraft. It accelerates rapidly, it's clearly going to turn quickly and the rate of climb is going to be spectacular. I would say that although it is at the beginning of its development, the Eurofighter 2000 is already demonstrating a great potential.

Volke Rühe turned down his invitation to the test flight. As one British official put it:

He simply cannot bear to associate himself with the aircraft.

Yeo's comments quietened the project's fiercest critics, but they did nothing to solve the problem of production share. Initially, the production work was to be shared out according to the number of aircraft ordered. Both Germany and the UK had ordered 250 of the 750 aircraft to be produced, i.e. exactly a third, but Germany had reduced its order to 120, causing its share to fall to 22 per cent and the UK's to rise to 42 per cent. DASA wanted to hold on to 33 per cent of the production, but BAe and others in Spain and Italy were unlikely to allow Germany to have the work, which they would see as undeserved, when they badly needed it in their own factories. In the end, the work-share percentages were agreed – UK 37, Germany 30, Italy 19 and Spain 14 – and the initial production orders settled down at 232 for the UK, 180 for Germany, 121 for Italy and 87 for Spain. This gave a total of 620 aircraft for which about 1,500 engines would be required, with production and delivery spread over fifteen years.

By 1996, the year originally planned for in-service operation, more prototypes were flying, for example from Alenia's Caselle flight test centre in Turin. How had the aircraft changed and developed from the original designs approved in 1985?

From the beginning a 'weapons system' approach had been adopted rather than a slightly haphazard bringing together of airframe, engines and equipment. There were thirteen stores stations on Eurofighter as opposed to nine on the F-18. Many weapon combinations were possible, including mixes of air-to-air and air-to-ground missiles. Two wing pods housed part of the defensive aids equipment, and Eurofighter also had good stealth design features to minimise detection by radar.

Only 15 per cent of the fighter's airframe was metal. There was extensive use of load-bearing carbon-fibre composites along with aluminium lithium, which had brought a 30 per cent saving in weight.

With regard to the engine, we have already seen how demands for high reliability, low cost of operation, and the need for extreme agility and ability to manoeuvre at extreme altitudes, as well as the need for rapid acceleration from subsonic to supersonic speeds, had been demanded in the original specification. Tolerance to distorted intake airflows was also deemed essential to permit extreme aircraft manoeuvres. The engine also had to operate effectively under zero and negative 'g' loadings, as well as during positive 'g' manoeuvres to the limits of pilot tolerance.

The EJ200 had a fan with a high pressure ratio to ensure low fuel consumption while in reheat. The convergent/divergent nozzle gave lower fuel consumption at high Mach numbers. It was designed for operation at high gas temperatures and high pressure ratios to provide a high thrust-to-weight ratio. Advanced cooling technology would provide a long turbine life. Rolls-Royce's civil experience with wide-chord aerofoils would give high efficiency and tolerance to foreign-object damage. Single-crystal turbine blades would confer long life at high turbine entry temperatures and consequently reduce life-cycle costs. Also, integral blade and disc assemblies ('blisks') had been introduced for the high- and low-pressure compressors also helping to reduce weight. As we saw, the engine had an advanced full-authority digital engine control (FADEC) system to permit more precise control functions to be used. The engine's accessories and on-condition maintenance items were easily accessible when the engine was installed, and an advanced engine health-monitoring system was incorporated, allowing checking by ground crew after each flight and easy and rapid engine changes.

Rolls-Royce was, officially, responsible for the combustor, combustion casing, high-pressure turbine, intermediate casing and the bearing support; MTU for the low-pressure compressor, high-pressure compressor and the variable inlet guide vanes; Fiat Avio for the gearbox, low-pressure turbine stator, low-pressure turbine rotor and the jet pipe front and reheat, while ITP was responsible for the bypass duct, exhaust duct and variable nozzle. Behind the scenes, largely as a result of the investment in the original XG-40 demonstrator, Rolls-Royce provided the technological support for the whole engine.

Rob Sellick, who worked on the EJ200 for Rolls-Royce from the mid-1980s and throughout the 1990s, said:

The programme moved slowly at times but at the development stage this may have been beneficial especially when you think of the dramatic advance in computers. Once you're into production there's an obvious tendency to freeze the development. Military engines are like Formula One engines. You're constantly on the margin and having to acquire and absorb new technology. For example in the EJ200 we put a high-speed shroudless HP turbine. This was a big technology challenge for us. We also had to change to an air-spray combustor when we realised the vaporising combustor was not going to work. That was another big challenge for us.

He went on to say of the changes during development:

Actually there weren't that many. The original engine specification showed vision and barely altered whereas the airframe changed a lot. Furthermore, we and our partners on the engines delivered on time and to budget and the engine is technologically good. The pilots love it.

The only compromise had been to drop the as yet unproven powder-metallurgy turbine disc and to revert to a more conventional wrought alloy.

As for the aircraft itself, this is what Group Captain Frith said:

223

As far as aerodynamic performance is concerned, Eurofighter 2000 will easily out-turn the F-15, F-16 and F-18 in both supersonic and subsonic flight. More significantly the turn rates of Eurofighter 2000 will match, or exceed, those of the Su27 Flanker and its developments. This applies both at low-level subsonic speeds, and at high supersonic Mach numbers at height.

With full internal fuel and operational load, the Eurofighter 2000 has a take-off roll of only 300 metres with its EJ200 engines giving over 40,000 lb of thrust ... Eurofighter 2000's ferry range without air refuelling is 2,000 nautical miles, clearly a useful feature for worldwide deployments. Although optimised for air superiority missions, the new multi-role fighter will carry 50 per cent more bombing ordnance than a Jaguar, over a larger radius of action.

After all the uncertainties, the defence ministers of the four participating nations signed an agreement in Bonn in December 1997 committing them to the production of 620 aircraft at a cost of £42 billion. Although not as stealthy as the F-22 – its shape would cause at least its tail fin to give radar reflections – it was, according to its engineers, 'as stealthy as it needs to be'. It was also, at £40 million, half the price of the F-22.

It could boast extreme agility with its intentionally unstable design, kept airborne by computers, and it was less 'sticky' than other aircraft, especially at high speeds. It could fly at more than Mach 2 and would be effective in combat at supersonic speeds. It also offered carefree handling so that the pilot would give instructions, sometimes by voice commands, and would leave the aircraft's computers to work out how to fulfil them, if possible. This would allow the pilot to carry out dangerous manoeuvres secure in the knowledge that the system would protect him. It also freed him to do other things. As John Turner, BAe's chief test pilot, said:

There is never enough time to think in a military cockpit. It is a waste of brain resource to spend time making things happen which you have already decided to do.

As regards useful and necessary information, Turner added:

The interface between the systems and the pilot is most important and has taken 10 years to develop. The cockpit displays show the information the pilot needs to know, when he needs to know it, in the clearest way possible.

'THE ENGINES WERE SUPERB'

On 1 August 1990, Saddam Hussein's Iraqi army invaded Kuwait, and we saw in Chapter One how the USA and UK responded. Rolls-Royce had been involved in supporting civil, military and industrial operations in the Middle

East for many years and had to think immediately not only of its customers but of the safety of its own personnel operating in the area. It was also clear very quickly that Rolls-Royce-powered aircraft and ships would soon be deployed, and indeed, on 8 August, the British Government made the decision to send forces to the Gulf. Four days later, RAF Tornados powered by the RB 199 and Jaguars powered by the Adour landed in the area. Soon, they were joined by more Rolls-Royce-powered aircraft, such as the VC10, and Victor tankers and Nimrod maritime patrol aircraft. Not far behind were Pegasus-powered AV-8B Harriers of the US Marine Corps, and Lynx and Sea King helicopters on board ships of the Royal Navy. There were also RB 211 RAF TriStars, which would provide tanking and strategic air support. Within a very short time, there were over a thousand Rolls-Royce aero-engines operational in the Gulf.

To co-ordinate the support that Rolls-Royce would give all these engines, a 'war operations room' was set up at Rolls-Royce's Military Engine headquarters in Bristol. This operations room liaised not only with the British but also the French, Italian, US and Saudi Arabian armed forces, and co-ordinated the actions relevant to the war of all the other Rolls-Royce sites. There was also an NEI Reyrolle team in Riyadh, Saudi Arabia, working on an important electricity substation, and they pressed on to make sure it was commissioned by mid-January 1991. Thompson Tankers of NEI completed an order for vehicles for the British forces in record time.

As always in time of war, programmes were speeded up. For example, the CRV7 air-to-ground rocket, produced by the Rolls-Royce Canadian company Bristol Aerospace and carried by RAF Jaguars, was hurried into service in November, and a series of performance enhancements were put in place on the RB 199 and Adour engines. The new 62B low-pressure compressor was provided for the RB 199s in the RAF's Tornado F3 to give improvements in performance during combat air patrols and in handling during air-to-air refuelling. An order for the German Luftwaffe Tornados was diverted to the RAF. Almost the first items needed were sand filters for the engines of the Lynx, Puma, Gazelle and Sea King helicopters.

Hussein ignored the demand of the United Nations that he withdraw his forces from Kuwait by 15 January, and on 17 January 1991 the Coalition air offensive was launched and was maintained for the duration of the war. The first offensive naval action was carried out by a Rolls-Royce Gem-powered Lynx operating from HMS *Gloucester* when it successfully engaged Iraqi surface vessels with its Sea Skua missiles. The reliability of the Rolls-Royce-powered aircraft was outstanding.

The air campaign began as a defensive one, but by November 1990, when it had become clear that Hussein was probably not going to back down, plans were drawn up for an offensive campaign. In charge of the US Air Force in the region was Lieutenant General Chuck Horner, a veteran of the Vietnam War and someone who was determined to exorcise what he saw as the failures of the USAF in that war. He set up a large planning cell in Riyadh in Saudi Arabia where the first 36 hours of the attack, and rolling plans every 24 hours after that, were worked out in detail. The American F-15s, F-16s, F117s and B-52s were supported by tankers in huge numbers, while the British operated RB-199-powered Tornados from northern and eastern Saudi Arabia, and Rolls-Royce Spey Buccaneers, Tornados and Adour-powered Jaguars from Bahrain. There were also six aircraft-carrier battle groups – three in the Mediterranean and three in the Red Sea. The US Marine Corps used Rolls-Royce Pegasus-powered Harriers. The cells in Riyadh also controlled forces from Saudi Arabia itself, Italy, Canada and Kuwait, as well as Rolls-Royce Dart-powered Alises of the French Air Force.

The initial aim of these UN forces was to close down the Iraqi airfields. On paper, the Iraqi Air Force was a serious threat, but the pilots lacked both training and practice. In the first week after the initial attack on 17 January 1991, Tornado GR1s, referred to as 'mud-movers', attacked the vast Iraqi airfields flying at very low levels, less than 200 feet above the ground at speeds up to 550 knots. Once complete air superiority had been established, low-level attacks were no longer necessary, and the Tornados, still flying both day and night, were supported by Buccaneers and Jaguars. The Tornado F3s, primed for defensive air-to-air battle, were scarcely in action as the Iraqis flew very few missions, and on those they did were usually shot down by American F-15s and F-16s. (Iraqi pilots had flown a number of F-15s to Iran at the very beginning of hostilities.) Nevertheless, these Tornados still flew 3,000 sorties.

Giving evidence to the House of Commons Defence Committee after the war, Air Vice Marshal Bill (later Sir William) Wratten, Air Commander British Forces Middle East, said:

After day four the Iraqi's only ability was in SAM [surface-to-air missiles] and AAA [anti-aircraft artillery]. The RAF's Panavia Tornado GR.1 crews delivered [JP233 hard-surface-damaging airfield-denial weapons] with incredible accuracy. Only a relatively few were not placed on the target.

He went on to point out that had the Iraqis shown a greater willingness to take on the Allies, continued low-level tactics would have been valid.

The Tornado GR1s flew more than 1,500 operational sorties and suffered six losses in combat. Five aircrew were killed and seven taken prisoner. Three of the six Tornados which were lost went down during the first three days of the war, in the battle to put craters in the Iraqi runways and taxiways.

During the early hours of 17 January, RAF Tornados attacked the three major Iraqi air bases with JP233s. The GR1s carried two JP233 containers under the fuselage, and either two 1,500-litre or two 2,250-litre drop tanks under the wings. After refuelling from Rolls-Royce Conway-powered Victor or VC10 tankers, the Tornados descended to cross the Iraqi border at only 200 feet in terrain-following, radar-controlled automatic flight with 'hard ride' selected, to follow ground contours as closely as possible. Navigating independently, the Tornados flew in four-ship attack teams in mutually supporting 'Card-4' formations with 12 to 20 feet between aircraft. Providing cover were American F-15 Eagles and F-17 Tomcat fighters, as well as F-4G Wild Weasels, Rolls-Royce Allison TF41-powered A-7 Corsairs and F-18 Hornets carrying high-speed anti-radiation defence-suppression missiles. Electronic jamming support was provided by EF-111s and EA-6Bs.

The standard Iraqi defence strategy was to 'hose the sky' with unaimed tracer rounds. Approaching the target, the pilots switched to maximum afterburner to attain the required speed, but then turned it off. As a pilot said:

There was no point in turning out the lights on the aircraft and then going over the airfield with 30 foot flames shooting out of your back end saying to the Iraqi gunners – 'Here we are.'

As they passed over the target at about 200 feet, the Tornados released 60 SG.357 runway-cratering bombs and 430 HB-876 area-denial mines. The process lasted about six seconds and sounded like a machine-gun.

At the same time, the US Marine Corps flew 3,383 combat sorties with their Rolls-Royce Pegasus-powered AV-8B Harriers, clocking up 4,112 flying hours in just 40 days while delivering 5.5 million pounds of ordnance. A Marine Corps maintenance officer said:

Readiness remained remarkably high during intense combat operations. The more we flew them the stronger they got.

And the commanding officer of Marine Attack Squadron VMA542 said:

The airplanes gave us absolute confidence to fly all over the area without a worry for mechanical or electrical failure. The engines were superb. There was no degradation of engine performance due to sand or extreme temperatures.

Altogether, there were no fewer than 2,790 fixed-wing aircraft in the United Nations forces, which flew 116,000 combat and direct support missions. Forty-two combat aircraft were lost. Derek Wilding, who ran the Rolls-Royce operations room referred to earlier, pointed out this was a loss rate of 0.36 per 1,000 sorties. (In Vietnam, it had been 3.5 per 1,000, and the rate predicted by the Air Warfare College was 10 per 1,000. In the Second World War, when Bomber Command of the Royal Air Force flew 364,414 sorties, they lost 8,000 aircraft and 55,573 aircrew: an aircraft loss rate of 45.5 per 1,000.) In spite of this remarkable performance in the Gulf War, there was still some criticism of the tactics used and the loss of six Tornados.

Wratten said shortly after the war:

The Rolls-Royce engines stood up extremely well. You cannot have availability rates above 90 per cent without the engines being part and parcel of it.

In his book *Harrier: The Vertical Reality*, Roy Braybrook noted that General Norman Schwartzkop, in his executive overview of the US Department of Defense Final Report on the Gulf War, highlighted the Harrier as one of six significant weapons systems of the war. Apparently, Secretary of Defense Richard Cheney narrowed that selection to three, but still included the Harrier.

Braybrook also wrote of its reliability:

Throughout the conflict maintenance crews were able to hold five … to ten aircraft per squadron in maintenance reserve yet still exceed the demands of the schedule. Availability (readiness rate) averaged 90% mission capable throughout the war. The aircraft actually improved during the war! The 66 land-based AV-8Bs consistently flew 120 sorties a day with highs of 160.

Throughout the course of Desert Shield/Desert Storm, only three engines had foreign object damage during normal operations. Those engines were easily repaired in the aircraft (file, polish and balance) and returned to the flight schedule. Two engines were FOD'd through maintenance error and material failure and some five others were removed for turbine failure (a problem common to the older style turbine blades). Sand and dust did not adversely affect avionics equipment nor did it cause accelerated wear to the engines.

The reliability did not happen by accident. Mike Mundy, one of Rolls-Royce's most experienced RB 199 engineers, pointed out that the sand in Saudi Arabia is not only very fine but rises as high as 20,000 feet. Rolls-Royce had already learnt from the Tornados in service with the Royal Saudi Air Force that this fine sand was forming a deposit in the HP turbine-blade cooling passages and that the blades were breaking down after only 25 hours in service. To overcome this problem, Rolls-Royce installed a device which washed the blades every 25 hours. They also turned the holes on the leading edge of the blade into a slot. During the Gulf War not a single Tornado engine was lost through sand damage.

And it was not only by powering manned aircraft that Rolls-Royce made a significant contribution. Rolls-Royce weapons systems provided CRV7 rockets, and a naval Sea Dart missile, powered by a Rolls-Royce Odin ramjet, successfully brought down a Silkworm missile aimed at a US battleship.

There were also over 100 Rolls-Royce-powered helicopters, mainly British Army Lynx and Royal Navy Lynx and Sea Kings involved in the fighting. Altogether they flew 26,000 engine hours.

At sea, Rolls-Royce engines powered ships of the Royal Navy as well as the navies of the Netherlands and France. The Spey SM1C, then Rolls-Royce's latest marine gas turbine, powered HMS *Brave*, giving the engine its first operational experience.

After the conflict, tributes to Rolls-Royce came in from Controller of the Navy, Vice Admiral Sir Kenneth Eaton, who said:

I particularly wish to acknowledge your work and co-operation in the areas of customer support and material provisioning.

And from Air Officer Engineering and Supply, Air Vice Marshal Michael (now Sir Michael) Alcock, who wrote to Rolls-Royce's director of customer support for military engines:

The flexibility and responsiveness of air power was clearly decisive in the battle for Kuwait.

The fact that the land war, when it started, lasted a mere hundred hours spoke volumes for the success of the Coalition airforces in the preceding air war.

HELICOPTER ENGINES

As we saw in Part Two, in the early 1980s Rolls-Royce felt that with the advance in their new engine technology there was an opportunity to win helicopter engine competitions against the already ageing GE T700 with its 1,700 shp. With its long-standing partner Turbomeca, with whom Rolls-Royce had successfully designed and built the Adour engine, Rolls-Royce designed the RTM322 with a capability of extending to 3,000 shp and beyond. The European Helicopter, EH101, designed to replace the Royal Navy's Sikorsky Sea King and the Italian Navy's Sea King ASW helicopters, called for engines of 2,100 hp to meet the demands of the Royal Navy and the Italian navy.

As we also saw, Rolls-Royce's ambitions for this engine stretched beyond the European Helicopter to the possibility of powering the Sikorsky Black Hawk, at that time using the GE T700. Gordon Page – at that time director of Rolls-Royce's Small Engine Division, which produced the helicopter engines at Leavesden, and now Chairman of Cobham plc – went to see Bill Paul at Sikorsky, who warned him:

However good your engine is, don't underestimate the task of trying to replace GE.

Rolls-Royce went to the trouble and expense of buying a Sikorsky Black Hawk and using it to demonstrate the RTM322 at both the Paris and Farnborough air shows. It also demonstrated the engine in the US naval version of the Black Hawk, the Sea-Hawk. As Paul had predicted, GE was not dislodged. There were other targets besides the Sikorsky helicopters. As well as the Anglo–Italian EH101, there was the possible single-engined development of the Agusta A129 Mangusta anti-tank helicopter. There was also the NH90 European transport helicopter for the 1990s. Furthermore, in November 1986, United Technologies took up their option for a licence enabling Pratt & Whitney to market and build the RTM322 for sales to the US and Canadian governments.

The RTM322, similar in concept to the Gem, was much simpler, with a single gas-generator rotor and only two bearing chambers; one of the great advances of the engine was its full-authority digital engine control (FADEC) system. This is what Douglas Nelms, who had flown VH-IB Huey helicopters in Vietnam, wrote about it in 1989:

The fuel control system on the RTM322, with its ability to maintain 100 per cent rotor speed (258 rpm) could actually save a combat pilot's life, since more than one pilot in Vietnam flew into trees, a hillside or even another helicopter while trying to clear an area with his rotor speed dropping, the audio warning sounding, enemy rounds slamming into his helicopter and his co-pilot yelling warnings into the inter-com. Often the greatest benefit of an engine is the ability to forget it, knowing that it will work when it has to.

As the RTM322 worked to get selected for the Black Hawk, in the summer of 1990 it was chosen as the engine for the Royal Navy EH101 Merlin Mk1 helicopter, displacing the GE T700 which had been used in the early EH101 demonstrator vehicles. An initial requirement for 200 engines was expected, and entry into service scheduled for 1995. It would be the most advanced helicopter in its anti-submarine role anywhere in the world. Helicopters operating in the early 1990s were still only semi-autonomous, relying on their mother ship to interpret information relayed back. On the other hand, the EH101's avionics would be so powerful they would obviate the need for any ship-based help to locate and destroy the enemy. The EH101 would be the first three-engined helicopter to be equipped with FADEC integrated with the flying control.

Just as with the Trent family of engines being developed by Rolls-Royce for the civil-airline market, the RTM322 was specifically designed to meet a number of helicopter applications, with single- or multi-engine applications in airframe with gross weights ranging from 10,000 to 35,000 lb. In production, Rolls-Royce would take 45 per cent of the work, Turbomeca 45 per cent and Piaggio of Italy the remaining 10 per cent. In simple terms, Turbomeca was responsible for the cold front end, while Rolls-Royce took the hot rear end.

In April 1994, the RTM322 was also selected for the NH90 helicopter, a collaborative venture between France, Germany, Italy and the Netherlands. The RTM322 had been an integral part of the NH90 development programme since 1992 and powered the maiden flight of the first prototype in December 1995. One of the key elements of the engine's advantages over competitive power plants was its lightness, which allowed extra fuel to be carried on missions. Another was that it was constructed from materials which did not corrode when exposed to sea, salt or sand. Keith Reid, Rolls-Royce Turbomeca's International Marketing Manager, said:

The design [of the RTM322] gives great potential for future incremented power growth without the need for major engine redesign. For instance, the RTM322-01/9, currently rated at 2,393 shp, could produce 2,650 shp by incorporating the same turbine materials, technologies and techniques used in other Rolls-Royce engines.

The engine was sized from the outset to enable it to produce outstanding performance, particularly in 'hot and high' climatic conditions. It has also been optimised to match the engine intake vortex separator selected by NH Industries, which ensures that foreign bodies, including sand, cannot be sucked into the engine. For all these reasons, the RTM322 is admirably suited to medium helicopter operations in Middle East and Far East countries.

In July 1997, the RTM322 achieved further success when, after a two-and-a-half-year battle – first to convince Westland Boeing that the technical merits of the RTM322 outweighed the competitive risk of introducing a new power plant, and then to convince the MoD both of this fact and of the case for a more efficient and capable, if more expensive, helicopter – the British Army chose the Westland/McDonnell Douglas WAH-64D Apache Longbow for its attack helicopter requirement. This meant that the GE T700 was displaced on the Apache in spite of what Bill Paul had told Gordon Page. The losers were the GEC/Bell's Cobra Venom and British Aerospace/Eurocopter's Tiger.

A contract was signed in Paris in June 2000 for the first batch of 298 NH90 aircraft, part of the immediate commitment by the four nations for 366 helicopters. The twin-engined aircraft was in the 10-tonne class and was designed from the outset as a weapons platform. It would be produced in two variants: first, as a tactical transport helicopter, and second as a NATO frigate helicopter. Germany would have the first tactical helicopter in 2004 and Italy its first NATO frigate helicopter in 2005. The order for the engines,

THE MAGIC OF A NAME

worth $1 billion over the lifetime of the engines, brought the total number of RTM322s to over 1,300. (In the late 1980s, when the RTM322 was struggling to win its first order, Sir Ralph Robins referred to it as 'the best engine we ever made that never sold'.) By this time, the RTM322 was powering the triple-engined EH101 Merlin HM Mk1s for the Royal Navy, the GKN Westland WAH-64 Apaches and had been selected for the RAF's Merlin HC Mk3 helicopters, which would enter service before the end of 2000.

The new Apache, named after the brave tribe of North American Indians, was an awesome machine. Its predecessor had won plaudits for its perform-ance in the Gulf War. The new variant could fly at up to 200 mph and loiter close to the battlefield for up to two hours, out to a range of 40 miles. Even more formidable was its Longbow millimetric-wave 360-degree radar that operated at a range of five miles and which could detect over 1,000 targets at any given moment. It also possessed target acquisition and designation systems and pilot night-vision systems, allowing the Apache to operate at night and in all weathers and, thanks to target magnification up to 40 times, with great accuracy in its offensive role. Its weaponry was frightening. Underneath its stub wings, it could carry up to 76 CRV7 multi-purpose rockets with a range of four miles, or up to sixteen Hellfire missiles that could attack tanks from a distance of five miles. Air-to-air missiles could be fitted to the wing tips. Under its nose, the Apache carried a 30-millimetre cannon capable of firing 625 rounds a minute with a range of two miles. Thanks to FADEC, the pilot could concentrate on flying the helicopter rather than the engine, and the RTM322 was providing much more power, especially in 'hot and high conditions'. Defence Secretary Geoffrey Hoon said of the helicopter:

Apache offers the Army of the 21st century a quantum leap in capability … It gives 16 Air Assault Brigade a capability that will make it the most potent combat formation for its size anywhere in Europe.

While the British Army was looking forward to going fully operational with its Apache AH Mk1s in mid-2002, the French and German armies were similarly gearing themselves up for operating the Eurocopter Tiger later that year. Between them, the Apache and the Tiger would fill gaps in European military capability and give both NATO and EU forces an extra dimension in peace-keeping roles. While the Apache was powered by the RTM322, the Tiger, in three variants – a German UHT or multi-role variant, a French HAP or escort version and a French HAC anti-tank model – would be powered by two 1,285 shp MTU/Turbomeca/Rolls-Royce MTR390 engines. Both Germany and France initially ordered 80 Tigers each and gave the production order for the engine in early 2000.

As with all matters military, the period from concept to full operation had been long. The decision to develop an attack helicopter jointly by the French and German governments had been made as long ago as 1984. The origins of the MTR390 engine also went back to the early 1980s when MTU and Turbomeca had worked on a collaborative design. Rolls-Royce joined the studies in 1986. The full-scale development contract for the engine was signed just before Christmas in 1989. Colin Green remembered that when Rolls-Royce joined its French and German partners, they seemed overjoyed – not just because of Rolls-Royce's expertise, but because all documents could henceforth be written in English rather than in French *and* German.

The first flight of the Tiger prototype had taken place on schedule, on 27 April 1991, at Aerospatiale's flight test centre at Mariguane in southern France. For two months before this, the MTR390 had been testing in an Aerospatiale Panther. This testing in the Panther continued until 1994.

The MTR390 engine programme was managed by MTU Turbomeca Rolls-Royce GmbH (MTR), a company registered in Germany. This company directed and co-ordinated not only the development and production of the engine but also the marketing, sales and customer support. It was hoped the engine would suit not only the Tiger but other military and civil helicopters. Aiming to produce an engine that was compact, simple and battle-tolerant, with a high specific power and low specific fuel consumption, of modular design with on-condition maintenance and with reliability and ample growth potential, the three companies decided on a configuration that used a two-stage fixed-geometry centrifugal compressor with a pressure ratio of 14:1. It also featured a single-stage, cooled gas-generator turbine which gave weight and cost advantages without any loss of performance, a two-stage, uncooled power turbine to increase efficiency, and an integrated main reduction and accessory gearbox which provided ease of access and was capable of a substantial power increase without major redesign. Finally, it would have responsive, high-reliability full-authority digital engine control (FADEC).

The work sharings split 40 per cent each to the German and French partners and 20 per cent to Rolls-Royce. The dual centrifugal compressor and gearbox would be made by Turbomeca, the combustor and single-stage gas-generator turbine by MTU and the power turbine by Rolls-Royce.

As we have seen, the fall of the Berlin Wall and the ending of the Cold War changed the attitude of the ministries of defence throughout the Western world towards all weapons, including helicopters. They viewed the idea of huge numbers of helicopters poised to attack advancing Soviet tanks as obsolete. They even asked, do we need military helicopters at all? For a time, all purchasing stalled. However, it became clear that helicopters would be needed – but to carry out the more sophisticated response required in dealing with localised conflicts, rather than advances of tanks in serried ranks.

Fortunately, the Tiger was flexible enough to make this adjustment, and, although the programme slipped in the early 1990s, the first production order was received at the end of the decade.

By this time, the family-design philosophy adopted by Rolls-Royce and Turbomeca with regard to the RTM322 was coming into its own. The four helicopter projects using the RTM322 which were under way were all demanding slightly different requirements. The engines for the Royal Navy's EH101 Merlin were rated at a baseline 2,200 shp, while those for the RAF were at 2,400 shp. Those for the Apache were rated differently, while those for the NH90 required 2,480 shp. By this time, Rolls-Royce Turbomeca was talking of an ultimate capability for the engine of nearly 3,500 shp.

As the RTM322 continued to pick up orders following its slow start, Jean-Bernard Cocheteux, President of Turbomeca, was asked in early 1999 if Rolls-Royce's purchase of Allison, with its strong helicopter-engine business, had caused any strains in the Rolls-Royce–Turbomeca partnership. He replied:

There are competitions involving engines by both Allison and Turbomeca. Our plan is to co-operate with Rolls-Royce on programmes when it is justified and profitable. Allison brings a potential advantage in opening the US market to the RTM322 which is now being offered on the Sikorsky S92 civil helicopter and on future versions of the Black Hawk utility machine. The fact that Allison is in the Rolls-Royce family is not necessarily a problem. We must be practical.

In 2002, following the reorganisation of the company that Chief Executive John Rose put in place, the helicopter-engine division has been turned into a 'customer-facing unit' in its own right and is run from Indianapolis. The model 250, which goes back to the 1950s, forms the high-volume nucleus of this business unit. The arrival of the lightweight turbine engine in the early 1950s transformed the possibilities for helicopters, and in 1957 the US Army held a competition to find a new generation of light observation aircraft. At that time, the Army was using Cessna L-19s and was not sure whether it wanted a fixed-wing aeroplane or a helicopter. What it did specify was that the engine should produce 250 hp and weigh no more than 250 lb. Allison entered the competition and won it with what became known as the Model 250, though the original development was carried out under the military designation, T63.

The early stages of development proved difficult, but in June 1960 the first successful engine run was made, and by this time the US Army had decided that the light observation role should be carried out by a helicopter. Allison was allocated a Bell HUL-1 helicopter, and it first flew with the T63 in February 1961. The Army then appointed three contenders – Hughes, Bell and Hiller – to build five prototypes each of the new helicopter. Eventually, the Hughes model won and, as the US involvement in Vietnam escalated, over 1,500 went into US Army service. The Army also called for increased engine performance, and Allison developed the 317 shp T63-A-5A to ensure that the minimum 250 shp would be possible under the hot and high conditions prevalent in South-East Asia. This new variant was certificated in July 1965 as the Model 250-C10B.

The two losers in the original helicopter contest, Bell and Hiller, developed their designs for the commercial market, Bell producing the Bell 206 Jetranger. This helicopter was hugely successful, and Bell went on to buy over 5,000 Model 250s to power it. Allison improved on the C10 to produce a C18, which won orders both in the civil and military markets. For example, MBB chose it for Germany's first post-war production helicopter. By the early 1980s, Allison was producing over 2,000 Model 250s a year.

The engine was continually improved – the C20 with 420 shp was surpassed by the 500 shp C28 and then the 650 shp C30. The C40/C47 family introduced FADEC into the series. The number of Model 250 engines in service was one of the attractions of Allison when Rolls-Royce acquired the company in 1995, and Rolls-Royce has certainly not been disappointed in the continuing popularity of the engine. The Model 250 has powered 130 different aircraft types, both fixed-wing and helicopter, and 80 of these aircraft types are still flying in 2002. The engine type is on the verge of passing 150 million flying hours. There are 3,850 civil helicopter users flying Model-250-powered aircraft in 106 countries, and 144 military and paramilitary operators in 92 countries. In total, 17,000 engines are still flying in no fewer than 140 countries.

Furthermore, the engine is set to break into new markets. The Model 250 is being used by the Northrop Grumman RQ-8A Fire Scout vertical take-off UAV (unmanned aerial vehicle), which is already in production for the US Navy. Initially, the US Department of Defense has ordered 69, but total US and export orders are expected to be over 200. In Japan, Fuji Heavy Industries' T7 is the new primary trainer for the Japanese Self-Defence Force. Forty-nine have been ordered, all powered by the 450 shp B17F variant of the Model 250. Variants of the engine are being considered by defence forces all over the world, and, in the meantime, the Model 250 continues to power the ubiquitous 206 Jetranger family of Bell helicopters. The 206 family is unique in having used all four series of the engine. Finally, the US Army is upgrading its OH-58D Kiowa Warrior fleet with the latest version of the Model 250-C30R/3, incorporating Full-Authority Digital Engine Control (FADEC). In 2001, Rolls-Royce signed a four-year support contract, the first fleet-hour agreement for US military helicopters.

Those in Rolls-Royce who, in the early 1990s, pointed to the Model 250 as one of the star attractions of Allison knew what they were talking about.

Another turboshaft engine supplied from Indianapolis is the AE 1107 for the V-22 tilt-rotor Osprey. What is a tilt rotor? The concept takes the best of fixed-wing and rotor-wing aircraft and combines them in one machine. The helicopter's disadvantages of low speed, limited range and the need for high engine thrust to provide lift are overcome by the Osprey's fixed wing. The fixed-wing aircraft's disadvantages during low-speed manoeuvring and its need for a runway are overcome by changing the Osprey's large rotor blades to the horizontal, allowing it to operate like a twin-rotor helicopter.

The first tilt-rotor designs were drawn as long ago as the 1940s, but it was not until the 1970s that the technology to make the design work successfully had been demonstrated. The Bell/Boeing V-22 Osprey has been developed since then, and, as it meets the US Marines' operational demands, the US Navy ordered 425 in 1996, to be delivered over 25 years. Those demands were seen as moving substantial numbers of personnel from ships to land-based military engagements beyond the range and capability of conventional helicopters. US defence strategies emphasised the importance of littoral operations, calculating that 70 per cent of the world's population, 80 per cent of its capitals, and the majority of nuclear reactors and weapons of mass destruction lay within 30 miles of a coastline.

The V-22 Osprey was being prepared to replace the tandem rotor CH-46 Sea Knight which harked back to the Vietnam War. As long ago as 1969, the US Marine Corps had recommended that the CH-46 be replaced, but it took 27 years, nineteen major studies and five analyses of the V-22's cost and operational effectiveness for the V-22 Osprey to be finally approved. Fortunately, by then, other parts of the US armed forces – US Special Operations Command, the US Navy and USAF – also saw the benefits.

The AE 1107 is the engine that provides the power and which allowed chief test pilot Tom Macdonald to say when testing:

We have demonstrated that V-22 more than meets the basic requirements. We have taken the aircraft to 294 knots at 18,000 feet and up to 349 knots in a dive. We have flown to a ceiling of 21,500 feet, conducted confined area landings and sea trials on USS *Wasp*, simulated air-to-air refuelling, flown 1,200-mile cross-country flights, carried 4,000 lb sling loads at 175 knots and flown as gross weight up to 51,150 lb. We have demonstrated troop insertions from the hover and shown that standard Marine Corps hardware is compatible.

As the Marines moved the V-22 through the Operational Evaluation (OPEVAL) phase of the programme to qualify it for introduction into field service, the programme encountered two tragic accidents. The first occurred during a two-aircraft troop-deployment exercise in which the second aircraft struck the ground at an unusually high sink rate upon landing, resulting in the loss of several lives. A few months later, a second aircraft on a night training mission was lost. In the first incident, the high approach speed was not arrested as intended due to the lack of familiarity with the flight characteristics of the aircraft. The second aircraft lost was attributed to a critical hydraulic-line failure, coupled with a software problem in the back-up failure-mode control system. The importance of the programme and its high visibility within the US Government resulted in several top-level investigations and reviews into the causes of the accidents and the viability of the concept. These reviews confirmed the soundness of the basic configuration but recommended that all major systems undergo additional extensive design reviews and more-detailed reliability testing. These efforts were designed to provide confidence in this unique and important Marine weapon system.

The other current Rolls-Royce helicopter engine to begin life in Indianapolis was the T800, a joint venture with Allied Signal, now Honeywell. The advanced T800 turboshaft was specifically developed to power the Boeing Sikorsky RAH-66 Comanche, which was the outcome of the US Army's LH (previously LHX) scout/attack helicopter programme.

The RAH-66 Comanche (RAH stands for Reconnaissance Attack Helicopter) has been developed by the US Army to fit with its post-Cold War strategy of reacting to regional conflicts using fewer personnel and long-range self-deployed aircraft based in the United States. Its attributes are stealth, long-range sensing, instant threat analysis, adverse-weather capabilities, daunting fire power, plus the power and reliability of the Rolls-Royce/ Honeywell LHT-801 1563 shp engine. It was originally to be powered by the 1,334 shp T800-LHT-800, but as development moved forward and more complex weapon systems were added the more powerful version was required. The need to sustain aircraft performance in hot and high operation has brought a new version, the T800-LHT-802, which offers an additional 100 shp in such operating conditions. US Army officials estimate they will need 1,200 Comanches by 2010, promising a bright future for the T800.

In the UK, the Gem is nearing the end of its original equipment life, though there are still about 500 Gem-powered helicopters in operation, and it is still giving valiant service in the Lynx and A129.

The Gnome is also still in service, mainly on the Sea King with British forces and in Scandinavia. The two-engined Sea King had proved its worth time and time again in the civil war in Bosnia in the mid-1990s. As one pilot said:

Our mandate was casevac [casualty evacuation role], for which the Sea King, with its excellent endurance, is ideal. To avoid mines we landed on roads and, in the winter conditions, the crews soon realised how much they were benefiting from their training in Norway ... Since we first arrived in 1992 our Sea Kings have made more than 4,500 sorties and been hit only 13 times. To minimise this risk we try to keep to a minimum altitude of 2,000 feet.

As protection the Sea King has armoured floor panels, flare and chaff launchers and a radar warning receiver that tells us if a radar is looking at us. If the frequency changes from search to fire control mode then we would use the chaff to break the radar lock on our aircraft. If a missile is launched at us the missile warning system automatically fires phosphorous flares to lure it away from the heat of our engines. In addition, there is the ALQ157 infra-red jamming system that confuses heat-seeking missiles.

Lieutenant Commander Tim Davies, an Air Engineering Officer working on the Gnome engines, said:

Our engines do not give us many problems. The sand filters have been a great success and incidents of foreign object damage have been zero – except for one engine that took a bullet down the front. Engines are going to life [service] at 1,250 hours – that's when we do part-life rework – and to 2,500 hours, which is full-life when rotables need to be changed. That's some achievement.

As we have seen, the RTM322 is thriving and won all five of the competitions held in Europe in 2001 so that it won orders to power twenty NH90s in Finland, eighteen NH90s (plus seven options) in Sweden, fourteen NH90s (plus ten options) in Norway, fourteen EH101s in Denmark, twelve EH101s in Denmark and twelve EH101s in Portugal. By the end of 2001, nine countries in Europe had selected RTM322-powered helicopters, underlining its position as the leading power plant for the European medium-sized helicopter market. More than a thousand RTM322s had been ordered or were on option, of which 300 had been delivered since the engine entered service in 1998.

Its main competitor in these competitions was the GE T700 powering the Sikorsky S92. Critical in the battle was the bigger core of the RTM322, giving it greater scope for an increase in power.

FLYING ON

We read a great deal about the Rolls-Royce Pegasus and the Harrier in Part Two. In the 1990s, both the engine and the aircraft proved their worth with air forces and navies round the world, including the Royal Air Force and Royal Navy, the US Marine Corps and the navies of India, Italy, Spain and Thailand. By the end of the 1990s, over 1,100 Pegasus engines had been produced and 1.5 million service hours accumulated.

The Harrier/Pegasus combination was invaluable in the Bosnia conflict in the mid-1990s. In spite of the proximity of airfields on mainland Italy, the French, British and United States navies all found seaborne airpower in the Adriatic essential, both to support the troops on land and to protect other ships at sea.

The future seemed to lie with smaller carriers and STOVL aircraft. By the end of the 1990s, only the US and French navies were operating huge carriers with conventional take-off-and-landing aircraft. Such carriers needed to be huge and were therefore extremely expensive both to build and to operate. For example, the US Navy carrier, USS *John C. Stennis*, operates an air wing of 74 fixed-wing aircraft but needs a crew of no fewer than 5,984: 3,184 to operate the ship and 2,800 in the air wing. The ship displaces 102,000 tonnes. The Royal Navy and other navies have built light carriers displacing between 10,000 and 20,000 tonnes and operating with the Harrier STOVL family.

Rolls-Royce did not ignore the development of the Pegasus and in 1999 was able to secure an order from the MoD for 40 upgraded Pegasus Mk 107s, with 86 options, to re-engine the Harriers, giving them greater thrust and reliability. Signed on 23 December, this £350 million contract was a welcome Christmas present for Rolls-Royce, secured under the MoD's 'Smart Acquisition' programme. The first engines went into service within eleven months.

The most successful advanced jet trainer and light combat fighter of the fifteen years up to 2002 has been the Hawk, powered by the Rolls-Royce Turbomeca Adour. Originally known as the HS (Hawker Siddeley) 1182, the Hawk first flew in 1974 and entered service with the RAF in 1976. It has sold throughout the world, as well as to the RAF, to Finland, Kenya, Zimbabwe, South Africa, Kuwait, Saudi Arabia, Abu Dhabi, Oman, Malaysia, Indonesia, Korea, Australia and to the Nato Flight Training Centre in Canada. It has also operated as the T45 Goshawk for the US Navy (see below). The new Adour Mk 951 with FADEC has given the Hawk a new lease of life.

The first of the large Saudi military equipment orders, Al Yamamah Phase One, included 30 Hawk Mk 60 two-seat trainers, and Al Yamamah Phase Two a further twenty. Malaysia was the launch customer for the Hawk 200 in its military variation and specified a version equipped with the Westinghouse APG-66(H) radar.

One of its advantages has been its cheapness compared with the Tornados or the US F-16s and F-18s. Another has been the continuing development of the Adour engine to give a thrust of 6,500 lb by 2002, compared with 5,700 lb in 1987, and also to provide a power plant with an overhaul life gradually moving from 1,200 hours in 1987 to 4,000 hours in 2002. Twenty years ago, the armed forces of the world scarcely considered life-cycle costs. Now they are a big consideration.

After nearly fifteen years of planning for its intermediate and advanced tactical aircraft training requirements, the US Navy took delivery of its first T-45A Goshawk trainer at the Long Beach, California, facility of the Douglas Aircraft company in April 1988. The McDonnell Douglas derivative of the British Aerospace Hawk had been selected as long ago as 1981 to replace the Rockwell T-2B/C Buckeye and Douglas TA-4J Skyhawk. McDonnell Douglas was already proving that a British Aerospace product, the Rolls-Royce Pegasus-powered STOVL tactical AV-8B Harrier, could be produced under licence in the USA in a successful and cost-effective manner.

The US Navy designated their aircraft the T-45A Goshawk, recognising that it differed somewhat from the Hawk. The conventional Hawk required some modifications to fulfil its Navy training role. It needed to be built to accommodate the stress of landings on aircraft carriers and to be able to recover successfully from a missed approach. The use of the cable to catch a hook on the underside of the tail to bring the aircraft to a juddering halt naturally meant much greater stress on the landing gear and the fuselage than would be the case on a normal runway landing. The T-45A's landing gear had to be modified considerably, as did the nose-gear to accommodate the modification. The T-45A also had to be modified to be able to fly at the lower approach speed of 115 knots as opposed to 140 knots.

Powering the T-45A was the Rolls-Royce Turbomeca Adour Mk 871, designated the F405-RR-401 engine, which we read about in Part Two. Originally developed as long ago as 1965, the Mk 871 was the latest variant. This variant at 6,030lb thrust was more powerful than the original Mk 861-49 (F405-RR-400) and was requested by the US Navy to cope with the tropical temperatures of the southern USA where their aircraft would be based. The Adour was seen as a major selling point by the US Navy thanks to its record of reliability. Service statistics from more than three million flying hours had indicated an engine removal rate far below average for a power plant of its kind. It could also show a near 100 per cent mission-success rate.

The Adour 871 also had a modified fuel-control system to reduce acceleration times. This control system included a fast-idle throttle stop which would be automatically engaged on the approach.

Furthermore, the Adour was easy to maintain in the field. Built on a modular basis, it consisted of eleven modules which could be removed and replaced easily under both organisational and intermediate levels of maintenance. The Adour's construction made for rapid turnaround time on repairs and a reduction in the number of spare engines required. And have the US Navy been pleased with it? They certainly have, praising it as the best engine they have ever used – and they have certainly used it. Whereas most military engines only fly 100 to 150 hours a year, the T-45s have been flying 700 hours plus. It is here that the attention to reliability and life-cycle cost has paid off for Rolls-Royce. They have faced severe competition from Allied Signal's F124 which has been offered, so far without success, to the US Navy. The success of the Adour in the US Navy's T-45As led to the Australian Government buying it as well.

THE LAST OF THE GREAT FIGHTER COMPETITIONS

The battle to win the contract to build the Joint Strike Fighter, financed mainly by the US Government with the British making a small contribution, was billed as 'the last of the great fighter competitions'. For those involved, it would certainly settle the issue of who would be the dominant US fighter manufacturer for the first half of the twenty-first century. The likely numbers were daunting – at least 3,000 aircraft – as was the list of aircraft it would replace: the Boeing F/A-18s, the AV-8Bs, GR7s, British Aerospace Sea Harriers, Fairchild A-10s and Lockheed Martin F-16s. The JSF's initial customers would be the US Air Force, US Marine Corps, US Navy, and the Royal Air Force and Royal Navy. Then there were the export customers whose existing F-16 and AV-8B aircraft would need replacing. And there would be others who wanted an affordable fighter capable of being launched from a carrier, carrying out close air support, suppressing enemy air defence and carrying out offensive strikes, or just for reconnaissance.

Plans for the JSF started in the mid-1980s, when it was proposed as a replacement for the Harrier. In effect, the US and UK armed forces wanted a supersonic Harrier. The US Defense Department Advanced Research Projects Agency (which became ARPA), NASA, USAF, USN and the UK Ministry of Defence joined forces on a broad-ranging Harrier-replacement study. Known as the Advanced STOVL (ASTOVL) feasibility study, it considered four main vertical-lift concepts: tandem fan, direct lift, remote augmented lift and ejector lift. As the recognised leader in propulsion technology for vertical lift, Rolls-Royce played a key part in these early studies, while the Allison Engine Company, as it was then called, was exclusively teamed with Lockheed on their shaft-driven LiftFan concept for augmenting lift thrust.

Comparing the Joint Strike Fighter with the Harrier AV-8B gave an idea of the advances being made. The speed of JSF was supersonic compared with Harrier's high subsonic – Mach 1.65 compared with Mach 0.97. The engine thrust would be 50,000 lb with afterburner and 39,000 lb in vertical-lift mode for the STOVL version, compared with 21,500 lb for Harrier. (The thrust of the two-engined Tornado was 35,000 lb.)

The operational range would be 450 nautical miles compared with Harrier's 300, its all-up weight (i.e. with weapons and fuel) 27 tonnes compared with 11, its length 50.5 feet compared with 48, its wingspan 35 feet compared with 25 and its wing area 460 square feet compared with 201. It was to be a lethal weapon, but one in which the pilot stood a good chance of survival; it was also to be affordable and operate as a stealth aircraft, invisible to radar. Its shape would not reflect radar beams, and its weapons would be carried internally to maintain the stealth configuration. Its main aim would be to hit targets on the ground, but it would also have air-to-air attack capability.

In 1988, the US Navy and US Marine Corps joined forces to outline the characteristics that would replace the AV-8B and F/A-18. This became the STOVL Strike Fighter (SSF) but was soon absorbed into the Common Affordable Lightweight Fighter (CALF) project. In 1989, the USAF became more closely interested when its studies showed that STOVL would offer significant benefits over conventional fighters. The USAF already had in place a project for a multi-role fighter to replace the F-16, but it was struggling on cost grounds.

NASA and ARPA began a three-year study into the two main vertical-lift concepts – direct lift, the tried and trusted method used by Rolls-Royce for the Harrier, and an augmented system that depended on a fan to generate vertical lift. The project looked into two methods for powering the fan using a shaft and hot engine gases.

The US Department of Defense formalised the ARPA project, calling the technology-demonstrator programme 'X-32' and dividing it into four major phases. The first phase, Phase 0, had looked at generic ASTOVL technology and had already been completed. Phase I would look at the feasibility of using derivative, advanced tactical-fighter engines in STOVL aircraft applications.

The two potential engines were the GE YF120 and the Pratt & Whitney YF119, which was selected for the USAF's Lockheed Martin/Boeing F-22 Raptor air superiority fighter. Phase II began in 1993, focusing on design and the validation of critical technology that would be used for propulsive lift. Two contracts were awarded to Lockheed and McDonnell Douglas to study shaft and gas-driven lift-fan concepts respectively. The US Congress also instructed ARPA to run a competition for a direct-lift study, and in March 1994 ARPA awarded a 50:50 cost-share agreement to Boeing. In May, Northrop Grumman joined the programme with a 'no-cost' agreement to examine a lift-plus/lift-cruise concept. In this concept, completely separate engines would be used for cruise and lift thrust.

Phase III would involve two flying demonstrators – a conventional take-off and landing X-32A for the USAF, and a STOVL X-32B for the US Navy, US Marine Corps and Royal Navy. At this point, Congress insisted that the CALF programme merge with the Joint Advanced Strike Technology (JAST) programme, which had emerged out of a number of abandoned USAF and USN projects. It was focused on technologies for a future multi-role bi-service combat aircraft, for 2008 and beyond. JAST was aimed at replacing a number of aircraft, including the F-14, F-111, F-15E, F117 and F-16.

This new programme, soon to be called Joint Strike Fighter, brought about a bigger flight-test effort with two finalists each building two demonstrators. One of each was to have ASTOVL capability, while the other was to be conventional. The US Navy also insisted on a carrier variant capable of operating from aircraft carriers without being dependent on vertical lift. The two finalists were Boeing, given the X-32 designation, and Lockheed Martin, given X-35. Boeing's design was a direct-lift-powered, delta-shaped aircraft with twin fins and a prominent chin intake. Lockheed's design incorporated a large, shaft-driven lift fan in STOVL form. Both concepts would use a derivative of the Pratt & Whitney F119 (now F135) engine, but in the later stages of the programme a consortium of GE, Rolls-Royce and Allison Advanced Development Company (by now owned by Rolls-Royce) would develop a competitor engine based on the GE YF120 (now F136) engine. (It would be Rolls-Royce's first collaboration with GE since their ill-fated joint venture on civil engines in the 1980s.)

Rolls-Royce was also involved in the Pratt & Whitney engine. Indeed, as the world's only manufacturer of a production vertical-lift turbofan, it had a key role on both programmes as the supplier of the lift modules and associated hardware for the STOVL variants of the demonstrators.

Boeing's STOVL design worked like the Pegasus-powered Harrier with the fan-duct flow being discharged through a laterally and axially aligned jetscreen to provide lift and prevent hot-gas injection from the main hot nozzles that discharged the gas jet. Rolls-Royce provided the spool duct, jetscreen and lift module and also the STOVL altitude-control nozzles and associated actuation. In STOVL mode, the main two-dimensional thrust nozzle closed, diverting the exhaust via large butterfly valves to Pegasus-style lift nozzles.

On the other hand, Lockheed Martin's STOVL design relied for vertical lift on a large 50-inch-diameter fan, made by Rolls-Royce Allison. The two-stage fan was capable of generating up to 19,000 lb of thrust (almost the total thrust of the Pegasus) and was used to control the pitch of the aircraft in STOVL mode. This gave the Lockheed aircraft much more lift margin, a key factor. The fan was driven by a shaft connected to the low-pressure turbine through a clutch and gear mechanism. Rolls-Royce was also responsible for the roll off-takes, which provide roll control, and for the three-bearing swivel duct. In conventional flight, this was used as a normal main exhaust, but in STOVL mode it could be vectored through 105 degrees to give the same hover manoeuvrability as the Harrier.

Both contenders would be expected to make their first flights at Palmdale, California, in April 2000. Test work would then transfer to the nearby Edwards Air Force base, and the more complex STOVL aircraft were expected to begin flight tests in the third quarter of 2000. A winner would be declared in 2001.

McDonnell Douglas's elimination from the programmes in November 1996 was a severe blow to them. Harry Stonecipher, the chief executive, said that the company's elimination was 'a massive loss which will be felt over the next decade'. It was felt quicker than that. During 1997, McDonnell Douglas was absorbed by Boeing.

Inevitably, as the demonstrator phase unfolded, a number of problems arose. There were rumours of Boeing and Lockheed running over-budget and investing their own money, a practice outlawed by the rules of the competition. In early 2000, US Defense Under-Secretary Jack Gansler announced he was going to review the 'winner takes all' basis of the competition. Some in the defence department had started to question the sense of this approach, as it might kill off companies that finished on the losing side. In May 2000, the *Sunday Times* announced: 'Boeing Heads For Victory in Fighter Order'. This assertion was apparently based on the fact that 'industry insiders' were saying that Boeing had established a 'clear edge' and that Lockheed 'would be unable to close the gap'.

Meanwhile, the flight-test programme was progressing, and in all flight tests the Lockheed concept was demonstrating that it had clear and tangible advantages, especially the Navy's carrier variant and its STOVL configurations.

ALIENS AND STRANGERS

As the day of decision – 26 October 2001 – approached, Boeing completed the flight-test programme of its X-32B demonstrator at the US Navy facility at Patuxent River, Maryland, with a sortie that included a short-take-off transition to conventional flight, supersonic dash and, finally, a conventional landing. Testing of the aircraft's direct-lift propulsion system – the third, and arguably most critical, flight phase – included over a hundred one-to-three-second transitions between wing, semi-wing and jet-borne hover. Meanwhile, Lockheed Martin completed its programme of flights with a short take-off in STOVL mode, a supersonic dash and a *vertical* landing. This so-called 'Mission X', to show the superior performance of the F35, had been conceived by ex-Marine General Harry Blot, himself a legendary Harrier pilot.

On Friday 26 October, Edward Aldridge, US Under-Secretary of Defense, announced the winner: Lockheed Martin. In spite of the review in early 2000, the DoD had decided to continue with the 'winner takes all' approach, and Aldridge said the DoD would not put pressure on Lockheed to share any of the contract, adding:

If they would like to do that then they are free to do that. We would not discourage it. But we are opposed to forcing the contractors into doing this.

Boeing was devastated. Nick Cook of *Jane's Defence Weekly* said:

Boeing's failure raises the spectre of the closure of its St Louis plant, the old McDonnell Douglas business.

By contrast, Lockheed was jubilant. In the development phase, the contract was worth $19 billion, and in the production phase it could be worth $200 billion over 40 years.

And where were the engine makers?

Colin Green, President of Rolls-Royce's defence business, said:

As an engineer, I am delighted by the choice. The F-35, with its Rolls-Royce LiftFan, is truly a new generation of vertical lift fighter aircraft while, as a businessman, I would have been just as pleased if Boeing had won as Rolls-Royce was a key subcontractor in both bids.

As John Whatley, Rolls-Royce's programme executive on the JSF, pointed out:

Between October 1996 and August 2001, we here at Bristol and our colleagues at Indianapolis designed, manufactured, qualified and flight-tested our engine components. It was a brilliant achievement from a clean sheet of paper as we faced what we call an 'aliens and strangers' situation.

And while Rolls-Royce expected $1 billion of business providing the lift systems during the development phase and, of course, much more from the production phase later, other British suppliers were also deeply involved. BAe Systems and Smiths Industries would be large beneficiaries, and, in addition, Flight Refuelling would provide the fuel system, Martin Baker Aircraft the ejection seats and Aerospace Composite Technologies the canopy.

Why did Lockheed win? Possibly it was because Lockheed built a prototype that was essentially an early version of what the JSF would be. By contrast, Boeing produced a far less developed demonstrator that was different from what it said it would ultimately create. It had a different wing shape and could not fly faster than sound. Possibly it had something to do with the USAF, which was by far the biggest customer, seeking 1,763 fighters against 408 for the US Navy, 609 for the US Marine Corps and 150 for the Royal Navy and Royal Air Force. The USAF's voice was probably stronger than the rest, and its interest in the STOVL version would have been markedly less. This would have given Lockheed an advantage as its aircraft was more modular, with fewer technical challenges and therefore less risk. Perhaps it was because the Lockheed fan system of lift provided about 10,000 lb more thrust in lift mode. Perhaps it was because Boeing's ugly shape had earned it a very unfortunate nickname and its carrier variant needed extensive redesign.

The truth is probably, as 'Pete' Aldridge said in announcing the decision, that in all phases of the evaluation the Lockheed aircraft had scored slightly, but consistently, better than its Boeing competitor.

And what was the JSF at this stage? We saw earlier what it was aiming to achieve and how its configuration and performance compared with the Harrier. There were three variants – first, conventional take-off and landing (CTOL), then aircraft-carrier based and, finally, short take-off/vertical landing (STOVL). As we have seen, they aimed to satisfy the needs of the US Air Force, Navy and Marine Corps, as well as the Royal Navy and Royal Air Force. There might be three variants but they would have commonality and would be built on the same production lines. The STOVL version would have a range of 800 nautical miles and the carrier-based version, 1,200.

Inside the single-seater cockpit, the pilot would have both 'heads-up' and helmet-mounted display. Information would come from early-warning aircraft, satellites and from other aircraft, as well as forces on the ground. It would be brought together with data from on-board sensors.

JSF would be able to carry 8 tonnes of weapons, including air-defence missiles, ground-attack missiles and precision-guided bombs controlled by satellite. It would also carry the Future Small Diameter Bomb, effectively an air-to-ground missile. The on-board computer power would be the equivalent of two Cray supercomputers.

Some were predicting that JSF would be the last conventional fighter to enter service with US armed forces. They felt that the technology being used in the 'unmanned aerial vehicles' such as Predator and Dark Star would have developed sufficiently to allow the next generation of combat aircraft, which would enter service around 2040, to operate with an on-board intelligent computer system flying most of a combat mission. Such aircraft would be linked by real-time telemetry to a human mission controller on a command aircraft safely positioned hundreds of miles away or, via a satellite link, even thousands of miles away, in the USA or the UK.

As well as the 3,000 aircraft needed by the USA and the UK, an export market for a further 2,000 to 3,000 aircraft was projected. The next phase, now called System Development and Demonstration (SDD), was opened up to foreign partners. The UK signed a memorandum of understanding as the sole partner at this level and would invest $2 billion for an 8 per cent stake. Italy and the Netherlands were expected to join once SDD began. Italy wanted to replace its AV-8Bs and the Alenia/Embraer AMX aircraft, while the Netherlands wanted to replace its F-16 AM/BMs. Turkey was also looking for an F-16 replacement. Talks had also been concluded for Denmark and Norway to join as a combined partner with Canada, as participants with a stake up to 2 per cent. Other potential purchasers were Australia, Brazil, Germany, Israel, Poland and Singapore.

The actual definite programme now stretched out for the rest of the decade. The selection of the JSF winner in October 2001 marked the end of the concept demonstration phase and the beginning of full-scale development of the Preferred Weapon System Concept (PWSC). The JSF Programme Office (JPO) called for the first test aircraft to fly 48 months from the time the system development and demonstration (SDD) contract was awarded. The initial production aircraft were scheduled for delivery in 2008 to support a US Marine Corps initial operational capability (IOC) in 2010. US Air Force IOC was set for 2011. The 126-month SDD phase would end in 2012 with the US Navy, Royal Air Force and Royal Navy also reaching IOC.

Flight testing would require fourteen PWSC development aircraft, comprising five CTOL versions for the USAF, four of the carrier-configured variant for the US Navy and five of the STOVL derivative for the US Marine Corps and the UK. The intention would be to build these aircraft as close as possible to the production standard, with common flight-test goals and a subset for each version. Tests would be centred on the USAF's Edwards base and the US Navy's Patuxent River facility but could also include Boscombe Down in the UK.

As we have seen, Rolls-Royce was deeply involved in the SDD phase for the coming ten years, and it would also be heavily involved in the subsequent production of 5,000 to 6,000 aircraft. The Pratt & Whitney F119 engine had been chosen for the SDD phase, and, as we have seen, Rolls-Royce would be manufacturing the shaft-driven lift fan, comprising the lift fan itself, the gearbox, the clutch/shaft nozzle and actuation, as well as the lift system, comprising the three-bearing swivel module and the roll post and nozzles. Once the production phase was reached, there would be a competition each year between the incumbent Pratt & Whitney engine, the F135, and an alternate engine, the F136, from the GE consortium, in which Rolls-Royce had a 40 per cent share. The settlement of this stake was due partly to Charles Hughes, Rolls-Royce's vice-president JSF, who had negotiated that GE would take Rolls-Royce's fan module on their engine back in 1995, but also to an existing agreement between GE and the Allison Engine Company, resulting from the latter's outstanding performance in the so-called US Integrated High-Performance Turbine Engine Technology demonstrator programmes. So the stage is set for another 'great engine war' the like of which has not been seen since the 1980s, when GE's F110 engine went head to head with Pratt & Whitney's F100 for the F-15 and F-16 fighter aircraft.

EXPANDED MILITARY MARKET COVERAGE

1980

Hawk · Harrier · AV-8A · MB339

Super Galeb · Orao · AMX · Tornado

Goshawk · Jaguar · Atlantic · A129

C160 · Lynx · G222 L · Sea King

TODAY

Eurofighter · Harrier · AV-8B · C130

Tornado · Goshawk · Hawk · C130A-H

Jaguar · Aermacchi · AMX · Orion

C-2A Greyhound · C-27J · Nimrod · E-2C Hawkeye

SK-60 · Jindivik · Comanche · ShinMaywa US-1A Kai

EH101 · NH90 · Osprey · Global Hawk

A129 · Lynx · Tiger · Super Lynx

Sea King · Apache · S92

CHAPTER EIGHT

POWER ON LAND
AND SEA AS WELL

THE MARINE SPEY
THE WR21
THE VANGUARD CLASS AND TRIDENT
PWR2
THE ASTUTE CLASS
'IMPORTANT IN TECHNICAL LEADERSHIP'
'WORTHY OF ITS DISTINGUISHED PAST'
MOTOR CARS AND DEFENCE
'MORE OR LESS VULNERABLE'
ULSTEIN – 'AN EXCELLENT FIT'
THE MARINE TRENT 30
THE INDUSTRIAL TRENT

THE MARINE SPEY

BY THE END OF THE 1980s, the gas turbine had become the dominant propulsion engine for major warships. Compared with the old-fashioned steam plant, it was light and compact, capable of quick starting, required little maintenance and could be operated by fewer hands. As we saw in Part Two, Rolls-Royce had been involved in supplying gas-turbine technology to warship propulsion since the Royal Navy's patrol craft HMS *Grey Goose* had been launched in 1953. By 1990, Rolls-Royce was working on developing an engine that would satisfy modern navies' concerns about the cost of fuel and have sufficient range to cope with global responsibilities. The company was working with Allison Gas Turbines on an intercooled recuperative (ICR) Spey marine-propulsion unit. How had it got there?

Back in the 1950s, the oil-fired steam turbine was the plant, with its poor efficiency at cruising speeds, that had to be surpassed. The first gas turbines used at sea were adapted from aircraft power units and were initially used in

249

combination with steam plants to provide fast start-up and higher top speed. Eventually, all-gas turbine systems were developed and adopted by the Royal Navy for use in the Type 21 frigates and Type 42 destroyers. Two Rolls-Royce Olympus turbines were used to drive a propeller at top speed, i.e. 'boost power', and two much smaller Rolls-Royce Tyne turbines to drive the propellers at cruise speed, i.e. 'cruise power'. This was known as COGOG or COGAG – COmbined power of Gas turbine for cruise Or/And Gas turbine for boost.

This COGOG arrangement became popular, though the Tynes were just a little too small for cruising, while the Olympus was more than adequate for boost speeds. What was needed was a new turbine of intermediate power. Rolls-Royce and the MoD worked together to find a suitable engine and chose Rolls-Royce's aero Spey which could be developed into a marine Spey. It was introduced at two power ratings – normal power of 12.75 MW and maximum of 14 MW. Designated the SM1A, it first entered service in 1985 in the Royal Navy's HMS *Brave* and the Japanese guided-missile destroyer *Hatakaze*. In both, the Speys worked in conjunction with other Rolls-Royce turbines: in the case of *Brave*, Tyne cruise engines and Spey boost engines, and in *Hatakaze*, Olympus for boosts and Spey for cruise. The SM1A was also supplied to other ships in the Royal Navy, the Japanese Maritime Self Defence Force and the Dutch Navy.

Bill Thomas, who was closely involved in the securing of orders for Rolls-Royce from the Japanese Navy, recalls the long-running efforts required:

My business dealings with Kawasaki Heavy Industries [KHI] started in 1970, just a few months after I had left the Royal Navy and joined the then Rolls-Royce Industrial and Marine Division as Chief Applications Engineer. At lunch one day, the Chief Engineer of the Division said to me 'I know something that you do not know'. 'That is not difficult,' I replied, 'but please tell me anyway'.

He said that I would be in Japan next week, and so I was, accompanying Ray Whitfield, the Managing Director of the division at that time. We met the Kawasaki team on the 19th Floor of the World Trade Center Building. From the window of the room I looked down at the jetty at Hamamatsu-cho where, during 1946, we had cleaned the boilers of the destroyer in which I was then serving.

This meeting was crucial in that both companies agreed to work together to market the Rolls-Royce Olympus and Tyne marine gas turbines. These engines, the big Olympus and the smaller Tyne, were already committed to two major classes of British warships, and it was thought that it might be possible to have them selected by the JMSDF [Japanese Marine Self Defence Force] for new Japanese vessels, of similar size, which were being planned for the JMSDF.

Very soon afterwards, Hajime Yamamoto San of the Prime Mover Division of KHI was sent to the Rolls-Royce factory at Ansty to study the gas turbines concerned. He spoke some English, and even in those early days we made a great deal of progress in sharing our combined knowledge and experience. Mr Yamamoto worked very hard, both on the engineering work and also at improving his English, and we soon became not merely collaborators but firm friends. We both held the simple view that friendship and mutual trust were vital if we were to succeed in selling in Japan. Close collaboration was also maintained between the Directors of KHI and successive directors of Rolls-Royce Industrial and Marine. Notable amongst the latter was Ralph Robins, now Sir Ralph Robins, Chairman of Rolls-Royce plc.

An essential part of the plan was shared manufacture, so that both manufacturers could benefit from the production work, and so that the potential customer would know that KHI were very heavily involved. This was not achieved without some of the Rolls-Royce workforce feeling that we were giving away too readily a great deal of hard earned expertise and also production work in this new engineering field. However, common sense prevailed, everyone realising that 'half a cake is much better than no cake at all'.

There followed roughly seven years of concentrated effort by both companies at all levels and countless engineering presentations were made to the JMSDF and JDA Officers concerned. These were 'master-minded' by Yoshiaki Okada San of the Prime Mover Division Head Office staff. I was fortunate in having been the Head of the Engineering Section of the New Ship Project Group when we designed the first three major classes of gas turbine powered warships for the Royal Navy. Thus I was able to inform our audiences, through Mr Yamamoto's excellent interpretation, not only about the gas turbines, but also about their integration into the ship designs, dealing with such matters as noise suppression, anti-shock mountings, air inlet and exhaust systems, main reduction gearing components and so on.

During these presentations we often shared a few jokes, and I like to think that the friendship between the engineers of both companies was evident to the potential customer, giving him comfort that neither would let the other down, and thus he would not be let down. Indeed, we had our troubles along the way, but these were always overcome together, without the need to resort to the fine print of the contract between us.

The first major event involving machinery occurred when a Rolls-Royce Olympus turbine was installed in the Kobe Works of KHI to be demonstrated to the potential customer. The engine had KHI manufactured air intake and exhaust silencing systems very similar to what is needed in ships. Power was absorbed in a dynamometer capable of taking the whole output of the Olympus of about 28,000 horsepower. Kawasaki arranged a magnificent day for our visitors, during which all had presentations on the gas turbine, tours of the KHI works and a very thrilling demonstration of the Olympus being started and brought to full power within seconds.

Masanobu Inubushi San, then the Head of the Gas Turbine section of the Prime Mover Division, took charge, his small figure contrasting with the power of the engine which he confidently put through its paces, winding the power up and down and then finally slamming the throttle shut and stopping. To the Japanese Marine Engineers watching, used to careful manoeuvring with steam boilers and turbines, it must have been a revelation. In steam ships it is normal for the watchkeepers to go down to the machinery spaces four hours before sailing time, but here was a machine which could be started in seconds. All that was needed in preparation was to start the machinery which would provide lubrication for the main reduction gearing and the power turbine, and this took only a few minutes. Full power could now be available before the seamen had time to raise the anchor or to release the hawsers securing a ship to its jetty!

While the demonstration day was entirely trouble free, it would be dishonest to pretend that there had been no problems with installation. Great care is needed in the design of silencers, which have to live in a very hostile environment of hot high velocity gas. Rolls-Royce had met trouble when the prototype Olympus for the Type 42 destroyer first ran in a test house at Ansty. After about twenty minutes the silencer broke its securing brackets. It was found that these had a natural frequency corresponding to the organ pipe frequency of the exhaust system! Thus a rapid redesign was necessary. When the KHI demonstrator first ran, the silencer was not as it would have been for a ship, but designed instead to suit the test house being used. Unfortunately its silencing was not all that had been hoped for. Mr Arthur Crossland, an Applications Engineering Manager from my team at Ansty, was in Kobe for the commissioning, and he and the KHI team redesigned the silencer and KHI built and installed the new one in a remarkably short time, so that it was ready for the great day. The Rolls-Royce engineers were astonished at how quickly the manufacture and installation was completed by KHI.

There is no doubt in my mind that this KHI demonstration played a major part in persuading the customer that they should use the KHI/Rolls-Royce gas turbines, and it was not long before the first ship set of Twin Olympus, Twin Tyne gas turbines was ordered. Again, another superbly managed demonstration at the Kobe works hosted by KHI, this time of one complete set of ship machinery. The heart of this machinery comprised an Olympus and a Tyne gas turbine, driving opposite ends of a shared reduction-gearing pinion. An excellent engineered self-shifting clutch, supplied by SSS Gears of UK, ensured a smooth transition from the cruising powered Tyne to the full power of the Olympus, with no risk of the large engine overspeeding the smaller. The clutch automatically disconnected whichever turbine was tending to be driven by the other. Again the gas turbines were started and accelerated to full power in turn. The rapidity with which they could be manoeuvred was extremely impressive to those more used to steam machinery.

A typical example of the mutual trust occurred once when I received a message saying that an Olympus gas turbine in one destroyer was suffering from 'hunting' idling speed. The ship concerned was about to take part in an exercise with American ships, and KHI was therefore concerned that it should perform well. Although the likely cause was a small air reservoir having lost its air pressure, and the likely cure was merely a couple of strokes with a bicycle tyre pump, Rolls-Royce sent a senior controls engineer to Japan on the next available flight. He recharged the air reservoir, and all was well. This was typical of the collaboration between the two companies. The important thing was to cure any problem, and not to wrangle about the financial responsibilities.

Marine gas turbines were developing fast. Even while the first Olympus and Tyne engines were being built for the JMSDF ships, Rolls-Royce was hard at work designing a marine version of the Spey aero engine. This was to have very much greater efficiency than the Olympus and would incorporate all the lessons learned with the Olympus engines in service with several navies. As with all gas turbine developments, substantial sales would be needed to make the new engine viable. Rolls-Royce was assured of sales to the Royal Navy, of course, but needed other outlets to supplement these. The Royal Netherlands Navy was interested in the Spey, and was kept informed of the development status. The JMSDF was also very interested, and was similarly informed in presentations by the KHI/Rolls-Royce team. Not surprisingly, neither of these two major navies wanted to become the first user of the Spey at sea, and looked to the Royal Navy to get sea experience first. It was thus imperative that a Spey should be put into one of the new Brave Class destroyers coming into service at that time. These had the then standard Olympus/Tyne machinery, and the only way of getting Spey sea experience was to redesign the engine system to include one Spey in place of one Olympus. There was obviously some risk and significant expense in such a task, not to mention a delay in the delivery of the ship concerned. Fortunately, Admiral Fieldhouse, then Controller (Chief of Material) of the Royal Navy, was a farsighted Officer. He realised instantly that unless a Spey was at sea with the Royal Navy quickly, the Dutch and Japanese would almost certainly commit to American engines. The KHI/Rolls-Royce team held its breath, and then rejoiced when the decision to install the Spey was announced. It is small wonder that Admiral Fieldhouse later became Lord Fieldhouse and Chief of the British Defence Staff.

It soon became necessary to provide more power, and a new Spey SM1C was developed. This unit increased power from 12.75 MW to 18 MW, and thermal efficiency from 33 to 35 per cent, while at the same time reducing fuel consumption by more than 5 per cent.

THE WR21

However efficient the Spey was, further development was going to be necessary to meet the power needs that would be required in the 1990s and beyond.

By the early 1990s, the US Navy was looking for a propulsion system that would produce a 30 per cent reduction in fuel usage as well as fuel-efficient operation at low power levels. The power requirement of warships differs from most other ships. Whereas merchant ships and cruise liners are designed to run at a chosen cruise speed, departing from it only when manoeuvring, warships are more demanding. Warships spend about 90 per cent of their time at cruising speed or less. Only occasionally is top speed required. After publishing a Request for Proposals in June 1991 which laid down a tight requirement for the development of an advanced-cycle gas-turbine propulsion unit for future warship applications, the US Navy's Naval Sea Systems Command awarded in December 1991 a $160-million contract to the Marine Division of Westinghouse, in conjunction with Rolls-Royce Industrial and Marine Gas Turbines Ltd., to develop an intercooled recuperative (ICR) cycle engine, the WR21, based on the RB 211 aero-engine. The intercooling referred to the cooling of the air flow after it had been compressed in the first section of the compressor. Recuperation, also known as regeneration, was the recovery of heat from the exhaust flow, which reduced fuel consumption.

Rolls-Royce had pioneered ICR technology as long ago as the 1950s. However, being based on aero technology, with relatively lightweight castings and roller bearings and designed for fast patrol boats, it was not felt to be robust enough for big warships, and the interest in ICR lapsed. However, it revived at the beginning of the 1980s, and since 1981 Rolls-Royce had been working with NAVSEA to look at ways of applying ICR technology to meet the US Navy's future needs. Initial studies were based on the marine Spey engines, but the US Navy's requirement for greater power led Rolls-Royce to turn to the RB 211.

Intercooling and recuperating a simple-cycle gas turbine improves the cycle by using an intercooler between the intermediate-pressure (IP) and high-pressure compressors (HP). This reduces the temperature of the air leaving the IP compressor so that it enters the HP compressor at near-ambient level. This reduces significantly the power needed to drive the HP compressor and, for the same cycle temperature, the engine can produce considerably more power. By also incorporating a recuperator to heat the air before it enters the combustion chamber, the combustion temperature required can be achieved with much less fuel. Intercooling and recuperation also improve fuel efficiency at reduced power levels. With the addition of variable-area nozzle guide vanes at the entry to the LP power turbine, the efficiency of the recuperator is improved, giving better fuel consumption down at the power levels used for cruising.

The core engine selected for the WR21 was a version of the very successful and reliable RB 211-535, though it also included a power turbine from the Rolls-Royce Trent. Parts of other Rolls-Royce engines were used so that the six major elements of the WR21 were based on the IP compressor, HP compressor and IP turbine from the RB 211-535, the HP turbine from the RB 211-524G/H, the combustion system from the marine Spey and aero Tay, and the LP turbine from the Trent.

The first ships to use the WR21 engine will be the Royal Navy's new Type 45 destroyers. These Type 45s will replace the T42s whose vulnerability was exposed in the Falklands War, when HMS *Sheffield* was destroyed by an Exocet missile with the loss of twenty lives and other Royal Navy ships were successfully attacked by fighter aircraft. The Type 45 destroyers will be equipped with the Principal Anti Air Missile System (PAAMS) weapon system. PAAMS will be capable of engaging several targets simultaneously and will be effective against the most advanced sea-skimming and high-diving missiles.

With a displacement of 7,350 tonnes, the Type 45 Class will be the largest destroyers ever built for the Royal Navy. Type 45 Prime Contract Office (PCO) Managing Director Brian Phillipson explained the need for size:

With the defence environment now one of considerable uncertainty and tight budgets, we need a robust design which will last the ships for their lifetime, without the necessity for major structural re-work in order to incorporate the changes of equipment which are bound to be needed as defence requirements change during the next 30 years. Other drivers on size include the requirement to get primary sensors high up, and the need to include new and much improved standards of crew accommodation. Another factor is our decision to go for integrated electric propulsion.

This is where the WR21 comes in. Having initially considered an all-diesel arrangement and then a combined gas-and-electric propulsion system, the PCO decided ultimately on an integrated electric-propulsion architecture. The electric power generation will come from two 25-megawatt-rated Northrop Grumman/Rolls-Royce WR21 gas-turbine alternators and two 2-megawatt diesel generators. [Northrop Grumman had taken over the Westinghouse engine division.]

The WR21 had been chosen because of the Royal Navy's existing support infrastructure for Rolls-Royce marine gas turbines, its ability to match the Navy's global operation profile and its ability to provide significant reductions in fuel consumption, as well as for its simplified maintenance and support. Finally, the WR21 met stringent environmental standards.

Under the contract awarded by the PCO in March 2001, Northrop Grumman and Rolls-Royce will supply six WR shipsets, i.e. twelve engines in total, for the first six ships of the Type 45 programme. The first delivery will be in 2003, and the Type 45s will enter service in 2007. A total of twelve ships are planned to join the fleet by 2014.

The next targets for the WR21 are the Future Aircraft Carrier and the Future Surface Combatant for the Royal Navy – both are expected to adopt the 'Electric Ship' concept – the US Navy's DD21 *Zumwalt* Class destroyer and ships of the French Navy. (In October 2000, Rolls-Royce and Northrop Grumman signed a licensing agreement with France's DCN for the marketing and manufacture of WR21.)

THE VANGUARD CLASS AND TRIDENT

As we saw earlier, the Royal Navy began to take an interest in submarines just over 100 years ago. In April 1901, Lord Selbourne, First Lord of the Admiralty, said:

Five submarine vessels of the type invented by Mr Holland have been ordered. What the future value of these boats may be in naval warfare can only be a matter of conjecture. But experiments with these boats will assist the Admiralty in assessing their true value.

Mr Holland's boat, built in the USA, was propelled by a 160 hp petrol engine and was capable of 8 knots on the surface and 7 knots submerged. It was soon superseded by British-designed vessels, and by the outbreak of the First World War there were 74 submarines operating in Britain, the most successful of which were the diesel-powered 'E' Class, with crews of 31 and ten times the power of the original Holland boats.

However, diesel-powered submarines could not keep pace with the Grand Fleet and were replaced by 'K' Class steam-powered boats with 10,000 shp turbines and a speed capability of 24 knots.

The two world wars demonstrated the efficiency of the submarine, highlighted especially in the Second World War when the German U-boat almost starved Britain into surrender. By 1945, the power of the submarine was not in doubt. Nevertheless, until the launch of the first nuclear submarine, the USS *Nautilus*, in 1954, the submarine remained a relatively slow vessel capable of operating for only about 24 hours under the surface. At a stroke, it was transformed into a warship capable of over 20 knots, with an ability to stay underwater for weeks at a time. By 1967, the Royal Navy's HMS *Valiant* was able to sail 12,000 miles from Singapore to Britain non-stop, submerged, in 28 days. In 1989, HMS *Superb* and HMS *Turbulent* met at the North Pole.

In the meantime, in December 1962, President of the USA, John F. Kennedy, and Prime Minister of Great Britain, Harold Macmillan, met at Nassau in the Bahamas and signed an agreement later ratified the following April by the Polaris Sales Agreement. Under the terms of these agreements, Britain took delivery of the Polaris A3 submarine-launched ballistic-missile system. Vickers Armstrong – later Vickers Shipbuilding and Engineering Limited (VSEL) and, even later, part of GEC and then BAe Systems – built two of the submarines and Cammell Laird built the other two. By 1967,

HMS *Resolution* was completed, and the following year she successfully fired a Polaris missile on the test range off Cape Kennedy on the Florida coast.

The Polaris A3 missile was a two-stage, solid-fuel ballistic missile. Nine-and-a-half metres in length and one-and-a-half metres in diameter, weighing 16 tonnes, it had a range of 2,500 nautical miles. It used a self-contained inertial guidance system independent of external commands or control. It was replaced in the US Navy in the early 1980s by the Trident C4 and then, in 1990, by the Trident D5. Manufactured in California by the Lockheed Missile and Space Company, the Trident D5 is 13 metres long, 2 metres in diameter and weighs no less than 60 tonnes. Each missile can deliver up to twelve warheads, which means a number of different targets can be attacked. Its range is over 4,000 nautical miles, and its accuracy can be measured in metres.

PWR2

The UK bought Trident to replace its Polaris missiles under the terms of the original Polaris Agreement and built a new class of submarine, the *Vanguard* Class, to carry them. This class boasted a number of improvements over existing nuclear submarines (the *Valiant* Class of the 1960s had been followed by the *Resolution* Class, the *Swiftsure* Class and the *Trafalgar* Class), most notably a much-improved nuclear propulsion plant. As with all nuclear submarines, the pressurised water reactor (PWR) was the driving force of the *Vanguard* submarine.

In simple terms, the PWR was a collection of fissile-uranium fuel elements producing huge amounts of energy to power the submarine (a tonne of fissionable material released the energy equivalent of two-and-a-half million tonnes of coal).

This PWR system was based on primary and secondary circuits. Water coolant travelled around the primary circuit, through the reactor pressure vessel where it was heated by the nuclear fuel elements and on through tubes in the steam generator. A high pressure was maintained in the primary circuit to prevent the coolant from boiling. In the steam generator, the heat from the primary coolant was used to convert water outside the tubes into steam, which was used to drive the main turbine engine. From there, a system of clutches, gearing and propulsion transmitted the power to the sea. Steam was also used to drive the turbo-generators which supplied the submarine with electricity.

The reactor and steam-generating facilities were operated through a number of automatic and manual controls, while a network of electronic and mechanical failsafe devices monitored the reactor at all times. Because of the large amount of energy stored in the uranium fuel elements, the *Vanguard*

Class submarines would be able to travel great distances and for many years without refuelling. The core used by the *Vanguard* Class, known as Core Z, offered nearly three times the life of the earlier Core A, and, through greatly improved power distribution, brought a significant reduction in noise.

HMS *Vanguard* was launched from the Vickers shipyard in Barrow on 4 March 1992. One hundred and fifty metres in length, with a maximum hull diameter of 13 metres and displacing 16,000 tonnes, it was the largest submarine ever built for the Royal Navy. It was the first submarine to use the Rolls-Royce-designed PWR2 reactor.

Between the Polaris-carrying *Valiant* Class and the Trident-carrying *Vanguard* Class, other nuclear submarines were commissioned by the Royal Navy. *Resolution* was followed by *Swiftsure*, and then came *Trafalgar*. Sir Robert Hill, who enjoyed a distinguished career in the Royal Navy before retiring as a vice admiral in 1993, said of the *Trafalgar* Class:

With superb modern sonars and armed with Spearfish torpedoes the Trafalgar Class submarines are formidable weapons of war. For marine engineers their most remarkable attributes are speed, range, endurance and reliability. They possess true mobility – the attribute that the profession of marine engineers exists to provide.

He was full of praise for the work of Rolls-Royce, saying:

As well as seeking noise reduction, the reactor plant designers had to respond to the pressing requirement for reactor core designs with ever longer lives. In the whole of the defence field, there can be few better examples of value for money than is represented by the work of the reactor core designers of Rolls-Royce and Associates. Over the years they have done a superb job which, because of security restraints, will only ever be appreciated by a small number of people in the company and the MoD.

Duncan Gorham, who worked at Rolls-Royce and Associates throughout the 1970s and 80s and into the 1990s, added:

It should be noted that the core factory produced about 70 cores, each containing over 200,000 fuel elements, and has enjoyed a 100 per cent quality and safety record.

Up to and including the *Trafalgar* Class, the power and the reactor-core-lifetime requirements of the Royal Navy's submarines could be met by reactor-plant equipment of much the same size as the original Dounreay prototype. However, once the decision had been made to replace Polaris with Trident, it was clear that a larger submarine with more power would be required. As PWR2 was planned, it was suggested that assembly would be far more economic if carried out at VSEL in Barrow and then the unit shipped to

Dounreay, rather than all components being transported individually to Dounreay before assembly, as with PWR1.

The primary unit, consisting of the completed reactor compartment, virtually fully tested but without the reactor core, would be built at Barrow before being shipped to the nearest suitable landing point on the Scottish north coast, which was Sandside Bay at Reay. From there, it would be transported overland to the newly constructed Shore Test Facility building at the Naval Nuclear Reactor Test Establishment at Dounreay. Similarly, four further units comprising the secondary plant would also be built at VSEL and transported to Dounreay. Needless to say, many people were convinced that this operation was fraught with hazard. As Sir Robert Hill pointed out:

Director General Submarines at the time was Mr Tony Warren RCNC. His fear was that the unit would be lost at sea and would have to be recovered from the bottom. A buoy was mounted on top to assist such an operation. A number of people feared that the air bag system simply would not do the job ... As Director of Nuclear Propulsion my own belief was that Greenpeace would harass and harry the operation at sea and on shore. Escorts and police cover were provided. However, so thorough were the planning and preparations that the operation went virtually without a hitch.

The PWR2 plant of the *Vanguard* Class would need refuelling only once during its operational life. (The refuelling process of the four Vanguard submarines will be carried out from 2002 to 2010.)

THE ASTUTE CLASS

Originally designed as a modest upgrade of the *Trafalgar* Class and known for much of its gestation period as B2TC (Batch 2 *Trafalgar* Class), the *Astute* Class eventually proved to be a significant development of the *Trafalgar* Class.

The biggest change was the installation of Rolls-Royce's PWR2 reactor, which had been developed for the *Vanguard* Class ballistic missile submarines.

In February 1997, Rolls-Royce Nuclear Engineering (the former Rolls-Royce and Associates) had secured a multi-million-pound contract to upgrade the Vulcan Naval Reactor Test Establishment at Dounreay and install the first of a new generation of long-life reactor cores. The new core would be designed to operate for the life of the submarine, as it would last six to eight times longer than the original core installed in Britain's first nuclear submarine, HMS *Dreadnought*. It could also be backfitted to all submarines equipped with Rolls-Royce's latest generation PWR2 reactor plant. It would require much less pumping power to keep the reactor cool, thus reducing generated noise and making the Royal Navy's submarine fleet one of the quietest, and therefore one of the most difficult to detect, in the world.

The reactor, known as Core H, would last the 25-to-30-year life of the submarines. This would lead to significant operational cost savings, as refitting and refuelling existing submarines kept them out of service for up to two years. For security reasons, specific details of the submarines were withheld, except to say that they would meet all tactical requirements and would sail faster, further and, thanks to reduced noise emissions, more quietly than *Trafalgar* boats. They would carry the US-made Tomahawk cruise missile which was capable of hitting targets accurately from a range of several hundred miles and which had been used effectively in the allied air offensive against Baghdad in the Gulf War in 1991.

The Minister for Defence Procurement, James Arbuthnot, told the House of Commons on 17 March 1997 (in what would be the last major defence announcement of the Tory Government before the election in May 1997):

I am pleased to announce that a contract has been placed with GEC-Marconi as prime contractor for the design, build and initial support of three Batch 2 *Trafalgar* Class submarines [HMS *Astute*, HMS *Ambush* and HMS *Artful*]. The new boats will be known as the *Astute* Class, and are expected to enter service early next century. The submarine will be built at GEC-Marconi's VSEL shipyard in Barrow.

The new vessels will be powered by the Rolls-Royce PWR2 nuclear reactor, fitted with the updated weapons system of Batch 1 *Trafalgar* Class submarines, and armed with the Spearfish torpedo and Submarine-Harpoon anti-ship missile. They will be able to carry conventionally-armed Tomahawk cruise missiles. [There would be space to carry a total of 36 weapons.] The *Astute* Class will replace the Royal Navy's existing *Swiftsure* Class boats as these vessels reach the end of their operational lives in the early part of the next century. They will perform a wide range of roles, including anti-submarine and anti-surface warfare.

While Rolls-Royce was continuing its long association with the nuclear defence market, it consolidated its position in the marine business by making the farsighted purchase of a company with whom it had enjoyed an association stretching back to the First World War.

'IMPORTANT IN TECHNICAL LEADERSHIP'

Vickers, Sons & Company Limited was incorporated on 17 April 1867 and gradually established itself in the difficult trading conditions of the subsequent twenty years. (The Vickers family had been involved in the steel industry since the 1820s, but the formation of the company in 1867 is probably the real starting point for the Vickers company.) In 1887, it entered the armaments industry when the Board invested in plant for the construction of guns and armour. It was a seminal moment. As J.D. Scott put it in *Vickers: A History*:

In the vital years from 1897 to 1914 this new and powerful combination of Vickers, Son & Maxim Limited [Vickers had bought Maxim] was to be one of the chief bulwarks of British naval strength ... It was, quite obviously and quite deliberately, challenging Armstrong Whitworth for the leadership of the British armament industry.

Britain was re-arming furiously in the first decade of the twentieth century as the naval threat from Germany grew, and while Armstrong's built the gun mountings for the *Dreadnought* battleships, Vickers built the engines as well as some of the ships.

For those brought up in the twentieth century it is difficult to believe, but Britain's traditional enemy in Europe was France, not Germany, and it was the threat from France that initially sparked Britain's rearmament programme in the final years of the nineteenth century and the first few years of the twentieth. France sparked the concern of the Admiralty in the 1890s by launching a series of big cruisers capable of 21 knots. These had been built when a group of French admirals decided that the best way of challenging the 'ruler of the seas' was with a pack of fast cruisers and torpedo boats that could cripple Britain's vital merchant trade.

The reaction of Britain was to build an anti-cruiser cruiser, faster and more heavily gunned than anything the French were building. The building programme was heavy – six ships in the *Cressy* Class of 12,000 tons were commissioned in 1898 and 1899 (two, *Hogue* and *Euryalus*, were built in Vickers' Barrow shipyard), four of the *Drake* Class of 14,000 tons in 1899, nine of the *County* Class of 9,800 tons in 1900 and 1901, six of the *Devonshire* Class of 10,850 tons in 1902, two of the *Duke of Edinburgh* Class of 13,500 tons in 1903, four of the *Warrior* Class of 13,550 tons in 1904 and three of the *Minotaur* Class of 14,600 tons in 1905.

However, by this time the potential enemy had changed from France to Germany. Concerned by the new closeness of Germany and Austria-Hungary with Italy in the wings, Britain and France drew closer together. (Edward VII is largely remembered for his frivolous behaviour as he waited in vain for his mother to step aside, but his work in helping to improve Anglo-French relations, when he finally succeeded to the throne in 1901, should not be forgotten.) As Martin Gilbert wrote in the first volume of his *History of the Twentieth Century*:

That October [1903] the two countries signed an agreement whereby disputes between them of a judicial nature, or relating to the interpretation of existing commercial treaties, would, if they proved intractable, be referred to the Permanent Court of Arbitration at The Hague. There were also areas in which one or other of the two countries felt their interest to be the dominant one, and in order that these regions should not be the source of any future conflict, negotiations were begun to reach agreements as to respective spheres of predominance. Britain wanted her rule in Egypt to be unchallenged by France; France wanted her control of Morocco to be an exclusive one. This was agreed.

On the basis of this exchange, several other smaller territorial conflicts were resolved, and an agreement was eventually signed in 1904, known as the Entente Cordiale. While in no way a military alliance or threat to any other Power, the Entente Cordiale brought France and Britain into close harmony. In its imperial activities, Britain could rely upon not being criticised by France, since both shared a belief in the concept of the Mission Civilisatrice of empire which had animated more than a century of exploration and expansion.

And in running this British Empire, Vickers was reaping benefit. The Maxim gun was used with devastating effect throughout Africa against natives armed mainly with spears and swords. An eyewitness of the final battle of the campaign against the Fulani in West Africa said:

As we approached close to the city, hordes of horsemen and footmen armed with spears, swords, old guns and bows and arrows appeared, charging the square over and over again, only to be mown down by machine-gun.

Vickers had acquired the firm Maxim Nordenfelt in 1897 for £1,353,000 [about £150 million in today's terms]. This gave it the right to manufacture and sell the Maxim gun, described by Scott as 'a truly revolutionary weapon'. He continued:

Both the Gatling gun and the continental mitrailleuse were simply 'revolvers', in the sense that they consisted of a number of barrels revolving round a central shaft. In both types the revolving was done by a hand crank, and the guns to that extent were not automatic weapons. The great principle of Maxim's machine gun was that it was the recoil of the weapon – a force which in all fire-arms up to that date had at best been useless and at worst dangerous – which was put to work, to eject the spent case and to insert a fresh cartridge in the barrel and to discharge this cartridge in turn. The Maxim gun was therefore a truly automatic weapon, the whole cycle of firing being dependent upon the explosive force of the cartridge, and being self-perpetuating.

The obvious company in Britain for the American businessman Hiram Maxim to approach was Armstrong, but Armstrong already made the rival Gatling under licence. Although Vickers was not yet in the 1880s an arms company, when the Maxim Gun Company Ltd. was formed in 1884, Albert Vickers became its chairman. In 1887, Maxim merged with another machine-gun company, Nordenfelt Guns and Ammunition. The amalgamated companies did not fare very well in the early 1890s, and this led to their takeover by Vickers in 1897.

In a bizarre twist of the mixture of international political and business relationships, in 1902 Vickers leased a fuze patent from the German armaments manufacturer Krupp. Under the agreement, every Vickers shell was stamped KP_z (Krupp patent fuze), eventually to be redeemed at 1s 3d a shell [6.25p or about £6.25 in today's terms]. After the First World War, Vickers paid the royalties in a settlement based on German artillery casualties. This placed Krupp in the slightly awkward position of having profited from the death of German troops. Undeterred, Krupp used the money within a year of the Armistice, along with subsidies from the Weimar Republic, to begin the secret re-armament that would lead to the next world war twenty years later.

In the Vickers' shipyards, the early years of the twentieth century were ones of frenetic activity, even if, for much of the time, the huge manufacturing capacity that Vickers had built was not fully utilised. This is what Scott wrote:

At the end of this period [1897–1914], as at its beginning, the Vickers contribution to imperial defence cannot be equated either with the actual building of warships complete, or even with the great unused capacity for the building of warships complete. The supply of guns and gun mountings, of warship machinery and of armour, continued to be important. Of the five suppliers of armour in this period (Armstrongs, Beardmore, Browns, Cammells and Vickers) Vickers were a close third in order of tonnage supplied ... But they were always important, particularly in technical leadership ... They [the Admiralty] made the Vickers plate the standard plate.

While Vickers was benefiting from the re-armament programme in the early years of the century, the nearby ship-building firm of William Armstrong was also building warships as fast as it could. (In the less war-torn but also less prosperous days of the 1920s, the two great firms would merge.)

The first ship to be launched from Armstrong's Elswick Yard in Newcastle upon Tyne was the torpedo cruiser *Panther*, built for the Austro-Hungarian empire. This ship was launched on 13 June 1885 and was followed by warships for many nations, including Britain, Japan, China, Argentina, Chile, Brazil, Norway, Portugal, Spain, Italy, Turkey and Romania. The USA also bought two vessels originally intended for the Brazilian Navy.

One of the most important customers was the Imperial Japanese Navy, which bought nine ships between 1893 and 1906. At the Battle of Tsushima on 27 and 28 May 1905 – perhaps *the* decisive engagement of the Russo-Japanese War of 1905 – ships built at Elswick Yard played an important role. The Japanese inflicted a crushing defeat on the Russian Navy, and four of

Admiral Heihachirō Togō's cruisers – *Asama*, *Iwate*, *Idzumo* and *Tokiwa* – had all been built at Elswick, as had many of the guns of the Japanese fleet. Three of the Japanese cruisers, *Idzumi*, *Naniwa* and *Takachiho*, had also been built at Armstrong's Low Walker works.

In this battle, Admiral Togō's ships sank eight battleships, four cruisers and five destroyers of the Russian Baltic Fleet commanded by Admiral Zinoui Rozhdestvensky, while the Japanese lost only three torpedo boats. The cruiser *Iwate* became a training ship in later life and survived until, 40 years after her first engagement at the Battle of Tsushima, she was sunk in 1945 by a US carrier-borne aircraft.

In 1911, Admiral Togō (one of the few foreigners to be awarded Britain's Order of Merit) visited Newcastle and stayed as a guest with Sir Andrew Noble, who after the death of Lord Armstrong in 1900 had succeeded him as chairman of Armstrong Whitworth. (Armstrong had merged with the Manchester-based Sir Joseph Whitworth in 1897. Noble, a former artillery officer and gun expert, had helped Armstrong build his firm into one of the largest gun-manufacturing complexes in the world.)

Between 1885 and 1918, no fewer than 90 armed ships, including battleships, were launched from Armstrong's. The first battleship to be built at Elswick was HMS *Victoria*, which cost £724,855 [about £80 million in today's terms] by the time she was launched in 1887.

Once war broke out in 1914, most of the Armstrong ships saw action, including the battle cruiser HMS *Invincible*, which, with her sister ship HMS *Inflexible*, defeated a German squadron at the Battle of the Falklands in 1914. The *Invincible* was later sunk at the Battle of Jutland in 1916, with the loss of 1,020 lives. Other Elswick ships at Jutland, the one big naval engagement of the war, were the battleships *Agincourt*, *Canada*, *Superb* and *Monarch*, and the cruisers *Hampshire* and *Birmingham*. All survived that battle, but the *Hampshire* was sunk a few days later when taking Lord Kitchener, Britain's Secretary of State for War in the early part of the conflict, on a mission to Russia.

The last warship built at Elswick was the aircraft carrier HMS *Eagle*. Originally laid down as a battleship for Chile, work was halted between 1914 and 1917, and she was subsequently bought for the Royal Navy. She left the shipyard as the first carrier to have a superstructure on the extreme starboard side of the ship. This became a standard design feature. The *Eagle* was eventually sunk by torpedoes in the Mediterranean in August 1942.

As well as a supplier for vessels on the water, Vickers became the sole supplier for those below the surface. The history of the submarine can be traced back to the sixteenth century. But as a serious weapon of war, its history is shorter, and its early uses were as weapons *against* the British Navy rather than for it. It was a Bushnell submarine in which Sergeant Ezra Leigh tried to blow up HMS *Eagle* in New York Harbour in 1776 during the

American War of Independence, and it was another American, Robert Fulton, who offered the submarine to the French in 1797 so that they could cut off British commerce.

Vickers came into contact with submarines through Nordenfelt, the same man and firm that had been involved with the Maxim gun. The Nordenfelt submarine was not a success, and it was with a submarine developed by an Irishman, J.D. Holland, which Vickers licensed from an American company, the Electric Boat Company (yet again, originally intended for use *against* the British), that Vickers made progress. A deal was signed on 27 October 1900, and soon five submarines with a length of 63 feet 4 inches and a width of 11 feet 9 inches were built in the Barrow shipyard. Their range was 600 miles on the surface, and they could run for four hours submerged. By the spring of 1906, Vickers had built 29 and, by the outbreak of war in 1914, an impressive 75.

At the same time, Vickers made sure it was one of the first companies involved in the new weapon of war, the aeroplane. Just as an arms race between Britain and Germany was developing at sea, a similar race was beginning in the air. The 1898 Hague Convention had banned the dropping of bombs from balloons or 'other kinds of aerial vessels'. At the Convention of 1907, of the 44 nations present only 27 voted for a continuation of the ban. Although Britain and the USA were two of the 27, ominously Germany rejected the ban. More ominously, war in the air was given international legitimacy by an agreement on what constituted legitimate targets. These were warships, harbours, military works, military or naval establishments, depots of arms or material and, significantly, workshops and factories 'which could be utilized for the needs of a hostile fleet or army'.

The first Vickers monoplane was built in 1911. At the Olympia Aero Show in 1913, the company exhibited the prototype of a machine that was used extensively in the early years of the First World War. This was the FB1 (FB stood for fighting biplane), a two-seater pusher biplane with a Vickers machine gun mounted in the nose and operated by the observer. During the war, Vickers designed about 30 different aircraft. The most famous, the Vimy, was the result of a request from the Air Board to design a twin-engined night bomber. Originally fitted with two 200 hp Hispano-Suiza engines, the Vimy could lift a third of a ton more than larger rivals when Rolls-Royce Eagle engines were fitted. The Air Board ordered 350, expecting to bomb Berlin with it and win the war. However, before they could be used the war ended, and both the Vimy and the Rolls-Royce Eagle engines became world famous for the more peaceful feat of flying Alcock and Brown in the first non-stop flight across the Atlantic. (See *The Magic of a Name: The Rolls-Royce Story: The First 40 Years* for the full story of this remarkable feat.)

The near-slump conditions of the 1920s brought crisis to the steel, shipbuilding and aircraft industries and forced Vickers into a merger with Armstrong Whitworth. In 1927, a new company, Vickers-Armstrong Limited, was founded, and, as re-armament became again a national priority, it prospered in the manufacture of a new generation of armaments, ships (including submarines), aircraft and tanks.

After the First World War, Britain took the lead, technically and tactically, in developing the mobility of tanks. Even before the end of the war, work had started on the Medium D with a maximum speed of 20 mph. The British Army ordered 160 of the new Vickers Medium tanks, officially the Light Tank Mark I, between 1923 and 1928, and these were almost the only tanks the British Army used until the early 1930s and were the only tanks produced in quantity anywhere in the world in the 1920s. Capable of speeds of 20 mph, they stimulated the Royal Tank Corps into developing mobile tactics.

Rolls-Royce and Vickers had worked together throughout the First World War on armoured cars. When the Royal Navy Air Service decided in 1914 that they needed armoured cars to protect their aircraft in war zones, they standardised on the Rolls-Royce 40/50-horsepower 'Silver Ghost'. Slightly modified chassis were despatched to the Vickers factory at Erith, where Vickers fitted the armoured plate around the radiator, bonnet and driver compartment and then added the turret. Initially, there was such a shortage of machine guns that Maxims had to be stripped from ships of the fleet. Once these shortages were overcome, the standard armament on the armoured cars was a Vickers machine gun. It was the first collaboration between Rolls-Royce and Vickers.

As the country re-armed in the 1930s, tank development and production was stepped up at Vickers, and the company manufactured about a third of all the tanks produced in Britain during the Second World War.

As M.M. Postan said in his book *British War Production*:

Organisation for tank design in the War Office was rudimentary in the extreme, and but for the solitary and pioneering efforts of the designers at Vickers-Armstrong the country would have possessed no facilities for the design and development of armoured vehicles.

In the air, the Supermarine company, which had been bought by Vickers in 1928, developed and produced in great numbers two of the most important combat aircraft of the Second World War, the Spitfire and the Wellington.

As we saw in Part One, the Spitfire, powered by a stream of increasingly powerful Rolls-Royce Merlin and Griffon engines, was critical in winning the Battle of Britain in 1940 and in gradually turning the tide against the enemy in the rest of the War. By 1945, Vickers had produced nearly 20,000 Spitfires and Seafires and 11,500 Wellingtons.

As well as the famous Spitfire and the Wellington, Vickers also produced the Warwick, some powered by two Rolls-Royce Vulture engines, others by two Bristol Centaurus engines, and the Windsor, powered either by four Bristol Hercules sleeve-valve engines or by four Rolls-Royce Griffons. It also produced the Viking, which was powered by two Bristol Hercules engines and was bought by British European Airways (BEA) after the war, as well as many other airlines throughout the world.

At the end of the war, Vickers could look back on six years of outstanding contribution. In the air, as well as the building of the Spitfires, Seafires and Wellingtons, its employee, Barnes Wallis, had invented the bouncing bomb that breached the Mohne and Eder dams in 1943 and had followed that remarkable achievement with the deep-penetration bombs Tallboy and Grandslam, which wrought havoc with the E-boat pens, the V.1 launching sites, the battleship *Tirpitz* and many enemy communications systems.

If Vickers made a huge contribution to war in the air, it was not less active in providing warships. From 1939 to 1945, the Vickers shipyards at Barrow and Newcastle delivered one battleship, five cruisers, nine aircraft carriers, one monitor, 22 destroyers, 146 submarines, 60 landing craft and barges and nine escort vessels, and in addition delivered ten merchant ships and a transport ferry. Turning to the British Army, the Vickers engineers produced tanks and guns by the thousand. From September 1939 to the end of 1940, the company's Crayford Works produced nearly 20,000 machine and gas-operated guns, about 50 per cent of national production. It was the same in field artillery.

Some would say that the war could not have been won without Vickers.

'WORTHY OF ITS DISTINGUISHED PAST'

At the end of the war, Vickers was forced to look for new products to replace the weapons of war. One of the areas in which it invested heavily was crawler tractors, as we saw in the second part of this history. Unfortunately, competition from the USA proved too severe, and the venture was abandoned. For a time, the aircraft-building side of the business was extremely successful as George Edwards (later Sir George Edwards OM) pushed through the Vickers Viscount, which, as we saw in Part Two, became Britain's best-selling passenger aircraft.

Powered by the Rolls-Royce Dart engine, the Vickers Viscount began service with British European Airways (BEA) on its London–Paris and London–Edinburgh routes in July 1950. It was the first aircraft powered by a propeller turbine to be used on a scheduled passenger service. The Viscount was a breakthrough in passenger air transport surpassing anything seen before in terms of comfort and reliability. Having cut 30 minutes from the London–Stockholm flight time, the aircraft prompted *The Times* to write:

267

The inaugural flight in both directions was characterised by the smoothness, effortless take-off and the quiet, almost vibrationless cruising which are already coming to be regarded as characteristic of the Viscount.

Altogether, 445 Viscounts were sold to 60 airline operators in 40 countries. It represented the zenith of British civil-aircraft production. Unfortunately, as we saw in Part Two, subsequent aircraft from Vickers were not very successful commercially. The Viscount's successor, the Vickers Vanguard, was launched into a world that had come to prefer pure jets as opposed to turboprops, and only 43 were produced. Vickers' final civil airliner was the VC10. Again, we saw the promise and the travails of this airliner, powered by four Rolls-Royce Conway engines. Initially given an order for 35 aircraft by British Overseas Airways Corporation (BOAC), a new chairman at BOAC, Sir Giles Guthrie, convinced by his engineers that the Boeing 707 was more economic, cancelled 17 of them. It was a body blow to the hopes for further sales.

On the military side, Vickers had developed the Valiant, the first of the 'V' bombers. It was from Valiants that the first British atomic and hydrogen bombs were dropped during the development tests in the Pacific in 1956 and 1957. The Valiant was joined by the Avro Vulcan and the Handley Page Victor to form Britain's airborne contribution to the nuclear shield during the Cold War.

By the mid-1950s, when Viscount Knollys took over the chairmanship of Vickers from Sir Ronald Weeks, *The Times* wrote of Vickers as a 'thriving and well-knit organisation, worthy of its distinguished past' (and employing no fewer than 90,000 people). At that time, Vickers-Armstrong was a federation of three powerful blocs – one in shipbuilding, one in aircraft manufacture and one in engineering. Indeed, in 1955 the three businesses were formed into separate companies, each with its own executive board.

As we have seen above, the aircraft side had made an excellent transition from building for the military to building and selling to the civil airlines. The shipbuilding side had also coped well. Naval contracts had declined, but the commercial shipping companies filled the gap for Vickers with tankers and liners. Vickers built the famous liners *Himalaya* and *Chusan* for P&O, *Orcades*, *Oronsay* and *Orsova* for Orient and *Empress of England* for Canadian Pacific. And the Royal Navy continued to order submarines. As we saw in Part Two, Vickers was deeply involved with Rolls-Royce from the beginning in the development of nuclear submarines.

In spite of this apparently rosy situation, it was clear that Vickers would have to diversify to lessen its dependence on defence and UK Government contracts. During the 1950s, although a Conservative Government was now in power and Vickers had been able to buy back its English Steel Corporation, which had been nationalised during the Labour administration from 1945 to 1951, even this Government was determined to interfere in the aircraft industry. By the end of the decade, the company had ceased to be a direct manufacturer of aircraft, and its aircraft interests had become a 40 per cent share in the British Aircraft Corporation.

Prompted by the Government, Vickers had engaged in talks with other aircraft manufacturers including de Havilland, English Electric, Hawker Siddeley and the Bristol Aeroplane Company. After much discussion, Hawker Siddeley bid for de Havilland, and Vickers, English Electric and Bristol put their aircraft manufacturing interests into the British Aircraft Corporation with shares of 40 per cent, 40 per cent and 20 per cent respectively. Chairman Lord Knollys said:

Vickers has an outstanding record in aviation, extending continually over 50 years. The Gun-bus, the Vimy, Wellingtons, Spitfires, Valiants, Viscounts have become part of aviation history. This great tradition and those who have helped to create and maintain it have been carried into British Aircraft Corporation … As a result of this merger our stake in aviation is maintained, but financial risks are spread and shared, and outstanding resources, human and technical, are combined to deal with the competitive situation of the future.

Shipbuilding continued to be a strength for Vickers. Following the liners mentioned above, in 1960 its Barrow shipyard was ready to launch *Oriana*, at 42,000 tons the biggest liner ever built in England. At Naval Yard, *Empress of Canada* and *Northern Star* were both nearly completed. Tanker orders continued, and in 1961 BP placed the order for *British Admiral*, the first 100,000-ton tanker to be built in Britain. Naval work was still available, and Vickers continued to launch frigates and submarines of the *Oberon* Class. Also in 1960, HMS *Hermes*, the last of the Royal Navy's conventional carriers, was launched from Barrow.

However, the future lay in nuclear submarines, and the building of *Dreadnought*, Britain's first nuclear submarine, began at Vickers' Barrow shipyard in January 1959. (It was Barrow's 295th submarine.) She was launched by the Queen on Trafalgar Day, 21 October 1960, and delivered to the Royal Navy in 1963. *Dreadnought* was followed by *Resolution*, *Valiant*, *Warspite*, *Churchill* and *Repulse*, these last four hunter-killers to be twice as big as *Dreadnought*.

The early 1960s, in retrospect, represented the high-water mark for Vickers in its post-war structure. Thereafter, life became tough in nearly all its divisions, tied as they were to the mature industries of yesteryear. The management was aware of the problem and called in the management consultants McKinsey, who confirmed what they had already worked out for themselves. As Harold Evans wrote in his book, *Vickers Against the Odds: 1956–1977*:

The basic problem, it was recognised, was inability to improve and expand existing business and to enter new business because of the low return on investment. Since 1959 capital expenditure alone had exceeded net cash flow by over £20m [£500 million in today's terms]. To meet these expenses, and to finance work in progress, a major increase in borrowing had been necessary, and in 1963 total borrowing stood at £68m, an increase of some £23m since the end of 1962. The increase would not have been necessary had the operating assets been able to earn between 12 and 15 per cent on capital, a target no more than equal to the average return in many UK manufacturing industries. In fact, the Group's return on capital had fallen from 8.8 per cent in 1960 to 5.5 per cent in 1963. With a return as low as this there was little scope for obtaining growth through internal financing.

The market price of our shares, it was noted, 'is only 50 per cent of the book value represented by the assets behind each share. This makes it extremely expensive either to raise outside capital or to acquire other companies. Doubling our profits would, in effect, cut in half the cost of any acquisition made through a share exchange'.

That Vickers' priorities were not quite in the right order was made clear by their buying property at Millbank on the Thames Embankment and building a prestigious tower block.

Nor did life become any easier in the second half of the 1960s. The Labour Party came to power again in the autumn of 1964, and nationalisation was back on the agenda. First, there was a serious threat to BAC through the cancellation in April 1965 of the TSR2 project. This was viewed by Vickers' man at BAC, Sir George Edwards, as a disaster. The TSR2 had been at the heart of the military aircraft programme for the previous six years, and a prototype was already flying. In his view, the very existence of BAC was at stake. Fortunately, contracts were soon awarded for the Jaguar and the Anglo-French Variable Geometry aircraft, and at the end of 1965 Saudi Arabia ordered Lightnings and Jet Provosts. The BAC 111 was beginning to sell, the Concorde project was proceeding well in its development stage, and the Guided Weapons division was winning orders for the Vigilant. The cancellation of TSR2 was a serious setback but did not bring BAC crashing down. Indeed, it prospered over the next few years. Its shareholding changed when GEC bought English Electric and Rolls-Royce bought Bristol. The Bristol 20 per cent was absorbed by GEC and Vickers in 1971, and they both owned 50 per cent.

On the tank front, Vickers was again reminded of the dangers of over-reliance on the government. When orders were placed for the new Chieftain tank, one-third went to Vickers and two-thirds to the Government-owned

Royal Ordnance Factory (ROF) in Leeds. The ROF also received the order for all the spares. When the second order was placed in March 1968, the whole of it went to the ROF.

Nineteen-sixty-seven, the year in which Vickers celebrated its centenary as a public company, was the year in which it said goodbye to steel production, the commodity on which the company had been founded in the 1820s. The new Labour Government was determined to nationalise steel again and removed, for £16.3 million [about £295 million in today's terms], one of the four legs of Vickers' stool. The Vickers chairman reckoned that the state had secured a bargain, saying:

The ESC [English Steel Corporation] group supplies a wider range of steel and engineering products than any other steel company or group in the United Kingdom: it is equipped to produce larger or heavier ingots, forgings and castings than any other British steelmaker: it is the major British producer of special steels: and in the new works at Tinsley Park it has Europe's most modern alloy steel plant.

Negotiating on behalf of the company with the Minister of Power was Sir Henry Benson, the Cooper Brothers accountant and the same man who, at the end of 1970, would advise Prime Minister Edward Heath that Rolls-Royce had no future in its present form.

The Vickers Board had to decide what to do with the money. It could return it to shareholders, invest in a growth business or pay off debt. By this time, its indebtedness, aggravated by poor profits over the preceding years and heavy losses on the VC10 project, left the Board with little choice: the money was used to reduce debt.

Another intervention that took place, by someone who was to play a large part in the activities of Rolls-Royce in the 1970s, occurred when Sir Kenneth (later Lord) Keith, in his capacity as chairman of Hill Samuel Bank, made representation to the Vickers chairman on behalf of some major institutional shareholders in Vickers. This led to the appointment of Peter (later Sir Peter) Matthews as the new chief executive at Vickers.

The early 1970s brought a resurgence, and by 1976 Vickers was making 38.3 million pounds' pre-tax profit. (The figure in 1966 had been only £3.94 million.) Over half of these profits came from its 50 per cent shareholding in BAC. Contributing strongly were BAC's central roles in the military aircraft programme, especially Jaguar and Tornado, in guided weapons, notably Rapier, and to a lesser extent in space satellites and equipment. By the end of 1976, orders in hand were £1,000 million [about £10 billion in today's terms], 75 per cent of them for export. Sir Arnold (later Lord) Weinstock was chairman of GEC, owner of the other 50 per cent of BAC, and, at the same time, he was a director of Rolls-Royce. There had not been a year since the beginning of the First World War in which Vickers and Rolls-Royce had not enjoyed a close relationship, whether through product or personality, or both.

It was unlikely Vickers was happy that more than 50 per cent of its profits came from an associated company, especially as it became clear from the Labour Party manifesto for the next election that, if they were returned to power, a Labour Government would nationalise aircraft manufacture and shipbuilding. And they did not have to ponder the possibility for long, as in February 1974 the Labour Party did indeed come into power, following Tory Prime Minister Edward Heath's belated attempt to control the steadily growing industrial anarchy by calling a hasty general election. The appointment of Tony Benn as Secretary of State for Industry made the possibility of nationalisation a certainty. We saw in Part Two that Benn felt scant sympathy for private industry and would have nationalised much more than the aircraft and shipbuilding industries if allowed to.

Benn immediately launched a programme designed to bring the private sector more closely under state direction. This programme included the establishment of a National Enterprise Board (Rolls-Royce was put under its auspices), a new Industry Act to give the Government wide powers to obtain information from companies and nationalisation of the aircraft industry as well as shipbuilding, ship repairing and marine engine manufacture. How did Vickers react to the prospect of the Government taking into public ownership its aircraft-manufacturing and shipbuilding interests? The aircraft business was not so emotive. It had already given up half its interest and would admit that GEC, with the redoubtable Weinstock as its chief executive, was the dominant partner. Shipbuilding, with 100 years of proud history, was rather different. Vickers' chairman was now Lord Robens, former civil servant and Member of Parliament and, most famously, Chairman of the National Coal Board from 1961 to 1971. He pointed to the record of ships launched from Vickers shipyards in the previous twenty years – one aircraft carrier, nine frigates, six destroyers, one cruiser, one corvette, eleven conventional, twelve nuclear and two coastal submarines, five passenger and sixteen cargo liners, 21 tankers and six other large vessels – and said to the shareholders:

If we thought that the nationalisation of Vickers shipbuilders would bring real benefit to the nation, we would gladly say so. For sentimental reasons Vickers might be very unhappy to give up this activity, in which it has achieved such an outstanding international reputation, but I have made it clear that commercially Vickers Limited would survive without difficulty on the basis of its many other activities, some of them more rewarding in terms of return on capital than shipbuilding. We do believe, however, that it is not in the public interest, or in the interests of managerial efficiency and technological strength, that Vickers shipbuilding should be brought under State ownership. I have explained why we believe this. No serious attempt has been made, however, by those who advocate nationalism of the business to state the grounds on which they do so other than in very generalised and ideological terms. The onus is still on them to make their case.

Devotees of parliamentary history will remember that the taking of the aircraft and shipbuilding interests into public ownership [by 1976, the word 'nationalisation' was deemed to be too old-style socialist] was the occasion of Michael Heseltine, at that time a Tory rising star, grabbing hold of the mace in the House of Commons.

The Labour Party's overall majority by 1976 was very small and faced the possibility of the Aircraft and Shipbuilding Industries Bill being defeated. To add spice, it became clear that one company in South Wales had been included when it should not have been, and another in Scotland had been left out when it should have been included. At this point, the Tory MP Robin Maxwell-Hyslop (who had worked for Rolls-Royce in the 1950s and 1960s) challenged the Speaker, saying that the Bill was 'hybrid' and should not proceed; he wanted to delay the Bill but was overruled. Nevertheless, it became clear that Labour was struggling to produce a majority. This is how the biographer of James Callaghan, then Prime Minister, related the outcome:

The government saved the day by sending through the lobby an MP whom the opposition knew to be paired. Tony Benn admitted that 'the fact is we cheated'.

Michael Heseltine then overplayed his hand by seizing the mace. In his autobiography, *Life in the Jungle*, he explained it in the following way:

I was acutely aware of the utter helplessness of the parliamentary Opposition, faced with a constitutional abuse of this sort. In the end, the House of Commons can only work because people stick to the rules. The Speaker is their custodian. If the government legislates to overrule the Speaker and does so by breaking its word, there is no knowing where that process will end. The symbol of the authority of the Commons is the mace and it was the authority of the Commons that had been abused. I picked it up with both hands and offered it to the jeering, ranting rows of Labour MPs. They were celebrating the unconstitutional enactment of legislation for which they had no majority. My critics and enemies have portrayed it as a mad, wild act.

If not mad and wild, it certainly proved to be counter-productive as it was used to divert attention from the real issue – i.e. that there was not a majority in favour of the nationalisation bill – and, indeed, it struggled in both the House of Commons and the House of Lords before finally becoming law in

1977. (The part of Vickers' shipbuilding operation that built the nuclear submarines, VSEL, was privatised again during the Thatcher administration in the 1980s, and then bought in the 1990s, first by GEC and then by BAe.)

Speculation that Vickers would become cash-rich once nationalisation of its aircraft and shipbuilding interests had become fact led to heightened interest in the City of a possible takeover. An entrepreneur of the day, David (not to be confused with Tiny) Rowland, so young that he was referred to by some, especially his victims, as 'Spotty', built up a stake of over 20 per cent through his vehicle, Williams Hudson. *The Guardian* noted that the Labour Government – keen itself, as we know, to buy half of Vickers – was concerned, writing:

Vickers is after all the largest supplier of ships to the Royal Navy, and is the sole builder of Britain's nuclear-propelled submarine fleet. In addition Vickers acts as an overflow for much of the work which the Ministry of Defence's own ordnance factories cannot deal with themselves. A large chunk of the Iranian order for Chieftain tanks [as we saw in Part Two, Rolls-Royce Motors Limited was also heavily involved in this order at its Shrewsbury factory] has gone to the group so that the order can be fulfilled within the specified time. Not only has Mr Rowland's reputation as an asset-stripper and profiteer obviously been fully noted by the defence top brass, but also there is a distinct flavour of 'foreign interest' about Rowland's unwelcome holding.

In the end, Rowland – like many similar characters, most notably Jim Slater, who depended for their apparent success on constantly rising share prices – was badly mauled by the stock-market collapse that began in the autumn of 1973 and continued until January 1975, and was forced to sell his stake to Lazards and Morgan Grenfell, taking a loss of £3 million [£54 million in today's terms].

MOTOR CARS AND DEFENCE

Nationalisation robbed Vickers of its core businesses, leaving only peripheral ones plus a handful of cash compensation.

All this exposed the vulnerability of Vickers, and it became apparent that if it were to retain its independence it had to make a decisive move to invest its compensation money. As we saw in Part Two, on 25 June 1980 it was announced that it had acquired Rolls-Royce Motors.

By this time, its businesses were Howson Algraphy, which manufactured lithographic plates for the printing industry; defence systems, which manufactured tanks; marine engineering, which consisted of a range of companies – Brown Brothers and Hasties, Stone Vickers, Michell Bearings and Jered

TOP: The Imperial Japanese Navy was one of Vickers' most important customers before the First World War, buying nine ships between 1893 and 1906. The cruiser *Iwate*, pictured here, fought at the decisive Battle of Tsushima in 1905 and, after becoming a training ship, was eventually sunk in 1945 by US carrier-borne aircraft.

BOTTOM: An Armstrong-built ship, HMS *Invincible* with her sister ship, HMS *Inflexible*, defeated a German squadron in the Battle of the Falklands in 1914. She was later sunk in the Battle of Jutland in 1916.

TOP: By the outbreak of war in 1914, Vickers had built 75 submarines.

BOTTOM: Vickers had acquired the firm Maxim Nordenfelt in 1897. Its machine guns were used by every British Army unit throughout the First World War, and many remained in use as the standard medium machine gun of the Army in the Second World War. In the First World War, the Rolls-Royce armoured cars carried a Vickers machine gun as their standard armament.

TOP: A Vickers light tank, Model 1937, with a 40 mm anti-tank gun.

BOTTOM: Vickers overcame not only the challenge from General Dynamics but also the scepticism of Margaret Thatcher – 'You do not … win wars on warranties' – to win the British Army contract for its new Challenger tank.

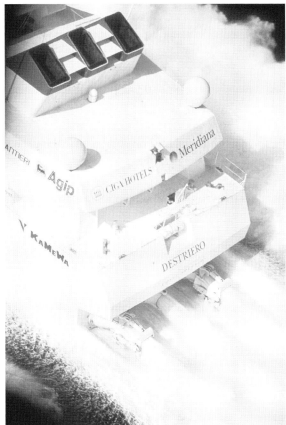

The jewel in the crown of Vickers' shipbuilding interests when
Rolls-Royce bought it in 1999 was the world-class propulsion
company, Kamewa. Kamewa Ulstein tunnel thrusters use CP,
or controllable pitch, propellers with highly skewed blades for low
noise and vibration levels, which can be reduced further by
an optional air-injection system. The majority of the world's fast
lightweight ferries are equipped with Kamewa's waterjets,
which are propulsion devices using waterpump technology, instead
of propellers, to provide thrust.

TOP: The emphasis in the future will be on faster ferries and ships. Rolls-Royce is well positioned to provide the most up-to-date power, propulsion and motion control systems.

BOTTOM: A total of 390 UT700-series vessels have been built, or are currently under construction, since they were first sold in the mid-1970s. The UT700 series was developed by the Norwegian marine company Ulstein, subsequently bought by Vickers in spring 1999.

TOP: HMS *Vanguard*, built by Vickers and powered by the
Rolls-Royce PWR2 reactor, was launched from the Vickers shipyard in
Barrow on 4 March 1992.

BOTTOM: The primary unit of PWR2 was built at VSEL's yard in Barrow
on a barge on a building slipway. The 'steam-swallowing' secondary
plant was assembled on another. When ready, both were launched and
towed out into the Irish Sea to meet Smit International's Giant 2.
Giant 2 then submerged until the two barges could be floated over her
platform deck, when she was brought to full buoyancy. When
Giant 2 arrived at Sandside Bay, she was still three miles from the Shore
Test Facility at Dounreay, and the plant, on its two barges, completed
its journey overland on inflatable rollers.

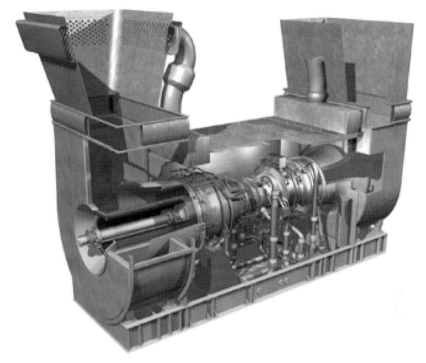

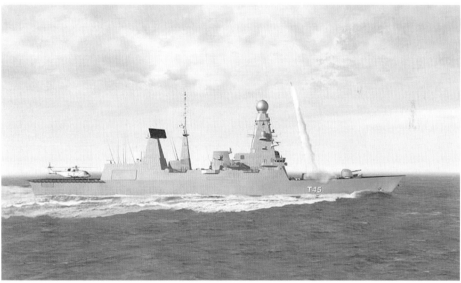

TOP: The Marine Trent 30 (MT30) will be the first marine engine based on the Trent aero-engine which Rolls-Royce has produced.

BOTTOM: The first ship to use the WR21 will be the Royal Navy's new Type 45 destroyer, the replacement for the T42 whose vulnerability was exposed in the Falklands War.

Saul Lanyado, President of Rolls-Royce Marine, watches Secretary of State for Defence, Geoff Hoon, sign the Nuclear Propulsion Submarine Support Contract on 9 November 2001. Rolls-Royce had won the MoD contract to service the Royal Navy's submarine fleet for the next three years.

Brown Brothers in the USA – which made naval and offshore equipment; and Vickers Furniture, which had become the market leader in office furniture in the UK.

Brown Brothers had developed the electro-hydraulic steering gear during the First World War, and subsequently over 20,000 vessels were fitted with Brown Brothers steering gear. During the Second World War, over 100 British Navy vessels were fitted with Brown Brothers equipment, and the close relationship between the company and the Ministry of Defence continued after the war, so that even today Denny-Brown fin stabilisers are standard equipment on all new British Navy ships.

It was in other areas, notably machine tools, that Vickers was hoping to sell its interests.

As we saw in Part Two, the merger was a hopeful case of blending Vickers' cash with Rolls-Royce Motor Cars' supposed good management. Even David (now Sir David) Plastow, who became managing director of the new group, said:

To be realistic there is no conventional synergy in the deal. We are taking two small engineering companies, and putting them together to make a sizeable one in international terms. In the end we will insulate ourselves from the business cycles and troughs.

As we saw, this hope was not realised as it foundered immediately on the rocks of the world recession of the early 1980s. This led to some severe restructuring, not only at Rolls-Royce Motors, which we read about in Chapter Five, but in other parts of the group. The diesel division, a part of Rolls-Royce Motors, was sold to Perkins Diesel, part of Massey Ferguson, for £20 million in December 1983, and Vickers' South African interests were also sold.

In 1985, after much of the restructuring of the early 1980s had been completed – twenty companies sold, the workforce halved to 15,000 – Vickers found itself under threat from the New York entrepreneur Saul Steinberg, who began to accumulate Vickers shares. In Steinberg's view, Vickers was not fully exploiting the Rolls-Royce name. Vickers management pointed out that any foreign owner would automatically lose the right to the Rolls-Royce name. Steinberg retreated, though not before he had sold his shares at a handsome profit.

As we saw, the Motor Car Division prospered, not only by restructuring but also by rediscovering the Bentley brand. Howson Algraphy held on to its place as number three in the world in the somewhat less glamorous arena of printing plates, after Fuji of Japan and the Kalle subsidiary of the German company Hoescht. Howson controlled 25 per cent of the European market.

In Defence, after much argument, Vickers beat off a strong challenge from

General Dynamics of the USA to win an order in 1988 for prototypes of its Challenger 2 tank for the British Army.

Winning the prototype order had been a close call. Vickers had squandered its reputation for building reliable tanks with the performance of its Challenger 1 tank. Its long pedigree in building tanks was not in doubt. As we have seen, it had been developing them since the First World War, but by the mid-1980s there were doubts in many quarters as to whether Challenger 2 would be built on time and whether it would be reliable if it were.

On 2 March 1987, Plastow met Lieutenant General Sir Richard Vincent, then Master General of the Ordnance and the man responsible for army equipment and weaponry. Plastow was concerned about his order book. Vickers' Newcastle plant was building tanks for export, as well as an initial run of 30 Challenger armoured repair-and-recovery vehicles ordered by the British Army. However, the former Royal Ordnance tank factory at Leeds, which Vickers had bought from the Government in 1986, had only three years' work left building Challenger 1. For his part, Vincent recognised the need for the Army to replace the ageing Chieftain tanks operating on the Rhine.

Plastow told Vincent he could solve both their problems by Vickers building the MoD an updated Challenger, which would be substantially redesigned and improved from the original. A sceptical Vincent indicated that it would need to be a great improvement. Chieftain had suffered from an unreliable engine and Challenger 1 a similarly flawed fire-control computer. The Army had been humiliated by coming last in a top international tank gunnery competition. Neither the engine nor the computer had been designed by Vickers, but the company was held responsible.

By the autumn of 1987, the MoD had decided it must replace the Chieftain and, under the new 'value for money' reforms set in place by Peter (now Lord) Levene, chief of defence procurement, bids were invited from others as well as Vickers. In came General Dynamics of the USA with a modified version of the M-1A1 tank and Krauss-Maffei, the German engineering and defence group, with an anglicised model of the Leopard 2. Both would provide stiff competition to Vickers, though both had their faults. The General Dynamics tank had thirsty gas-turbine engines, and there was some doubt about the quality of the Leopard's armour.

The propaganda war waged through 1988, and Plastow was summoned to an interview with Prime Minister Margaret Thatcher at 10 Downing Street. She told him that she and some of her colleagues were not convinced that Vickers could fulfil the contract. Plastow replied that the project would be underwritten by a catalogue of warranties and guarantees. To this, Thatcher replied imperiously:

You do not, Sir David, win wars on warranties.

In the end, when the Cabinet's overseas and defence committee failed to reach a decision, the issue went to full Cabinet. It was a true dilemma. As one senior army officer said:

Our hearts tell us to go with Vickers but our heads say we should go with the Americans.

And there was plenty of pressure applied to the Cabinet. More than 100 MPs publicly backed the British 'world-beater'. Pressure also came from the Prime Minister, who rebuked many of her Cabinet colleagues for not having done their homework properly. The first two full Cabinet discussions on the subject were cut short without any conclusion.

As Christmas 1988 approached, the Secretary for Trade and Industry, Lord Young (famed as the man who brought the Prime Minister 'solutions', whereas everyone else just brought her questions), spoke up for Vickers and for the British solution; the failures of the past should not be blamed on Vickers and a failure to support them would snuff out a strategically important chunk of Britain's ability to provide for its own defence. Thatcher, while not wholly convinced, was impressed enough to give Vickers not a full order but a deadline of 21 months to build nine prototypes.

It was a tough timetable, yet General Dynamics and Krauss-Maffei did not give up. They continued to lobby while Vickers strove to produce the prototypes on time. On 2 August 1990, a dramatic event, which helped Vickers, occurred when Iraq invaded Kuwait. Over the coming months as the British Government debated whether to send ground forces to the Gulf, Vickers prepared Challenger 1 for desert warfare, well aware that success could lead to the full order for Challenger 2.

On 13 September 1990, the top Vickers team was summoned to 10 Downing Street. The Prime Minister was again scathing in her criticism of the Challenger's availability, record and demanded assurances of 80 per cent availability if Challengers were sent to the Gulf. The Vickers team said they would deliver, but she insisted they sign personal assurances and warned them that, if things went wrong, she would hold them personally responsible for the rest of their lives.

Challenger was shipped to the Gulf and served with the Seventh and Fourth armoured brigades accompanied by Vickers support teams. On the morning the land war started in early 1991, 98 per cent of the 225 tanks mobilised were available, and 95 per cent completed the 176-mile drive into Iraq. Lieutenant General Sir Peter de la Billière, the British Commander, later described Challenger's performance as 'a major achievement'. It helped that the Challenger armoured repair-and-recovery vehicles, using the same engine that would go into Challenger 2, also performed well.

However, Vickers' struggles to win the order were not over, and further intense lobbying of the new Prime Minister, John Major, was required before the order was signed in June 1991. The contract was for 130 to 140 tanks, with a value of £400 million. (Plastow had even told the Prime Minister at a CBI dinner that the British Government was becoming a laughing stock in the Middle East thanks to its indecision.)

Winning the tank order had, as always with large defence decisions, been a long-running saga. Plastow criticised the MoD for the time it had taken to make its choice, saying:

The delay has damaged Vickers in overseas markets; that is our only complaint but the decision on Challenger 2 reopens the opportunities for British tank exports. The market is estimated to be worth £12 billion over the next 10 years and we shall now go out and win a share of that market for Britain.

It gave up on office furniture and sold the division, including the generic Roneo, in 1988. The medical division was being nurtured but contributed only 10 per cent of the £70 million profit of 1988. This was better than the marine division, which contributed a measly £1.7 million. However, the £15-million acquisition of the Swedish variable-pitch propeller manufacturer Kamewa gave the division a leading product in the world market.

On the lithographic front, the core business was soon deemed to be non-core and was sold for £245 million in May 1989 to the US giant DuPont. Vickers feared that Howson's position was being threatened by new plants being built by its bigger rivals.

'MORE OR LESS VULNERABLE'

This further injection of cash following the sale of the furniture business set the tongues wagging as to what Vickers might acquire. 'Nothing silly', said Sir David. Some wondered whether Vickers itself might now be acquired. The *Investors Chronicle* said:

It is an open question whether this deal makes Vickers more or less vulnerable.

There were various possibilities. It could have moved to build on its world lead in baby incubators. However, the price earnings ratios being demanded for medical-equipment businesses were thought to be 'crazy'. Aerospace was also a possibility as Vickers had a £40-million-turnover business supplying gas-turbine components to most of the world's aero-engine makers including Rolls-Royce. In Defence, there was VSEL, the privatised warship builder, which included the former Vickers' shipyard in Barrow-in-Furness. There was also United Scientific, owner of armoured-vehicle maker Alvis.

While it pondered, Vickers acquired on the personnel front Sir Colin Chandler, the former marketing director of British Aerospace seconded to the Ministry of Defence in 1985 to act as its head of export services department. He had been a central figure in negotiating the Al-Yamamah deal, Britain's two-stage defence agreement with Saudi Arabia expected to be worth £15 billion. The *Financial Times* speculated that:

Vickers, which has about a quarter of its business in defence and aerospace, clearly hopes that his experience in the Middle East will be brought to bear to exploit markets for battle tanks and armoured vehicles. The company is engaged in a race against the clock to clinch a £1 billion-plus UK tank contract against US and West German competition. It is halfway through the 21 month period given it by the UK Ministry of Defence last December to demonstrate the prototype performance of its Challenger 2 tank. The UK contract is considered crucial to its export prospects.

And Vickers quickly started to spend the money brought in by the sale of Howson Algraphy. It bought the Ross Catherall Group for £106.2 million, which took it into the field of super-alloys, ceramics and other materials for the aerospace industry, as well as investment castings for automotive turbochargers. Next was the Italian luxury-boat manufacturer Cantieri Riva, which Vickers bought for £9.1 million. Plastow justified this purchase on the basis that it would add value to the well-established Rolls-Royce Motors marketing network, saying:

Riva hasn't been selling in the US, and of course Rolls-Royce has been selling there for many years. Because the wealth of people is growing, the top of these markets has grown as well.

Riva was one of Europe's leading builders of luxury powerboats in the 26-to-60-feet range, which were popular with celebrities and industrialists. Prices ranged from £170,000 to more than £1.5 million. Founded as long ago as 1842, by 1990 Riva was building about 60 boats a year at its plant on Lake Iseo, 50 miles from Milan. Its latest product range included the Riva 32, a joint venture with Ferrari Engineering.

As well as offering marketing expertise to Riva, Vickers also hoped to provide engineering expertise. Its Kamewa subsidiary was a world leader in waterjet technology used in powerboats.

After Riva, Vickers bought the high-performance engine maker Cosworth Holdings, which it bought from the media group Carlton Communications, who had acquired it with its purchase of UEI. Carlton had bought UEI for its digital processing expertise, not for its interests in high-performance engines. This had some people dreaming of a new British prestige sports car.

A Cosworth-powered Tyrrell Ford had come second at two Grand Prix in the first half of the 1990 season, and it was hoped by some that a sporting Bentley, or something similar, would soon be on offer. Apart from making engines for Formula One cars and the Sierra Cosworth, Cosworth supplied engines or parts to many other car manufacturers including Mercedes-Benz, Jaguar and Opel.

By this time, Vickers was confronting the New Zealand entrepreneur Sir Ron Brierley, who had built up a 17.25 per cent stake and who was making the same point that Steinberg had made earlier. In his view, Vickers was not exploiting to the full the value of the Rolls-Royce name. As we saw in Chapter Five, Brierley failed to convince the Vickers shareholders of his good intentions.

In the first half of the 1990s, as we know, Vickers was badly affected by the severe recession that followed the overheating of the late 1980s and decided it must sell Rolls-Royce Motor Cars. The story of this sale was told in detail in Chapter Five.

Following the sales of Rolls-Royce Motor Cars, Cosworth Engineering and the medical division, Sir Colin Chandler claimed that Vickers was now down to its constituent parts, and to help him run it he appointed a Belgian, Baron Paul Buysse, as group chief executive. Buysse had run the power-drives division of BTR but had recently left with £1.14-million compensation. He asked Buysse to look at ways to build up the Kamewa marine-propulsion division and to review options for the Ross Catherall turbocharger and aerospace businesses. Chandler felt this would leave him free to concentrate on the future of the defence business.

Vickers realised that Vickers Defence Systems had to comprise more than Challenger tanks, and in 1999 it embarked on a series of joint-venture and acquisition initiatives. An agreement was drawn up with the French defence company GIAT Industries for the two companies to collaborate on a bid for the French VCI wheeled-infantry carrier programme and to integrate the Vickers tactical bridge, BR90, on a Leclerc chassis to offer to the French Army. An agreement was also made with MOWAG of Switzerland to contribute to the development of the Piranha IV family of wheeled vehicles for the UK and targeted overseas countries, and another with MOWAG to promote the Eagle II, a 4×4 wheeled battlefield liaison vehicle, into the UK market.

Reumech's OMC and Gear Ratio businesses in South Africa, including the Ermetek design capability, were acquired. This brought an entry into the mine-protection field, as well as a large family of wheeled vehicles with both military and civil applications. A Memorandum of Understanding (MoU) was signed with Singapore Technologies Automotive to develop jointly the Bionix light-tracked armoured-vehicle family for the UK and European markets. An MoU was also signed with Krauss-Maffei Wegman of Germany to promote the APCV2, a new 4×4 armoured-personnel carrier, into the UK market. A further MoU was signed with the Adval Group to create a joint-venture company to provide comprehensive training services to the UK and overseas markets.

In spite of this acquisition and the joint ventures, Chandler knew that, in the long run, Vickers could not survive on its own. Prophetically, he said in August 1998:

We want to be involved in the consolidation process that the British Government is encouraging. Eventually, we will be part of a larger defence company, first in Britain, and then Europe or the United States.

In the period before Vickers put Rolls-Royce Motor Cars up for sale in the autumn of 1997, Rolls-Royce plc twice looked at the possibility of buying the whole of Vickers. In 1995, BMW suggested to Rolls-Royce that one way forward would be for Rolls-Royce to buy the whole of Vickers, supported by BMW taking an equity stake in Rolls-Royce, and that BMW would then buy Rolls-Royce Motors from Rolls-Royce plc. This did not appeal to Rolls-Royce plc as, at that time, there were no business sectors that Vickers served which would contribute significantly to Rolls-Royce's corporate strategy.

In the spring of 1997, BMW and Rolls-Royce looked again at the possibility of bidding for Vickers. This time the engineering group GKN was involved. The *Sunday Times* caught a whiff of possible activity and, under the headline 'GKN Runs Its Rule Over Vickers', Andrew Lorenz wrote on 27 April 1997:

GKN is believed to be tracking Vickers, whose share price slump last week has left it vulnerable to a takeover bid ... GKN's main interest in Vickers is to merge the tanks business with its own defence subsidiary, maker of the Warrior, Saxon and Piranha armoured vehicles. With Warrior orders running out later this year, GKN faces big costs for cutting back its Telford armoured vehicles factory. By contrast, a British army order for Challenger 2 tanks runs until 2000, and Vickers is pushing hard for tank export orders ... Analysts believe a bidder would find ready buyers for other parts of the Vickers operation; Germany's BMW wants to buy Rolls-Royce [Motor Cars], while Vosper Thorneycroft would be interested in the KaMeWa ship propellers operation. Smiths Industries and several American firms are potential buyers of Vickers' medical division.

On 1 May, after discussion between John Rose and C.K. Chow (the chief executive of GKN), Charles Coltman, Rolls-Royce's Director of Strategic Planning, Dr Hagen Luderitz of BMW and David Turner of GKN met in London. The possibility of a bid for Vickers was discussed, and the three put forward their own interests if such a bid went ahead. Rolls-Royce did not have a *specific* interest in any of Vickers' businesses. However, it would accept the propulsion and Ross Catherall business. On the other hand, Rolls-Royce was keenly interested that the brand equity of the Rolls-Royce trade-mark represented by the motor-car business should be maintained at the highest possible level. They accepted that BMW was ideally suited to achieve this objective and were therefore wholly supportive of BMW's ambitions to own the motor-car business.

For its part, BMW's strategy was to address the automotive markets with different brands, each representing specific marque values. BMW should be seen as 'dynamic, exclusive and elegant', its subsidiary, Rover, as 'relaxed, comfortable, British'. BMW saw the Vickers motor-car business as representing values of prestige and luxury not fully addressed by the existing brands of the BMW Group. It felt that it had acquired with Rover elements of Britishness in its corporate image and was ideally suited to add Rolls-Royce Motor Cars to its product portfolio; it felt that Vickers accepted this. On the other hand, BMW was not interested in Cosworth and certainly not in Riva.

GKN seemed to be a bit lukewarm about the whole idea. In Dr Luderitz's summing up after the meeting:

Armoured vehicles are the backbone of GKN's defence business. The warrior business with Kuwait will be finished soon. Continuation of the armoured vehicle business, as it is, is not possible. New orders require new products. A decision about GKN's future strategy has not been taken; even the basic work to arrive at a strategy has not been done. One possibility to continue the armoured vehicle business would be the acquisition of Venice's [code word for Vickers] defence business. Although GKN does not have an interest in tanks, they would take the business. They may have an interest in Cosworth engineering, probably less in the casting business.

If a bid was to be made, GKN wanted Rolls-Royce to be the lead company, and *vice versa*. The three parties agreed to carry out further evaluation.

The next big development, as we saw in Chapter Five, was Vickers putting Rolls-Royce Motor Cars up for sale in October 1997. This prompted speculation that there would be further merger activity between GKN and Vickers on the defence business front, but this time it was thought Vickers would be doing the buying.

ULSTEIN – 'AN EXCELLENT FIT'

The rationalisation of Vickers continued in 1998 with the sale of Cantieri Riva to Stellican, a London investment company headed by Stephen Julius. The price was believed to be £4 million – far from the £9.1 million Vickers had paid in 1990. The truth was that the company had never fitted into the group, and serious cross-selling to Rolls-Royce motor-car owners had never been attempted.

The jewel in the crown of Vickers' shipbuilding interests was the world-class propulsion company Kamewa. Founded in 1849 as Christinehamns Jernwägs Werkstad (Christinehamn's Wagon and Track Repair Shop), Kamewa (Karlstads Mekaniska Werkstad) had developed first as a wagon and track repair shop, then in the 1860s as a producer of steam-driven loco-motives, followed by the manufacture of turbines and steam ships in the 1870s. In the early twentieth century, the company concentrated on the develop-ment and production of steam turbines before turning to the design, development and production of the adjustable Kamewa propeller in the 1930s.

This propeller was inspired by a Russian whom Kamewa's chief engineer, Elov Englesson, met on a trip to the Baltic States in the mid-1930s. Englesson had been working with an Austrian engineer, Professor Victor Kaplan, on an adjustable propeller, designed to counter the effects of cavitation. (We have already seen in Chapter Two that Charles Parsons struggled with the same problems.) The Russian expressed surprise that Englesson had not used the Kaplan technique to design adjustable-pitch ship propellers. Englesson set about designing hydraulically adjustable blades to replace those adjusted manually by the engine-room crew. Testing his system in 1938, he told the press:

Even the largest motor-driven ships will be able to manoeuvre from the bridge using this device. The ship's engines can be used in all weathers, higher speeds are obtained and wear is reduced. It allows much better utilization of the installed engine power, and the likelihood of incorrect manoeuvring is greatly reduced.

In 1936, Kamewa had been bought by the larger Johnson Group. As this group operated a substantial shipping fleet, orders for the adjustable propellers were assured. Orders were received in 1940 from Sweden to fit twenty minesweepers, and in 1944 the first ocean-going vessel, the M/S *Suecia*, was fitted with Kamewa propellers. By the 1950s, the company was supplying a number of commercial shipping lines and also some of the world's navies, and in the 1960s propeller volume outstripped that of turbines. In the 1970s came the skewed blades that reduced both noise and vibration, an attractive innovation for shipping companies operating large luxury liners.

The other big development at Kamewa in the 1960s was the introduction of thrusters. The shipping boom of that decade, with its big increase in both passenger and freight ferry transport, and the advent of 'ro-ro' (roll-on, roll-off), demanded fast and smooth shuttle traffic. This in turn meant an increase in demand for manoeuvrability, and thrusters would help as a steering aid for docking or manoeuvring in narrow passages and crowded sea lanes.

Initially called a 'bow thruster' then a 'steering thruster', the thruster eventually settled down as a 'tunnel thruster' (the propeller being located in a tunnel). Kamewa offered a package with the main propeller for propulsion and a tunnel thruster for manoeuvring. After some teething problems, mainly associated with seals, the Kamewa soon became a huge success, catering for the fast expansion in the European ferry market. Kamewa thrusters also became very popular with companies involved in the offshore oil and gas industry and with large cruise ships. *Carnival Destiny* was the largest ship in the world when launched in 1996 but was overtaken by *Eagle* in 1998; both were equipped with Kamewa thrusters.

Kamewa also built what are known as either rotatable, Ro-thruster or Azimuth thrusters, and in 1995 Vickers acquired its main competitor in this area, Aquamaster-Rauma, to give the group an unequalled range in thruster production.

The other big attraction of Kamewa was its waterjet division. It began developing waterjets in the 1960s, and its first unit was installed on the Swedish Navy landing craft *Tärnan* in 1971. However, it was not until the 1980s that both the luxury market and the naval market began to place orders in any number. In the late 1980s, Kamewa supplied four coastal corvettes of the Swedish Navy with 2000 kW waterjets and in 1993 received an order to supply twelve patrol vehicles of the Singapore Navy. In the same year, the ferry ship *Aquastrada*, capable of carrying 100 cars and 500 passengers, ordered three Kamewa waterjets with a total output of 25,000 kW. The success of this ship brought orders from Stena Line and also for two Italian ferry ships, *Taurus* and *Aries*, which can carry 1,800 passengers and 460 cars at speeds up to 40 knots.

Buysse's brief was to build up Vickers' marine business on the back of the successful Kamewa, or divest the group of the business. He chose the former plan, and at the end of 1998 it was announced that, after several months of negotiation, Vickers would acquire the Norwegian shipbuilding and marine-propulsion company Ulstein. Vickers would take the marine-propulsion business, and the shipbuilding business would be sold to a new company. The cost to Vickers would be £304 million plus £54.8 million of debt. After some months of negotiation, the deal was signed on 30 November 1998 and completed on 4 May 1999.

Vickers' reasoning behind the purchase was the conclusion that there would be a growing demand for passenger and cargo transport by water, mainly because of environmental considerations and developing technology which would enable vessels to travel at higher speeds in most sea conditions. Furthermore, ship owners and shipyards would demand integrated propulsion and positioning systems for their vessels. To exploit this new situation, Vickers and Ulstein were in an excellent position to conceive together and realise technological innovations and design, and develop speedily the integrated marine-equipment solutions required. Ulstein had particular expertise in supplying equipment to vessels employed in the offshore oil-and-gas-production field. With steady growth in the world demand for energy, and technological advances in the field of deep-sea extraction, the future for this market should be very promising.

Ulstein Mek Verksted had been founded as a fishing-boat repair company by Martin Ulstein at Naustneset in Ulsteinvik on the west coast of Norway in 1917. It was not until the 1950s that the firm branched out into construction, launching the car ferry *Torulf* in 1957. It branched out into propeller production in the 1960s, but its great leap forward came in the 1970s with the development of the UT704 supply boat, which cashed in on the growing offshore oil-and-gas industry. The construction of these support vessels formed the mainstay of the company throughout the 1970s and 1980s. Ulstein also grew by acquisition in the 1980s, buying and developing a number of marine-equipment companies.

By the late 1990s, Ulstein was organised into five divisions. The first was design and ship systems, in which Ulstein developed and marketed a range of ship design packages and marine-consultancy services. Over 300 offshore service vessels in its UT700 series had been ordered. The second division was propulsion, where Ulstein developed, built and serviced a range of marine-propulsion systems, focusing on reduction gears, controllable-pitch propellers, compass and tunnel thrusters, and electronic control systems. There were production centres in Norway, Scotland and Canada, and in March 1998 Ulstein had bought Bird-Johnson in the USA, a manufacturer of propulsion systems for both the civil and defence markets.

The third division designed, developed and manufactured deck machinery and steering-gear systems for merchant and fishing vessels, offshore service vessels and rigs. The fourth developed, built, marketed and serviced diesel engines for the marine market and gas turbines for onshore power-generation units. Finally, the fifth division built advanced, specialised vessels for the international market, mainly within the offshore sector. Vickers was not acquiring this last division.

The investment bank ABN AMRO realised immediately that this purchase transformed Vickers, and in a piece of research published in December 1998 wrote:

The acquisition of Ulstein will move Vickers from a 'speculative' to a 'fundamental' play on its world leading position in the marine propulsion market ... We believe that Ulstein is an excellent fit with KaMeWa and Aquamaster-Rauma. Ulstein successfully fulfils the strategy of moving the Marine division into a position to supply complete propulsion systems. In the process, Vickers creates a world leading business with a range of products and capabilities that will be very difficult, perhaps impossible, for others to rival ... Recommendation: Buy.

And that's exactly what Rolls-Royce did. On 20 September 1999, it was announced that the Board of Vickers would recommend its shareholders to accept a cash bid of £576 million.

As we saw in Part One, Rolls-Royce and Vickers had come quite close to a merger at the end of the First World War. In those days, Vickers was a much larger and more diverse company than Rolls-Royce, and the 'merger' would almost certainly have been a Vickers takeover of Rolls-Royce. That was the way Rolls-Royce's Managing Director, Claude Johnson, saw it after a meeting on 17 April 1917 with Sir Victor Caillard, a Vickers director, Ernest Hopwood, the Managing Director of Wolseley, and Edward Manville, the Chairman of Daimler. He wrote to his fellow directors:

It appeared to me peculiar that Vickers were represented by three people at the conference, and that one of them, Sir Victor Caillard, should produce from his pocket a typewritten statement of the statistics which each company should supply. I came to the conclusion that Vickers arranged the meeting [this was not correct – the original suggestion came from Siddeley] and that it was to the interest of Vickers (and probably not of Rolls-Royce) that the combination should be formed. Under the circumstances Vickers would probably desire to swallow up Rolls-Royce as part of a combination which they would control rather than face Rolls-Royce in open markets.

The result was that talks were broken off, though there were further discussions in 1919 between Rolls-Royce and Vickers, with the object of forming Vickers Rolls-Royce Aviation.

In 1999, studying what Vickers comprised following its divestments and acquisitions, Rolls-Royce came to the conclusion that the industrial and financial logic for combining the businesses was overwhelming. It would create a global leader in marine-power systems. The acquisition was consistent with Rolls-Royce's business strategies, in that it would leverage Rolls-Royce's gas-turbine technology, would broaden its routes to market, build on its core skills, create new market opportunities and increase the aftermarket potential. At the price Rolls-Royce proposed to pay, it would also enhance earnings immediately.

Rolls-Royce was a pioneer in marine gas turbines, as was Vickers in marine waterjets. Vickers had consolidated its position in rotating thrusters and ship deck machinery in 1995 by acquiring Kamewa's competitor, Aquamaster, based in Rauma, Finland. Together they would be offering unique technology, including the only advanced-cycle marine gas turbine. Vickers had also bought in the late 1980s the Edinburgh-based Brown Brothers, specialists in steering gear for naval vessels and stabilisers for both naval and commercial vessels.

The marine market was growing at 4 per cent per annum, with the segment for faster ships growing at 8 per cent. In diesel engines, through Allen & Crossley, which it had acquired when it bought NEI in 1989, Rolls-Royce made engines in the 3-to-10-megawatt range while Vickers made them in the 8-megawatt-plus range; in gas turbines, Rolls-Royce manufactured in the 3-to-50-megawatt range, while in propulsors Vickers manufactured waterjets, thrusters and propellers; in ship design and systems, Rolls-Royce would contribute power systems, control instruments and gearboxes, while Vickers would bring ship design and electronic-and-gearbox systems; in steering gear, Vickers made steering gear and stabilisers; and in ancillary equipment, Rolls-Royce would contribute deck machinery, microturbines and permanent magnet motors, while Vickers brought deck machinery.

For example, such integration would mean that on a naval frigate, while Rolls-Royce would supply the gas-turbine generators, gearboxes, electric motors and generators, power electronics and main gas turbines, Vickers would supply the diesel generators, shaft-line controllers, propellers, shafting and bearings, the steering gear and stabilisers, and together they would provide design and integration, project management, ship control and instrumentation, procurement and equipment supply, installation and commissioning, and winches and handling.

And what was the reaction when the deal was announced? *Lex* in the *Financial Times*, whose respect is hard to earn, rather liked it, saying:

Given the Vickers' depressed valuation [after, in *Lex*'s view, over-paying for Ulstein], the price should not be too much of a concern. Even after the 53 per cent premium [to Vickers' pre-bid share price], Vickers is being taken out at a discount to Rolls itself.

The other financial newspaper owned by Pearson, *The Economist*, concentrated on the potential of the new ships being planned by FastShips Inc., writing:

Rolls's interest lies in a little office in Philadelphia, where five entrepreneurs are planning to revolutionise marine-freight transport. Their company, FastShips Inc., is trying to raise $1.5 billion to build four vessels, each of which will carry 1,432 containers (weighing 10,000 tonnes) across the Atlantic in four days at 40 knots. That is twice the speed of normal container ships for only a fraction of their cost. To do this, FastShips needs marine versions of the huge jet engines that power airliners; and it intends to buy 25 such jets from Rolls-Royce at a cost of £600 million ... Buying

Vickers will give Rolls-Royce a marine-propulsion business that can provide whole systems rather than just turbines or other engines.

In February 1999, Kamewa signed an agreement to develop the world's largest waterjets. When the FastShip takes to the sea, the five Rolls-Royce MT50 gas turbines combining with five Kamewa waterjets will move as much water as goes over the US side of Niagara Falls at any given moment.

When the financing is fully in place, four ships will be built to sail between Philadelphia and Cherbourg. They were going to be built at the NASSLO shipyard in San Diego, but now the plan is to build them in the Philadelphia shipyard owned by the Norwegian company Aker. As Saul Lanyado, President Rolls-Royce Marine, points out:

It is not only the ship's speed that's important. It's the whole package, the speed of loading and unloading and delivery to the customer. Fast cargo is being seen as more and more important. As roads become more and more congested fast sea transport, especially coastal waters, could be a viable alternative. As for the military, after September 11, the Department of Defence in the USA have shown a heightened interest in the rapid movement of supplies and personnel.

By the end of 2001, everything was in place for the building of the first FastShip except the final signing of the financial agreements. On 18 November 2001, under the heading 'Jet Ships Will Cross Atlantic in Three Days', the *Sunday Times* wrote:

A jet-powered ship capable of crossing the Atlantic in three days, halving current journey times, is to be built in the new year by a consortium including Rolls-Royce. The vessel – the length of three jumbo jets – could make its maiden voyage within three years, heralding one of the most significant developments in ocean travel in the past 100 years.

The article went on to say that though the idea had always been aimed at the cargo market, the fear of flying for many after the events of 11 September 2001 had convinced the consortium that a market existed for passenger versions of the ship. Roland Bullard, President of FastShip, also believed the ship could be easily converted to military use, another concept whose appeal had increased after September 11th.

As Rolls-Royce Finance Director Paul Heiden told the author in the spring of 2002:

Whether FastShip comes to fruition or not, the fact remains that ships will go faster in the future, perhaps twice as fast, and this requires four times the power. This will require gas turbine rather than diesel engines. Furthermore, as well as giving greater speed, gas turbines are attractive to shipowners because, with the growing use of electricity on ships, they can be sited anywhere, probably on deck, and free up space for extra passengers or cargo. On the naval side, there is a move towards prime contractorship and we saw an opportunity to supply complete systems.

However, to do this, we must be supplying about 60–70 per cent of the 'kit'. With the acquisition of Vickers, we are in a position to do that.

Returning to Rolls-Royce's acquisition of Vickers, the *Daily Telegraph* was happy with the logic of the purchase of Ulstein, saying:

There are some deals which are obvious and which the City's experts still fail to see coming. Adding Rolls-Royce's gas turbine expertise to Ulstein of Norway's market-leading position in marine propulsion makes clear commercial sense.

The Times approved:

Rolls is keen to balance its business in the skies with that on the seas and combining with Vickers is a neat and comfortable way of doing just that.

Following the acquisition, the marine interests of Rolls-Royce and Vickers were organised into two groups: Naval Marine, which was effectively the former marine interests of Rolls-Royce, and Commercial Marine, those of Vickers. Commercial Marine comprised five strong brand names – Kamewa, Ulstein, Aquamaster, Bird-Johnson and Brown Brothers, which, between them, enjoyed market-leading positions, holding a 45 per cent share of controllable-pitch propellers, a 60 per cent share of waterjets, a 45 per cent share of thrusters, a 30 per cent share of pod propulsion (electrically driven propulsion capsules) in commercial marine, a 60 per cent share of offshore anchor winches, a 25 per cent share of stabilisers and a 30 per cent share of naval gas turbines.

The merging of Rolls-Royce's and Vickers' naval and commercial marine businesses will bring the benefits of considerable synergy between the two. For example, fast jets have applications for both naval and commercial ships, and the company's 30 marine servicing centres round the world could handle both naval and commercial ships. Currently, in the naval market, 96 per cent of ships are powered by diesel engines and only 4 per cent by gas-turbine engines.

In the commercial market, the dominance of diesel, at 98 per cent, is even greater. Rolls-Royce envisages a growth to 7 to 8 per cent market share for gas turbines over the coming decade, and Vickers, following its purchase of Kamewa and Ulstein, provides Rolls-Royce with the platform to capture much of this growing market.

THE MARINE TRENT 30

The Marine Trent 30 (MT30) will be the first marine engine based on the Trent aero-engine which Rolls-Royce has produced. However, the practice of using technology developed in the aero sector and then applying it to the marine industry has long been established in Rolls-Royce. The Spey, Olympus and Tyne all followed that route.

In developing the Marine Trent 30, Rolls-Royce set itself the goal of producing a marine gas turbine which would meet the needs of the commercial marine market, have the maximum of parts in common with the well-proven Trent 800 aero-engine and draw on experience gained in developing the Trent industrial engine. The resulting unit will be supplied as a complete package for generator drive or for propeller (cube) law mechanical transmission, suitable for a range of applications including propulsion of cruise ships, fast commercial vessels and LNG (liquefied natural gas) carriers. It is also designed to meet naval requirements.

Availability, reliability and maintainability have been key words in establishing the design parameters of the new gas turbine, with overhaul intervals and time between failures that will allow the engine to compete well with its diesel alternatives. The MT30 will be competitive with other gas turbines on the market down to 25 MW and its thermal efficiency in line with high-speed diesel engines, thanks to its up-to-date technology.

At the heart of the MT30 is a gas-generator section that uses the latest design techniques, materials and production technology. It is essentially the core unit of the aero-engine minus the fan section. An eight-stage variable-geometry axial low-pressure compressor, driven by a single-stage LP turbine, feeds air to the high-pressure spool, comprising a four-stage compressor and single-stage HP turbine. Between the HP compressor and HP turbine is the annular combustion chamber. LP and HP spools rotate in opposite directions, and temperatures and pressures are substantially lower than the aero-engine take-off rating in the interest of long life.

Hot gas from the gas-generator section supplies a four-stage power turbine. For generator drive the shaft speed is 3,600 rpm. A full speed of 3,500 rpm has been selected for the power turbine for mechanical drive as this gives the lowest specific fuel consumption. Waterjet drive can be a demanding operation, since large load changes can occur almost instantaneously if air is drawn into the jet unit in severe sea conditions. Accumulated knowledge from other parts of the Rolls-Royce marine business has been applied to make sure the MT30 will withstand a lifetime of tough operating conditions.

By June 2002, a fully instrumented test cell was nearing completion at the Rolls-Royce site in Bristol, and the first unit in the two-engine test programme is due to start running during the summer. While the first engine is stripped for detailed inspection, the second will start certification running for marine type-approval, with Det Norske Veritas as classification society.

Rolls-Royce has become involved with shipowners in a number of projects covering vessels to be powered by the new engine, and production engines are scheduled to be available from the first quarter of 2004. Once prototype testing work is complete, the test cell will be used for acceptance trials of completed production engines. The test-bed is equipped with a generator and load banks that enable all types of load profile to be run. The layout is flexible and has the advantage that when a production unit is on test it can be coupled to the customer's own generator, enabling the whole system to be tested prior to dispatch. The customer's proposed fuel can also be used, giving added assurance.

The MT30 will be supplied as a package on a bedplate with an acoustic enclosure that is fitted with automatic fire detection and extinguishing and which houses the auxiliaries, and the inlet and exhaust diffuser. The complete unit weighs about 26 tonnes dry and is 9.1 metres long, 3.8 metres wide and 4.0 metres high. When a gas-generator change is needed, the exchange unit is air-freightable.

An important part of the package is the integrated control and monitoring system, housed in a free-standing cabinet. It includes an independent power supply so that a failure of the ship's electricity supply does not prejudice the safety of the gas-turbine package. An optional engine and health-monitoring system will also be available. The main package can be installed in a single lift at the shipyard, while the control panel and the starter and lube-oil modules can be mounted where convenient in the engine room.

High levels of reliability have been achieved by the 250 examples of the aero Trent that are in service. The marine version of the engine has about 80 per cent commonality of parts – in many cases, the only difference is an additional manufacturing process to apply coatings for protection against the marine environment. This gives an excellent basis for an efficient and cost-effective marine prime mover for mechanical or electric transmissions.

THE INDUSTRIAL TRENT

Running a multinational company selling nothing more exciting than products based on cocoa and milk can produce problems that explode in the face of top management. Nestlé discovered this when the powdered-milk-to-babies-in-Africa scandal broke. For a company such as Rolls-Royce, involved in the infinitely more demanding development of gas-turbine engines constantly operating at the cutting edge of technology, the risks are very much greater.

In the summer of 2000, the Chairman, Sir Ralph Robins, announced that Rolls-Royce would write off no less than £130 million to cover support, warranty, inventory, project completion and the upgrading of Rolls-Royce's industrial-Trent gas turbine. What had gone wrong?

The development of an industrial version of Rolls-Royce's world-beating Trent aero-engine had all started well enough at the beginning of the 1990s. Following Rolls-Royce's acquisition of NEI in 1989, interest had been stimulated in the possibilities which existed in any industry which could use gas-turbine power. Rolls-Royce had confined itself mainly to the oil and gas industry through its company Cooper Rolls, though it had supplied packaged power sets using Olympus engines, many of which are still running, in the 1960s and 1970s. Now, with NEI's extra capacity and Rolls-Royce's successful Trent aero-engine, the decision was taken to adapt the Trent and produce a large gas turbine for industrial power generation and for utilities requiring peak-hour generating capacity.

Development work had already begun on the WR21 engine for the Royal and US Navies and, as there was not enough capacity at the Ansty plant to develop both, Rolls-Royce Gas Turbine Engines was set up at Rolls-Royce's plant in Montreal in 1992 to continue the development work on the industrial Trent after the feasibility study had been completed at Ansty.

Rolls-Royce knew that the biggest market for the industrial Trent would be in North America and forged an alliance with Westinghouse. In May 1993, the two companies signed a fifteen-year agreement covering technology transfer, joint development of combustion-turbine technology and marketing of combustion turbines and combined-cycle power plants. Technology transfer via licensing had long been an integral part of the power-equipment industry. For example, Westinghouse's early steam turbines were based on designs by Sir Charles Parsons (see Chapter Two), and it had made a number of agreements with Mitsubishi companies in Japan and with Fiat Avio in Italy. Westinghouse realised it needed access to aero-engine technology, which meant co-operation with GE, Pratt & Whitney or Rolls-Royce. It chose Rolls-Royce.

From Rolls-Royce's point of view, co-operation with Westinghouse would give it not only access to Westinghouse's existing heavy-duty gas turbines and technology in combined-cycle power (the increasingly popular gas-turbine/steam generator/steam turbine combination), but also to Westinghouse's marketing presence in the all-important North American market. Managing Director of Rolls-Royce's Industrial Power Group, Richard Maudslay, said:

By 1996 we will have available both a 50 MW industrial version of the Trent and our existing 28 MW industrial RB 211 and we want both to be strongly marketed in

North America. [Available since 1974, the industrial RB 211 was operating in nearly 250 locations by the early 1990s.]

The new combined team quickly won a contract from the Tennessee Valley Authority to provide two replacement generators to be built by Westinghouse and four steam turbine rotors to be built by Rolls-Royce, with Westinghouse installing and servicing the equipment.

However, this was only a retrofit. The real test – development of the new industrial Trent – still had to be completed successfully, and it was only in 1996, when an operational readiness review was carried out, that it became clear that this development was not proceeding according to plan.

Mike Howse, currently Director of Engineering and Technology at Rolls-Royce, said that the technical challenge of developing an industrial version of the Trent was enormous. The emission on the aero version was about 300 parts per million (ppm) of NO_x, whereas the permitted level on the industrial version was 25 ppm. He said:

The problem was that we did not put people with the right mix of experience on to the problem. It was not that they knew they had a difficult problem to solve, they didn't even realise there was a problem. Also, and slightly perversely, they wanted to be different from the aero engine approach so, when they did start to realise the problem and its extent, they didn't call on the aero engine people for help.

To get the 25 ppm NO_x required in most parts of the world, it was necessary to have a very good mixing between gas and air to avoid variations and prevent the temperature rising too high. Unfortunately, the engineers in Canada produced an engine that, if it met the NO_x required, vibrated and shook itself to pieces.

While the development work was proceeding, eight contracts were won to supply ten units, and the first, at Whitby in Canada, went into service in May 1998. This was followed by others – at Seal Sands and Derby in the UK in October 1998, at Heartlands in the UK in February 1999, at Exeter in the UK in September 1999 and at Bristol in the UK in December 1999. Units were also sold to SK Power in Denmark and TCE Bear Creek in Canada, due to begin service in 2002.

The 'noise' levels had been solved, but the units did not comply with permitted NO_x emission levels, and Rolls-Royce undertook to support the operation of the plants until the necessary compliant hardware could be retrofitted.

By 2001, Rolls-Royce had solved the noise feedback loops by developing a new approach to the premix process which damped out the feedback of combustion pressure fluctuations into the premix ducts. This new system also employed a turbulent-mixing approach which provided extremely good mixing, resulting in very low NO_x emissions. Testing demonstrated single-digit NO_x (i.e. less than 10 ppm) capability with virtually no combustion noise. However, auto-ignition in the mixing ducts, which was burning out the combustor, still remained an unsolved problem. By early 2002, this problem was close to being solved, and satisfactory production was in sight.

As we have seen, the delays had proved expensive. Not only was there the £130 million of write-offs to absorb, there was also the lost orders. Nevertheless, the future now seemed bright. There was no doubting the technical superiority of the Trent over its competitors. In power output, it enjoys a 16 per cent advantage over the basic GE LM6000. Furthermore, whereas the LM6000 is near its limit, the Trent has the scope to grow in power and efficiency. In operation, the Trent will be the best in its class in start-up time in the peaking market, and its higher mass flow gives the Trent an advantage over its competitors. In terms of cost, the Trent will match the LM6000 on a dollar-per-kW installed basis and on maintenance will also be competitive on a miles-per-kWh basis.

In the 35-to-75-megawatt market at which Rolls-Royce is aiming the Trent, the dominant force is General Electric. Of the 260 orders given in 2000, admittedly a very good year, GE received about 160 for its LM6000 43-to-48-megawatt industrial gas turbine and about 60 for its Frame 6B 42-megawatt turbine. Pratt & Whitney received twenty, Siemens three and Alsthom eleven. Rolls-Royce expected the market to remain in the 100-to-150-units-per-year area for the next twenty years. The company expects to achieve a material share of the market. With a selling price of £15–20 million per project, the potential for turnover and profit is significant.

CHAPTER NINE

THE FIRST HUNDRED YEARS

'I HAVE FOUND THE GREATEST ENGINEER IN THE WORLD'
A FAMILY OF ENGINES
'"GO HOME, MR WELCH" IS A PERFECT TITLE'
'A BALANCED BUSINESS'
WORLD-CLASS TECHNOLOGY
THE FUTURE

'I HAVE FOUND THE GREATEST ENGINEER IN THE WORLD'

WE HAVE NOW REACHED the spring of 2002, exactly 100 years since Henry Royce began to design his first motor car, and we should look back and see what Rolls-Royce has achieved in those hundred years.

On 4 May 1904, thanks to entrepreneur and businessman Henry Edmunds (later to be known as 'The Godfather' of Rolls-Royce), the aristocratic motor-car salesman, the Honourable C.S. Rolls, was introduced to the engineer Henry Royce. Later, Edmunds would write in his memoirs:

I well remember the conversation I had in the dining-car of the train with Mr Rolls, who said it was his ambition to have a motor car connected with his name so that in the future it might be a household word, just as much as 'Broadwood' or 'Steinway' in connection with pianos; or 'Chubbs' in connection with safes. I am sure neither of us at that time could see the wonderful development of the car which resulted from my introduction of these two gentlemen ... I think both men took to each other at first sight.

For his part, Rolls, having seen Royce's car which he had been developing since 1902, returned to London, went to see his business partner, Claude Johnson, and told him:

I have found the greatest engineer in the world.

Rolls arranged that the firm of C.S. Rolls & Co. would have the sole selling rights of the marque, one of the conditions being that the car would be sold under the name 'Rolls-Royce'.

Rolls began selling Rolls-Royce cars, and on 15 March 1906 the company Rolls-Royce Ltd. was formally registered. One of its first actions was to find new premises to increase production, as Royce's factory, little more than a workshop, in Manchester was not adequate. Derby and Leicester competed to become Rolls-Royce's home, Derby winning by offering electrical power at especially low rates. The new factory was opened on Thursday 9 July 1908 by Sir John (later Lord) Montagu, a great enthusiast of the motor car. In his speech, Rolls set the tone for the future, saying:

Instead of turning out cars in huge quantities at a low price, we are turning out comparatively a small number of cars by the very best and most careful methods of manufacture. It is, in fact, the comparison between the ordinary watch and an English lever.

The other most important early decision was to concentrate on one model. Royce had developed a range of cars based on his first model, but in late 1906 put all he had learnt into the new six-cylinder 40/50 hp model. Claude Johnson recognised that this was superior to anything else on the market – indeed, Royce himself said that it was the best thing he had ever done – and insisted that all other models be dropped to concentrate on this model. Royce's 40/50 hp six-cylinder Rolls-Royce, which became known as the Silver Ghost, was probably the most famous car ever built. The first one appeared in 1906, and over 6,000 were built over the following twenty years, both in the UK and at Springfield, Massachusetts, in the USA.

While Johnson, with his marketing flair, was establishing Rolls-Royce's reputation for producing 'the best car in the world', the firm itself suffered two severe setbacks. Rolls, whose restless spirit had moved him on from motor cars to the even more modern means of conveyance, the aeroplane, was tragically killed in a flying contest at Bournemouth on 12 July 1910. He was only 32, but he had achieved enough in his short life for his name to become known throughout the world and equated with excellence for the rest of the twentieth century and, we trust, for the whole of the twenty-first century as well.

Recovering from this shock, the firm was struck again in 1911 when Royce was taken seriously ill. Long years of overwork and irregular meals had taken their toll, and the doctors feared for his life. Johnson, horrified at the prospect of losing the company's design genius, took Royce on an extended holiday through France and Italy and on to Egypt. Enchanted by the south of France, Royce decided to build himself a house at Le Canadel on the Côte d'Azur and spent the rest of his life either there or in the south of England. He only returned to the Rolls-Royce works in Derby once, but established a coterie of design engineers to work with him in the warmer climes of southern England and the south of France.

In the years leading up to the outbreak of the First World War in August 1914, Johnson and Royce concentrated on improving the Silver Ghost and maintaining its high profile in the market. One devotee was Lord North-cliffe, creator and owner of the *Daily Mail*, who wrote in 1912:

The six-cylinder Rolls-Royce is taking the place of the railway train as the most luxurious form of travel in town, or between town and country or for cross-country journeys … Disinterested experts, who have tried every other make of car, after driving the Rolls-Royce always admit that it is a revelation of suppleness, luxury of suspension, silence, smokelessness and all-round excellence.

Unfortunately, this happy world was to end and never return when on 4 August 1914, a European war – soon to escalate into a world war – broke out and lasted for four years, killing millions of young men. As a manufacturer of luxury cars, Rolls-Royce faced yet another serious crisis. Initially, and surprisingly, the Chairman decided that the company 'would not avail itself of the opportunity, now possibly arising, of making or assembling aero-engines for the British Government'.

However, Royce and Johnson were persuaded by the War Office to tender for the manufacture of 50 aero-engines to a design by Renault of France. Furthermore, Royce, who almost certainly did not agree with his Board's decision about involvement in aero-engines, began to design an aero-engine himself. So rapidly did he work that the engine, to be named the Eagle, was on the test bed by February 1915. Bill Gunston, the prolific writer on aircraft and aero-engines, wrote in his book *Rolls-Royce: Aero Engines*:

Under Hives the progress of the engine was nothing short of brilliant. The 'Old Man's' instructions were followed meticulously and nothing was left to chance. Speed was increased almost immediately to 1800 rpm, and by August 1915 to 2000 rpm, the maximum brake horsepower then reading 300.

The Eagle first flew in the Handley Page bomber, the 0/100. Other users included its derivative, the Handley Page heavy night bomber, the 0/400; the Airco DH4 day bombers; the Felixstowe series of large flying boats, the F.2 and F.3; and the Fairey Campania float seaplanes. It also powered the Fairey IIIF when the Portuguese Navy crossed the South Atlantic from Lisbon to

Brazil, as well as the Vickers Vimys in which Alcock and Brown crossed the North Atlantic, Ross and Keith Smith flew to Australia, and van Rynevett and Quintin Brand flew to Cape Town. In total, about 50 different aeroplane and airship types used the Eagle, and the official number of engines manufactured was 4,681.

After the Eagle came the Hawk, Falcon and Condor. Launched as a trainer, the Hawk was the first choice of the Royal Naval Air Service to power its Blimps, which were used to patrol coastal waters and protect convoys from U-boat attack. The Falcon was effectively a smaller Eagle and was designed primarily for fighter applications, of which the most famous was the Bristol Fighter. The Condor, the last and largest of Royce's first generation of aero-engines, was intended for long-range bombers, but the Armistice was signed in November 1918 before they were ready for action.

After the First World War, Rolls-Royce had to decide whether it should concentrate on manufacturing aero-engines or return to cars. The prospects for aero-engines were bleak. The view of the British Government was that Britain would not be involved in another major war for at least ten years, and it ran down its armed forces accordingly. Civil aviation had barely begun, and Rolls-Royce was therefore left with no choice. It should return to its roots – the manufacture of luxury cars. Not that it had anything to fear; its reputation had been enhanced, not only by the performance of its aero-engines, but also by the performance of its cars used in theatres of war.

The French War Minister, Alexandre Millerand, already owned a Rolls-Royce when war broke out. His driver wrote to the company after the war:

I travelled with him 35,000 kilometres in three months, all over France but principally at the front. Both our two cars travelled without a single breakdown and always behaved perfectly.

Lawrence of Arabia wrote:

A Rolls in the desert was above rubies … Great was Rolls and great was Royce! They were worth hundreds of men to us in those deserts.

The immediate aftermath of the war produced a boom, but this was very quickly followed by a slump, and in May 1921 the price of the Silver Ghost chassis was reduced to clear stocks. Meanwhile, Royce, ever mindful of economic necessities, designed a smaller car, the Twenty, which was launched in 1922. Not everyone, even with the company, approved of this car, some referring to it as 'Sweet Lavinia, the gutless wonder'. However, Sir Max Pemberton, Royce's biographer, was full of praise:

It is with very real pleasure that I write to you about the remarkable performance of the 'Twenty' ... This car has accomplished 100,000 miles, it has done so without any road stop whatsoever and the engine is as quiet as the day it left your factory.

The next two cars to come from Royce were the new Phantom (called the Phantom I) launched in 1925, and the Phantom II, introduced in 1929. As these cars were being developed, Rolls-Royce was also manufacturing cars in the USA, having set up a plant in Springfield, Massachusetts, in 1920. The plant suffered a number of handicaps, most notably the slowness of securing decisions from the UK. Nevertheless it spawned some of the most elegant coachwork seen on Rolls-Royces between the wars. It was already struggling to make money in the boom years of the American economy in the 1920s. When this boom ended abruptly with the Wall Street Crash at the end of 1929, the Springfield plant was closed down.

The Rolls-Royce operation in the USA was not the only casualty of the depression that hit the world at the beginning of the 1930s. Bentley, the manufacturer of glorious, high-performance cars, suffered severe financial difficulties and was bought by Rolls-Royce. The two greatest names in luxury motor cars were now joined and faced the economic uncertainties of the 1930s together. As they did so, the irreplaceable Henry Royce, by this time made a baronet for his contribution to Britain winning the Schneider Trophy in 1929, died at his home in West Wittering. Could Rolls-Royce go forward without its mentor? After all, as Ivan Evernden, who worked with Royce in the 1920s and continued to serve Rolls-Royce until the early 1960s, said:

Henry Royce ruled the lives of the people around him, claimed their body and soul, even when they were asleep.

Fortunately, there were others of great ability to carry on the good work: Albert Elliott, Ernest (later Lord) Hives, Bernard Day, R.W. Harvey-Bailey, Maurice Olley, Lt. Col. Timothy Barrington, Arthur Rowledge, Arthur Robotham, Cyril Lovesey, Ray Dorey, Arthur Rubbra, Jimmy Ellor and many more. Arthur Sidgreaves held the ship steady as managing director, and there was Hives, known to all as Hs, who took over as general manager in 1936. He took the company by the scruff of its neck and prepared it for what would be a fight not only for its own survival but also the survival of Britain itself. He reorganised Rolls-Royce completely and focused on two objectives: to prepare for war, and to rationalise the range of cars and take cost out of their manufacture.

Though concentrating on car production in the 1920s, Rolls-Royce had not abandoned aero-engine development and production altogether, and in 1928 the Air Ministry ordered the company to develop an engine, to power the Supermarine S6 designed by Reginald Mitchell, that would enable Britain to retain the Schneider Trophy – the world's most prestigious air contest devised by the Frenchman Jacques Schneider just before the First World War. Royce took Rolls-Royce's Buzzard, still called the 'H' engine and, with limited time available, souped it up to create the 'Racing H', ultimately called the 'R' engine. The S6, fitted with Rolls-Royce's 'R' engine, won the Trophy in 1929. Further work was done on the engine and airframe, and Britain won again in 1931. This development work proved vital in preparing both aircraft and engine designs for the fighters that were going to be needed as world war loomed on the horizon.

Both the Government and the Air Ministry had to be convinced of the growing threat from Nazi Germany once Adolf Hitler had come to power. Finally, in 1934, Sir Robert McLean, the chairman of Vickers, after unfruitful discussions with the Air Ministry, decided with Arthur Sidgreaves, the managing director of Rolls-Royce, to develop what he called 'a real killer fighter'. Reginald Mitchell would design the aeroplane, and Rolls-Royce would develop the engine. The aeroplane became the Spitfire; the engine became the Merlin. At the same time as these two new weapons of war were being developed, the Hawker Hurricane was also being designed by Sydney (later Sir Sydney) Camm and manufactured by the Hawker Engineering Company.

By 1936, the danger from Germany's rearmament programme was apparent to almost everyone, and the Air Ministry placed orders for Hurricanes and subsequently Spitfires, both to be powered by Rolls-Royce Merlins. Fortunately, in Hives Rolls-Royce possessed a man of exceptional organising ability, and he set about gearing up not only the Derby factory but also shadow factories at Crewe and Glasgow. Even so, it was a miracle that there were enough Hurricanes, Spitfires and Merlins to power them ready by the summer of 1940 when Hitler tried to gain mastery of the skies over south-east England in preparation for an invasion. We shall never know whether Prime Minister Neville Chamberlain had been playing for vital time when he met Hitler at Munich in September 1938, or whether he really thought he had bought 'peace for our time'. The fact remains that the RAF only just beat off the Luftwaffe in what became known as the Battle of Britain in August and September 1940, and it was thanks to the skill and courage of the pilots, the 'Few', and the performance of the Spitfire and Hurricane fighters powered by Rolls-Royce Merlin engines.

Once that hectic scare had passed and Hitler had turned his attention to the invasion of the Soviet Union, the war spread throughout the world – the Middle East, the Far East and Africa as well as Europe. The Merlin powered not only Spitfires and Hurricanes in all these theatres but also the Lancaster bomber, the Mosquito fighter-bomber and the North American P-51

Mustang. When the Mustang first appeared in Britain, having been bought by the British Purchasing Commission in the USA, it was powered by the V-1710 manufactured by the Allison Engine Company. However, when Ronnie Harker, Rolls-Royce's liaison pilot, tested it at Duxford, Cambridgeshire, in 1942, he recommended it be fitted with the Merlin engine. He wrote later:

I asked Witold Challier, our Polish performance expert, to estimate what the Mustang would do when fitted with a Merlin 61. He reported that there would be a greatly improved rate of climb and an increase of some 40 mph in top speed at 25,000 feet and above. The estimate, together with the fact that her tank capacity would give her longer range, meant that the Mustang, when fitted with the Merlin, would be superior to any other fighter at the time.

Harker's recommendation was taken up by both the RAF and USAAF, and the production of Merlin engines was increased yet again. The engine was produced not only at Rolls-Royce's Derby factory (32,377 engines) but also at the shadow factories in Crewe (26,065) and Glasgow (23,647), as well as at the Ford Motor Company's factory in Manchester (30,428) and in Detroit by the Packard Company (55,523).

While these 168,040 piston aero-engines were being manufactured, Rolls-Royce had also made sure it was involved in the new development in aircraft propulsion, the jet engine.

In the late 1920s, two men, both working for the British Government, independently put forward ideas for propulsion by a means different from the reciprocating engine. Dr A.A. Griffith, of the Royal Aircraft Establishment's Engines Experimental Department, published a paper, 'An Aerodynamic Theory of Turbine Design', which proposed the use of a single-shaft turbine engine with multi-stage axial compressor as a means of driving a propeller through a reduction gear. The paper and its supporting test work were reviewed by the Engines sub-committee of the Aeronautical Research Committee in April 1930 and concluded that:

At the present state of knowledge the superiority of the gas turbine over the reciprocating engine cannot be predicted.

As a result, the RAE did not fund further investigation into this development until 1936.

Meanwhile, in 1928, a young RAF officer, Frank (later Sir Frank) Whittle, had also written a paper, 'Future Developments in Aircraft Design'. He envisaged aircraft flying at speeds of 500 mph at a time when fighters of the RAF could not reach 200 mph. At this point, he was not sure of the method of propulsion, although he was already considering rockets and gas turbines driving propellers. A year later, in October 1929, he suddenly realised that the gas turbine could be substituted for the piston engine because the exhaust would propel the aircraft, making the propeller redundant.

The story of the early 1930s was one of frustration for Whittle, but in 1935 he was approached by an old RAF Cranwell colleague, Rolf Dudley Williams, who – in conjunction with another former RAF pilot, J.C.B. Tinling – wanted to finance the development of Whittle's idea. Between them, they raised the money to form Power Jets Ltd., and Whittle was able to commence development.

Hives stepped into the development of the jet engine, first by recruiting A.A. Griffith so that he could continue work on his axial-compressor units and second by negotiating with Spencer Wilks, the managing director of Rover, who was helping Whittle produce his first engines. At a dinner at the Swan and Royal in Clitheroe in December 1942, Hives said to Wilks:

Why are you playing round with the jet engine? It's not your business, you grub about on the ground. I'll tell you what I'll do. You give this jet job, and I'll give you our tank engine factory in Nottingham.

That was it. The deal was done. Rolls-Royce was properly in the gas-turbine business, and within fifteen months the first Meteor aircraft, powered by Rolls-Royce Wellands (the production version of Whittle's W.2B engine), were delivered to the RAF. Within a few weeks, the aircraft were transferred to 616 Squadron at Manston, and they began operations against Germany's V.1 flying bombs on 27 July 1944. However, the war ended before the new jet aircraft saw much action. Nevertheless, the gas turbine was clearly the engine of the future, and, once the War was over, Rolls-Royce was soon keen to exploit it by finding customers throughout the world, most especially in the USA. The company was helped initially by Philip Taylor, the former chief engineer of Curtiss-Wright, who introduced Rolls-Royce both to the US Navy and to the US aero-engine manufacturer Pratt & Whitney.

A Rolls-Royce Derwent-powered Gloster Meteor had set a new air-speed record of 615.81 mph in September 1946, and Hives knew he had a world-beating product to sell. Pratt & Whitney, although they had plans to be abreast, or even ahead, of other gas-turbine manufacturers by 1950, saw the taking of a licence for Rolls-Royce's Nene engine as a useful stop-gap and signed an agreement in May 1947. They called the Nene the J42 Turbo Wasp and produced 1,137 of them under licence, together with 4,021 of the larger Tay, the J48, also known as the Turbo Wasp, before relying on their own developments and becoming a competitor to Rolls-Royce, which they have remained ever since. Rolls-Royce continued to try to secure a long-term future in the USA by signing a ten-year licensing agreement with Westinghouse. This yielded little except useful minimum royalty payments.

In the meantime, Rolls-Royce's development of new gas turbines continued apace. The first new engine, aimed at the burgeoning civil market, was the Dart, a turboprop engine. Thanks to the encouragement of George (late Sir George) Edwards, at that time manager and chief engineer of the Aircraft Division of Vickers, it was chosen to power Vickers' new passenger airliner, the Vickers Viscount. The Viscount was a huge success, due, in part, to the Rolls-Royce Dart engines. In August 1953, as the orders rolled in for the Viscount, *The Times* wrote:

A third of BEA's total network – about 5,000 miles of unduplicated routes – is now being flown by Viscounts ... Since it was first introduced on BEA's services on April 18 last the Discovery class Viscount 701, with its smoothness, quietness and relatively high speed, has proved not only popular with passengers but profitable for the operators ... Peter [now Sir Peter] Masefield (Chief Executive of BEA) praised the reliability of the airline's Rolls-Royce Dart engines, which, he said, had been 'remarkably free of troubles'.

While the Dart was winning plaudits all over the world, Rolls-Royce developed its first A.A. Griffith-inspired axial-compressor engine, the Avon. Development began during the war, but there were considerable teething problems, and it was not until 1948 that it made its first appearance at the Farnborough Air Show. The following year, it stole the show when a Gloster Meteor, powered by two Avons, displayed a climbing power unmatched by anything else from the UK or from the USA – or even from the Soviet Union, for that matter. From 1950 onwards, the Avon was powering the country's most important military aircraft, the English Electric Canberra bomber, the Vickers Valiant bomber and the Hunter and Swift fighters. On the civil front, de Havilland ordered the Avon for its second series of Comets.

Joe Sutter, who became chief designer at Boeing and who is best remembered for his work in developing the 747, said of the Comet:

Boeing came to look at the Comet at Farnborough. It made such a big impression [that] they decided the civil business was the place to be. We built the 367-8Q prototype or Dash-80 where I was in charge of the aerodynamics. The Dash-80 became the 707.

By the time the Comet was re-launched, after its disastrous crashes in the Mediterranean in 1954, the Boeing 707 had captured the market for turbojet-powered airliners. The success of the 707 was symptomatic of a very difficult decade for the British and, indeed, the European aircraft industry as it struggled to compete with its mighty and rapidly growing equivalent in the USA. As we saw in Chapter Six, the European industry was fragmented. Jean

Pierson, Managing Director of Airbus Industrie from 1985 to 1998, summed it up:

From the point of technology, the Europeans were capable, and comparable with the United States. But the Europeans competed against each other and fragmented the market in Europe.

In the early 1960s, Europe was offering no fewer than ten different turbine-powered airliners, of which the leading three were the French Caravelle, and the British Trident and BAC 111. Total sales of these aircraft were 625 – only enough for one to break even.

It was no better on the military front. The British economy struggled to adapt to the post-war world, and defence budgets were constantly being slashed. As a result, first, the military aircraft industry was decimated by the decision laid out in Duncan Sandys' White Paper of 1957, which said that, in future, Britain's defence would depend on thermonuclear power. Manned aircraft were to be phased out and replaced with missiles, or 'rockets' as Sandys called them. Second, the one-strike aircraft that was to be built to replace the V-Force bombers – the Victor, Vulcan and Valiant – the TSR2, was cancelled by the Labour Government in 1965.

Faced with the virtual collapse of the indigenous civil-airframe manufacturing industry, and vacillation and cutbacks in the defence industry, Rolls-Royce made the courageous decision to risk all on a new, revolutionary engine that would establish the company in the large US market and would therefore maintain Rolls-Royce's place as one of the world's leading aero-engine makers.

In May 1963, Rolls-Royce's leading engineer, Adrian Lombard, who had come to the firm when Hives took over Rover's involvement with Whittle's engine at Barnoldswick during the war, presented a case to the Rolls-Royce Board that he should develop an engine that would replace Rolls-Royce's first bypass engine, the Conway. The real innovation in this engine, which became the RB 211, was its three-shaft design. The Board had little choice but to sanction the development, as forecasts were showing that the future for aero-engines in the civil market would be for engines up to 50,000 lb thrust and that most of them would be sold in the USA. Rolls-Royce did not have such an engine, and without one it could not hope to stay in serious competition with Pratt & Whitney and General Electric.

The history of the 1960s for Rolls-Royce was one of great courage and dedicated hard work, both in development and marketing. Initially, both the new wide-bodied aircraft being designed by the newly formed Airbus Industrie and the tri-jet being designed by Lockheed in the USA were targeted by Rolls-Royce for its new three-shaft engine. The big push came on the RB 211 for the Lockheed L.1011, called the TriStar. The engine was a high-bypass engine and included new features not found on any previous Rolls-Royce engine. The first was the three-shaft concept, the second the extensive use of composite materials such as 'Hyfil', and the third the use of an annular combustion chamber in a high-pressure engine.

It had extremely ambitious design objectives compared with the Conway. It aimed to reduce fuel consumption by 20 to 25 per cent with low installed drag and to reduce engine noise at sideline, flyover and approach conditions by 10 to 15 PNdB. The aim was to devise a 'smokeless' engine and minimise unburnt hydrocarbons, carbon monoxide and oxides of nitrogen, and to evolve a robust mechanical arrangement enabling high pressures and blade speeds, operating in a high-temperature environment. Most important, the aim was to provide the potential for thrust growth and achieve a substantial reduction in specific weight, while achieving good flight response, control and handling characteristics, as well as tolerance to intake-flow distortion. These ambitious targets were to be achieved with an engine that was easy to build and strip – a requirement that would make the engine cheaper as it would have fewer parts – yet one that would not compromise on reliability or safety.

While the engineers in Derby, initially led by Adrian Lombard (who tragic-ally died of a heart attack in 1967), worked to turn this ambitious design concept into reality, David (later Sir David) Huddie led the sales team in the USA that worked tirelessly to convince Lockheed that this was the engine for their new TriStar. The competition from General Electric was severe. Not only did they reduce the price of the engine they were offering, they also played the balance-of-payments and US-employment cards. In spite of these handicaps, Rolls-Royce won. In March 1968, it secured the commitment from Lockheed, who in turn secured the necessary orders from Trans World Airlines (44 aircraft), Eastern Airlines (50) and the British company Air Holdings (50). Lockheed ordered from Rolls-Royce 150 ship sets of three engines each.

The *Financial Times* recorded the enormous sales effort and meticulous attention to detail that had secured the order:

Beginning in September 1966, Rolls-Royce personnel began a round of 230 journeys across the Atlantic which were to cost more than £80,000 in air fares and expenses alone. At any one time there were 20 members of Rolls visiting the US as part of the sales drive – the undramatic process of talking not just to top men, but talking to men from the grass roots as well, right round the country. [This is what Phil Gilbert, Rolls-Royce's lawyer and adviser in the USA since 1946, had advocated, and Rolls-Royce carried out his advice.]

One of the results of Rolls-Royce's 'cold analysis of past failures' [Huddie's words] was to make contact with technicians and engineers at every level of decision making, and to anticipate their problems. Each aircraft manufacturer and each of a dozen or so interested airlines were bombarded with specifications for the RB.211, which made a pile over two feet high. Each document was bound in black with the individual company's name embossed in gold. [The present Chairman, Sir Ralph Robins, ran a Special Project group precisely to co-ordinate this activity. David Huddie said later, 'When I was away, inter-departmental affairs didn't get done, so I put Ralph on to it and boy, did he do it well!']

Rolls-Royce had gambled and won, though it had been forced to abandon its efforts to supply the engine for the new Airbus A300. However, the engine now had to be produced, and it had to be delivered to a very tight timetable. Unfortunately, it did not make it. Huddie would say later:

I'm not blaming anyone else ... We had promised a bit more than we could perform. Things were not deplorable. Flight engines were four months late. Four months is four months but it is not deplorable. The deplorable thing was the cost ... The accountants never got cash-flow into our heads.

This attempt to break into the all-important US market ended, in the short term, in tragedy. On 4 February 1971, Rupert Nicholson of Peat Marwick Mitchell & Co. was appointed receiver of Rolls-Royce. Everyone at Rolls-Royce was stunned; indeed, the whole country was stunned. How could Rolls-Royce, our saviour only 30 years ago, go bust? Maybe the whole country's gone bust.

Fortunately, some people kept their heads, most notably the receiver Rupert Nicholson, who quickly sorted out what was necessary to keep the company going, and Dan Haughton, the President of Lockheed, who worked with the Rolls-Royce engineers to ensure that the final glitches in the RB 211 engine were solved and that they were produced in time to power his new TriStars.

The 1970s was a decade of steady recovery under the flamboyant and morale-raising chairmanship of the banker, Sir Kenneth (now Lord) Keith. The RB 211s were indeed produced and shipped to Lockheed, the Rolls-Royce engines already in service throughout the world, especially in the armed forces of many countries, continued to be serviced, and new orders were gradually secured again. The Rolls-Royce Motor Car Division, which had operated from Crewe since the immediate post-war years, and the Rolls-Royce Oil Engine Division at Shrewsbury were floated separately on to the stock market by the Government.

If there were sixteen years in twentieth-century Britain when a company had to be under the control of the Government, 1971 to 1987 was as good a

TOP: In July 1995, the US Department of Defense selected the Teledyne Ryan Aeronautical for Phase Two of the Global Hawk high-altitude-endurance unmanned aerial vehicle (UAV) programme. Rolls-Royce Allison modified its AE 3007 to power the UAV to altitudes of 65,000 feet. In 2001, the Global Hawk became the first unmanned aircraft to depart from one continent under its own power and land on another.

BOTTOM: Charles Coltman has worked throughout the 1990s and into the new millennium on Rolls-Royce's future strategy.

ABOVE AND OPPOSITE: There was some doubt about whether there was a future for a VLA (Very Large Aircraft), though not at Airbus, which pressed ahead with its A3XX. The early buyers – Singapore Airlines, Qantas, Virgin Atlantic and Lufthansa – all ordered the A380, as it was named, and specified Rolls-Royce's Trent 900 engine.

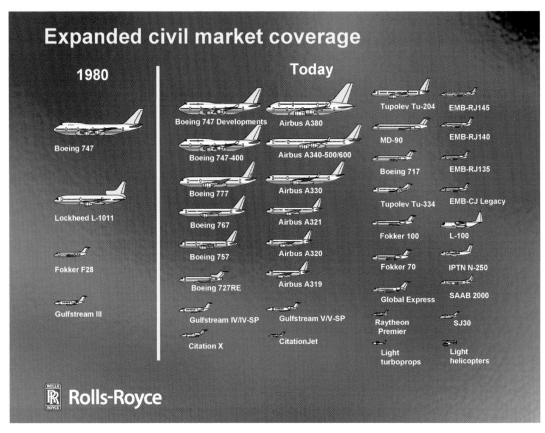

ABOVE AND OPPOSITE: The progress that Rolls-Royce made in this
twenty-year period, both in terms of market share and
presence on the world's leading aircraft, is well illustrated in
these two charts.

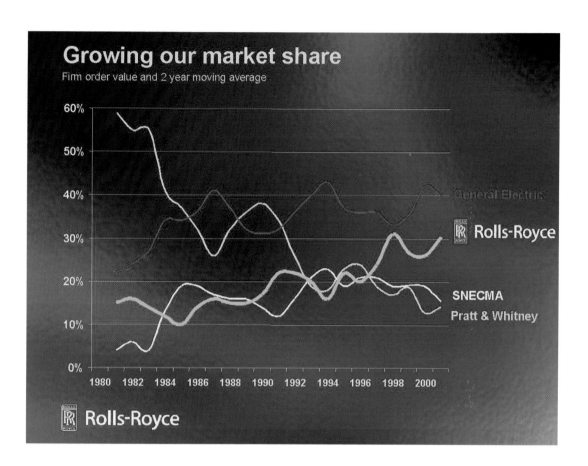

Seen here with two Rolls-Royce graduates at the Farnborough Air Show,
John Rose was appointed Chief Executive of Rolls-Royce in 1996
and, working alongside the Chairman, has positioned Rolls-Royce for the
twenty-first century.

OPPOSITE TOP: Rolls-Royce Finance Director Paul Heiden at the opening of
the new cell dedicated to the production of complex cores for the
industrial gas-turbine market at Ross Catherall (originally within the
Vickers group and now a subsidiary of Rolls-Royce).

OPPOSITE BOTTOM: John Cheffins, currently Rolls-Royce Chief Operating
Officer, with Dr Cheong Choong Kong, the present Chairman of
Singapore Airlines, in front of a Trent 800 – the engine that powers SIA's
Boeing 777s.

To the great regret of everyone at Rolls-Royce, Sir Ralph Robins is to
retire before the AGM in 2003. This book is a testimony to his
remarkable achievements in the last fifteen years, when he has been,
first, Managing Director and then, from 1992, Chairman. Compare the
Rolls-Royce of 1987 with the Rolls-Royce of 2002 and you will
see that he stands alongside those other great men of Rolls-Royce
– Sir Henry Royce, the Hon. C.S. Rolls, Claude Johnson and
Lord Hives – in establishing Rolls-Royce as *the* great British
engineering company.

choice as any. The country went through probably its worst patch in that century, bedevilled by weak management and truculent trades unions. By the time Margaret Thatcher came to power in May 1979, many were fearing that the country would not only continue to decline relatively, compared with its overseas competitors, but was about to decline in absolute terms as well.

It is fashionable now to deride Margaret Thatcher, though it is noticeable that *Labour* Prime Minister Tony Blair speaks highly of her achievements. Most people in the wealth-*creating* part of the economy look on her as the saviour of a country that in their view was 'going to the dogs'. Hugo Young, a *Guardian* journalist, who was certainly not one of her most fervent admirers, wrote in his book *One of Us*:

She brought to that post [Leader of the Conservative Party] no great technical expertise, but a handful of unshakeable economic principles. They were not particularly original purposes. But they were commitments made with the fire of the zealot.

She herself, faced with lukewarm support from her Cabinet colleagues, said:

If you're going to do the things you want to do – and I'm only in politics to do things – you've got to have a togetherness and a unity in your cabinet. There are two ways of making a cabinet. One way is to have in it people who represent all the different viewpoints within the party, within the broad philosophy. The other way is to have in it only people who go in the direction in which every instinct tells me we have to go. Clearly, steadily, firmly, with resolution. We've got to go in an agreed and clear direction.

One of the clear directions was that whole sections of the economy that were under Government control – British Gas, British Telecom, British Airways, British Petroleum – were sold to the public. Henceforth, boards would have to answer to shareholders, not civil servants, and would have to make profits. Rolls-Royce was deemed ripe for this privatisation, and the company itself welcomed it with open arms when the day arrived in April 1987.

A FAMILY OF ENGINES

As Rolls-Royce faced the future as a 'public' company, it needed, as after both wars and in the 1960s, to make some key strategic decisions. Compared with Pratt & Whitney, which was part of the large US corporation United Technologies Corporation Inc., and the aero-engine division of the vast General Electric, it was a small company. Could it compete? And if it was going to try, should it be with a limited number of engines or with a whole range?

There was no question about whether it was going to try to compete. It had already rejected the idea of being a subcontractor to General Electric on large engines, and it was now going to develop one of its own. Nevertheless, it had to make two fundamental decisions. Should the engine be brand new or a derivative, and should it be three-shaft or two-?

The decisions were quickly made. The engine should be a derivative and it should retain the benefits of being three-shaft. As for the big strategic decision on whether to have a whole range of engines, this conundrum was solved by the development of its new engine, which it called the Trent, into a family of engines based on one core.

The advantages of the derivative and three-shaft concept were so great that there was little debate. As Mike Howse, current Director of Engineering and Technology at Rolls-Royce, said:

The three-shaft engine concept comprises a low-pressure system and a gas generator made up of an intermediate (IP) and high-pressure (HP) system. These three systems can then be individually designed to run at their optimum aerodynamic loading which gives high efficiency and a low number of compressor and turbine stages. This was one of the design intents when the concept was formulated in the 1960s ... The three-shaft design is shorter, more rigid and lighter than the two-shaft equivalent. It performs its duties with fewer stages, fewer aerofoils, fewer total components, giving low unit cost.

Having made the decision to develop the Trent family, Rolls-Royce had to face up to the cost of the investment necessary. This led the company to make another investment, which came to look increasingly suspect. On 10 April 1989, Sir Francis Tombs announced that Rolls-Royce had acquired the engineering company based in the north-east, NEI. There were two major benefits from Tombs's point of view. NEI was not in the aero-engine business, and it would therefore provide some balance to that business, long recognised as cyclical. (Most capital plant businesses are cyclical, so it was to be hoped that NEI would be on a different cycle from Rolls-Royce.) The second benefit was cash flow and profits. It was hoped that NEI's net cash flow would be positive and its profits stable while Rolls-Royce was investing heavily in the development of its new large engine, the Trent.

In the short term, these benefits did accrue to the combined group, and the recession of the early 1990s, compounded by the reduction in military engine business following the ending of the Cold War, made the cash and profits even more important as Rolls-Royce's aero-engine business suffered. However, as the recession lifted, it became clear that the prospects for growth at NEI were not comparable to those of the aero-engine divisions. NEI had not invested sufficiently in the 1980s, and its market share in most of its businesses was so small that it was a price follower, rather than a price leader. For example, in steam turbines its market share was less than 1 per cent, and prices were falling at 10 to 15 per cent per year due to the increasing globalisation of such giants as ABB, GEC-Alsthom, Siemens, General Electric, Mitsubishi, Toshiba and Hitachi. Rolls-Royce gradually sold most of the constituents of NEI, including the once mighty and innovative Reyrolle-Parsons. Sir Ralph Robins, the Rolls-Royce Chairman, said:

We will focus on sectors where we are a major player in the world, which we were not in large steam turbines.

Thanks to the investment in the Trent engine, by the mid-1990s Rolls-Royce certainly was a major world player in the aero-engine business. By then it had developed the Trent 600, which was going to be launched by Air Europe on the McDonnell Douglas MD-11, the Trent 700, aimed at the Airbus A330, the Trent 800, aimed at the Boeing 777, and the Trent 500, aimed at the Airbus A340-500/600. There were two early setbacks. The launch customer for the MD-11 and the Trent 600, Air Europe, went into liquidation. This may have been a blessing in disguise as Rolls-Royce would be the first to admit that the engine was still suffering from a number of glitches. More serious was the decision in August 1991 by Rolls-Royce's traditionally loyal customer, British Airways, to power its new Boeing 777s with General Electric's GE90 engines.

The consequences of this decision were potentially serious as others, most notably All Nippon Airways, followed BA's lead and rejected the Trent. The Chairman remained calm, saying:

We must keep our nerve. The BA decision was a big disappointment but not a killer. You can't read the whole market on two or three early 777 decisions.

He was right. Just a month later, Thai Airways International specified the Trent 800 for their 777s, and in December so did Emirates. In April 1992, Cathay Pacific also specified the Trent for its order for 777s. This brought Rolls-Royce's share on the 777 up to 28 per cent. This was all very encouraging, but the Trent 800 order which really set the pulses racing was the one from Singapore Airlines in December 1995. SIA ordered no fewer than 77 Boeing 777s: 34 firm and 43 options, with up to 157 engines.

This order was extremely significant, as big a breakthrough as BA's decision to buy GE had been a setback in 1991. It prompted Robins to say:

SIA is a benchmark airline. Its decision will have an impact everywhere.

He was right again. Malaysian Airlines followed suit in January 1996, Singapore

Aircraft Leasing Enterprise the following month, and in 1997 the leading US airlines, Delta and American, also specified the Trent for their 777s. When British Airways, which had experienced some problems with the GE90, also specified the Trent for their next tranche of 777s, a City analyst was able to write:

The deal is a major victory for Rolls. Its defeat at the hands of GE … always looked a strange decision by BA and now all the main members of the Oneworld alliance will have Rolls-powered 777s. Rolls is on course to take 50 per cent of the big-engine market, making it the market leader.

Adding to its strength was the success it was also enjoying with the Trent 700 where it was securing orders on the Airbus 330. Furthermore, it won a very significant advantage with Airbus when the European airframe manufacturers made Rolls-Royce's new Trent 500 the only engine available on its new A340-500 and -600 aircraft. At the Paris Air Show in June 1997, Airbus announced that it had selected the Trent 500; by early September, it announced its first firm orders for the aircraft, and by the end of that month had secured orders for 100 aircraft, prompting Rolls-Royce Chief Executive, John Rose, to say:

This is the strongest launch we have ever had for a new engine programme. It's tremendous news for the Trent family.

The new extension to the Trent family was the Trent 900, which was developed to power the new 'Very Large Aircraft', the A3XX, planned by Airbus. By the end of 2000, Airbus had received enough orders to launch the programme and to call the aircraft the A380. Initially, Rolls-Royce secured all the engine orders with the Trent 900, though the engine alliance with GE and Pratt & Whitney began to catch up in 2001. In May 2002, Rolls-Royce were delighted to secure a commitment to the Trent on the fifteen A380s ordered by the large and prestigious Lufthansa, traditionally a GE customer.

By 2002, the wisdom of developing the Trent 'family' of engines had become fully apparent. The Trent 800 had the same HP system and IP turbine as the Trent 700, though it had an increased-capacity IP compressor and a five-stage LP turbine. The Trent 500 had the same 97.5-inch fan diameter as the Trent 700 and a reduced-flow core derived from the Trent 800. For airlines considering Airbus's A340, the attraction of the Trent 500 was Rolls-Royce's ability to scale proven designs from existing Trent family members while incorporating the latest technology where appropriate. The Trent 900 continued the theme. It used the same 110-inch-diameter fan, structure, systems and accessories as the Trent 800, with scaled-down IP and HP compressors, a new five-stage LP turbine and reduced-loading IP and HP turbines.

While Rolls-Royce was developing its family of Trent engines in the 50,000 lb thrust and upwards range, it made three decisive moves to increase its strength in the lower thrust area. It developed, in conjunction with Pratt & Whitney of the USA, Fiat Avio of Italy, MTU of Germany and the Japanese Aero Engines Corporation, a 22,000-to-33,000 lb-thrust engine, the V-2500. After some serious problems in the development stage, the engine has won some very large orders to power the A319, A320 and A321. At the beginning of the 1990s, Rolls-Royce teamed up with BMW to develop a series of engines in the 14,000 to 23,000 lb range, effectively a successor to the Tay, and was extremely successful in winning orders to power the Gulfstream V, the Bombardier Global Express and the Boeing 717.

Three years later, Rolls-Royce bought the US engine company Allison, with whom it had enjoyed happy relations for many years. This was a strategically brilliant acquisition, giving Rolls-Royce not only a significant presence in the USA, increasingly important in the US defence market, but also a strong position with Allison's A3007 engine in the fast-growing regional airliner market. It also brought it a large installed-engine market, most notably through the long-running Model 250 helicopter engine.

On the military-engine front, Rolls-Royce had decided to go down the collaboration route. It continued to supply and service the Adour, its collaborative engine with Turbomeca, and the RB 199, its collaborative engine with MTU. On helicopter engines, it worked with Turbomeca on the RTM322, and with Turbomeca and MTU on the MTR390. In the USA, it worked with Honeywell on the T800. On the two new fighters, Eurofighter and the Joint Strike Fighter, it worked with MTU, Fiat and ITP on the former, and Pratt & Whitney and GE on the latter.

'"GO HOME, MR WELCH" IS A PERFECT TITLE'

As Rolls-Royce moved into the new millennium, delighted with the growing success of its Trent family of engines and increasingly convinced that they were right with their strategy of spreading their coverage of the gas-turbine field by the purchase of Allison and Vickers, a further threat to their competitive position appeared out of the blue in the form of a bid from General Electric for Honeywell.

The bid had been prompted by an almost agreed merger between Honeywell and the owner of Pratt & Whitney, United Technologies. Jack Welch had heard of the impending merger from a journalist and immediately appreciated its significance. He wrote in his autobiography:

We had looked at Honeywell earlier in the year [2000]. I thought it might be a good fit with GE. Honeywell's business was complementary to our own in three key areas – aircraft engines, industrial systems and plastics [and avionics, though Welch does not say so for reasons we shall see].

At the product level, there was no direct overlap. Honeywell, for example, is a leader in the small business jet engine field. GE is the leader in large jet engines.

GE decided it could not stand by and allow United Technologies to take Honeywell, and it made an offer that valued Honeywell at $45 billion – $5 billion more than UTC's offer. GE realised, especially in view of the merger between Honeywell and Allied Signal a year earlier, that the competition authorities might insist on some divestments, perhaps in the helicopter-engine area, but it did not expect any real difficulties either in the USA or in Europe.

Although the proposed deal may not have had too many product overlaps, it would give GE a dominant position in offering engines, particularly large engines, to the airlines of the world. Not only would it be able to offer its GE90 engine as well as the CFM56 it manufactured with SNECMA, it would also be able to offer the avionics of Honeywell. Combined, this could add up to 55 per cent of the net present value of an aircraft and its support. This would mean that GE would be in a position to dictate what aircraft were made in the future. On top of this, GE's finance arm, GECAS, was not only a finan-cier of aircraft and aero-engine purchases, it bought aircraft in its own right.

Flight International had no doubts about the scope of the engine range if the deal went through:

GE appears to have found the perfect match for its powerplant family. Honeywell's small and medium-thrust business and regional engines range from the 3,500 lb (15 kN)-thrust TFE731 to the new AS900 at 9,000 lb. GE's engine line starts with the hugely successful CF34 at 8,700 lb and extends all the way to the mighty GE90-115, at 115,000 lb the most powerful jet engine ever developed. There are similar cosy fits on the turboshaft side between Honeywell's TPE331 and T800 and GE's CT7/T700 engines. Even in the military arena, Honeywell's F124 engine sits in a thrust niche below the bigger company's F404/414 and F110.

GE can therefore anticipate significant market penetration with its wide-ranging new engine family, which now matches the enormous breadth of the combined Pratt & Whitney Canada (P&WC) and P&W product range as well as that of Rolls-Royce.

A combined valuation at the share prices prevailing in early 2001 would capitalise GE and Honeywell at $100 billion against Rolls-Royce's $5–6 billion. The GE–Honeywell combination would be dominant in the aero-engine business, and a number of companies – Rolls-Royce, Thales, Pratt & Whitney, Litton Industries, Rockwell Collins and Luftfahrttechnik (subsidiary of Lufthansa) – made strong presentations to the European Commission.

Fortunately, such presentations from competitors are allowed in Europe, whereas in the USA the attitude of the Justice Department is that evidence from competitors should be ignored. The US practice has not always been thus. In 1975, the US Justice Department opposed, on anti-trust grounds, a joint venture between Rolls-Royce and Pratt & Whitney (Canada) to build an executive jet engine, the RB 401. Indeed, Welch proved to be correct in his assumption that he would have few problems with the US authorities. He wrote later:

We got some good news on May 2 when the US Justice Department approved the deal – after we had agreed to sell Honeywell's military helicopter engine business and open up our servicing business on small jet engines and auxiliary power units.

However, the reception in Europe was different. In Europe, an argument based on dominance of an industry can be considered even when that evidence is presented by competitors. The Commissioner, Mario Monti, advised by a merger team led by Enrique Gonzalez-Diaz, looked into ramifications very thoroughly and told GE that they wanted to study the 'range effect' of combining GE's and Honeywell's overall presence in the aircraft industry.

Realising that this was not going to be the pushover expected, GE began to offer concessions. Welch wrote:

I worked with the teams [of GE and Honeywell executives and advisers] until midnight to put together a mutually agreed submission that raised our offer [of divestments] threefold to $1.3 billion and included for the first time some critical avionics products.

This did not receive a favourable reaction from the Commission, and on 12 June GE increased their offer to $1.9 billion and, when a similar reaction was forthcoming, raised it again to $2.2 billion. However, at the final meeting with Monti and his team, which included Gonzalez-Diaz, Alexander Schaub (director-general of competition) and Götz Drauz (director of the merger task force), it was made clear that GE's final proposal was inadequate. For Monti and his colleagues, the fundamental problem remained that the GE offer did not dissociate GECAS from the rest of the GE product range. Welch was shocked and wrote later:

I took notes as Commissioner Monti suggested we divest one Honeywell business after another.

The divestitures he was suggesting added up to somewhere in the neighborhood of $5 billion to $6 billion and basically took any notion of a merger between GE and Honeywell off the table.

'Mr Monti, I'm shocked and stunned by these demands,' I said. 'There's no way I could consider this. If that's your position, I'll go home tonight. I've got a book to write.'

Across the table, Alexander Schaub, a heavyset, round-faced German, broke out laughing.

'That can be your last chapter, Mr Welch,' he said. '"Go Home, Mr Welch" is a perfect title.'

In spite of this rejection, GE and Honeywell did not give up. They under-stood the importance of the position of GECAS and were prepared to sell 19.9 per cent to one or more third-party investors of GE's choice and to have one independent director on the five-person GECAS board. However, in offering this, they wanted to reduce the $2.2-billion divestment of Honey-well business already suggested to $1.1 billion. This offer was put to Monti, who again rejected it.

In a final desperate attempt to save the deal, Mike Bonsignore, Honey-well's chief executive, asked GE to return to the $2.2-billion offer and to modify the GECAS proposal so that the European Commission would have to approve the minority investor and independent Board member. He also lowered the price GE would have to pay for Honeywell to 1.01 from 1.055 GE shares for each Honeywell share.

This was not acceptable to GE, never mind the Commission. Welch wrote later:

In short, in response to the commission's position, Honeywell was proposing all the previous divestments plus an onerous GECAS concept … It was unacceptable. I called the GE board, explained our position, and got its approval to turn down Honeywell's proposed revision of the merger agreement. This was not a hard decision. The commission had destroyed the strategic reasons for doing the deal.

As a finale, GE and Honeywell have appealed against the decision by the European Commission. At the very least, GE would like the removal of the word 'dominant' from the Commission's ruling.

'A BALANCED BUSINESS'

Meanwhile, Rolls-Royce was showing that it could cope with a slowing world economy. After its profit warning in August 2000, shareholders waited nervously for the report of Sir Ralph Robins and John Rose in August

2001. The strong growth of the world economy, most especially the USA, had ground to a halt in 2000, and air-passenger numbers were falling. Nevertheless, Robins and Rose were upbeat about Rolls-Royce's prospects. They expected to increase civil-engine deliveries to 1,400 in the year 2001. This was a remarkable increase on the 400 of 1996 and the 100 of the late 1980s. The company would not predict exactly how many engines it would deliver in 2002 but was confident of increasing its growth in earnings. The benefits of a higher installed base of engines were beginning to show through in higher sales and profits from the aftercare market.

That was Friday 24 August. Two weeks later, on 11 September 2001, at 9.00 a.m. Eastern Standard Time, a United Airlines airliner crashed into the top of one of the twin towers of the World Trade Center in New York. At first, many thought it was an accident. Indeed the initial announcement on BBC Radio 4 was almost light-hearted – 'An aircraft has flown into the World Trade Center, we'll let you know if there are any fatalities.' When, a few minutes later, an American Airlines aircraft flew into the other tower, the world realised this was no accident. Nor was this the end of the horror. In Washington, American Airlines flight 77 was deliberately crashed into the Pentagon, and it was reported that another airliner had crashed in Pennsylvania. It was surmised later that this aircraft might have been on its way to crash into the White House; however, passengers alerted on their mobile telephones to the other hijackings attacked their own hijackers, and in the ensuing mayhem the aircraft crashed. America was at war, but with whom and why?

All flights in the USA were grounded, and all flights on the way to the USA were diverted. The New York Stock Exchange did not open for the day, and remained shut until the following week. In the rest of the world, the value of all shares, but most especially those that had any connection with air travel, plunged. This was the greatest crisis the world had faced since Kennedy and Kruschev squared up to each other over Soviet nuclear missiles in Cuba in 1962. When both towers of the World Trade Center collapsed completely, the world watched CNN in horror, wondering how many people were buried in the rubble. Fifty thousand people worked in the two buildings, and there had been precious little time to escape. There were fears that as many as 20,000 had died. The figure was gradually revised down and down from the earliest estimates, and finally settled at just under 3,000. To put it in perspective, 30,000 had died in one day's battle in the American Civil War, and 2,400 were killed when Pearl Harbor was attacked in 1941. But the Civil War took place in the far-off 1860s, and Pearl Harbor was in faraway Hawaii. This was New York and Washington. As the *New Statesman* put it:

Throughout Tuesday, there was a slow, steady moan of stunned surprise that gradually metamorphosed into roars of outrage and anger … the nation began to realise that thousands of Americans lay dead beneath rubble in New York and Washington, and that (a) they were impotent to do anything about it, and (b) the weapons of people used so diabolically might just as well have been missiles launched from overseas. Thus the impossible had happened. America had become like other countries Americans watched on the news.

Millions and millions of words have been written on the horrific events of 11 September 2001, or '9-11' as the Americans call it to denote the month and the day (it is also appropriate because 911 is what you dial in an emergency in the USA). In this book, we must confine ourselves to the effects on Rolls-Royce, though there is little doubt that it was a seminal moment in the world's history and that everyone will remember what they were doing when they learnt of the attacks.

First, it had unquestionably altered the USA's perception of itself in relation to the rest of the world. It had assumed that its military might added to its geographical position – being separated from the rest of the world by two large oceans – made it invulnerable. A small number of patient and deter-mined martyrs had shattered that sense of security. Second, the belief that the USA was a force only for good in the world, or, as President Bush put it, 'the brightest beacon for freedom and opportunity in the world', and that it there-fore could not possibly be hated so much by some, was also shown to be false.

The benefit of 9-11, if there could be one, was the new realisation by the USA and its allies that they could not ignore the poverty and deprivation of many people throughout the world, however far away they were and however apparently powerless. At the end of the nineteenth century, the British aristocracy had realised that prosperity needed to be shared if they were not to finish up swinging from the nearest lamp-post. The Russian aristocracy had not appreciated this and had paid the price with their lives, or at the least been exiled. Now, the wealthy countries of the world needed to spread their wealth – or live with it constantly under threat.

Such policies were for the medium and long term. In the short term, the immediate task was to stabilise the finances of the world and to try to make sure the recession that was undoubtedly coming did not turn into a 1930s-style depression. Many countries were on the verge of a recession anyway; 9-11 would just serve to make it worse as investment decisions were put on hold. Led by Chairman of the Federal Reserve Bank, Alan Greenspan, interest rates were reduced in every industrialised country. In the airline industry, drastic cuts in manpower were carried out by airlines, airframe makers and aero-engine manufacturers. Dire forecasts were made. The International Air Transport Association estimated that the global-airline sector could have to face the effects of losing up to $10 billion because of lower revenues and the rise in maintenance and security costs. The obvious comparison to make was the Gulf War in 1991. However, most thought the effects would be worse.

The effect on Rolls-Royce, as on every business in the civil aerospace industry, was severe, and everyone realised it would be. Airlines, the airframe manufacturers and the component suppliers, including the aero-engine manufacturers, were all, almost without exception, forced to announce cutbacks in output and redundancies among their workforces.

Rolls-Royce could not escape, but, as Chief Executive John Rose pointed out, ten years earlier such an event would have had a much more severe impact on the company. He wrote:

The tragic events of September 11, 2001 have cast a shadow over the year. They affected individuals, industries, institutions and countries in many ways and generated greater levels of economic uncertainty than have been experienced in recent years.

The most profound impact on our company will be experienced in the civil aerospace sector where our airline customers felt the consequences immediately. They saw reductions in travel on a scale unprecedented in the last 50 years, with predictable consequences for their operations and fleet planning. The suppliers to the industry will also be adversely affected until demand for air travel returns to normal levels and surplus capacity has been absorbed.

Over the past decade we have transformed our company by pursuing a consistent strategy. We have created a balanced business portfolio and a strong management team. We have built a robust business by growing organically and through focused and well-integrated acquisitions which have broadened our product range and opened up new markets.

The acquisitions of the Allison Engine Company, Vickers, Cooper Energy Services' compressor business and National Airmotive and their successful integration into Rolls-Royce opened up new opportunities for our civil, defence, marine and energy businesses. In addition, we have enhanced our focus through the disposal of 40 non-core businesses over the past decade. The result is that the civil aerospace sector now accounts for 54 per cent of our Group sales. This balance has helped reduce some of the financial impact of September 11, allowing us to manage our business through the crisis and remain on course to deliver our strategic objectives.

The senior management at Rolls-Royce took a measured approach, waiting for about six weeks in order thoroughly to assess the impact of the tragedy. Employees and unions were fully consulted, and, although significant redundancies were announced, the handling of the necessary cutbacks was so sensitively managed that the only union comment at the Rolls-Royce AGM in May 2002 was positive and supportive.

Clearly, orders for new aircraft, and therefore new engines, did not dry up completely. In December 2001, Indigo, a corporate-jet service based in Chicago, ordered 75 twin-engined Embraer Legacy corporate aircraft to be powered by Rolls-Royce AE 3007 engines. In March 2002, South African Airways ordered nine Airbus A340-600s to be powered by Rolls-Royce Trent 500s. Also in March, the longstanding customer Gulfstream Aerospace Corporation ordered up to 600 upgraded BR710 engines – 300 firm and 300 options – to power its new twin-engine Gulfstream V-SP business jet aircraft. Produced at Rolls-Royce Deutschland's new facility at Dahlewitz near Berlin, the BR710 was the sole power plant for the Gulfstream V and Gulfstream V-SP.

With more good news for Dahlewitz, the US airline Midwest Express announced in April 2002 that it was increasing its order for Boeing 717s to 25 firm with 25 options from its original tentative twenty-aircraft option. The 717 is powered by BR715s also made at the Dahlewitz plant. It was also announced in April that Middle East Airlines (MEA) would lease three Airbus A330s from International Lease Finance Corporation and that they would be powered by Trent 700s. MEA were the twenty-third operator of the A330 to choose the engine. Finally, in early May, Lufthansa chose the Trent 900 for its order of fifteen Airbus A380s. This order from the large and prestigious airline, won against stiff competition from the Engine Alliance, the joint venture between General Electric and Pratt & Whitney, was particularly satisfying as it re-established Rolls-Royce's lead in winning engine orders for the new high-capacity aircraft.

WORLD-CLASS TECHNOLOGY

As Rolls-Royce, along with the rest of the world, adjusted to the world 'post-9-11', the Chairman, Sir Ralph Robins, approaching his seventieth birthday, announced that he would retire before the AGM of 2003.

What can we say of his chairmanship, which began in 1992 and will end, after ten years, sometime in 2002 or the first half of 2003?

As any Rolls-Royce shareholder will tell you, it has not witnessed a great leap forward in the Rolls-Royce share price, which Robins finds very disappointing, although since 1992 the performance has been markedly better than since privatisation in 1987, which is the starting date normally used when looking at Rolls-Royce's price performance. However, the aero-engine business has always been a long-term one, and Robins has always been determined to build Rolls-Royce for a secure long-term future. As a senior executive of a competitive aerospace group told the *Financial Times* in August 2001:

Rolls-Royce is one of Britain's great unsung engineering successes of the last decade.

As we have seen, Rolls-Royce was only supplying a very small number of civil airlines in the 1980s and was powering sixteen military aircraft. By 2002, the number of civil aircraft powered by Rolls-Royce engines has grown from the four of 1980 to over 40, and the number of military types from sixteen to over 30.

Nor has it only been in the aerospace business that Rolls-Royce has placed itself at the forefront of the global market. The acquisition of Vickers, much misunderstood at the time, has transformed the size and potential of Rolls-Royce's marine business. As Chief Executive John Rose said in the 2001 Annual Report:

We are now a world leader in the provision of marine power systems, providing a comprehensive range of products capable of managing all aspects of electrical and propulsive power. We supply over 2,000 naval and commercial marine customers in more than 200 countries. Our investment in new products will enable us to take full advantage of the increasing use of gas turbines for commercial shipping as well as the opportunities created by the re-equipment programmes being implemented by the world's navies. We have also been particularly successful in the offshore oil and gas marine market which is expected to remain buoyant as oil exploration continues at high levels.

In assessing Robins' chairmanship, he also said:

We have nearly doubled our turnover, more than doubled our firm order book and increased underlying profit before interest and tax from £125 million to £594 million.

In creating a more balanced business we have also changed the mix of our sales. Services have grown from £1.0 billion in 1991 to £2.3 billion in 2001 and now account for approximately 40 per cent of total sales. Our service activities will continue to grow as a result of deliveries of new engines, the increasing maturity of our installed base, and the growth of our repair and overhaul activities. The high level of proprietary technology embedded in our products enables us to offer a growing range of value-added services.

Our civil aerospace market share for new engines has increased by 40 per cent over the last decade and we now consistently achieve 30 per cent of the world market. This increase has been driven by our investment in new and derivative civil engines and our resulting ability to power a wider range of aircraft. This broadening of our product range has resulted in our installed base more than doubling over the last decade to 9,000 jet engines and our annual rate of deliveries more than trebling to 1,362 in 2001. Although we now expect to deliver approximately 900 civil engines in

2002, a 40 per cent reduction on our internal forecast made before September 11, this will still represent 27 per cent of the commercial jet engine market.

He told the *Financial Times* in August 2001:

He has taken the company from a very lowly position in the mid 1980s and has been hugely brave in taking it into the position it is in today. He will be a hard act to follow.

With hindsight, and with the Trent family of engines winning increasing market share, it may look obvious now that investment in the engine was the natural way to go. However, in the dark days of the early 1990s, when world recession meant a dearth of orders, and development problems were costing Rolls-Royce not just millions but hundreds of millions of pounds, not all the Rolls-Royce directors were in favour of continuing the Trent-programme investment. A senior Rolls-Royce executive told the author in 2001, and, just in case he had missed the point, again in 2002, that it was Robins who kept the vision and insisted that the investment continue. As a close colleague said of him:

Sir Ralph has balls of steel.

Another said:

We are fighting two powerful competitors, but many people like doing business with Rolls-Royce because of its integrity. The Chairman epitomises that integrity.

Lord Marshall, Chairman of British Airways, said:

He's been the principal architect in restoring Rolls-Royce's credibility and success. It's during his stewardship that Rolls has really come back.

The *Financial Times* put his massive achievement succinctly when it wrote:

He will emerge from a career at Rolls-Royce with the rare distinction of being one of the few people to have proven capable of building a British company into one of the world's leading engineering groups … While much of UK industry has passed into foreign hands, Rolls-Royce remains proudly British, with world-class technology and a name that stands for quality the world over. Its rivals, GE and Pratt & Whitney, have seethed as Rolls-Royce has grabbed engine orders from under their noses. Rolls-Royce is now second only to GE in the number of engines it sells.

Robins himself is clear in his own mind of the important position of Rolls-Royce in British industry, saying:

We are a very important company in the sense that the only thing this country can do in the future is produce high-converted-value product. We aren't going to make much out of steel or coal mining.

When he announced his retirement in March 2002, *The Independent* wrote:

Rolls is the only British engineering company of world stature … Sir Ralph is that rare animal, a British engineer who has successfully run a big quoted company and kept it independent when others have either been gobbled up or lost the fight to the Japanese and the Americans. For that, he deserves his place in the corporate history books more than most.

THE FUTURE

Predicting the future is fraught with danger, but all businesses have to make forecasts, and in the aero-engine business, where development costs are extremely high and can only be recovered over a number of years of sales and servicing, forecasting is a vital task for any company that wants to prosper.

Advances are being made in information technology, especially in the field of communication, which *may* reduce the need for business travel. However, when the economic cycle is on the up, businessmen travel because they see the cost as insignificant. When the inevitable recessions arrive, there may be a reduction in travel – 'can't we do this on the phone, or by e-mail?' – but getting that order will be seen as so vital that the salesman still feels the need to pitch to his customer face-to-face, though he might consider travelling economy rather than business or first class. As for travel for leisure purposes, the world becomes gradually more prosperous and that points to a steady increase in leisure travel. Congestion at major airports is taking some of the pleasure out of air travel, but demand will almost certainly ensure better air-traffic-control systems as well as larger aircraft, leading to a reduction, or at least a slower growth, in the number of traffic movements.

Since the 1960s, aircraft noise levels have reduced by no less than 75 per cent, mainly thanks to the increase in bypass ratio in large turbofan engines. Nevertheless, there will be continual pressure to reduce noise levels further.

At the end of the year 2000, Rolls-Royce forecast that passenger air-traffic growth over the next twenty years would be 5 per cent per annum and that of air freight would be 6 per cent. The terrible events of 11 September 2001 have obviously dented this forecast in the short term, though there are many that believe that the overall growth rate will not be significantly affected over the twenty years. Five per cent growth may not sound very much, but it means that air traffic will be over two-and-a-half times the level of 2000 by 2020.

Rolls-Royce is well positioned to take advantage of this growth. In the near term, the Boeing 747-400 and 777, and the Airbus A330 and A340 and their derivatives, will satisfy the market needs for long-haul flights for up to 450 passengers. The A380 will satisfy the market for carrying up to 650 passengers over similar long distances. The A330 may be reaching its limits, but new versions of the four-engined A340 are being developed with the Rolls-Royce Trent 500 to provide greater range and extra payload. The Boeing 777 is also being developed to remain competitive and, consequently, will require more thrust from its Trent 800s. The Trent 8014 has already run up to 110,000 lb thrust.

The narrow-body market is changing fast with many of its older aircraft – DC-9, Boeing 737 and 727 – nearing the end of their lives. The 180-seat market is catered for by the Airbus A321, Boeing 757 and 737-900. The 130-to-150-seat market is also well catered for by the A320, A319 and other new 737 families. In the 70-to-110-seat area, the Boeing 717 and Airbus A318 cover the larger end, while the Bombardier CRJ 700 covers the smaller. There is potential for more aircraft in this market segment. In the regional market of aircraft in the 35-to-50-seat area, Embraer and Bombardier are competing fiercely.

Thanks to its strategy of pursuing a complete family of engines, Rolls-Royce is positioned to provide engines for all these market segments – the Trent 500, 600, 700, 800 and 900 for the long-haul aircraft, and the AE 3007, BR710 and 715 and V-2500 for the narrow-bodies.

We have already seen in this book how the three-shaft engine architecture, unique to the RB 211 and Trent engine family, has a number of inherent advantages for large turbofan engines. These can be summed up as: shorter engine, fewer stages, improved performance retention and greater growth potential.

For short-haul operators, acquisition and maintenance costs are the dominant drivers in aircraft economics, with flight-cycle usage between 45 minutes and two hours, compared with six to eight hours on long-haul operations. Engines designed for these shorter operations are of a lower overall pressure ratio, turbine entry temperature and bypass ratio. This, allied to their smaller size, makes the two-shaft layout the ideal configuration. In this class, Rolls-Royce has the V-2500, the BR710 and 715, and the AE 3007. The V-2500 is currently powering the A319, A320, A321 and MD-90 at different ratings of thrust, and there is potential to increase its thrust to 36,000 lb. The BR710 and 715 share a common core and have been developed from experience gained on the Tay, V-2500 and Trent, thereby ensuring a low-risk derivative design philosophy. The AE 3007 shares a common core with the AE 2100 turboprop and the T406/AE 1107 turboshaft.

In the drive to improve the economics of its engines, Rolls-Royce is constantly looking at the all- or more-electric aircraft. In this scenario, the aircraft systems are electrically powered and driven by an all- or more-electric engine that makes wider use of electronic controls and integrates electromagnetic technologies to offer life-cycle cost benefits. The maximum benefit for the all-electric aircraft comes from the propulsion system and airframe integration, by using electrical systems throughout the aircraft driven by embedded electrical generators inside the engine. Electromagnetic bearings will replace current bearings, eliminating the engine's oil system. Engine operability will be improved as generated electrical power is shared between shafts, enabling reoptimisation of the gas generator for surge control and enhancements to the re-light envelope. Predicted benefits suggest the equivalent of a 15 per cent reduction in fuel consumption. These improvements come about largely because of the elimination of the engine oil system, as well as the removal of engine and aircraft accessories, in turn bringing weight savings and lower engine maintenance.

More innovative aircraft designs such as the 'flying wing' also promise a significant improvement in aircraft performance by the blending of the wing and fuselage structures into a 'lifting body'. This would enable the moving of the engines to the rear of the aircraft and above the wing to provide noise shielding. This layout would enable the incorporation of a contra-rotating fan at the rear of the engine, with each stage driven by its own turbine. The fan turbines would then be driven by a two-shaft gas generator with improved efficiency. Such an aircraft and engine combustion could reduce fuel burn by as much as 30 per cent, or even 40 per cent if combined with the all-electric engine technologies.

The Cranfield College of Aeronautics is undertaking a three-year research programme, supported by Rolls-Royce and BAe Systems, to look at blended wing-body (BWB) configurations, and the Toulouse-based design office of Aerospatiale Matra is also looking at the possibilities of flying-wing designs. In the USA, Boeing and NASA are also studying the BWB concept. NASA BWB programme manager Frank Cutter pointed out that the BWB configuration eliminated interference drag and lowered induced drag:

Instead of the fuselage being along for the ride, it contributes to the lift and, with the resulting large internal volume, the BWB would be highly efficient.

Will supersonic aircraft have a place? The limited demand for supersonic travel at a premium price has already been proved by Concorde. However, because of the very high development costs, a large supersonic passenger aircraft seems unlikely. Nevertheless, supersonic business jets seem a possibility. Low development costs are essential, and Rolls-Royce is studying a possible engine with a Trent core with a new LP spool and swept fan, sized to enable the engine to achieve a cruise speed of Mach 1.8. This engine would have a Concorde-style exhaust system, comprising a variable-area primary nozzle and pivoting secondary nozzle where 'buckets' form a convergent/divergent nozzle for supersonic cruise and close together to form a thrust reverser for landing.

Gulfstream has been showing an interest in developing a supersonic business jet (SSBJ) for some time. Senior Vice-President, Programmes, Pres Henne, told *Flight International* in December 2001:

It's a market that's waiting for us if we can do it. The schedule we are looking at is a 2010–2012 entry into service.

At the same time, Boeing is working on the development of its sonic cruiser. This aircraft will cruise at Mach 0.95, have a range of 9,000 miles and will cut journey times on long-distance routes by as much as 20 per cent. However, each aircraft is expected to cost as much as £200 million, and Boeing will therefore want to be very sure there is sufficient market before embarking fully on the enormously expensive development.

All of these developments are under way and are easily imaginable.

Some are talking of more radical developments such as 'virtual reality', whereby hardware integration using computer power will provide any full-sense awareness that is wanted, and 'molecular-level manufacturing', which holds out the promise of making precise products using tiny amounts of energy and leaving no waste.

A radical step forward in the method of air travel, which has remained largely unchanged in the last 50 years, would be for people to have their own personal aircraft allowing them to fly at reasonably high speeds of, say, 300 mph to thousands of small airports. Such a revolution would reduce journey times dramatically, as currently more than half the time in 'air travel' is spent not travelling at all, but waiting around on the ground.

Burt Rutan, the founder of the Scaled Composites prototype development company, thinks that:

We will see, by 2010, a fully integrated revolutionary aircraft. It will have a cockpit without an instrument panel and with a pilot interface so simple and intuitive that a person with 2 hr. of training can safely navigate and conduct his own collision avoidance. It will come equipped with synthetic vision, so clouds or darkness do not block the pilot's view of outside features. IMC [Instrument Meteorological Conditions] piloting tasks will be identical to VMC [Visual Meteorological Conditions]. The aircraft will have collision avoidance via 3D audio alert and visual target icons overlaying actual traffic. If a pilot fails to heed a threat, the autopilot will intervene to avert collision.

The pilot will control the aircraft via attitude command rather than rate command, eliminating the requirement to learn and maintain exacting piloting skills. His reliable turbofan engine will be affordable and quiet.

With all these enabling technologies demonstrated, individually operated personal aircraft could begin to substantially replace our inconvenient, bus-like airliners. By 2025, we will mass-produce these aircraft, discard our conventional ATC [air traffic control] systems and build large numbers of new, small airports. We will then view the airline terminal in the same way we now view the bus terminal. By 2040, the transition will be complete, with only a minority of people using airlines for domestic air travel.

Who can say whether any or all of these developments will come to pass?

More likely is rather more gentle progress to faster, larger, more comfortable aircraft powered by more fuel-efficient, and certainly quieter, engines. Fortunately, as we have seen, Rolls-Royce is well placed to provide a significant share of those engines. The company has made the investment organically, by acquisition and through partnership, to reap the benefit from the almost certain expansion of the civil-airline industry.

In 1998, the Chief Executive, John Rose, had re-organised Rolls-Royce radically into a series of 'customer-facing' units. It was a fundamental change from the previous project-centric approach and entailed a corresponding change in organisation to support it. Rolls-Royce now saw it as essential for its future prosperity to identify, as precisely as possible, the needs, concerns and future requirements of its existing and potential customers, and to gear the whole structure of the company towards satisfying those needs, concerns and requirements. To take one example, Rolls-Royce has made a huge investment in developing its family of engines and can now look forward to a profitable period for many years servicing the aftermarket for those engines, supplying spares and so on. However, the FAA, through the Parts Manufacturing Authority, can allow others to supply spares which can, in some cases, deprive Rolls-Royce of those sales. This has led Rolls-Royce to approach its customers, understand their future requirements and tailor packages whereby Roll-Royce will service the engines for life.

The guiding principles of the Rolls-Royce organisation would be to instil trust in the customer in Rolls-Royce excellence and to improve the focus of the business units within Rolls-Royce to achieve customer satisfaction. By creating a flat, simplified and transparent organisation, decisions would be reached more speedily and personal accountability would be achieved. The engineering integrity of Rolls-Royce products would be maintained and improved, the company's cost base lowered and its delivery systems made world class.

Looking back over the last ten years, John Rose told the author in June 2002:

A decade ago we had a very small installed base in terms of the number of engines. We were over-dependent on defence business to fund a serious entry into the civil market. We were barely supplying the large airlines of the world and we faced one of the giants of the corporate world – General Electric – as our main competitor. It was a daunting prospect. Nevertheless, we have made it. We jumped over that huge barrier-to-entry and we are already reaping the rewards. We have increased our output by 50 per cent over the last five years and we are already investing the rewards from that success in new opportunities for the future.

If we had realised how high those barriers-to-entry were, we might never have taken the risks. But we did – we invested in the Trent, we founded a joint venture with BMW, we bought the Allison Engine company, we convinced Singapore Airlines, American, British Airways and many others that the Trent was the engine best-suited to their needs, we bought Vickers to give us a leading position in marine propulsion systems. And we did all this against competitors who enjoy a better funded research and development environment than we do. We had to act as though we were global, with all the attendant costs, before we really were. But now we are truly a global power systems force with an international presence and international leadership. We are no longer a stuffy, blue-chip, UK-centric engineering company, which might have been a fair description a decade ago.

In the final analysis, a company is all about its people, and there can be few to benefit as much as Rolls-Royce does – and always has – from the dedication and passion of its people. Certainly, I have not come across one, and I have written about more than 40. The inspiration was provided in the beginning by Royce himself, and, when the company opened its new factory in Derby in 1908, many of Royce's employees walked all the way from Manchester so that they could continue to work for him. The loyalty and dedication continued through two world wars, when many worked all hours God gave to provide the engines to beat the enemy. Ernest Hives himself travelled weekly to Glasgow – and wartime train travel was a wearing experience – to encourage his workforce to turn out more and more Merlin engines.

And in the last 50 years, the devotion to and passion for Rolls-Royce has continued undimmed. No matter how inspirational the leadership – and inspirational it has been, especially in the last fifteen years – it would have yielded little if the majority of Rolls-Royce personnel, both in the UK and in the many countries overseas in which the company now operates, had not given their all to make Rolls-Royce the truly global player it is today.

BIBLIOGRAPHY OF
BOOKS CONSULTED

Adams, Jad, *Tony Benn*, Macmillan, 1992

Anderson, Bruce, *John Major: The Making of the Prime Minister*, Fourth Estate, 1991

Andrews, C.F., *Vickers Aircraft Since 1908*, Putnam, 1969

Barnato-Walker, Diana, *Spreading My Wings*, Patrick Stephens Ltd., 1994

Braybrook, Roy, *Harrier: The Vertical Reality*, RAF Benevolent Fund Enterprises, 1996

Butler, David, and Kavanagh, Dennis, *The British General Election of 1987*, Macmillan Press, 1988

Butler, David, and Kavanagh, Dennis, *The British General Election of 1992*, Macmillan Press, 1992

Butler, David, and Kavanagh, Dennis, *The British General Election of 1997*, Macmillan Press, 1997

Childs, David, *Britain Since 1945*, Routledge, 1992

Clark, Alan, *Diaries: In Power*, Weidenfeld & Nicholson, 1993

Dugan, Sally, and Dugan, David, *The Day the World Took Off: The Roots of the Industrial Revolution*, Channel 4 Books, 2000

Evans, Harold, *Vickers Against the Odds: 1956/77*, Hodder & Stoughton, 1978

Evans, Mike, *In the Beginning: The Manchester Origins of Rolls-Royce*, Rolls-Royce Heritage Trust (Historical Series Vol. 4), 1984

Evans, Sir Richard, and Price, Colin, *Vertical Take-Off: The Inside Story of British Aerospace's Comeback from Crisis to World Class*, Nicholas Brealey Publishing, 1999

Fara, Patricia, *An Entertainment for Angels: Electricity in the Enlightenment*, Icon Books, 2002

Foden, Giles (ed.), *'The Guardian' Century*, Fourth Estate, 1999

Frawley, Gerard, *The International Directory of Civil Aircraft: 2001/2002*, Aerospace Publications, 2001

Gilbert, Martin, *A History of the Twentieth Century: Volume Three: 1952–1999*, HarperCollins, 1999

Gilmour, Ian, and Garnett, Mark, *Whatever Happened to the Tories: The Conservatives Since 1945*, Fourth Estate, 1997

Gordon, Andrew, *The Rules of the Game: Jutland and British Naval Command*, John Murray (Publishers) Ltd., 1996

Gunston, Bill, *History of Military Aviation*, Hamlyn, 2000

Gunston, Bill (ed.), *The Encyclopedia of Modern Warplanes*, MetroBooks, 2000

Gunston, Bill, *Rolls-Royce Aero Engines*, Haynes Publishing, 2001

Harkins, Hugh, *Eurofighter 2000*, Midland Publishing, 1997

Hayward, Keith, *Government and British Civil Aerospace*, Manchester University Press, 1983

Hayward, Keith, *The British Aircraft Industry*, Manchester University Press, 1989

Heath, Anthony (ed.), et al., *Labour's Last Chance?*, Dartmouth, 1994

Hennessy, Peter, *The Prime Minister: The Office and its Holders Since 1945*, The Penguin Press, 2000

Heseltine, Michael, *Life in the Jungle*, Hodder & Stoughton, 2000

Holt, Richard, *Second Against Equals*, Profile Books, 2001

Hutton, Will, *The State We're In*, Jonathan Cape, 1995

Isaacs, Jeremy, and Downing, Taylor, *Cold War*, Transworld Publishers, 1998

Kavanagh, David, and Seldon, Anthony, *The Major Effect*, Macmillan, 1994

Keys, Dick, and Smith, Ken, *Down Elswick Slipways*, Newcastle City Libraries, 1996

Kynaston, David, *The City of London: A Club No More: 1945–2000*, Chatto & Windus, 2001

Lawrence, Philip, and Braddon, Derek, *Strategic Issues in European Aerospace*, Ashgate Publishing, 1999

McSmith, Andy, *Faces of Labour: The Inside Story*, Verso, 1996

Needham, Richard, *Battling for Peace*, The Blackstaff Press, 1998

Nott, John, *Here Today, Gone Tomorrow: Recollections of an Errant Politician*, Politico's Publishing, 2002

Oldfield, David, *The European Fighter Aircraft*, PhD Thesis at University of Bath, 2000

Postan, M.M, *British War Production*, Her Majesty's Stationery Office, 1952

Preston, C.E., *Power for the Fleet*, Eton Publishing, 1982

Redding, Robert, and Yenne, Bill, *Boeing: Planemaker to the World*, Thunder Bay Press, 1997

Sabbagh, Karl, *21st Century Jet: The Making of the Boeing 777*, Pan Macmillan, 1995

Scott, J.D., *Vickers: A History*, Weidenfeld & Nicholson, 1962

Serling, Robert, *The Electra Story*, Doubleday, 1963

Serling, Robert J., *Legend and Legacy: The Story of Boeing and its People*, St Martin's Press, 1992

Welch, Jack, and Byrne, John, *Jack*, Headline Book Publishing, 2001

Weyl, A.R., *Fokker: The Creative Years*, Putnam Aeronautical Books, 1965

Whitney, Daniel D., *Vees for Victory! The Story of Allison V-1710: 1929–1948*, Schiffer Military History, 1998

Young, Hugo, *One of Us*, Pan Macmillan, 1990

I also studied all relevant articles in *Flight International* and *Aviation Week* covering the period from 1987 to 2002. The staff on both journals were extremely helpful.

The *Rolls-Royce Magazine*, published quarterly for the last twenty years, has also been extremely helpful in providing factual information and interesting anecdotes.

INDEX